D0868381

# Poe-Land

# Poe-Land

*The Hallowed Haunts of Edgar Allan Poe*

J. W. Ocker

THE COUNTRYMAN PRESS
WOODSTOCK, Vermont

Copyright © 2015 by J. W. Ocker

All rights reserved. No part of this book may be reproduced in any form or by any electronic or
mechanical means including information storage and retrieval systems without permission in
writing from the publisher, except by a reviewer, who may quote brief passages.

Interior photographs by the author unless otherwise specified
Book design and composition by Eugenie S. Delaney
Cover illustration and design by Brian Weaver

Published by The Countryman Press, P.O. Box 748, Woodstock, VT 05091
Distributed by W. W. Norton & Company, Inc., 500 Fifth Avenue, New York, NY 10110
Printed in the United States of America

Library of Congress Cataloging-in-Publication Data are available
Poe-Land
978-1-58157-221-6

10 9 8 7 6 5 4 3 2 1

To Hazel Lenore
You have been part of a very weird year.

*You lived, sir, and wrote during an earlier, simpler moment
of darkness when a drunken Fortunato had to be bricked into
a wall by an individually skilled artisan. Now we immure
whole neighborhoods in one day's urban renewal. You must
realize, The Fall of the House of Usher only cleared the way
for another highrise. The Descent into the Maelstrom is the
daily ride to work. The Pit is one of our two major political
parties, the Pendulum the other. The Masque of the Red
Death is held annually for combined interfaith charities.
The System of Doctor Tarr and Professor Fether has been
medically approved. Though we are more hesitant now about
rushing the Tell-Tale Heart to transplant. The MS. is Found
in a non-returnable bottle. The Purloined Letter is junk mail.
The Bells are recorded. The Black Cat has been "fixed."*

The Late Great Creature
*Brock Brower*

# Contents

*George Julian Zolnay bust of Edgar Allan Poe, Alderman Library,*
*University of Virginia, Charlottesville*

# Introduction

*My Earthly Lot Hath—Little of Earth in It*

DGAR ALLAN POE WAS AN ODDITY. His life was odd, his literature is odd, his legacy is odd.

He was an author of unique genius, and if it's lazy for me to use that shorthand, then he was one of unique ability, unique vision, unique expression. He didn't so much write words as weave them together into strange fabrics that compel you to either tapestry them onto a wall and marvel or smother someone to death with them and marvel.

He had a vision so insistent that he had to invent or evolve entire genres of literature just to express it. With "The Murders in the Rue Morgue," he created the modern detective story, meaning he made possible about 80 percent of contemporary literature and television programming. No Poe, no Poirot, no *Magnum, P.I.* And that's three mustaches the world would be impoverished without.

He sent a man to the moon thirty years before Jules Verne did and more than half a century before H. G. Wells did. He destroyed our planet in a comet-born apocalypse, a trope of the science fiction genre that we're still troping today. And horror stories—well, if Hell is a hall of fame for earth's horrors, then Poe has his own demon wing there.

And that latter bit really doesn't fit. His dexterity with words could have floated him among the loftiest of poets for sheer beauty and craft, and he was a poet, for sure, as that was where his passions settled naturally. But he could have been the American Shakespeare. The American Shelley. The American Slick Rick. Yet, he turned that genius to stories and poems of horror. Or at least, that's where his genius refracted the most light. In death. In gloom. In despair.

He focused that high ability on what has traditionally been considered low literature and what today has been neatly circumscribed as the horror genre, and which is still often kept at a safe distance from its playmates. By doing so, Poe elevated the genre and forced many to take it more seriously than they otherwise would have while inspiring many others to pursue it as worthwhile. His genius is so inescapable that we find it necessary to introduce stories of madmen, of murder, of exotic torture and obsession with death to our children in school just because we need to show them what great literature is or else fail in our roles as educators, decent people, and apex predators.

And yet, despite the fact that his horrors have granted him eternal life as far as we can bestow it, most of his work is comedic, silly, full of puns and trivialities. I think if he had been barred from claiming the mantel of poet, he would have claimed that of satirist or humorist, a film negative of Mark Twain.

But if humor was all he'd written, nobody would have cared about Edgar Allan Poe. His comedies are trifles. His horrors are exquisite.

Another odd aspect of his work is that when Poe wrote well, he wrote like the English language was newfound. When he was bad, he wrote with a dull axe in both fists. I don't know if I can ever read *The Narrative of Arthur Gordon Pym* again. And, honestly, if threatened with living entombment, I could probably make a longer list of his bad and mediocre works than one of his good and great works. Plus there were his plagiarisms, which were frequent and blatant enough to relegate him to one of the laughingstocks of literary history, yet we brush them aside like it's okay for a guy like Poe to have that kind of body beneath his boards.

Certainly, the inconsistent quality issue might not be Poe's fault. Every author has levels of quality that range throughout his or her career. It's just that those with a larger body of work can better hide or context the juvenilia, the paycheck work, and the bad decisions (or can afford to at least destroy them in a fire, as Ray Bradbury is supposed to have done). Poe's base of work is small, and he was forced to pad it just to have something to stick silverware into. And it doesn't help that his work is held in such high regard that we lust after every scrap of paper that he so much as poked with a quill.

But all that still doesn't plumb the depth of this angel of the odd.

His work is heralded by the dustiest of scholars. The most ivory towered of academics. Even when various critical tides turned against him over the years or when he was ravaged by those prominent literary voices who were somehow born without a Poe gene, his work still bore the showy stamp of approval of the most cultured culturati.

And yet he is just as much a part of pop culture as the latest dance song or Internet meme or reality television show. Everybody knows Poe. And, sure, there is a pantheon of writers and artists that everyone can recognize by name and sig- nature work, but those men and women aren't held with the same passion. From the teenagers who have barely existed long enough to have sampled anything in life to the elder librarians who have read every word printed on silverfish food, an astounding number of people of an astounding variety of tastes and lifestyles love Poe. Or identify with him. Or recognize him as some kind of symbol.

I mean, he's a Halloween decoration. Take that, every other writer.

Just over the course of the writing of this book, which covered all of 2013 and some of 2014, there debuted a prime-time network series inspired by Poe, an NFL football team named after his most famous poem won the Super Bowl, and a major U.S. city put together the funding for a statue of the man to adorn one of its most prominent spots.

Heck, in July of 2013, an original manuscript handwritten and signed by Poe for his poem "The Conqueror Worm" went up for auction in Massachusetts, his birth state. The five stanzas pulled in $300,000.

More than two centuries after his birth, Edgar Allan Poe is bankable—in the entertainment industry, the sports industry, the tourism industry. Check the web. He even has a pretty fulsome merchandise line. His action figure is staring morosely at me on my desk as I write this introduction.

Of course, he never got any revenue from raven-adorned T-shirts or plush black cats. He lived a life of poverty and relative obscurity, the value of his work to a burgeoning world of American literature, and to human letters in general, going mostly unacknowledged during his lifetime. And while that's not too strange in the literary world, where many live and work without acclaim and yet still secure a legacy of fame posthumously, Poe's pendulum swings wider and stranger than most in this regard. The position he and his work hold today and the position they held in his lifetime are so out of proportion as to give credence to the idea of cosmic jokes.

But there's more to his legacy than just his work. We regard him not just as a poet and an author, but as a figure. I don't know what Virginia Woolf looked like. Charles Dickens is a vague beardy impression. My own great-grandfather might as well be faceless for all I know of him. But Poe's dour countenance is as easily recognizable as the latest United States president. We are hyper-aware of the man who wrote the words even as we read them. We can't peruse "The Fall of the House of Usher" without imagining Poe as either the visitor or Roderick Usher himself. Unless we're imagining the latter as Vincent Price, I guess.

Our movies and books are full of stories that use Poe himself as a character. Partly, that's because there seems to be a lot of Poe's life in his characters, from intense, uncomfortable-to-behold romances to the terrors of death and losing those held dear. I'm guessing an actor would be happy to play the role of Prince Prospero or William Wilson, but he would be ecstatic to play the author himself. And from Klaus Kinski to John Cusack on the screen and John Astin to Jeffrey Combs on the stage, quite a few actors have worn the dark mustache and could testify.

Which is strange to be so enamored by the character of a person whose main activity in life was scratching at paper while hunched in a chair.

And that's because we have this Myth of Poe, an image of a man tormented by both life and art, a melancholy creature, pathetic, ill-starred, and death-beset, perched precariously on a tight-rope pen, his only salvation from the abyss of suffocating darkness and insanity below. A man whom that darkness eventually overcame in an end so tragic and outré that its details were hidden from history.

I'm not saying there's no truth in that myth. Scholars have debated since his death whether that impression of Poe is true, false, or an inextricable knot of both. Whether he wrote such tales as "Berenice" and "Ligeia" in a fit of morbidity or as a simple lark or as a cold and carefully crafted exercise in effect. But we do love the myth.

Another odd aspect of Edgar Allan Poe's life, literature, and legacy is that he and his work seem of no real place, a strange thing for a writer. Many of his contemporaries have become synonymous with the locales they lived in and wrote about: Dickens in London, Irving in New York, Hawthorne in Massachusetts. Poe, on the other hand, was a man of limbo.

During his short life his search for both success and subsistence led him up and down the East Coast, from his birthplace in Boston all the way down to an island in South Carolina, and he set his stories in a range of similar locales, including Europe, where he lived for five years when he was a child. But he spread himself so thin across the states it's as if that was the cause of his mysterious death in Baltimore. He just ran out of Poe at that point in time and at that place.

Edgar Allan Poe was an oddity.

And it will take an oddity of a book to tell his story.

Because of both his nomadic life and the strong passions that he and his work still kindle today, we have the opportunity to tell his story in a different way than the conventional. We don't have to tell it chronologically, from start to finish. Or literarily, through the lens of his writings.

We can tell it geographically.

Today, every city whose cobblestones he so much as drunkenly scraped a foot across or within whose borders he brilliantly slung black ink into blacker text has attempted to claim a part in his legacy. No less than four cities where he lived have official Edgar Allan Poe museums, and many more places tout artifacts and sites connected to him or have erected memorials in his honor.

For this book, I traveled some one thousand miles of the East Coast and crossed an ocean to visit these hallowed haunts of Edgar Allan Poe, the places where he spent time, and which have since been beatified into landmarks to physically preserve his memory. These memorials include everything from statues of the poet's person to artifacts from his body, life, and death to the humble houses that kept the rain off his head and the final place where the molecules that organized into one of America's greatest poets went their separate ways.

Because Poe visited or lived at these places at multiple, nonconsecutive times throughout this life, we won't be telling his story in order. For instance, take the chapter on his life in Massachusetts. In it, we'll meet him as an infant, as a young man entering the U.S. Army, and as an older, respected lecturer and unrequited lover. Then we'll travel to other cities and time-travel to other points of his life.

As a result, we end up with a peculiar timeline for the author. Sure, he's born at the beginning of this book, as with any traditional biography, but he dies just over halfway through. And it ends in anticlimax, with him under palm trees and warm sunshine in the subtropics of South Carolina.

Now, I admit, telling a story geographically sounds like it could be confusing and, let's face it, bland. So let me state it another way.

We can tell his story experientially.

I have found by firsthand experience that, better than biography, better than literary criticism, better than watching fictionalized dramatizations of his life, tracking Poe through his hereafter of monuments, artifacts, museums, and preserved sites is really the best way for us, today, to access and connect to Poe at a real level.

Instead of just reading about where or how he wrote "The Raven" and how its publication affected his life and American poetry in general, we can sit in front of the very fireplace that inspired the words "And each separate dying ember wrought its ghost upon the floor."

Likewise, we can read about the sickness and death of his young wife, Virginia, and read the poems he wrote about her, but to walk into the room where it actually happened, and kneel by the bed that she died in, is a more tangible way of experiencing Edgar Allan Poe.

So, in a way, we can do more than just learn about Poe. We can go see him. We can live him. It just takes a few road trips.

In addition to telling Poe's story geographically and experientially, we're also going to be telling Poe's story posthumously. And I don't mean that word literally, even though it is true. I mean that we'll look at his life by looking at his afterlife, contemporarily.

For this book, I've done more than seek out the physical traces that announce to the world that "Poe Was Here." I sought the people who are responsible for scrawling them across the landscape. I've talked to those who are preserving Poe's physical legacy, from the sculptors of his monuments, to the private collectors who treasure locks of his hair, to the docents who dedicate their lives to Poe's, to the actors who have become him to keep both Poe and themselves alive.

By doing so, maybe we can gain some insight into just why so many people today remain so invested in Poe, more than a century and a half since his death, and despite the thousands of amazing authors who have been born since his lonely little October funeral. We'll see why it's not enough that his work is preserved for the duration of culture but also everything from his bed to his breeches and every place he ever exchanged oxygen for carbon dioxide.

Now, despite that hyperbole, this book is not an attempt to track every one of Poe's footfalls. It's not an attempt to investigate every spot or building whose continued existence is only incidental to the fact that Poe knew of it, nor am I visiting every site connected to those whom Poe met. Instead, it is the places and artifacts that were purposefully or consequently hallowed because of their connection to Poe—with plenty of exceptions when interest pulled me in those directions.

Nevertheless, it's a lot of Poe.

But this book is not a biography, even if the subject, with his maelstrom of a life, is exceedingly suited for it. As Poe himself wrote in his *Marginalia,* "We should pass over all biographies of 'the good and the great,' while we search carefully the slight records of wretches who died in prison, in Bedlam, or upon the gallows."

Sure, at its most basic level, this book will tell the story of Poe's life. But to encapsulate a man—an evolving, inconstant, and whim-prone creature—is impossible, silly, and an extremely important thing to do. Far more important than what I'm comfortable with shouldering.

Still, in the same way that every biography creates a new version of its subject, and every new version helps add facets (and smudge older ones) to what is necessarily a complex human being, I hope this book creates another Poe to stick amongst the scores of Poes out there on the shelves of libraries and in the netherspace of digital storage.

I want to show you my Poe. The one I constructed from the very boards he walked across. The very bed he dreamed in. The very ink from his pen, hairs from his head, and the chamber in which he honeymooned.

This book should also in no way be considered journalistic, even though there will be gentle investigative elements. Also, because it sounds vaguely insulting. I'm not sure why. However, I do interview many people throughout this book as I try to discern more specifically—since I already understand it primally—why they spend so much of their lives ensuring that someone else, someone already famous and globally esteemed, lives on far beyond them at a particular place.

Finally, this book is not a guidebook. Every site and artifact in it, where it's not on somebody's personal property, will have all the information anybody needs to visit it. But I don't really arrange that information in an easy-to-use format. Unless I end up doing that in an appendix at the end. Actually, that's a good idea. I'm going to do that. But it still won't be a guidebook, no matter what the back cover ends up saying.

And while I'm pretty confident about what this book is not, I'm a little wobbly on what it is. I think the best way to describe it would be a travelogue or travel diary, a personal narrative of my experiences visiting the places that sanctify Poe's memory and the people responsible for doing so. And since these will be my experiences, I guess you should know a bit more about my attitude toward Mr. Edgar Allan Poe and the biases I bring with me on this journey.

As you can no doubt tell by the tenor of this introduction, I'm fascinated by Poe and his work. A fan, to put it simply. I like his work, at least his darker stories and poems, the ones that give impeachable evidence of a man in supreme control of a language and a feel for the macabre. I like the story of his life, that of a man trying to find a few crumbs of comfort and recognition and expand what can be done with literature. I like his myth, the drunken, tormented, insane creature wringing out a dark life into dark ideas. And I like all the blurry bits in between. I like Poe. So there'll be a lot of hagi in this ography.

But I'm not a scholar. Not an expert on Poe or literature. I once submitted a paper on him in a college literature class where I misspelled his middle name as "Allen" every single time (the trick, I've since learned, is remembering that Edgar Allan Poe only has an "e" at each end). I also won't be trying to shed light on any of the controversies of his life . . . whether he made it back to Europe as an adult, when he was being satiric and when sincere in his stories, what his exact level of fame was during his lifetime, whether he was really an alcoholic and a drug-fiend, which school of criticism is the most effective at quickening his work.

I'm just a guy who likes Poe and especially likes his place in culture right now. A guy who has lived in two of the same states as Poe and worked for years in a third. A guy who, as a result of this book, lived Poe for a year . . . geographically, experientially, posthumously.

A guy who marvels at the glorious oddity that is Edgar Allan Poe.

And Edgar Allan Poe was an oddity. But what he left behind is even odder.

Welcome to Poe-Land.

*Side of electrical box, Edgar Allan Poe Square*

# CHAPTER 1

# Massachusetts

## *A Chaos of Deep Passion, from His Birth*

I STOOD ON THE EDGE OF THE SMALL, triangular plaza formed by the busy intersection of Boylston and Charles Streets. Behind me, across a ground laid with red bricks, was a strip of retail . . . a luggage store, a trolley tour office, a tobacconist, a burrito joint. It was early spring, and the small area of the plaza sectioned off for outside dining was full. The front of the plaza faced the southwest section of the Common, where the small, 260-year-old Central Burying Ground makes its staunch, somber stand against the recreating crowds. Turning just a few degrees to the left, I could see the adjacent Public Garden, the Common's more recent and upscale sibling. I was standing on Edgar Allan Poe's piece of Boston.

Four feet above my head, almost hidden in the shading foliage of the Callery pear trees, his banner flew from a black lamppost. The white letters on the blue street sign spelled out his name under the seal of Boston, adding the extra surname of *Square.* The sign does its best to fight for attention with the cluster of roadway signs sharing the post.

For the past 160 years, this spot and its surrounding area have been the playground on which Poe's legacy in the city has seesawed. But soon, probably as you're reading this, Poe's place in Boston will finally be secured . . . and in a big way.

Over the years that I've been visiting the spot, the plaza has become more Poe-themed. When I first set foot in the square in 2008, there was a lone, decades-old plaque dedicated to him on the side of a building. By the end of 2009, the 200th anniversary of his birth, the aforementioned sign that officially dubbed the plaza Edgar Allan Poe Square had been unfurled. And, in 2010, an artist painted all the sides of a trashcan-sized electrical box at the edge of the square with a fresh coat of Poe. It bore a pallid bust of Pallas with an ebony bird on her head, a gold bug above the inscription HIC NATUS UBIQUE NOTUS (Born here, known everywhere), Poe's own mournful countenance and elegant

signature, and a snippet of his poem "The Spirits of the Dead" in a facsimile of his own flowing handwriting. As of 2013, the mini-mural was still there, slightly molested by weather. The "Gold-Bug" and the "Raven" panels had started to chip, and a single, simple graffiti tag marred the space beside his head where I assume his devil sits. The tag included a dripping, black bullet hole in Poe's temple.

It was like the plaza was slowly blooming, but instead of signaling spring, these small honorariums to Poe were the signs of a coming. For what is a long time coming.

## In the Beginning, Poe

I don't think Edgar Allan Poe ever forgave Boston for its singular crime against him . . . being the city of his birth. That's right. The bad sign that Poe was born under was WELCOME TO BEANTOWN.

Poe was born on January 19, 1809. His parents lived in a boardinghouse at 62 Carver Street, about a block or two from Boston Common. His roots didn't penetrate very deep into the city, though. His mother, Elizabeth Arnold Poe, was from England. His father, David Poe, was from Baltimore. They had been living in Boston for three years, but both were traveling actors. Boston was the musical chair on which they were sitting when Edgar was born and where they would spend the months after his birth before taking off for New York.

The life of these actors was an active one, and Mr. and Mrs. Poe traveled to whatever city gave them the opportunity to pay their bills and strive for immortality in the arts, not realizing that their best chance for the latter was the small child they birthed during that New England winter. The couple hopped up and down the East Coast, from Boston to New York City to Philadelphia, Richmond, Charleston, other cities. Wherever there was a welcoming stage, they went.

It was an itinerancy that Poe would mirror in his own life, almost to the city, as he looked for his own kind of welcoming stage.

David Poe was Elizabeth's second husband. Her first was Charles Hopkins, another actor, who died in October of 1805. He was twenty. She was eighteen. Less than a year later, she married David Poe. For the three years previous to Edgar's birth, Boston was their home. Edgar's older brother, Henry Leonard, was born there in 1807. His younger sister, Rosalie, would be destined to have a southern accent after her birth in Virginia in 1810.

Then, before he reached the age of three, Edgar became both an orphan and a Virginian.

His father disappeared sometime during the acting stint in New York, less than a year after Edgar's birth. What happened to him isn't known for sure. Theories generally include the only two options: flight or death, with the former often attributed to overwhelming debt, a disappointing career, an unhealthy affinity for alcohol, and stressful family responsibilities. These were the same burdens his son would go on to shoulder his entire life.

Edgar's mother died in Richmond on December 8, 1811, after a long illness. She was twenty-four years old. Edgar would grow up in that city under the foster care of a merchant named John Allan and his wife, Frances, while his sister was taken up by another Richmond family and his brother was raised by relatives in Baltimore.

But Poe couldn't quite shake Boston.

The Boston area was always an option for him as a home, but that's all it ever remained. If you add up all of Poe's time living in the city, it comes to less than a year; however, that year is spread throughout the course of his whole life and is full of people and events important to his overall story. He visited the city as late as a year before his death on October 7, 1849.

And for most of the century and a half after the death of this dark poet, Boston couldn't have cared less that one of America's greatest writers had breathed Boston's atmosphere first.

## *They Paved Over Poe and Put Up a Parking Lot*

It's a strange thing. If you've been to Boston, you know it's a city of civic braggadocio. Its residents are intensely proud of the prominence of their city in American history, of the legacy of science and invention and scholarship just over the Charles River in Cambridge, of its sports teams. The red line of its Freedom Trail is less a guide for tourists than it is an emphatic underline.

And, yet, Boston has done nothing to officially claim a part in the legacy of one of America's brightest, if also blackest, literary lights. Let me put that into perspective. The city enstatuated a line of ducks in its Public Gardens to commemorate a children's book. In the Dorchester neighborhood towers an eleven-foot-tall bronze pear because a variety of that fruit was cultivated there. The city even erected the planet's first statue of the Viking Leif Erikson. Because the legacy of Vikings in Boston is that important.

But that doesn't mean every single person in Boston forgot about Poe. Just that even the most meager efforts have gone unsupported and sometimes have even been thwarted.

In 1913, shortly after the centenary of his birth, Boston named the intersection of Broadway and Carver Street, near where he was born, Edgar Allan Poe Square. This act was either Boston getting caught up in all the Poe interest that came about around this time as the country reevaluated the author's work, or it was some ignorant soul who just needed to stick a name on a square and was unaware of the Poe taboo.

Either way, the lapse was addressed seven years later, when Boston renamed the square after Matthew E. Ryan, a local veteran and victim of World War I.

In 1924, a group named the Boston Authors Club chose literature above local pride and installed a plaque in Poe's honor in the same general area. It contained no images, was formatted like an eye chart, and read:

NEAR THIS SPOT

NINETEENTH

JANUARY

MDCCCIX

WAS BORN

EDGAR

ALLAN POE

ROMANCER

POET CRITIC

THIS TABLET IS

PLACED HERE

IN HIS MEMORY BY

THE BOSTON

AUTHORS CLUB

The plaque didn't stick, probably disappearing during the travesty of what happened to his birth home. For not only did Boston quickly revert to its normal policy of Poe non grata, it obliterated his place in the city.

In the late 1950s/early 1960s, they tore down the house where he was born. In its place, they spread a layer of asphalt.

Right. They paved over Poe and put up a parking lot.

And I had to see that for myself.

The missing tooth of a spot is two blocks or so down Charles Street South from today's Edgar Allan Poe Square. Walking there, I passed more retail and restaurants, a P.F. Chang restaurant guarded by an eleven-foot-tall statue of a Metzengerstein-like horse, and a parking garage, and then crossed over Stuart Street. Retail soon gave way to a pair of out-of-place townhouses.

More than just destroying the landmark of Poe's house, Boston, in the modern version of sowing land with salt, ripped up most of the block on which the house sat to make way for municipal facilities. In so doing, the city altered a landscape that Poe probably wouldn't have remembered from his childhood, but more than likely visited during his adult years, mistily nostalgic or, more in the vein of the Myth of Poe, bemoaning the fact that he'd ever been born.

I was looking for one address in particular: 60 Charles Street South. That's the address of Poe's neighbor.

In a bit of what seems almost like nose-thumbing, the residence right beside Poe's birthplace of 62 Carver Street survived, still bearing its original number, even though its street name has changed. Today, it has only one neighbor, on its north side: 58 Charles Street South, the birthplace of nobody in particular. Its south side ends in an ugly, blank, ragged wall of brick that looks as if it's still getting used to the sun exposure. Something was obviously ripped away there. It was a stark contrast to the nice, historic-looking façade of number 60.

Adjacent to that brick wall, and possibly sharing it, 62 Carver Street, the house where Poe let loose his first cries against the world, once stood. A photo from the 1930s reveals it to be a plain brick building at the end of the row. Beside it was a parking lot lined with a six-foot-tall chain-link fence cherried by barbed wire.

Today, the fencing has encroached to occupy the space where Poe was born. It's also been raised four more feet, blanketed with a dark scrim that barely obscures what's behind it, and adorned with signs that warn NO TRESPASSING. VIOLATORS WILL BE PROSECUTED.

The house was Usher'd when it was acquired by the Boston Edison power company in 1959. Today, a different power company, NSTAR, owns the site and only a portion of it remains a parking lot. Most of the space previously occupied by the house is taken up by a monstrous metal power transformer that's terrifying and dangerous-looking. If this were a movie, it's not something you'd want to place on the site where the vengeful ghost of a horror master might haunt.

Standing outside the fence, I tried to gauge my reaction. I wasn't as sad as I thought I'd be, honestly. I mean, objectively, how bad is it that we lost the house where Edgar Allan Poe was probably born?

There are three ways to rephrase that question to get a substantial answer. The first is: How bad is it in general, in the grand scheme of life, the universe, and everything? The answer to that is easy. Not bad at all.

The whole thing could be framed as a corporation versus culture story, I guess, to give it a little more resonance, but in the end it is just a building. And a building where Poe spent only his earliest infancy. We don't adore that Poe. Only his parents did, and possibly only one of them. Preserving such a place in light of what that squirming, pink, and I assume mustachioed, creature turned out to be would be cool, but we've got bigger issues to deal with. And people need power.

Next, is it bad for the legacy of Poe? Again, not really. Poe's legacy will always be a literary one. As far as the physical legacy goes, we have a good passel of preserved Poe sites and memorials to fall back on. Like a whole book's worth. Erasing one more spot of Poe does little to lessen that physical legacy . . . as long as we stop erasing at some point, of course.

Finally, is it bad for Boston? To that I'd say, definitely. Of the current extant Poe houses in the country—New York's, Philadelphia's, and Baltimore's—none are in an ideal location. All three are far from any tourist center and, even worse, are in relatively unwelcoming areas of those cities. Boston, on the other hand,

*Site of Poe's birthplace*

could have had a literary mecca just two blocks from the tourist sweet spot that is the Boston Common, making the area an even more desirable destination. Plus, it's hard to tout yourself as a high-culture city with such a black mark on your résumé. Everybody in HR will make fun of you for that.

All that said, there is something tragically romantic about Poe's birth home being gone. It fits the Myth of Poe that we all love. Woebegone both in life and afterlife.

I didn't spend too much time gazing up at that transformer, both because there wasn't much to see and because it could probably be considered suspicious activity, and instead of going back the way I came, toward the plaza, I continued to head south. Half a block in that direction and in a direct line of sight with the vacancy that was once Poe's birth home was a sign that said MATTHEW E. RYAN SQUARE.

## *Acting and Plaquing Poe*

In 1989, thirty years after Poe's Boston digs were rubbled into oblivion, some people tried again to name something in the city after him, this time a small alley, complete with a brand-new plaque. They had better success. Although the alley name went the way of everything else in the city named after Edgar Allan Poe, the plaque remains to this day . . . possibly because it's kept a low profile.

You can find it on the exterior wall of the aforementioned burrito joint, at the intersection of Boylston and Charles Streets. That space has been a few things over the years: a florist, a luggage shop, but since the end of 2008 it's been a restaurant chain called Boloco. At the corner of the building, about seven feet up the wall, is a large but unobtrusive bronze plaque camouflaged against the brown-painted exterior.

The plaque looks a bit like an old-time wanted poster. It bears an image of the bust of Poe at the top, his face bookended by his birth and death years. His crimes include:

EDGAR ALLAN POE
POET STORYWRITER CRITIC
BORN ON CARVER STREET JANUARY 19, 1809,
TO DAVID AND ELIZABETH (ELIZA) POE,
ACTORS AT THE BOSTON THEATRE,
IN 1827 PUBLISHED HIS FIRST BOOK
*TAMERLANE AND OTHER POEMS*,
AT A SHOP ON THE CORNER OF WASHINGTON
AND STATE STREETS AND ENLISTED IN THE
U.S. ARMY AT FORT INDEPENDENCE,
BOSTON HARBOR. LECTURED IN BOSTON
OCTOBER 16, 1845. PUBLISHED 'LANDOR'S COTTAGE,'
HIS LAST TALE, IN BOSTON'S
*FLAG OF OUR UNION*, JUNE 9, 1849.
DIED AT BALTIMORE OCTOBER 7, 1849.

And then, below a small relief of a raven adapted from the Édouard Manet ex libris illustration for an 1875 French edition of Poe's "The Raven":

EDGAR ALLAN POE
MEMORIAL COMMITTEE
JANUARY 19, 1989

The Poe in the plaque gazes despondently across at the Common and, more directly, at the white pillar that marks the tomb of Charles Sprague in the Central Burying Ground. Charles Sprague was a one-eyed banker poet and Poe contemporary. Poe knew his work, and hated most of it. Sprague earned a better monument than Poe did, just by dying in the city.

I've been to this site dozens of times over the years. It's a crawly anthill of tourists and locals, and I have never seen anybody walk up to that plaque. The truth is, unless they're an ardent and eagle-eyed species of Poe fan, anybody in the vicinity of the plaque is probably there because they have a craving for Mexican tube sandwiches.

The restaurant is prouder of the plaque than Boston is. On an earlier visit to the site, I posted my destination on Twitter and promptly received a response from a corporate Boloco account to the effect of, "We call that one Poe-loco."

Poe would have loved that response. He used puns frequently enough that it should've hurt his reputation as a dark, sober soul. In his story "The Devil in the Belfry," he called a town where the residents were obsessed with clocks Vondervotteimittiss. In "The Man that Was Used Up," he named a sculptor Chipon-

*1989 Poe plaque, Edgar Allan Poe Square*

chipino. And, of course, there's the name of the eponymous character from "Some Words with a Mummy" . . . Allamistakeo. When biographers say that Poe was often his own worst enemy, they rarely bring up this particular fact. But they should.

I'll digress just to say that a great way for Boston to make up for snubbing Poe for so long would be to get Boloco to create a burrito called the Crazy Poe. "Sorry we tore down your house, man. We named a stuffed tortilla after you. Hope we're cool."

This Poe plaque has fascinated me since I first saw the memorial. It seems somehow both defiant in the face of apathy and embarrassed for its attempt. Kind of like how I assume those people who twirl advertising signs on street corners feel. I also might be reading weird moods into the expression frozen on Poe's bronze face, as I'm wont to do with any depiction of Poe's countenance.

My interest in this simple plaque that was the only public acknowledgment of Poe in Boston in the latter half of the twentieth century eventually led me to the man responsible for its existence. His name is Norman George.

George was born in Alexandria Bay, New York, and moved to Boston in the late 1960s to attend Boston University. The most relevant part of his biography is that he is more than a Poe fan. For twenty-five years, Norman George was a Poe performer.

Now, Poe performers are a species of actor that revels in acting out Poe's work or biography, often as a one-man show, in the character of Edgar Allan Poe. The fact that there are enough Poe performers to think of them as an entire species speaks a lot to the market. People want to see Poe in the flesh, even if the real Poe has none anymore.

Poe performers are rarely just capitalizing on a demand, however. These guys love Poe. They aren't content with reading his work or watching adaptations of it. Not even with traveling the country visiting Poe sites. They need to be Poe. Need to show other people what Poe means to them by telling Poe's story and performing Poe's works through Poe's own mustache.

Heck, I think the secret to Poe's appeal could be found in this strange breed of man and, I would later discover, woman. Were we to round up all the people propelled by their inner fires to portray Poe on stage and subject them to intensive psychological analysis, the latest in brain scan technology, and maybe some gentle dissection, we may find a clue to Poe's odd hold over his admirers.

That would've been a much better book, I think.

In George's case, his fascination with Poe started as a young boy watching the American International Pictures horror movies based on Poe's stories, the ones directed by Roger Corman and starring Vincent Price. That led to reading Poe's actual stories. And that led to him attempting to track down Poe's birthplace at a young age. He told me, "When I was fourteen, my father took me down to Boston for a Boston University football game. While we were there, we looked for Poe's birthplace but just couldn't find it."

That's not your fault, Norman. That's Boston's.

George had acted since high school, and in 1983 the two passions finally collided.

In this, the year of the final episode of *M\*A\*S\*H,* the debut of Michael Jackson's moonwalk and McDonald's Chicken McNugget, and the first flight of the space shuttle *Challenger,* Norman George found himself walking around Boston, where he lived, fresh from the grocery store and wearing a T-shirt with Poe's face on it.

He was stopped by a local historian who asked where George got the shirt. An affinity was established, and George invited the man to his place to show him his collection of more than five hundred books and publications dedicated to Poe. After a bit of conversation, the historian mentioned that he was looking for an actor to give a performance as Poe for an event he was hosting.

George rushed to his bathroom mirror, placed a couple of fingers on his upper lip as an impromptu mustache, and tried his best to look underfed and underappreciated.

And thus Norman George was reborn as Edgar Allan Poe.

"I'd acted. I was obsessed with Poe. Even orated some of his stories in high school as part of an acting program," he told me in an interview that started over the phone and finished in a hotel restaurant in Chelmsford, Massachusetts. "But I'd never thought to really put the two together."

George's first performance as Poe came on Halloween of that year. For the performance, he composed a dramatic act called *Poe Alone: The Last Appeal.* The conceit of the show was that Poe was in Richmond toward the end of his life, attempting to drum up funds for a literary journal that he had been trying to jump-start his entire professional career. It would be his last lecture before that fateful stop in Baltimore.

"I took liberties with it, because had I tried to do a typical, two-hour Poe lecture, the audience would have fallen asleep. I wanted it to be plausible—the style, the content. I wanted him to have a Richmond accent."

After that Halloween, George performed the show hundreds of times in fifteen states. One 1989 *New York Times* article I read about him observed that he "earns far more being Poe than Poe did."

Pictures of George as Poe show a reasonable facsimile of the poet. George's transformation was admirable in the almost impossible attempt to show forty years of misery and hardship with just makeup and facial expressions. Mostly, from what I've seen, the biggest difference between Poe and most Poe performers seems to be that every Poe performer is proud of being Poe. I'm not sure we could always say the same of Poe himself.

The role launched George into a grand Poe adventure. In his travels and performances, he got to meet famous Poe scholars, like Daniel Hoffman, author of one of the more unique Poe books out there in *Poe Poe Poe Poe Poe Poe Poe* (and who passed away just a few months into the start of this book), as well as a range of Poe appreciators and museum staff. In one of his most memorable experiences, and the one that makes me jealous enough to be tempted to malign him in these pages, he got to stay the night in the parlor of the Bronx cottage that was Poe's last house and the place where Poe's wife, Virginia, died.

When I met him in Chelmsford, I was curious as to why he'd given up Poe, which he'd done about five years earlier. I thought maybe he'd put on weight. That he wasn't Poe-shaped anymore. I didn't think it was age. John Astin, of Gomez Addams fame, didn't even start his one-man Edgar Allan Poe show until he was almost seventy.

The man I met was gray-headed and bespectacled, thin. He was in his early sixties, well before the expiration date for performing Poe. He was also soft-spoken and seemed to me more English teacher than drama teacher.

When I asked him why he stopped doing Poe, he didn't give me a reason. Just kind of brushed it off, like that raven had flitted. But as much as the role might have consummated George's own Poe fandom, it was the starting point of the Boston Poe plaque.

According to George, he visited the Boylston/Charles Street location when it was a luggage store, looking for a valise to carry some papers he needed for his Poe act. He happened to mention to the person working at the store that the building was close to where Poe was born, information that was then passed along to the building's landlord, Michael Moskow. He encouraged George to commission a plaque for the building and offered to help fund it as well. Then George, perhaps remembering the disappointment he felt as a fourteen-year-old unable to find Poe's birthplace, went further.

He spearheaded the formation of a group called the Edgar Allan Poe

Memorial Committee and approached the office of Raymond Flynn, the mayor of Boston at the time. He got as far as one of the aides, but that was far enough. One call later, and the alley beside the building was officially renamed Edgar Allan Poe Way. "That's how politics works, I guess," George said. Maybe he'd found a Poe fan somewhere in the mayor's office.

The plaque itself was cast by Robert Shure, whom I was also able to catch up with. Like George, Shure is a native New Yorker who came to Boston for school. He apprenticed at the studio of Adio di Biccari and Arcangelo Cascieri in South Boston and eventually took over their studio, moving it just outside of Boston to Woburn and renaming it Skylight Studios. The Poe plaque was one of the last projects he finished at the original location.

George found Shure through the recommendation of Cascieri, whose goddaughter had created the costumes George wore in his Poe act.

Art and restoration projects from Shure's studio can be found all over the world, but most of its work is concentrated in Massachusetts. In Boston, Shure and his studio are probably best known for the large Ted Williams plaques at each end of the Ted Williams Tunnel and the Massachusetts Fallen Firefighters Memorial outside the state house. Few connect him with the lowly plaque on the far side of the Common.

Shure cast the plaque using text written by George, and the image of Poe was based on a 7.5-inch-diameter bronze medallion designed by Edith Woodman Burroughs in 1909 for the Grolier Club, a New York–based bibliophile society established in 1884 and still around today.

I asked Shure if he'd seen the Poe plaque recently. "I have. Seems to be corroding," he told me both sadly and matter-of-factly. "It needs to be maintained with coatings of wax every year or two and then cleaned and polished to preserve it." The plaque apparently ended up being a more fitting tribute to Poe's legacy in Boston than either he or George intended.

They unveiled the plaque in 1989 at the Old South Church on Washington Street for Poe's 180th birthday to one of the biggest crowds ever assembled there. The ceremony included a lecture on the images of Edgar Allan Poe by photohistorian Clifford Krainik (who owned the Poe medallion borrowed for the plaque) and a performance of *Poe Alone* by George. The event got national publicity. I was even able to dig up an old *People* magazine article on it. That's right. Poe was celebrity enough for *People*. The article referred to Poe as one of Boston's "least favorite sons."

As a nice, final touch, a program from the event was placed in a plastic bag and sealed behind the plaque.

So that's how a Poe performer got a Poe plaque in a prominent spot of a notoriously Poe-less city. But there's still that one question that'll hang over this entire book. Of all possible objects of obsession that life offers, why Poe? George's answer to me: "His originality. He was just so original. You can't find anything like Poe anywhere." In the *People* article, a two-decades-younger George explains it a bit more introspectively. He found in Poe "a sense of apartness I identified with, having been an only child." Better interviewer, I guess.

And even though the sign that denoted Edgar Allan Poe Way is no more, the plaque is still there, so unobtrusive that it seems to honor some Bostonian of mere parochial interest instead of one of the most influential writers the world has ever known.

Although the plaque has been the only public Poe memorial in Boston for most of the twentieth and twenty-first centuries, it hasn't been entirely alone in its vigil. There is another, private, relatively longstanding Poe acknowledgment not two blocks south.

Fayette Street is a three-block stretch of late-nineteenth century residences in the pleasant and expensive Bay Village neighborhood of Boston. Number 15 on that street doesn't stand out too much from its neighbors. Like most of them, it's built of red brick and trimmed in black.

However, to the left of the iron scrollwork gate that guards the entrance is a bronze medallion the size of a saucer. On it is the morose visage of Edgar Allan Poe, his prominent forehead somewhat weathered, his hair crowned by the letters of his name, and his face bracketed by Roman numerals representing his birth and death years. By his left cheek is a symbol that looks vaguely like a tree encircled by a wreath. On the other side of the entrance is a typed sheet of residents for the building's seven apartments, beneath the name, "Poe Condominium."

Turns out, the symbol isn't a tree. It's the crest of the Grolier Club. The disc is one of the Grolier Club medallions used as inspiration in the Poe plaque.

Other than ringing all the door buzzers and explaining this entire book project over a staticky intercom or staking out the building and accosting its tenants as they entered or exited, I wasn't quite sure how to get the story of why that medallion was attached to that condominium. I only knew that the small piece of bronze transformed the

*Grolier Club medallion,*
*15 Fayette Street*

entire building from just another place in Boston to a mysterious point on the Poescape, and I wanted to know more about it.

Fortunately, I was saved from possible restraining orders by Norman George. He directed me to a man named Robert Davis.

I met Robert for dinner at a seafood restaurant on Boston's Long Wharf, where Poe's own mother first stepped foot on American soil at age nine. He told me over e-mail that he'd be carrying a book with Poe's face on it so that I'd recognize him. I sent him an image of Pee-Wee Herman. He didn't get the joke, and was looking for a skinny guy with bulging eyes and a red bow tie. "I wasn't sure what I was getting into," he said when he finally saw that I looked slightly more boring than that.

But Davis had humor enough. Later in the dinner he would throw an actual brick onto the table.

Davis had the look of what some might call an old-timer, and he must have been in his seventies. He was a retired writer and editor, a native Bostonian who graduated from Northeastern University with a degree in English-Journalism in 1959 PPW (pre Pee-Wee Herman).

Davis met George when they worked for the publishing house Little, Brown and Company. They eventually became roommates, and Davis would help George with his Poe act by writing essays for his playbills. Davis also wrote about the other Edgar Allan Poe for various newspapers and magazines. He was listed on the roster of George's Edgar Allan Poe Memorial Committee as "Historian."

"I liked Poe before I met Norman, but was mostly into Ray Bradbury and pulp sci-fi. But Norman, he was a total freak about Poe, and really turned me onto the guy in a big way." Of course, one doesn't need to share a refrigerator with a man dressed as Edgar Allan Poe to get from science fiction and Bradbury to Poe.

Poe is often credited as being an early contributor, if not a founder, of the science fiction genre long before technology took over the world and really inspired authors to start codifying the genre. When not burying people alive or making dead people live, Poe was sending men to the moon and uncharted regions of the earth and spending entire pages on the science that made the journeys possible. Toward the end of his life, he tried to create a unified theory of the universe in his prose poem *Eureka,* his second longest work next to *The Narrative of Arthur Gordon Pym of Nantucket,* which itself is one of those aforementioned proto-science fiction stories.

So it's no surprise that Ray Bradbury, an original voice and heart in the science fiction and horror genres, was always vociferous about Poe's influence on his stories. In his introduction to the 1966 science fiction anthology *S is for Space,* he listed him as an influence along with Jules Verne, H. G. Wells, and Mary

Shelley. "Edgar Allan Poe was the bat-winged cousin we kept high in the attic room." Thirty years later, in a new forward to his macabre anthology *The October Country,* Bradbury wrote that Poe had grown to become more of a patriarch on the Bradbury family Halloween tree: "My proper home was Usher, my aunts and uncles descended from Poe."

Where the two diverge on the family tree is that Bradbury wrote from a totally different place. Every word Bradbury wrote, no matter how sinister, no matter how fraught with soul-peril, seems to have been written with a child laughing over his shoulder, whereas any laughter that Poe might have heard as he composed his tales was of the maniacal sort. The two would be perfect for a revamp of *The Odd Couple.*

Back to Robert Davis, his specialty was the more obscure aspects of Poe life, and his pet piece of obscurity was Calvin F. S. Thomas, the teenaged Boston printer who, in 1827, published the first work of a teenaged Poe. It was a ten-poem pamphlet entitled *Tamerlane and Other Poems,* and it came out right around the time that Poe joined the Army.

"I once flew up to Buffalo just to see the site of Thomas's grave at Forest Lawn Cemetery," said Davis. I knew the cemetery. Had been there myself. Its 269 acres is full of macabre wonders like the Blocher Memorial, an entire deathbed scene of life-sized marble figures in a glass-and-stone-enclosed bell chamber, and Frank Lloyd Wright's Blue Sky Mausoleum, a set of crypts arranged like gentle stair steps that lead down a hill to a pond. Interred in that cemetery is the dentist who invented the electric chair, an explorer who may have faked the first trip to the North Pole, the thirteenth President of the United States, and the singer famous for the song *Super Freak.*

Basically, there are a lot of reasons to visit that Buffalo cemetery. Davis's special trip might have been the only time in its history that the grave of an obscure Boston printer was one of them.

Today, the spot where Thomas's Boston print shop stood is 1 State Street, an eighty-year-old building on the lion side of Boston's lion-and-unicorn-topped Old State House, just steps away from the site of the Boston Massacre. I worked for years just down the road from the site, and I'd dodged many a tourist and many a colonial-dressed tour guide there on my way to lunch before I ever learned what had transpired at that location once upon a time: the official beginning of Poe's writing career . . . unmemorialized, of course.

Davis had published a piece on Calvin Thomas in *The Boston Globe* on June 6, 1988, the day before Sotheby's sold a recently discovered first edition of *Tamerlane and Other Poems.* It was only the twelfth known to exist and had been found in a stack of agricultural pamphlets in a Hampton, New Hampshire, junk shop, where it was purchased for $15. It sold at auction to a private collector for just under $150,000. Two decades later, another first edition was sold to a private collector for more than $660,000.

Another bit of obscurity Davis knew about was the Fayette Street Grolier Club medallion. He told me that the residence once held the studio of a Boston-born artist named Kahlil Gibran, who had been named after the famous poet, who was also his cousin and godfather. Kahlil's landlord, a Poe fan, had purchased one of the Grolier Club Poe medallions, and, knowing Poe had been born nearby, asked Gibran to affix the medallion to the front of the house.

"Unfortunately, the medallion led some to assume that Poe had been born at 15 Fayette," Davis told me. "That couldn't have happened because 15 Fayette was under water in the year of Poe's birth." The area had been a part of Back Bay before being landfilled and developed in the early 1800s.

Gibran died in 2008, leaving this story as simple as a private memorial. But I'll always be tempted to tell people that 15 Fayette is a private club of eccentric Poe fans who style themselves after the characters in the funeral-home wine-cellar court of "King Pest."

Davis also showed me some of the articles he'd published about Poe, including a humor piece intended to be a conversation between Michael Jackson and Poe in 1999, when rumors abounded that Jackson was going to star as Poe in a major motion picture. Then he reached into the satchel that he'd brought and pulled out a red brick. A brass plaque attached to it read:

SALVAGED FROM THE LAST MANHATTAN
RESIDENCE OF EDGAR ALLAN POE.
85 AMITY STREET. GREENWICH VILLAGE
POE MUSEUM, RICHMOND, VIRGINIA,
AND THE MYSTERY WRITERS OF AMERICA.
NUMBER 204.

What I said out loud was "That's freaking awesome." In my head it was, "Damn it, you're messing up my chronology." And I meant both.

The brick was exactly what it said on the plaque; the building had been torn down in 2000 to make way for New York University's law school. Davis had gone there to report on the controversy for *The Mystery Review,* a now-defunct Canadian journal, and had been part of the protest against its demolition. But that's a New York story. We'll get to that one later.

But it's a good place to end this part of the Boston Poe story, with Norman George's Poe plaque and the Fayette Street Grolier Club medallion being the sum total of Poe's physical legacy inside Boston proper for more than half a century, all the way to 2009, in fact. It's no giant piece of metal fruit, but it's something.

## Poe vs. Boston

The whole situation is strange. Why would a city used to flaunting its best jewelry regardless of the party being thrown not adorn itself with its finest literary charm?

Well, traditionally, the storyline has been that Poe hated Boston, so Boston hated him right back. It's clean, it's interesting, and I only kind of buy it. Let's look at the action before the equal and opposite reaction.

While the Boston area was always an option as a place to live for Poe, it was also always a thorn and a goad. Poe's feeling of ill-will toward the city of his birth seems to be supported by a lot of evidence, straight from Poe's own black beak.

In the November 1, 1845, issue of the *Broadway Journal,* a publication he eventually owned and whose pages formed the battlefield for his one-sided war against Henry Wadsworth Longfellow, he wrote:

> **We like Boston. We were born there—and perhaps it is just as well not to mention that we are heartily ashamed of the fact. The Bostonians are very well in their way. Their hotels are bad. Their pumpkin pies are delicious. Their poetry is not so good. Their Common is no common thing—and the duck-pond might answer—if its answer could be heard for the frogs. But with all these good qualities the Bostonians have no soul . . . The Bostonians are well-bred—as very dull persons generally are.**

All right, well, Poe hated Boston. Got it.

Oh, wait. Context.

The quote was part of a long, public response to a literary engagement he had at the blunt peak of the fame he achieved during his lifetime. "The Raven" had been published in January of that year in New York, causing a sensation that made him a wanted man for parties and lectures. For the Boston Lyceum association, he delivered an address that may or may not have been a success, depending on who tells the tale.

Poe was the second speaker of the night and was supposed to have delivered a new poem for the occasion. Instead, either out of spite or artistic desperation (but more than likely the latter), he brushed off one of his oldest and longest poems, a confusing piece of juvenilia called "Al Aaraaf." It's the story of a supernova in Arabia. Or something. Critics are still trying to figure it out. He also spent his time on the dais disparaging Boston Transcendentalism, and then finished the night with "The Raven." The next day, some critics disparaged his presentation, claiming that many people left before Poe could even get to the popular bird in black.

Poe took offense and greatly disagreed with the negative characterization of the night. And also said horrible stuff about the city. The thing about being a genius with words is that it's real hard to turn down fights that use them as weapons. God knows what he would've done with social media in his arsenal.

But it wasn't his first time slagging Boston. He didn't need public provocation. He regularly called the city "Frogpondium" in print, a reference to a stagnant pond on the Common and an inference that its literary establishment was little more than croaking frogs—loud, obnoxious, and parochial. Today that frog pond is a frog-themed recreation area—a wading pool in the summer and an ice rink in the winter. Large, cartoony bronze statues of frogs decorate the whole area. Again, as has been its wont, Boston memorialized a frog pond before Poe.

That context is important when assessing Poe's attitude toward Boston. His beef was less with the locale and its people and more with the literary scene. Poe wasn't a big fan of poetry with morals or lessons or those who used poetry as a platform. So he found the works of such New England poets as Ralph Waldo Emerson, Charles Sprague, and Henry Wadsworth Longfellow—basically anyone he deemed a Transcendentalist, a term his pen transmogrified into a curse word—anathema to good poetry.

He wrote about this voluminously and acerbically in the literary magazines that he edited throughout his career and it fit right in with his reputation as a caustic critic. They called him the Tomahawk Man, and it's too bad they didn't make T-shirts in those days.

Honestly, a lot of Poe's motivations here were badly seasoned with a bitter envy that his work wasn't achieving the renown of these poets who were composing what he thought were fundamentally inferior works. Had Boston demarcated a nice, grassy spot on its literary landscape for him, he'd have been a Bostonian with pride. Probably would have kissed Longfellow right on his bearded cheek and called him Santa.

In fact, whatever Poe's attitude toward Boston was on any given day, he had an obvious affection for the city.

When, at the age of eighteen, he fled Richmond and the rocky relationship with his foster father John Allan, he went straight to Boston, despite all the cities along the way.

Not too long after he arrived in Boston, he published *Tamerlane and Other Poems*, which he bylined anonymously as "A Bostonian." Admittedly, it was more of a marketing move than one of solidarity, but it did publicly acknowledge his kinship.

He was published regularly in Boston magazines throughout his life. In fact, as the Poe plaque already pointed out, he published the last tale of his life, "Landor's Cottage," in Boston's *Flag of Our Union* in June of 1849. It wasn't a magazine he particularly liked, but it did pay.

Toward the end of his life, he even had designs on moving back to the area. That decision was more about a girl than a place, a girl we'll talk about more later in this chapter, but still, his lifetime of loathing apparently wasn't so deep that he wouldn't move to the source of it. Or maybe the pumpkin pies were just that good.

And more than having a mere affection for the city, Poe had a reason to yearn for it.

Poe identified the city with his mother. It's become a part of Poe lore that one of his few mementos of her was a small watercolor picture of Boston Harbor she painted the year before his birth. On the back of it, she was supposed to have written, "For my little son Edgar, who should ever love Boston, the place of his birth, and where his mother found her best and most sympathetic friends."

Eliza Poe had more reasons than her son to love Boston. She birthed two of her three children there, and it was the last place she had a whole family before her death. Boston was also the first bit of America she saw, when she came over from England at the age of nine with her mother, also named Elizabeth and also an actress. Eliza's debut American performance was in Boston, just three months after landfall. Heck, Poe's gig for the Boston Lyceum was on the same stage his mother had acted on, at the long-gone Odeon Theatre (called the Federal Street Theatre back in his parents' day) at what is now 1 Federal Street. His mother had even performed there while pregnant with Edgar.

Just that mere identification with Eliza Poe should have been enough to elevate Boston to Shangri-La for Poe. And maybe in his more hopeful moments, it was. However, more often than not, it was just one more of the circles of a hell made up of every place he ever lived.

And that's another angle. Poe's inability to put a blurb on the cover of a Boston visitors guide could also be attributed to the fact that he simply had some real bad times there.

After fleeing Richmond and his guardian, John Allan, for Boston, Poe scraped by for about six weeks until he got desperate enough to join the military, upping his age to twenty-two and offering his name as Edgar A. Perry. He was stationed at Fort Independence on Castle Island for most of his time in the city.

His *Tamerlane and Other Poems* made no impact on Boston's literary scene. Any scene, really. Well, except the one 200 years later where literary collectors are buying copies of it for north of half a million dollars.

Boston is also the proud home of Poe's only known suicide attempt, so important for the Myth of Poe. Poe regularly made highly dramatic, end-of-life pronouncements in his letters for want of love or money or literary validation. Every situation was a matter of life and death, from unrequited love to actual matters of life and death. In this particular case, it's debatable whether he tried his hardest to kill himself or if he was taking one of his ploys a little further than mere words.

This was about a year and nine months after the death of his wife, and Poe, for much of that time, had been playing the field. By this point he had narrowed it down to two women, neither in an ideal situation for being his paramour—one was married and the other was withholding her finances from him and insisting he never drink.

Partially out of desperation and mostly to get the attention of that first woman, Poe purchased a couple of ounces of laudanum in Providence to cure him of "the fever called Living," took off for Boston, and wrote a letter to her, announcing his intention to kill himself, hoping she'd show how much she cared by coming to his deathbed after his overdose. He took half of the drug, and then got too sick to do anything else, including either sending the letter or dying. After a few horror-filled days, he sheepishly left the city and returned to Providence. He never stayed another night in Boston for the short rest of his life.

You could almost put together a tour of Poe's low points in Boston. Except that, like his birth home and Calvin F. S. Thomas's print shop and the Odeon Theatre, none of the places stand anymore. Except for Fort Independence. Sort of.

## Fortified in Massachusetts

I'll admit that it's somewhat iffy to characterize Poe's time in the Army as a low point. He certainly joined for lack of options, and his future actions would prove he didn't want to be a soldier, but it was one of the few times of his adult life when he wasn't trying to hold everything together by decaying threads. He had food, shelter, and employment and didn't have to worry about suddenly not having any of that.

And he did well, starting out as private in the First Regiment of Artillery and quickly working up to the rank of sergeant major and a clerk's job, away from the sooty hands and strained backs of cannon loaders. After five months at Fort Independence, his regiment moved to Fort Moultrie in South Carolina for a year and then Fort Monroe in Virginia, before he exited his five-year tour three years early. He topped off his military career, or, more accurately, beheaded it, at the West Point officer's academy in New York.

Today, Fort Independence still sits like a paperweight on Castle Island

*Fort Independence, Castle Island*

in South Boston, although things have changed. Castle Island is no longer an island. It's now connected to the mainland as the result of a land reclamation project. The fort itself, like so many of its kind along the East Coast, is now a historic monument and public park. And the whole thing has been completely rebuilt since Poe shoved heavy black iron spheres down the throats of heavy black iron tubes.

In fact, the modern-day Fort Independence is the eighth incarnation of the fortification. The first, back in 1634, was just a humble bit of wood and earth. In 1827, Poe served at the seventh Fort Independence, a five-sided affair similar to the current fort, though smaller and made of brick instead of granite.

Poe, like most who had been stationed at the fort over the course of its life-time, had it relatively easy as far as military action goes. The fort never saw any real warfare in its 350 years, only a slightly destructive retreat by the British in 1776 and many centuries of harsh New England winters.

I visited Fort Independence hoping to discover some Poe references. I found one . . . at the monkey bars.

It was the day before Memorial Day, a sunny affair in a year that basically skipped spring. You could tell that people were excited to be out because they weren't deterred by the series of invisible face jabs that was the high wind coming off the harbor. People were fishing and picnicking, jogging and flying kites, laying out in the sun, and just generally doing non-warlike things all around the five walls of the fort.

The only way to see the interior of the fort is by guided tour. They're free and offered regularly throughout the summer and early fall months. I joined one, finding myself in a group of some thirty other people for what I learned was the first Fort Independence tour of 2013.

I've been through my share of early American forts, and Fort Independence is typical. It's a pentagonal enclosure of granite walls surrounding a wide, grassy space. At each corner is a bastion named for some famous personage of Boston history: Winthrop, Adams, Dearborn, Shirley, and Hancock. No Poe Bastion.

My group was taken through a series of rooms, and then we ascended a set of stairs and were led around the flag-bedecked top of the wall. From there we could see the building-scape of Boston and most of the harbor and its islands, complete with the spherical tanks of the sewage treatment plant on Deer Island and the winking eye of Boston Light on Little Brewster Island, site of the oldest lighthouse base in the country and the second-oldest lighthouse structure.

My apologies for making the same reference twice in a single chapter, but I felt a bit like Pee-Wee Herman waiting to be shown the basement of the Alamo. "Where's the Poe Room? Aren't we going to see the Poe Room?"

But the poet-soldier never came up, although a spot where they once filmed a shaving cream commercial did, and I saw no trace of either his name or face. His only mention was in the cream-colored Fort Independence pamphlet, in a paragraph under the heading "Interesting Incidents": "The duel between Lts. Massie and Drane in 1817 has resulted in a legend that still lives. Edgar Allen [*sic*] Poe served on Castle Island for five months in 1827 under the name of Perry, and his story of 'The Cask of Amontillado' is alleged to have been influenced by the Drane-Massie duel."

That happens a lot at Poe sites. It's not enough to claim Poe himself; you have to claim his horrors, too, even if you have to stretch that claim to Mr. Fantastic proportions. Disappointed, I left the fort and headed down to the nearby playground to meet my wife and child.

And there I found Poe.

From my previous ramble atop the walls of the fort, I had seen the playground below. It was laid out in the same shape as the fort, with a concrete stub of a pillar set in each bastion.

At ground level, I could see pentagonal stainless steel plates bolted to the top of the short pillars. On each of the manhole-sized plates were etched five illustrations and five facts about the fort, the island, and the harbor itself: trivia like President Adams giving the fort its name in 1799, that Donald McKay's clipper ships were built in the area (an item memorialized on the far side of the island with a massive stone obelisk), or the sighting of a sea serpent in the harbor in 1818. And right there in the corner of one was the enduring countenance of Poe gleaming in stainless steel hot enough in the noon sunshine to scorch a child: EDGAR ALLAN POE WAS STATIONED, UNDER AN ASSUMED NAME, WITH THE 1ST ARTILLERY AT THE BRICK FORT INDEPENDENCE IN 1827.

It's a minor mention, but it made me happy. And, honestly, it's fitting in context. The fort on the island has 350 years' and half a dozen wars' worth of history. Poe spent five unremarkable months there.

But what I can forgive the fort for I cannot quite forgive Boston, which buried his legacy so much more deeply than Baltimore buried his body.

## A Beat Poet

Boston isn't the only place in Massachusetts where you can see Poe's name etched into durable materials. The nearby cities of Lowell and Westford, northwest of Boston, have both attempted to pick up what they can of what Poe's birthplace has for so long dropped.

Poe's relationship with these Boston suburbs started as a lecture stop and ended with a woman. In 1845, Poe's star rose as high in his lifetime as was allowed with the publication of what would become his signature work, "The Raven." Lots of places were inviting him to lecture about poetry and recite the

*Poe trivia at Castle Island playground*

poem. In 1848, while living in New York, he was invited to Lowell. It was there that he met Nancy Heywood Richmond.

After the passing of his wife in 1847, Poe found himself in the market for a new muse. Ideally one he could idealize. And if she had cash, that would be cool, too. Thanks to his literary magazine career, he knew lots of women poets and had paramours in Providence, Richmond, New York, and probably other places. Even proposed to a couple of them. And yet, while all this was going on, the woman he really wanted was Nancy. She lived in Lowell. And she had a husband.

To read Poe's letters to Nancy, or, as he affectionately called her, Annie, is to see exactly the type of Poe we all hope for: Passionate, histrionic, sad, desperate, and odd. For instance:

> **Ah, Annie Annie!** *my* **Annie! what cruel thoughts about your Eddy must have been torturing your heart during the last terrible fortnight, in which you have heard *nothing* from me—not even one little word to say that I still lived & loved you. But Annie I know that you *felt* too deeply the nature of my love for you, to doubt that, even for one moment, & this thought has comforted me in my bitter sorrow—I could bear that you should imagine *every other evil except that one*— that my soul had been untrue to yours. Why am I not *with you now darling* that I might sit by your side, press your dear hand in mine, & look deep down into the clear Heaven of your eyes—so that the words which I now can only *write*, might sink into your heart, and make you comprehend what it is that I would say—And yet Annie, *all* that I wish to say— all that my soul pines to express at this instant, is included in the one word, *love*—To be with you now—so that I might whisper in your ear the divine emotions, which agitate me— I would willingly—oh *joyfully* abandon this world with all my hopes of another—but you *believe* this, Annie—you do believe it, & will always believe it—So long as I think that you *know* I love you, as no man ever loved woman—so long as I think you comprehend in some measure, the fervor with which I adore you, so long, no worldly trouble can ever render me absolutely wretched. But oh, *my darling, my* Annie, my own sweet *sister* Annie, my *pure* beautiful angel—*wife* of my soul—to be mine hereafter & *forever in the Heavens*—how shall I explain to you the *bitter, bitter* anguish which has tortured me since I left you?**

And that's just the first part of a very long letter to this married woman.

Nancy found him fascinating and welcomed him into her life, but didn't do the one thing he really wanted her to do. In a letter to his mother-in-law Maria Clemm, he writes, "Do not tell me anything about Annie—I cannot bear to hear it now—unless you can tell me that Mr. R is dead." Mr. R is, of course, Charles Richmond, Nancy's husband.

Still, Poe found a way to contort his life to fit hers much the same way he contorted his life to fit into the lives of Maria and Virginia. Poe visited Nancy regularly in his last two years of life, trying to woo her without seeming like he was trying to woo her. Perhaps that's why he gave her the pet name "Annie"—to create his own version of her that was his alone.

Annie was the woman for whom his suicide letter, and his suicide attempt in general, was intended. He wanted to get her to make good on the promise she'd made to come to his death bed, even if he had to make or fake that death bed.

And it was for Annie that, well, "For Annie" was written, a poem in which dying in her arms is his ideal state of existence with this woman.

Lowell and Westford still bear traces of this strange time in Poe's strange life, perhaps marked best by the single photo of Poe taken in Lowell. It's one of the more familiar and forlorn images we have of the poet, and it was taken just a few months before his death. In it, it's easy to imagine the type of figure that inspired Proverbs 31:7: "Let him drink, and forget his poverty, and remember his misery no more."

The city of Lowell has had a bit of a rough reputation in the past, but these days it's mostly known for being the home of Beat Generation novelist Jack Kerouac. A monument in a park named after him consists of a series of eight-foot-tall triangular stone pillars, each one inscribed with passages from his work.

And while I did swing by Kerouac Park to see it, the first thing I did upon entering Lowell was hit up the Dunkin Donuts downtown because, well, that's what you do in New England. But also, because it's a Dunkin Poe-nuts. In front

*Marker at site of Annie Richmond's childhood home*

of this shop, at the busy intersection of Church and Central Streets, is a three-foot-tall pink stone column. The top of it is slightly angled, and on its polished surface are the words:

FORMER SITE OF THE
WASHINGTON HOUSE
AND TAVERN
1832–1960
VISITED BY CHARLES DICKENS
AND EDGAR ALLAN POE

A PAINTING REPRESENTING
THIS SITE DURING THE 1800's
CAN BE VIEWED BEHIND THE
TELLER'S COUNTER INSIDE
THE FIRST BANK BUILDING

*Washington House and Tavern site marker*

The Washington House and Tavern was a massive white building with lots of windows. About a dozen chimneys pierced the sky above it. A portico ran around the base of the building's second story. It was at this tavern where we get a fun little bit of Poe apocrypha.

For years during the latter half of the 1800s, an original manuscript of a poem was supposed to have hung on the wall of the tavern of this building. It's come to be called "Lines on Ale."

> Fill with mingled cream and amber,
> I will drain that glass again.
> Such hilarious visions clamber
> Through the chamber of my brain—
> Quaintest thoughts—queerest fancies
> Come to life and fade away;
> What care I how time advances?
> I am drinking ale today.

The story goes that the poem was written by Poe to pay a bar tab. And as much as I would love to have a world where rhymes were currency at bars, recent scholarship has proven these lighthearted few lines to be somebody else's work. And while I'd like the story even better if Poe jotted them down from memory and passed them off on his own because he really wanted to drink ale that day, it seems the poem might post-date him. Poe never really waxed poetic about booze anyway . . . unless you count Nepenthe. No donuts in his poetry either.

But buildings from Poe's day still stand in Lowell, most notably the Wentworth Building at the corner of Shattuck and Merrimack Streets, where Poe gave his lecture, after which he met Annie.

And I figured while I was in Lowell, I should probably meet her myself.

Lowell Cemetery is usually only known for its lion and its witch, much like Oz or Narnia. The 170-year-old cemetery at 77 Knapp Avenue is well treed and sprawls pleasantly on 85 acres above the Concord River.

Its lion marks the grave of James Cook Ayer, a nineteenth-century entrepreneur who made his fortune in medicine. That's why he could afford to decay under a massive white lion carved out of twenty tons of Italian marble. His store is mentioned in an advertisement for Poe's Lowell talk as a place where people could get tickets for the event. And, while lion statues are a dime a pride, there's something about the size and color combined with the fact that it's a corpse weight that really make this piece remarkable. The sculpture has even been adopted by the cemetery as its symbol.

Of course, that's because its other notable piece of funerary art is simply terrifying.

*Wentworth Building*

Dubbed Witch Bonney, it's a bronze statue of a woman with outstretched arms holding a flowing cape or long shawl above her head. It's the Dracula pose, but its spookiness also comes from the green and black patina earned by a century or so of guarding the family plot; that patina is especially evident around her eyes, which are a soulless black (my Crayola box says that's actually a color). Its presence on a hill in front of a white-columned structure gives it further emphasis.

Bonney gets her name from the family buried in her plot. She gets her legend because she's a spooky old statue that stands out in a cemetery without any other spooky old statues.

The legend is a familiar one: Disrespect it and harm will befall you. One

*Annie Richmond's grave*

unique wrinkle in Witch Bonney's story, though, centers on her blouse. It's draped low enough to give the appearance that it's only held up by her nipples. The story goes that it drops farther every year, and that when it finally drops to her waist, the witch will rise to wreak half-naked havoc on the town.

Annie's grave is in view of both funerary statues.

The Richmond family tombstone is large and squat and bears about nine names across two sides of the marker. Annie's side faces Verbena Path, on which the stone is set. She died in 1898, almost fifty years after Poe's death. The most surprising element of her grave is that she's buried under the name Annie L. Richmond, inscribed right under the name of her husband, Charles, who died a quarter century before her.

In fact, after Poe's death, she legally changed her name to his pet name for her. Whether that was a tribute to a lost love or an attempt to jump on the coattails of a man whose fame was rising, we'll never know. In a letter she wrote in 1877, she described her memory of Poe: "He seemed so unlike any other person I had ever known that I could not think of him in the same way—he was incomparable—not to be measured by any ordinary standard—& all the events of his life, which he narrated to me, had a flavor of unreality about them, just like his stories." Unreal stories like his last published one, "Landor's Cottage," in which he set

Annie, "the perfection of natural, in contradistinction from artificial *grace*," in an idealized setting unsullied by plot.

My next stop was Westford, about ten miles southwest of Lowell, to the site of her birthplace, but only because one man from Lowell thought it worth commemorating.

## Edgar Allan Poe vs. That Damned Westford Knight

I briefly met Brad Parker during a celebration of Poe's 204th birthday at the Boston Public Library's Central Library, a massive, regal set of structures (it's technically made up of two connected buildings) with window ledges covered in the names of great writers and thinkers. Poe's name is there, on the side of the building that faces Boylston Street, under Emerson and Hawthorne and above Thoreau . . . so memorialized with a bunch of people whose work he often didn't like, something that happens a lot to Poe.

During Poe's birthday bash, Parker and I made plans for a more formal meet-up, and that ended up being at a restaurant in Park Square, about a block away from Edgar Allan Poe Square.

Parker was born in Lowell. He got a degree in American History and Civilization from Boston University in 1968. He's retired now, but still brandishes a large, gold class ring on his finger. Parker's career was a relatively unconventional one. He spent six years teaching English in Japan and ten years working at the Thoreau Lyceum, a literary center in Concord dedicated to Henry David Thoreau, as well as at the nearby Old Manse, home of Ralph Waldo Emerson and Nathaniel Hawthorne (although not at the same time). He even portrayed Thoreau at Walden Pond, the former-wilderness area made famous by Thoreau's *Walden,* his memoir about the two years he lived there. "I'm not really well-read," Parker told me.

But I was there to talk about the Westford Poe marker, a monument that existed almost solely because of him.

It wasn't the first Brad Parker–motivated monument I'd seen. He'd hooked Bette Davis up as well. She was born in Lowell, and her birth home now bears a giant bronze plaque on the façade between the first and second stories. "I put two stars on it, one for each of her Academy Awards."

Parker's a man who likes to commemorate. And a man who likes his home.

His current obsession is Jack Kerouac. When I met Parker, he was writing a book on Kerouac. His second. His first was self-published in 1989. During our conversation, he'd often twist the topic back to Kerouac, like any good, obsessed seeker would do. "It's going to be called *Sleeping with Kerouac: A One-Stop Jack Book.* It's going to be all over the place, and I might never finish before I die, but that's fine if fate demands such."

*Poe's name engraved below a window at Boston Public Library*

He'd also published in 1984 a book about Poe called *Lowell's Greatest Romance: The Saga of Eddie & Annie.* He'd brought his last copy to show me. It was a short, sixty-page booklet with a black cover.

It was pretty obvious that Parker's actions were based on a combination of local pride and love of history, but when I asked him why he liked Poe specifically, he said, "The same reason everybody likes him. He's a mystery writing about mystery."

It was a good answer, but I didn't let on. "That's cool. I dig Poe, too. But I'd never think to stick a monument to him in the ground."

"Well, it was that damned Westford Knight."

The Westford Knight might be the town's most popular, if obscure, attraction. It's located beside the sidewalk on Depot Street and is purported to be the grave of a Knight Templar. According to the story, his name was Sir James Gunn, and he was part of an expedition to North America led by a Scottish earl named Henry Sinclair a century before Christopher Columbus's journey. A naked stretch of stone is supposed to bear a rough image of a knight with a sword and Gunn's coat of arms.

But you have to squint to the point of blind imagination to see it, honestly, and the evidence seems to show that the stretch of rock was six feet underground during the fourteenth century. Still, the town chained off the rock and set a stone marker there to mark the stone. A complementary chunk of rock bearing the image of a boat, an arrow, and the number 184 is supposed to be a waymark from that expedition and is on display at the nearby Westford J. V. Fletcher Library. It was across from the bathroom when I visited.

Parker lived in Westford for thirty-four years and had heard the legend too many times. "It was so obviously false, and they had a real visit from a famous person in Edgar Allan Poe that they could commemorate."

So, in 1983, he did some research, determined the site of the Heywood farm, got a granite company to donate the stone, paid $300 to get it chiseled, and then he and his seventy-nine-year-old father, Royce Parker, planted that sucker in the ground where the front door would have been. The original house was long gone, but its barn and shed had been incorporated into a new home in 1950 or so.

Parker threw a dedication ceremony for the marker, talked the local leadership into declaring a Poe Day, and hired a pair of actors to play Poe and Annie, who were brought to the event in a carriage drawn by a pair of Morgan horses. He'd met the Poe actor recently and by accident. He had been walking on Commonwealth Avenue in Boston, when he ran into a man carrying grocery bags and wearing a T-shirt with Poe's face on it. They got to talking about Poe, and the man took Parker back to his place to show off his book collection.

The man's name was Norman George. And that makes Brad Parker the grandfather of the Boston Poe plaque. And the Westford Knight its great-grandfather, I guess.

I asked him if he ever visited the three-decades-old Westford Poe marker anymore. "I used to. I'd always touch up the raven with some black Rust-Oleum. Probably need to go up there again."

I'd been to the site a few times, but decided to go again after meeting Parker. The address of the house is 11 Graniteville Road. The gravestone-shaped memorial sits in a small clump of trees to the side of the house, but since it's within the bounds of a circular driveway, it's slightly awkward to stop by and check out. It also makes me wonder what it's like to live with a Poe memorial in one's yard. Beneath the image of a black raven is the inscription:

EDGAR ALLAN POE
WAS HERE
1848–1849
READING POEMS—EXPLORING THE TOWN
NURTURING HIS FRIENDSHIP WITH
NANCY HEYWOOD RICHMOND ("ANNIE")

The raven did, in fact, need a new coat of Rust-Oleum, but it looked as if the thirty-year-old marker had faithfully maintained its vigil to an important piece of Poe's life. It didn't look like it was going anywhere soon, even if its raven is molting.

## Bad-Ass Poe Is All Out of Bubblegum

After that brief foray into the suburbs of Boston, it's time to bring the story back into the city. For more than a century, where it was even known that Poe was a New Englander, the storyline has been that Poe hated Boston and Boston hates Poe. But, like I said, I don't buy it. I'm okay with the first part—that Poe's bad experiences in the city combined with his professional jealousy overwhelmed his affection for it and caused him to renounce his citizenship, even as he made plans later in life to move just north of it to be closer to Annie Richmond.

But the second half of that story—that an entire city officially and bulldoggedly ignored his legacy, generation after generation, so that all he gets is a scattering of fan-sponsored memorials and a small engraving at a playground? That I'm not so sure of.

Even if a continuing line of Longfellow's descendants laced Boston's water supply with ill-will toward Poe, that shouldn't be enough to stop the city from capitalizing on him. "Poe," should say the Paul Revere statue behind the Old North Church, "you couldn't make enough money to even reach poverty in your life, but you're making a Bos-ton of it for us today." Poe pun.

It's a mystery I don't think is solvable because it's probably due to a snake nest of factors . . . but it's also a mystery that, as of the writing of this section, is about to become irrelevant.

For decades, when other cities were celebrating his birth in winter or mourning his death in fall, Boston just turned on the Celtics game. But, today, that's all water under the Zakim Bridge. Poe vs. Boston is no longer the story. It's the preface. A long one as I've told it, I admit, but nonetheless so. Poe is being redeemed as "a Bostonian" in a big way.

In 2011, the Boston Art Commission and the newly christened Edgar Allan Poe Foundation of Boston issued a call for proposals to design a memorial for Poe to be placed prominently in Edgar Allan Poe Square.

More than 250 proposals came in from around the world, and the winning design was . . . bad-ass.

It came from Stefanie Rocknak. A sculptor and professor of philosophy at Hartwick College in Oneonta, New York, she offered Boston a life-sized, upright figure of Poe. That by itself is probably not worth winning the grant . . . even though in my Poe travels I haven't come across a full-sized standing figure of the man. It's the attitude of the statue's proposed design that set it apart.

In Boston come fall of 2014, Poe will be bronzed mid-stride, his hair blowing back and coat flying behind him like a superhero's cape. In fact, there is a bit of a comic book flair about the figure. In his hand is an open portmanteau full of manuscripts, which flutter out and behind him in a trail that would cross panels in that medium. His ever-present black-feathered familiar bursts oversized from the case as well, as if to acknowledge "The Raven" as the most fully formed of his works.

The idea is that he's just off the train, brimming with success, renowned for his writing, walking briskly and proudly to the place of his birth (apparently nobody has told him it's a power transformer). The metal will be covered in a gray patina to give Poe a ghost-like appearance, a specter of what should have been for a man of his talent.

I call it "Bad-Ass Poe." I see him toting his poetry and stories like a machine gun, strutting down the street to the strains of James Brown's *How Do You Like Me Now?*, unleashing nightmares and quoting Rowdy Roddy Piper. This is the second coming of Poe, his triumphal return, the global phenomenon, the one we never saw—the one who has finally received the recognition he deserved in his lifetime and is coming home to claim his birthright . . . or to rub it in Boston's face; I'm not sure. But he is a cocky bastard.

According to Rocknak's proposal, "Boston is not claiming Poe, Poe is claiming Boston."

Either way, Boston is getting a Poe statue to go along with its bronze duckies. A full-sized Poe statue puts Boston in the elite. Baltimore has an awesome one in a passable location. Richmond has a passable one in an awesome location. Both are seated, sedate figures. And Boston aims to get one unlike anything we've ever seen around Poe.

At the 204th birthday event at the Boston Public Library, I got to see a nineteen-inch-tall wooden maquette of this piece, and it seems to be everything the Internet jpegs promised. I wanted to know more about how this statue project came to be, so while there, I placed Dr. Paul Lewis in my sights, even though it wouldn't be until almost a year later that I finally sat down and talked to him.

Lewis is a professor in the English Department at Boston College. In early 2009 he worked with a doctoral student at the school named Katherine Kim on a celebration of the Poe bicentennial and curated a small exhibition on Poe and Boston at an on-campus library. With the assistance of Boston College students and independent scholars Dan Currie and Rob Velella, the exhibit was then expanded into *The Raven in the Frog Pond: Edgar Allan Poe and the City of Boston*, which ran at the Boston Public Library from December 2009 through March 2010.

Around the time Edgar Allan Poe Square was dedicated in 2009, Currie and Lewis came up with the idea of installing a permanent work of art to memorialize Poe's ties to Boston. They started the Edgar Allan Poe Foundation of Boston to push for the idea, with Currie as its first president and Lewis as the chairman.

By the time I got the opportunity to talk to either one of them, Currie had retired from the position after four years, though he continues to champion Poe's place in Boston.

I met Lewis at his office at Boston College. It was located on the fourth floor of the college's brand new Stokes Hall. The office was small, with touches of Poe here and there—a few images of the poet, a fake raven perched on a shelf. Nothing overt.

Lewis himself was thin—actually narrow might be a better word for him—balding, with a neatly clipped gray goatee. Were I to guess his occupation without knowing who he was, I probably would have gone with something in the medical field. Maybe a radiologist or a coroner. Or honestly, exactly what he is . . . a distinguished college English professor in a major urban center.

He grew up on the Upper West Side of Manhattan, but much of his education and academic career took place in more northern climes: New Hampshire and Manitoba. His CV actually has more humor than horror, with such publications as *Cracking Up: American Humor in a Time of Conflict* and *Disaster as a Laughing Matter*. It also credits him for coining the term "Frankenfood" for genetically modified crops.

Every year around Poe's birthday, when the usual "Why does Poe Hate Boston?" article pops up in the local newspaper, Lewis is often the go-to guy. He's kind of adopted Poe, just as he's adopted Boston. In the warmer months he offers walking tours of Poe's Boston. He even participated in a pair of public debates, in Boston and Philadelphia, over which city deserved Poe's legacy. I listened to a recording of the one in Philadelphia. He made a real good showing with a thesis that Poe became what he was because he was at odds with the Boston literati. I'm paraphrasing here, but he basically said Poe needs Boston like the Batman needs the Joker. Or vice versa.

"Tell me your Poe story."

"I was kind of a morbid teenager and into horror films . . . the classic ones, not today's gory movies." The screen led him to the page, where he discovered Gothic fiction, which was where his academic career started. "My dissertation in the mid-'70s was on Gothic fiction and Poe was a chapter in it. He was a pivot point from gothic fiction to literary humor for me."

His Poe advocacy, however, started out as Boston literature advocacy. "Boston does far too little to celebrate its literary heritage. The Freedom Trail is mostly historical, as it should be, but they've got an amazing literary story and it really should be told. Of course, Poe is the black sheep of that story. That makes him interesting. "

"And pretty unique, right?"

"Oh, no. Poe wasn't unique. Poe was very much a product of his time and place. He wrote both within and against genre constraints. Original, sure, but he's not unique."

"But there's a professional football team named after a poem he wrote."

"Oh, that's unusual, and Poe's unusual no doubt. But there's a difference between 'unique' and 'unusual.'"

It was a precision I expected from an English professor and a cautious academic in general, but not from a man who had spent years promoting the legacy of Poe and who was now working to secure it. He went further when I attempted to push the uniqueness with my usual statement about teaching his most horrific stories to adolescents.

"The reason students love him is that they come home from middle school with that assignment, and it's so different from what they're used to, but they're getting assigned his most cherry-picked works, like "The Tale-Tell Heart," as opposed to *Eureka* or *The Narrative of Arthur Gordon Pym* or any of his works where he's faux-erudite and hard to read."

Still, this was a man working hard to honor that fake scholar—and in a big way. After all, getting a public statue created and installed involves way more than just whipping a sheet off at the end.

"The statue has been a lot more work than I realized, what with insurers, lawyers, public scrutiny, fundraising, contractors—and I've become a lot more involved than I planned to, especially with Dan stepping down." Fortunately, they had recently filled the foundation presidency again with a man named John LaFleur.

"So what are you trying to accomplish with the statue?

"It closes a circle. The statue is about Poe and Boston, not just Poe. It's about his triumph and is part of a larger process of celebrating Boston's literacy legacy. I'd like to think of it as the centerpiece of this."

Before I left, I had one more question for the man whose published works have titles that reference Sarah Silverman and Borat. "Do you find Poe funny?"

He inclined his head for a moment, and then in his careful, academic way said, "I find Poe funny, but after studying him for thirty-five years . . ." He started again. "Humor depends on surprise. Let's say I don't find him primarily funny. Poe does have an interesting sense of humor. He anticipates the dark, Freddy Krueger type of horror. He could write gothic fiction and mock gothic fiction. Write detective fiction and mock detective fiction. He understood the connections between humor and fear."

It reminded me of that episode from *The Munsters* where Herman Munster is reading "The Murders in the Rue Morgue," gets annoyed at the noise Grandpa Munster is making, and says, "I'm trying to read. With all that noise I can't concentrate on the jokes."

I thanked him for the interview and the Freddy Krueger reference, and then left. I had one more person on the board of the Edgar Allan Poe Foundation of Boston to meet.

His name is Rob Velella, and he was part of the team that helped Lewis with the Poe exhibit at the Boston Public Library. If Lewis is the quintessential literary professor, Rob is more like . . . I don't know. He treats nineteenth-century authors like your cool musician friend treats obscure bands, voraciously learning everything about them and then evangelizing them. He's described his work as "bringing nineteenth-century writers back from the dead." Oh, and he's also a Poe performer.

I looked up Velella by typing his last name into Google. It returned lots of pictures of purple jellyfish-type creatures. Eventually I found his site, The American Literary Blog. That was enough research for me to go talk to him. We met downtown at a Mexican restaurant that used to be the bookshop of Elizabeth Peabody, Boston's first woman publisher. Back in the 1840s, she co-published a magazine with Ralph Waldo Emerson, and her shop was a crossroads of transcendentalist writers and thinkers, the kind of place that would have burned Poe's skin like holy water on a demon had he tried to enter.

Velella was from Waltham, Massachusetts, looked to be in his early thirties, and had straight dark brown hair to his shoulders and a thick mustache. Multiple people told me I should "talk to Rob" when they found out about my Poe book. When the lecturer at the 204th anniversary at the Boston Public Library didn't know the answer to an obscure question about Poe, without hesitation Velella piped up with the correct answer.

Of all the people I'd talked to, his Poe story was the most unique. And hilarious. His exposure to Poe wasn't through the Roger Corman horror films or through being introduced to the stories in middle school or junior high. It wasn't until he was in college at UMass Lowell that Poe got under his floorboards.

"I started off as a music major, and I was miserable. I hated it so much. So I finally switched to English. I became the president of the literary society my freshman year. I went up to one of my professors and told him that we should do an event, that Halloween was coming, and did he know of any respected writers that have like any short, scary stories?" He laughed at the memory. "That was it."

And then he found himself in Philadelphia for graduate work and just couldn't stay away from the city's Poe National Historic Site. He started volunteering there, racking up some three hundred hours in his first eight months. Then he moved back to Boston, accidentally timing it for the two hundredth anniversary of the poet's birth.

"When I moved back here, I'd just gotten my master's. My thesis was a capstone project, where I researched, wrote, designed, and produced an Edgar Allan Poe-themed desktop calendar. To sell it, I started doing lectures and got in touch with Paul Lewis and ended up getting involved in a Poe exhibit he and Dan Currie put on called *The Raven and the Frog Pond*."

"And then you just became Poe one day?"

"Well, I had tons of literary history in my head, but I wasn't a teacher, so I didn't know what to do with it. So I started dressing up." And it wasn't just Poe. Nathaniel Hawthorne and Henry Wadsworth Longfellow often look back at him from his bathroom mirror. But more often than not, and especially in October, it's Poe.

"So what do you call it . . . are you a Poe actor? Impersonator? Performer?"

"I just say I portray Edgar Allan Poe. I'm not an actor. I don't like impersonator because it sounds cheesy, like an Elvis guy in Las Vegas. I don't even think of myself as a performer. I just think of myself as a literary historian who presents literary history differently." He went on to describe his version of Poe. "I like to make him complicated. I don't focus on the negative stuff. I know there are people that do. There aren't a huge number of Poe impersonators out there, but there's enough that it takes more than two hands to count them."

"There's enough for it to be a thing."

"Yeah, it's totally a thing. I mean, it's not like Abraham Lincoln where there's one in every town. I even thought about creating a network—a Poe impersonator club—you know, like a guild." This guy lives such a different life than I do.

Currently, Poe isn't who fascinates him. He's working on a book about Rufus Griswold, Poe's literary executor and character assassin, who did more for the Myth of Poe than generations of teenagers and horror movies combined. According to Velella, "Griswold might be more Poe than Poe."

Apparently, the editor and anthologist opened his own wife's tomb out of despair to hold her corpse. His house blew up with him in it, though he survived. His daughter died in a train accident and then was revived hours later. He wasn't buried for six years after his death, lying in a receiving tomb before being lain to rest in an unmarked grave. The Boston Public Library inherited the Griswold literary estate, so Boston's a good place to live when you're researching the guy.

But Griswold wasn't the one getting a statue. I asked Velella about his experience on the board of the Poe Foundation.

"We all knew it was going to take a long time, but at this point, we're all like 'Holy crap, we've been working on this for years.' But Boston needs it. We're undermining our culture by not supporting these literary figures. Most of the statues in Boston, and many places for that matter, are political figures. That's great and all, but these literary figures are the ones who really help create how each generation defines itself. A century from now, regardless of what people think of *Twilight* and *Harry Potter* and those kinds of books right now, those are the books that helped define this generation just based on how popular they were."

And that set up the perfect segue to talk about Poe's odd popularity in the modern world. Velella admitted he didn't think there was a good answer, but then proceeded to give me a good one, one that echoed Parker's sentiment as well. "Not only is he a tormented writer, but he's writing tormented stuff. At least what we remember of his work. I mean, Longfellow suffered from bouts of depression, but then he writes 'Into each life some rain must fall' or 'The lowest ebb is the turn of the tide.' So you're like, forget it, this guy's not committing to his own real emotions.

"James Russell Lowell had a difficult life. He attempted suicide twice that we know of. But if you ask any random person if they know who Lowell is or anything about his work, you won't get a thing. With Poe, the mythology of the man really intersects with the work that we remember him for. Although, if Poe had lived another ten or fifteen years he would have been significantly more successful."

He then explained to me that the decade directly after Poe's death saw a massive boom in publishing technology, in addition to laws that protected authors and larger readerships as the prices of books dropped and literacy rates increased. "Writers started becoming successful in America for the first time. Of course, if Poe had been successful in the 1850s, he wouldn't be as famous as he is today. If he was like this well-adjusted comfortably wealthy guy, we would have a harder time talking about him.

"When I do library talks, the average age is like ninety. That's the library crowd. But when I do Poe shows, the average age drops to twenty. When I do Longfellow—and I do him as a young man, and he does have a compelling story—

it's a more geriatric crowd that comes to that. Nobody in their twenties comes up to me and tells me what a huge Longfellow fan they are."

He sounded pretty bummed about that, so for the rest of the lunch, we swapped stories of visiting graveyards along the East Coast, something we had in common, and then afterwards he took me to the Omni Parker Hotel on School Street to see a mirror from the room where Charles Dickens stayed that was rumored to reflect Dickens's ghost.

As for the bronze ghost of Poe, the Poe Foundation had just about met its funding goal as of the writing of this section, and the sculpting of the statue was underway at Rocknak's New York studio. They had received donations from Michael Moskow, who funded Norman George's Poe plaque, prominent New England horror author Stephen King, and even Boloco kicked in some funds. But most of the money, Velella told me, just came from Poe's massive crowd of fans who contributed small amounts here and there.

The statue is slated to be unveiled in October of 2014, so I basically, wrote this book a year too early.

Like it was during his life, Poe's afterlife in Massachusetts has been a turbulent one. He's been ignored, claimed, kind of claimed, slighted, celebrated. He deserves the triumphant return that the Poe Foundation is giving him, the opportunity for him to finally walk confidently down the street like he's leading a literary movement instead of groveling for literary acknowledgment.

And he is leading. Poe's influence on culture is practically unbounded, but his influence in New England is most clearly seen through the slew of important New England–born and adopted horror authors that he Usher'd in: H. P. Lovecraft, Stephen King, Edith Wharton, Henry James, Shirley Jackson. Edgar Allan Poe broke ground for all of them, releasing the monsters that made the horror genre the rich, powerful one it is today.

*Jovanka Vuckovic's Poe and Lovecraft leg tattoos*

# Rhode Island

*Wild Weird Clime that Lieth, Sublime, Out of Space—Out of Time*

A CROWD LARGE ENOUGH to make the emergency-exit diagram on the wall required reading sat in folding chairs in the basement of a 175-year-old library in Providence, Rhode Island. A set of stairs extended itself into the middle of the room like a starship ramp, and the surrounding walls were covered floor-to-ceiling in books, except for one section, where a massive, centuries-old painting of George Washington dominated the room, or would have at any other time except that warm August night.

Everybody in that room—those seated in chairs, those lining the staircase, those standing in the back—were staring in anticipation at a mysterious form covered in a somber black shroud beside a simple lectern, waiting for it to be unveiled like it was a surprise funeral.

Finally, the shroud was whipped away to reveal the bronze bust of one of the most famous and influential horror authors of all time.

Edgar Allan . . . Howard Phillips Lovecraft.

## Brothers in Horror

Edgar Allan Poe never lived in Providence, but the city was a fulcrum of his final years on the planet. It was here that he courted Sarah Helen Whitman, a local poet whom he met thanks to a flirtatious poem she wrote about him. The two grew close, even as his attention began turning toward Annie Richmond just fifty miles north. But, unlike with Annie, Poe officially proposed to Whitman.

However, while Whitman is the appropriate context for Poe's Providence story, I can't tell it without giving it a grander one . . . by nesting it within the story of H. P. Lovecraft, the horror author whose stature in the genre has risen so high, the only rung above him is the one on which Poe himself perches, thumbing his nose.

Lovecraft was born in Providence in 1890, forty years after Poe was dropped with little fanfare into Baltimore dirt, but the lives of the two men bear an uncanny similarity that makes one wonder exactly what the appropriate conditions are for inspiring supreme expressions of horror.

Both men were born in New England. Poe didn't live there long, moving to enough other places to, well, fill a book. Lovecraft lived his entire life in the capital city of the smallest state in the union, with the exception of a short, unhappy couple of years in Brooklyn, New York.

Both men lost their fathers at young ages. Poe was orphaned at age two, when his father disappeared and his mother died of tuberculosis. Lovecraft lost his father at age three to a mental institution called Butler Hospital. His father died there five years later. His mother was around until he was thirty or so, although her life also ended in a mental institution, the same one where her husband died.

Both men lived in abject poverty their entire lives and for much the same reasons. Poe and Lovecraft had elitist streaks of varying widths throughout the courses of their lives that fed into their inability to accept or keep "common" occupations. They could only write . . . which they did between hunger pangs and humiliations.

Both men died in their forties. Poe was forty, Lovecraft forty-six.

Both men left legacies that are hysterically disproportional to their lives. Neither made it big in their lifetimes, although Poe was better known in his day than Lovecraft was in his. Today, of course, they are both giants of their genre whose shadows hide horrors that have inspired every teller of terror tales today.

Both men went unacknowledged in their birth cities long after their fame had reached apexes that everybody else could see. Poe—we covered that story. And Lovecraft, we're getting to it.

Both men were keenly interested in science, with Poe's interest incarnating itself into works of science fiction like "The Unparalleled Adventure of One Hans Pfaall" and works of nonfiction like *Eureka.* Lovecraft's interest in science came out in a body of work that can just as comfortably be classified as science fiction as it can be horror.

And, of course, both men wrote horror stories . . . genre-defining ones. And it is here where these men took separate, though adjacent, psychiatrist couches. Poe's horrors sprang from the psychoses of men. Lovecraft's from the indifference of the cosmos. Poe rips away your faith in humanity. Lovecraft, your faith in the universe. In Poe, you die at the hands of a madman. In Lovecraft, you die by your own hand in the face of your own insignificance.

In some ways, they couldn't have been more different in the terrors at the tips of their pens, except that Poe's influence on Lovecraft and his work was written in invisible ink between every line. Sometimes Poe lurked in the shadows and corners of Lovecraft's stories. Other times he was the Rod Serling to his *Twilight Zone* episodes.

But you don't have to do a story-by-story comparison to see the importance of Poe to Lovecraft and the esteem in which the latter held his literary progenitor. In Lovecraft's short survey of weird fiction, *Supernatural Horror in Literature,* Poe gets an entire chapter, about 10 percent of the book.

In it, he calls Poe an "opener of artistic vistas" and a "deity and fountainhead of all modern diabolic fiction" (in his letters, he calls Poe his "God of fiction" and "the apex of fantastic art"), all names I hope you're reading in the voice of a ring announcer.

Lovecraft adds that "Poe did that which no one else ever did or could have done; and to him we owe the modern horror-story in its final and perfected state."

In three words, Lovecraft dug Poe. Strip away the tentacles, scales, claws, and wings on the miniature stone idol of Cthulhu on his pedestal and you'll find a little statue of Poe glowering back at you

In fact, in reading Lovecraft's take on weird fiction, we see some of Poe's favorite precepts: the idea of the "creation of a sensation" as the primary reason for a tale, over plot and character; the idea that stories shouldn't teach, but instead exist solely as aesthetic experiences; and the importance of analytic thought behind the creation of those experiences.

I'm very close to quoting that entire chapter of *Supernatural Horror in Literature,* so let me move on from belaboring a point that nobody disagrees with in the first place.

Finally, and most relevant to this book, although they missed each other in time, they crossed paths in space at multiple places. As I've mentioned, Poe visited Providence half a dozen times in his final years, and Lovecraft loved to trace those places in his home city that Poe haunted.

Heck, Lovecraft went on his own tour of Poe-Land itself, visiting Poe sites along the entire East Coast. In a 1934 essay called Homes and Shrines of Poe, he describes what he found throughout his treks, bemoaning the lack of markers at most of the sites, but describing the Richmond Edgar Allan Poe Museum (back then called the Edgar Allan Poe Shrine) and the recently opened Edgar Allan Poe House in Philadelphia with an awe barely obscured by the matter-of-fact tone of the piece.

Basically, he wrote my book eighty years ago and in about two thousand words.

So it was with some sense of appropriateness that my travels to Edgar Allan Poe sites brought me to Providence at the same time that NecronomiCon Providence, an inaugural conference dedicated to the man who has been called the "Providence Poe," was being held in the city.

# Lovecraft-Land

It was the end of August, and I arrived on the first day of the four-day conference. The keynote speech was that night, as was the unveiling of the H. P. Lovecraft bust that was its signature event and a big reason I was attending.

NecronomiCon Providence was organized by Niels Hobbs, a New England–based marine biologist who likes both his life and his fiction full of tentacles. The name of the convention is a pun on *The Necronomicon*, a "book of the dead" invented by H. P. Lovecraft that, in his stories, is written by a mad Arab and contains some of the darker secrets of the universe, including accounts of the elder gods that impinge from just outside the pages on most Lovecraft stories.

I decided the first thing on my conference agenda would be to avoid the conference. Instead, I would find some of the important Lovecraft sites and see where they intersected with Poe. That meant College Hill, the capital of Lovecraft-Land.

It's extremely difficult to see every Lovecraft site in a single go. Because Lovecraft lived almost his entire life in the city, based much of his work on the city, and wrote voluminously in his personal letters about his time in the city, just about everything in Providence, and especially College Hill, is a Lovecraft site. But I'll tell you how I did it that first day of NecronomiCon.

For the sake of readability, I'm going to present this tour like I wish I had done my research: thoroughly and in a well-organized manner that maximizes efficiency. The truth is I did extremely slipshod research before arriving, did some more on-the-go with my smartphone as I walked the streets, criss-crossed and back-tracked, lost my bearings one or two times, and took pictures of anything anybody else seemed to be taking pictures of. It's just that easy to find Lovecraft sites in the area. Also, I stuck to buildings that were still around, as a few Lovecraft sites have been torn down.

So let's go.

Fleur-de-Lys Studios looks like it has a backstory straight out of Grimm's Fairy Tales. The tall, thin building set on the side of the hill on Thomas Street is a bumblebee-colored edifice covered in plaster reliefs of animals and goddesses and other architectural embellishments to the point that it looks like the abode of an eccentric millionaire or an extraterrestrial dignitary or an outsider artist.

Its purposes are actually artistic. It was built in 1885 under the direction of Sydney Burleigh to be a personal studio, a haven for artists in general, and the headquarters of the Providence Art Club. Today, the club still exists and has expanded to other buildings on the street, although none so outlandish as the Fleur-de-Lys.

Lovecraft hallowed it by making it the address of Henry Anthony Wilcox, a strange young artist in "The Call of Cthulhu," who receives images in his dreams

*Fleur-de-Lys Studios*

that inspire him to sculpt the "horror in clay" that is the image of Cthulhu itself and our own first peek at the titular, gigantic, octopus-headed god who has since become the mascot for all things Lovecraftian. You can buy him in plush form these days.

The Fleur-de-Lys sits across the street from the First Baptist Church of America, which is both a name and a fact. This tall, white church was built in 1775, and the irreligious Lovecraft mentions it in his letters, calling it the "supreme landmark of Providence" and recounts the time he tried to play *Yes, We Have No Bananas* on the church organ. Later on that first day of NecronomiCon, his ghost would play it again during the convention keynote address there.

Benefit Street runs behind the church, and it's a beautiful stretch of College Hill lined with historic, colorful homes—well worth strolling even if you aren't looking for the horrors behind the old facades.

*First Baptist Church of America*

*Knowles Funeral Home*

Just a few steps from the church, at 187 Benefit Street, is a residence with gray siding and an incongruous, bulbous section of windows above its front door. Back in Lovecraft's day, this building was the Knowles Funeral Home, and it was here that Lovecraft's own funeral was held after he died on March 15, 1937, from intestinal cancer at the Jane Brown Memorial Hospital.

Moving north on Benefit Street, just past the gray mini-castle of the State Arsenal and the former rectory that is now the Old Court Bed and Breakfast, is 135 Benefit Street, a large, cheery, yellow house built in 1763 that Lovecraft transmogrified into the Shunned House in his story of the same name. "The Shunned House" is a stay-overnight-in-a-haunted-house story, and reading Lovecraft's take on it will explain all by itself why we've turned Lovecraft's name into an adjective.

It was at that point where I ran into Edgar Allan Poe.

## A Match Unmade in Providence

The large, red house at 88 Benefit Street was constructed in the late eighteenth century. The residence is plain but elegant, with white trim, and is almost completely hidden behind the single tree that grows between it and the road. In July 1845, Edgar Allan Poe found himself walking past this house during a stop in the city. It was the home of Sarah Helen Whitman, a widow and a poet who was six years older than Poe to the day. He saw her in the garden of the house, but didn't meet her.

Whitman was a fan of Poe and three years later wrote a poem called "To Edgar Allan Poe" for one of the literary parties that were in fashion in New York. In it, Whitman goths about sacrificing her Heaven to keep a sad, lonely, Christ-like Poe company in the hopes they can attain a Heaven together. Poe wasn't at the gathering, but heard about the poem, and immediately started a correspondence with Whitman that turned into outright courting. Poe had been a widower himself for a little less than two years at this point.

Poe would visit her at her home on Benefit Street, and they would hang out at nearby places . . . like the graveyard behind her house.

The Cathedral of St. John faces North Main Street, but it backs right up to the backyard of 88 Benefit Street. The church was built in 1810, replacing another church that dated to the early eighteenth century. It was called King's Church before being called St. John's.

Of course, you can't have an old church without an old cemetery St. John's cemetery is a small one, with about four hundred burials ranging from the 1730s to the 1940s. It's all but hidden from the surrounding roads, and the only way to enter it without going through the church is via a small pathway near 66 Benefit Street, just a few houses down from the Whitman House.

Here Poe and Whitman would walk among the stones and generally do what lovers do. About a century later Lovecraft would wander among the same tombstones, give or take a few, minus the lover. As a result of hearing about

*Home of Sarah Helen Whitman*

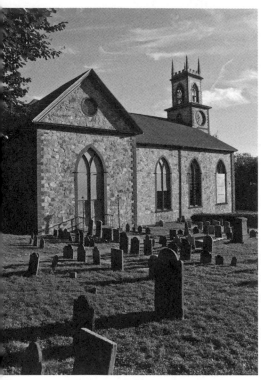

*Cathedral of St. John*

people being spooked by what he called the "hidden churchyard," Lovecraft once joked in a letter that "there must be some unsuspected vampiric horror burrowing down there & emitting vague miasmatic influences." Oh, that Lovecraft.

But he didn't visit the place for its vampiric horror. He visited it because of Poe. There's a picture from 1935 of Lovecraft posing beside the Whitman House and, in another letter he wrote of the graveyard itself, "Poe knew of this place, & is said to have wandered among its whispering willows during his visits here 90 years ago. Last August I shewed this place to two guests, & we all sat down on an altar-tomb & wrote rhymed acrostics on the name of Edgar Allan Poe."

I didn't attempt any rhymed acrostics on my visit, but I did marvel at the after-presence of Poe. By this time in my Poe trek, I'd marveled at that after-presence quite a few times in quite a few places, but in this instance it seemed different. This time it was in a graveyard, and I was surrounded by the mute witnesses of his passing. This poet who wrote so much about entombment and death, this man, who has rightly or wrongly come to personify grief and morbidity in our culture, had walked in this place that was a symbol of both. For the real-life Poe, the graveyard wasn't his element. But for the Mythic Poe, it was exactly that.

However, unlike Lovecraft, I had the additional pleasure of knowing that this graveyard was a crossroads of two of our best nightmare-makers. Lovecraft loved the idea that Poe walked in that graveyard, and we love the fact that they both did.

I visited the graveyard during the day, and it's a charming one, but it wasn't spooky, and I can't imagine it being very spooky even at night. It's too small, so you can't get lost in it, and any escape you might have to make from ghouls and night-gaunts is pretty easy, what with the back windows of the houses on Benefit Street standing watch on one side and the bustle of Main Street traffic on the other. Still, it does have a nice secret-garden quality, one enriched by the knowledge that both Poe and Lovecraft compacted the dead just a bit more here with their footfalls.

For Poe and Whitman, the romantic ambiance of the Providence cemeteries was too much, and they were soon engaged. There was a lot to be said for Poe marrying Whitman. She liked literature, had a good bit of money, and respected his abilities as a poet. The only problem was her family and friends. Also Poe.

The facts in the termination of their engagement are a bit fuzzy, and a lot of that has to do with Whitman outliving Poe by a good three decades, so only her side of the story lives on in any detail . . . but the lines are there to be read between.

Whitman's family and friends didn't like Poe, especially her mother, who lived with her on Benefit Street. They had heard rumors about Poe's drinking and other dalliances. It was all very junior high and all pretty much true, if blown out of proportion. However, Whitman's mother probably had good reason to be skeptical of this recently widowed pauper. To Poe, Whitman was no more than a sensible option for him, not exactly what he wanted, but good enough considering his circumstances . . . that is, until she wasn't.

Whitman, at the advice of her mother, drew up a prenuptial agreement to keep him from her cash and then made him promise to stop drinking. Just a few days and (allegedly) a single glass of wine later, they were dis-engaged. Personally, and for no reason other than it makes for a good story, I like to think the glass of wine was less a matter of Poe's inability to self-restrain and more an unchristening. With this wine, I thee de-wed.

Of course, it wasn't really that simple. As these things usually are, the breakup was a messy one. The wedding was so close to happening that they had chosen a reverend and a date, and had even placed an announcement in the newspapers. Word of his drinking came not from his own tell-tale heart, but from an anonymous note Whitman received while the two were visiting a local library. Poe talked so often about having enemies that it makes one suspicious of how he was defining the term, but there were certainly a few people who didn't want him marrying Whitman.

When Poe went to apologize for his behavior, one account says Whitman could not handle the drama and inhaled ether from a handkerchief until she passed out. Later, more unreliable stories claimed that the Providence police had to be called to forcibly remove Poe from her house.

And thus was the ugly end of Poe's Providence story, but not of my own Poe story in that city. I still had a few important Poe (and Lovecraft) sites and artifacts to see, including one of my favorite Poe artifacts in this entire book.

## Lovecraft-Land, Part 2

As I walked the streets of College Hill, I'd run into an organized Lovecraft tour every once in a while. You could tell it was a Lovecraft tour by the T-shirts.

Sometimes the squid hats. You don't get many opportunities to wear Lovecraft gear in a relevant context.

I don't like group tours, but in one way it made complete sense to see Lovecraft-Land as part of a group—the sweaty solidarity of walking the calf-destroying streets of College Hill. The place is called a hill for a reason, as the whole neighborhood slopes at a drastic angle down to the Providence River, and that plus the unrelenting August heat made walking by myself a bit demoralizing, like being off-center in an unsympathetic universe.

It also didn't help that my own private route was unavoidably headed toward Jenckes Street. Jenckes Street is on a demon of a hill. Like walking up the humped back of one of Lovecraft's barely described behemoths, except that at the end you don't get the relief of being devoured soul-first.

Off the intersection of Jenckes Street and Prospect Street is a gorgeous red-brick mansion set behind black wrought-iron gates. The address is 140 Prospect, and it was used by Lovecraft as the home of the titular character in his novella *The Case of Charles Dexter Ward.*

The story is about a man who resurrects his evil magician ancestor, who returns the favor by taking over his descendant's body as a first step to taking over the world. In it, Lovecraft gives the address as 100 Prospect Street, but the "double-bayed brick façade" of the building clearly belongs to what was both then and today known as the Halsey House, a few blocks down. During my visit I noticed tiny handprints in the red brick of the sidewalk near the black gates that

*Halsey House, site of Lovecraft's* The Case of Charles Dexter Ward

glistened faintly like slug trails. When you're in a Lovecraft state of mind, that's the kind of stuff you notice. The story also references 133 Prospect Street, the "little white farmhouse" mentioned for no reason other than to even more firmly ground the story in Providence.

After that intersection Jenckes Street becomes Barnes Street, and it's at 10 Barnes that one of the three remaining Providence homes of Lovecraft stands. He had a room on the first floor of this large, three-story Victorian house in the late 1920s and early 1930s, and it was here that he wrote "The Call of Cthulhu," along with others of his tales.

From there, had I the stamina, I could have trekked the three quarters of a mile northeast, to Brown University's Ladd Observatory at 210 Doyle Avenue. Lovecraft was given regular access to it by a family friend, and it is perhaps here that he gained his awe and terror of space, using it as he did as a canvas to fill with cosmic monsters.

Instead, I backtracked a bit and headed to Prospect Terrace Park, to sit down on a bench and rest, sure, after my ascent of Jenckes, but also because it was one of Lovecraft's favorite places to frequent. It's easy to see why. The small patch of grass overlooks all of Providence . . . if you can see around the giant statue of Roger Williams set at its edge.

The remains of the city's founder are actually entombed in the base of the somewhat cartoonish and awkwardly posed statue. It's his third resting place, having been originally interred on Williams's own property and then moved two times after that.

From there it was on to 65 Prospect Street. This house is the second of Lovecraft's still-standing Providence residences, and the last one he lived in. Originally, the house was located at 66 College Street, right behind Brown University's John Hay Library, but was moved as the university expanded to assimilate the area. Lovecraft also used the house in his story "The Haunter of the Dark."

Two blocks later, I arrived at the intersection of Prospect and Angell Streets. Here, a shiny new sign designated the area as H. P. LOVECRAFT MEMORIAL SQUARE. Seventy-five years after the death of the author, the humble piece of aluminum is the first real acknowledgment of Lovecraft by the city, and it was bolted to the pole mere days before I visited to coincide with the conference.

*Last home of H. P. Lovecraft*

Seeing his name lettered in yellow on a blue street sign seemed incongruous. None of the Lovecraft sites I had visited thus far were labeled in any way as Lovecraft sites. Many of the houses did have historic plaques on them, but just to honor the early Providence families who built and lived in them. Even Lovecraft's last house, the one that was moved to its current address of 65 Prospect Street, was preserved for historic reasons and not literary. The plaque on that house names the place the Simon B. Mumford House, even though an online search of the term only really pulls up its Lovecraft connection.

I know how Lovecraft felt as he traced down Edgar Allan Poe sites a century earlier only to learn that many weren't marked as such.

But here, at this less-than-pretty intersection, at least, was progress. Sure, it was the type of progress that, if Boston's turbulent history with Poe were any indication, could be quickly erased, but it was still a cool thing to see. The guy created an octopus-god. Now he gets his own intersection.

Had I followed Angell Street west from H. P. Lovecraft Memorial Square, I could have checked off a few more Lovecraft sites. About half a mile away is the "sumptuous but hideous French-roofed mansion" at 276 Angell referenced in "The Shunned House." Another half mile beyond that is the original site of Lovecraft's birthplace, at 454 Angell. That building was Boston'd right around the time that Poe's own house was demolished. Another third of a mile after that is the third still-standing Lovecraft residence at 598 Angell. Butler Hos-

*House referenced in Lovecraft's "The Shunned House"*

pital, where both his parents died, is on Blackstone Boulevard, 1.7 miles north of where Angell intersects Butler Avenue.

But I couldn't take such a long detour, even partially. I had an appointment looming. A very exciting appointment.

So instead of taking Angell Street at the square, I took Prospect. Along the way were two more Lovecraft sites, both at Brown University. The first was the John Hay Library, at 20 Prospect. This stately library was visited by Lovecraft, who, as I mentioned, lived just behind it during the last years of his life, but it is more important to his legacy as the repository of his papers—original manuscripts, letters, first editions, even a few artifacts are preserved within the walls of the university institution. The letters are especially interesting. Lovecraft wrote these paper missives like they were e-mails. Some estimates have his total letter count, including letters that are lost, at around eighty thousand, a staggering and unbelievable number considering his short life and also accounting for the fact that he didn't have to punch a clock.

Unfortunately, the library had closed three months earlier as part of a year-long renovation, but I was able to wend between the construction fences to at least see the Lovecraft plaque on a small patch of grass to the right of the entrance.

Set on its edge there is a rectangle of stone about the size of a large dog. On it is a bronze plaque dedicated to the author. Beneath his profile are the words:

HOWARD PHILLIPS LOVECRAFT

(1890–1937)

U.S. AUTHOR

I NEVER CAN BE TIED TO RAW NEW THINGS,

FOR I FIRST SAW THE LIGHT IN AN OLD TOWN,

WHERE FROM MY WINDOW HUDDLED ROOFS SLOPED DOWN

TO A QUAINT HARBOUR RICH WITH VISIONINGS.

STREETS WITH CARVED DOORWAYS WHERE THE SUNSET BEAMS

FLOODED OLD FANLIGHTS AND SMALL WINDOW-PANES,

AND GEORGIAN STEEPLES TOPPED WITH GILDED VANES—

THESE ARE THE SIGHTS THAT SHAPED MY CHILDHOOD DREAMS.

DEDICATED ON THE CENTENNIAL OF HIS BIRTH

AUGUST 20, 1990

BY

THE CITY OF PROVIDENCE

BROWN UNIVERSITY

AND

FRIENDS OF H. P. LOVECRAFT

*H. P. Lovecraft plaque*

*Providence Athenaeum*

The quote is from *Sonnet XXX: Background,* from a series of thirty-six sonnets Lovecraft wrote, called "Fungi from Yoggoth." Oh, that Lovecraft.

The Friends of H. P. Lovecraft are the reason the humble memorial exists, alone for more than two decades in publicly honoring the horror master in his hometown. The group was led by Jon B. Cooke, Will Murray, and S. T. Joshi, the latter being the guy who made Lovecraft scholarship cool.

From there, I passed the ornate, wrought iron and red brick of Brown University's Van Wickle Gates. One of the more famous photographs of Lovecraft shows him seated on one of the concrete benches built into and flanking those gates. In the picture, he warmed the one to the left of the gates as you face them.

And with that, I was on my way to the Providence Athenaeum.

## A Library of Horrors

The Providence Athenaeum surprised me. I was expecting the building at 251 Benefit Street to be grandiose, maybe like the John Hay Library, just around the corner. Instead, it was a dark, squat, granite building whose Greek Revival architecture was totally out of place in College Hill. It looked more like the headquarters of an ominous secret society than a welcoming institution of learning.

But the history of the library is a grand one. Created in 1836, its lineage goes back even further, to 1753, and its precursor, the Providence Library Company, one of the first libraries in the country. Today, the Athenaeum has retained its unique character. It's an independent membership library that's nevertheless open to the public for visiting.

Most relevant to me, it was another Poe-Lovecraft crossroads.

Poe visited this library, hitting on a woman.

Lovecraft visited it, not hitting on one.

The Providence Athenaeum was another make-out spot for Poe and Whitman, and one that comes with a great Poe anecdote. At one point, while visiting the library, Whitman asked Poe if he had read a new poem called "Ulalume." It was the melancholy tale of a man who inadvertently wanders to the grave of the love he had buried there a year before. She thought it'd be right up Poe's dark and twisted alley.

The two went over to the stacks and pulled out the December 1847 issue of *The American Review* to see the anonymously published poem. At that point Poe whipped out a pencil, claimed authorship, and autographed it right in the book.

It's a wonder Whitman didn't renounce the prenuptial and buy him a case of port right then and there. It's a great move. My wife still thinks I wrote *Beowulf*.

But Poe really did write "Ulalume." He'd just published it anonymously as a marketing ploy. It's one of his best poems and focuses on his most obsessive theme . . . the death of a beautiful woman. Whitman probably already guessed it was his.

The Athenaeum was the best of places and the worst of places for the two because it was also here that the two broke up when somebody slipped Whitman a note informing her of Poe's one-man wine-tasting event.

I'd like to say Lovecraft's time in the Athenaeum was similar, but few of his works were published in his lifetime, and the ones that were wound up in publications that, at the time, would never have taken up shelf space in an auspicious library.

In addition, Lovecraft wasn't exactly a ladies' man. He lived most of his life as a bachelor, except for a two-year marriage to a woman named Sonia Greene, and they spent half that time apart. Like Ohio to New York apart. Lovecraft moved with her to Brooklyn during the marriage and soon after, she left for a job in Ohio.

Meanwhile, Lovecraft found himself horrified by the squalor and multicultural character of the area. He took what inspiration he could from the place for a few new horror tales and then pulled his New England umbilical cord taut to slingshot back to Providence, from which he never moved again. His New York City abode still stands in the Brooklyn Heights neighborhood, although like the Providence Lovecraft homes, no marker proclaims the fact.

The main room of the Providence Athenaeum rises two stories high, but not in the elegant way of some major city libraries. Despite its highfalutin name,

*Interior of Providence Athenaeum*

this place is cozy. You immediately see books, not architecture. It's the type of library you'd see in a kid's movie in which some magic tome awaits deep within its recesses.

From the main floor you see two glorious floors' worth of books, with the second floor shelves accessible from the north and south wings of the building. The library's most notable interior feature are the white busts of famous thinkers, writers, and leaders that line the ends of the shelves, high up on the second story and just under a ceiling full of skylights.

This building was only a decade old when Poe ascended its steps, and it was a much different library back then. The building was only a single story, none of the wings had yet been built, and the stairs leading to the basement weren't there either. At the time, the basement was accessible only by an exterior entrance and wasn't even part of the library. It was owned by the Franklin Society, a philosophy and natural science club. The library eventually purchased that space and shoved books down there, too.

And it was down to that basement that I was headed, to the Philbrick Rare Book Room.

Besides housing the special archives, the Philbrick Rare Book Room is also the library's exhibit space. It's a small room with a pair of glass cases in the doorway and a bigger one in the back. Most of the room is dominated by a single round table. On either side of the room are staff offices, separated from the main area by panes of glass.

On that day, the three glass cases were full of Lovecraft, all from the John Hay Library Lovecraft collection, while a small TV on a side table played the 2005 silent film version of "The Call of Cthulhu."

The exhibit featured some amazing artifacts. There were letters and sketches Lovecraft wrote and drew, fanzines he'd put together, first editions of his work, and even a pair of tiny ceramic cats he owned. There were also more modern pieces honoring the author: statuettes and artwork and books.

The most fascinating piece, though, at least to me, was a small card on which Lovecraft had drawn the Cthulhu idol from "The Call of Cthulhu." What it showed wasn't a terror indescribable by human tongue, but a cartoony beast that looked as if it had been created by a middle school student during math class. It was goddamn delightful, especially contexted as it was with some of the modern interpretations of the creature, depicting it as the apocalypse incarnate. The image was inscribed by Lovecraft to one of the many pen pals he had throughout his life:

> **To R. H. Barlow, Esq., whose Sculpture**
> **hath given Immortality to this trivial**
> **Design of his oblig'd obdt Servant.**
> **Cthulhu**
> **H. P. Lovecraft**
> **11th May, 1934**

After gazing at the displays long enough to have officially crossed the line into heist planning, I met a woman with long blonde hair and an English accent. Kate Wodehouse was an art history major originally from England who had lived in Providence for close to two decades. These days, she was the collections librarian for the Athenaeum. I'd been in contact with her for months about dropping by to see the library's Edgar Allan Poe collection, for even though the Athenaeum was merely borrowing the Lovecraft collection from the temporarily closed John Hay Library, it boasted its very own Edgar Allan Poe collection.

"Poe stuff, right?" she asked after connecting my name to my e-mails. "Right over there." Turns out, she wouldn't have to take too many trips into the vault for me. A long glass-topped display case set on the center table was full of Poe artifacts. And it wasn't in honor of my visit. The library had decided to display them with the Lovecraft artifacts because it just made sense. Like telling Poe's story through Lovecraft's. It was yet another testament to how entwined the legacies of these two men have become. She opened the case. "While you look at these, I've got a few other things you should see."

I didn't know what she was about to get, but all I needed in life was in that case.

There were first editions of Poe's works, including the "prose poem" *Eureka*, in which Poe seeks to expound the secrets of the universe, and the 1845 *The Raven and Other Poems* sans a front cover. There were a couple of books of poetry by Whitman herself, as well as her 1860 *Edgar Poe and His Critics*, a short work in which she defends Poe's character from the popular misconception of him as an immoral creep that started with Rufus Griswold's posthumous smear campaign.

There was also a photograph of Whitman and an 1848 copy of the "Ultima Thule" daguerreotype of Poe. This was the one taken of the poet in Providence just days after his suicide attempt and just a year before his death. It was named such by Whitman herself as a reference to a passage in his poem "Dream-Land."

The most prominent artifact in the case was an 1876 print of Édouard Manet's famous *ex libris* raven, which was one of a series of illustrations for a French translation by poet Stéphane Mallarmé of "The Raven." The print was actually autographed by Mallarmé to Whitman.

But the crowning piece of that collection, and one of my favorite artifacts I mention in this book, was the autographed copy of "Ulalume." That's right. What

*Poe's "Ulalume" autograph, courtesy of the Providence Athenaeum*

sounds like an apocryphal story of the author is actually true . . . or at least has a powerful piece of evidence in its favor.

*The American Review* was bound in book form, and his poem is near the end. It's the version of "Ulalume" with an additional final stanza that was later removed, the one that blames (or praises) the woodlandish ghouls for hiding the tomb of his lost love from him.

And there, right at the end of the page and beneath the last line in that version of the poem, "From the Hell of planetary souls?", was the excessively neat autograph of Poe himself.

It wasn't the florid signature we're used to, with its stylized underline and perfect attention given to every letter, but it did display Poe's penchant for an almost machine-like script. The penciled "Edgar A. Poe" looked like it was written above a ruler, and the only defect is the stem of the "d" in "Edgar." A faded rectangle surrounds the autograph, as if at some point somebody had tried to clean or preserve it and merely discolored the page.

It was Whitman herself who is responsible for sanctifying the artifact. She went back and found it after his death and told the story to her friends.

Before I could stuff my pockets, Wodehouse came back bearing a massive book in her arms. She set up a stand on the table and laid her burden down. It was an old log book from the Athenaeum, and she pointed to an entry near the top of one of the pages. The log was signed by Poe (this time in a fancier script that initialed his first and middle name to "E. A. Poe") for a book called *Stanley, Or The Recollections of a Man of the World*.

It was the first volume of a two-volume novel by Horace Binney Wallace, an author who was born in Philadelphia in 1817 and committed suicide in 1852 in Paris at the age of thirty-five. Wallace was published in some of the same magazines as Poe and had corresponded with him. Poe liked Wallace's body of work enough that he stole bits of it for his "Marginalia," a collection of short, unrelated thoughts and opinions, often on literature—ostensibly the kinds of things one would jot in the margins of a book—that he published in various magazines during his last years. Wodehouse then pointed to an entry a few lines below Poe's own. Whitman had later checked out the same book.

She then showed me a brown silk scarf that belonged to Whitman, as well as a more modern-day oddity. It was a homemade scrapbook from the 1950s that had been put together by a woman named Virginia Louise Doris. It was called *The Raven Circles* and was filled with pictures and text concerning Edgar Allan Poe's life in Providence. Had she lived in the Internet age, Ms. Doris would have undoubtedly run a fan site for the poet. It was a vivid example of yet another kindred soul mesmerized by a man who couldn't keep anybody's attention while he was alive.

Wodehouse also made sure to introduce me to one of her colleagues, Christina Bevilacqua. Bevilacqua was from Poe's adopted hometown of Richmond and was the resident expert on Poe's only novella, *The Narrative of Arthur Gordon Pym of Nantucket.*

I disparaged *Pym* in the introduction to this book, and maybe because of that I couldn't help but observe how often that work popped up in my travels and research. *Pym* is undeniably a beloved topic in the field of literary criticism, and its influence on literature is palpable. It inspired Melville as he wrote *Moby-Dick.* Jules Verne liked it so much he wrote a sequel to it. And Lovecraft was inspired enough by it to write his own tale of Antarctic exploration, called "At the Mountains of Madness." But it was while talking to Bevilacqua that I finally realized I'd have to read the book again before my adventure in Poe-Land was over. As we finished talking, she showed me a white pocketbook with tiny Poe faces all over it that she had bought as a gift. "Know what the pattern's called? Poe-ka dot."

Before I left the Athenaeum, all Poe- and Lovecraft-drunk and dreading having to reread *Pym,* Wodehouse wanted to show me one more thing. She led me out of the Philbrick Rare Book Room to ascend back to the main floor of the library. As we walked, she pointed to a large chest decorated in Egyptalia. "That was here back when Poe visited." It held documents about Napoleon's invasion of Egypt and another text that described the country. Poe very well might have pulled out the books to read. This was, after all, the guy who wrote "Some Words with a Mummy."

But the trunk wasn't what she wanted to show me. As we arrived on the main floor of the lobby, she had me turn around to face the front door and look up. There, near the ceiling in an alcove, were Poe and Whitman themselves, looking out over the library.

Wodehouse took me up there so I could examine the ghosts more closely. The alcove was a short hallway of a room, crammed with books and more of the library's signature white busts. In the alcove window was a pair of large pictures on stands. One was an oil painting of Whitman. The other, a photograph of Poe.

The photograph of Poe was an enlarged version of the Whitman daguerreotype, which was taken in Providence just days after the Ultima Thule daguerreotype was shot. However, this one doesn't show a miserable Poe; instead it's a more laid-back Poe. He was wearing a great coat, the buttons on his undercoat badly fastened, and his look of uncomfortableness with the world—the trademark of all his daguerreotypes—slightly mitigated.

The portrait of Whitman was an original painting created in 1838 by Cephas Giovanni Thompson. This is the image of her you always see online. She wears a cap that is supposed to be the mourning cap for her husband, who died in 1833, but is bright and pink and looks ready for an Easter Sunday. Her hair falls from it in curly brown ringlets, and her gaze is directed to the edge of the frame. This is Whitman ten years before she would meet Poe.

Eventually and too soon, I had to say goodbye to Poe, Whitman, and Wodehouse. But it was only temporarily. The next event on my agenda would happen back at the Athenaeum, but I had some time and a few gin and tonics to kill before it would start. As I left the library, I walked past a lurid green-and-yellow poster of Lovecraft surrounded by fish-like demons and the very building I had been exploring for the past two hours. The poster was advertising the Lovecraft bust unveiling that was scheduled in the library's basement later that night.

## Head and Shoulders among His Peers

I keep calling it the library's basement, but the level in which the Philbrick Rare Book Room is located is actually the ground floor. It's just that the main entrance of the Providence Athenaeum is up a set of stairs that bypasses that level. The basement has windows and its own entrance, and is divided into sections. The main room of the library basement is adjacent to the Philbrick Rare Book Room and looks, well, like a library . . . lots of books. That night, it also had lots of people, all of them busy finding seats and settling in to watch the unveiling of a memorial that promised big things for the legacy of H. P. Lovecraft.

Thanks to Niels Hobbs and some of the organizers of the unveiling, I squeaked in on a press pass. And good thing, too. Even though the event was free, attendance was constrained to ticket holders for space reasons. There must have been between 150 and 200 people flooding that small room.

At the front, the shrouded form sat there, completely obscured beneath its black veil, which I was later told was just a tablecloth borrowed from a nearby hotel. However, there wasn't a single person at the event who didn't know exactly what was under that veil and what it looked like. We had all been following its creation avidly for the past few months on Facebook and Twitter and, before that, Kickstarter.

The Lovecraft Bust Project was started, and finished, by Bryan Moore. Moore is a sculptor whose knives are usually put in the service of the toy and collectibles industry, but he wanted to do something grander. To help get the funding he needed for the project, he teamed with Jovanka Vuckovic, a filmmaker who rose to prominence in the horror community through her role as editor of *Rue Morgue* magazine, one of the top horror magazines in the industry, named, of course, after Poe's story about a killer ape. She was well connected and had experience successfully producing projects crowd-funded by Kickstarter.

For the Lovecraft Bust Project, they set their Kickstarter goal at $30,000. Per the terms of Kickstarter, they had thirty days to raise the money, and if they missed the goal by even one dollar, all donations would be void.

The project was fully funded within forty-eight hours, and, by the end of the whole thirty-day run, they'd nearly doubled the goal.

I got to talk to both of them during the night, but just briefly. It was their party, after all. Later, during NecronomiCon proper, I got to sit down in the dealer room and talk to them more in depth.

"So I get the why of this project. It's Lovecraft. We all dig him. That's why we're here. But my question is 'Why now?' Why do we suddenly have a Lovecraft bust?"

"I had just moved from Los Angeles to Iowa, bought my first home, and then a couple of key freelance projects fell through, so I had some time," said Moore. "And I was ready to do some fine art. I'd done some Lovecraft products in the past and I didn't know of any other Lovecraft bust, so it made sense to try him."

Moore was tall, fifty years old, with short, salt-and-pepper hair and a matching beard. He didn't look like a Satanist who sculpted toys for a living. He'd been with the Church of Satan for about ten years, but had officially distanced himself from it, even though he still dug the philosophy. He helped spearhead the fortieth anniversary gathering of the Church of Satan on June 6, 2006, in Los Angeles. "Look it up on YouTube," he told me, "and there's old Bry, reading the Satanic High Mass."

Moore had started his career in practical movie effects working on such projects as one of the *A Nightmare on Elm Street* sequels, *Jumanji,* and *Mortal Kombat,* as well as TV anthologies like *Tales from the Darkside* and *Monsters.* He then switched to the toy industry and eventually started his own freelance outfit, called Arkham Studios. A Lovecraft invention, Arkham is the fictional Massachusetts town featured in some of his stories and the place where his fictional Miskatonic University is located.

Moore was sitting behind a dealer table. For the unveiling he had worn a suit and tie, but now he lounged in a simple black shirt. Beside him sat Vuckovic.

"How'd you meet Jovanka?"

"Vampira's funeral."

"Wait. What? How did you know Vampira?" Vampira was the alter ego of Maila Nurmi, a 1950s horror hostess who dressed like an anorexic Morticia Addams and was the precursor to Elvira, whom she once sued for copying her shtick.

"I'm a hearse collector." Every question Moore answered made me want to change the direction of the interview. Basically, because of that hobby, he had taken part in 2005 in what was at the time the world's largest hearse procession.

It was hosted by the Peterson Automotive Museum in Los Angeles, and there were eighty-four death taxis in it. The eighty-two-year-old Nurmi was the grand marshal of the macabre parade.

Moore struck up a friendship with her, taking her out for rides in his hearses, including one from the 1994 Tim Burton biopic *Ed Wood*. Nurmi is also known for acting in director Ed Wood's infamous *Plan 9 from Outer Space* back in the late 1950s. Burton's then-wife, Lisa Marie, played her in the biopic.

Nurmi died on January 10, 2008, in Los Angeles. "One day she was riding with me in the front of the hearse, and then six weeks later she was riding in the back of one," said Moore. And it was there, at Nurmi's funeral in Hollywood Forever Cemetery, that he met Vuckovic.

Vuckovic is—well, she's a presence. I had written a few articles for her years before during her stint as Editor-in-Chief of *Rue Morgue* magazine, but Necro-nomiCon was my first time meeting her in person. Her hair was yellow at the crown and then conflagrated into long, thick tresses the color of B-horror movie blood. She's also covered in tattoos, most of them horror-inspired. On the back of her left calf is the face of Edgar Allan Poe above the word "Nevermore." On the back of her right is the face of H. P. Lovecraft in a halo of tentacles. Her legs are basically a metaphor for this entire chapter.

She talked liked someone who knew how to take charge, and that's exactly what she did with the business aspects of the Lovecraft Bust Project. "There were three things we needed for this to work: a concept, quality, and visibility. For example, we needed a good Kickstarter video. If you can't put together good videos, how's the Kickstarter and horror communities going to trust you to put together anything? So we got Frank here."

"Frank" was Frank H. Woodward, and he was sitting on Vuckovic's other side. Woodward is a documentary filmmaker best known for *Lovecraft: Fear of the Unknown.*

"Yeah," Moore concurred, turning to Woodward. "Sorry we messed up your name on the plaque. It was our one mistake." He was talking about the plaque listing the project's team members that's affixed to the pedestal holding the bust of Lovecraft. Frank H. Woodward will go down in posterity with H. P. Lovecraft as Frank W. Woodward.

But even with all the help that the team received and all the support from major figures in the horror community, putting together the project was still no easy matter. "Man," said Moore, "running a Kickstarter campaign is rough. It was a full-time job, a freelance project with no guarantee of getting paid. And the sculpture part—the fun part and the whole point of the thing—had to come last as far as priorities." Moore even found himself hospitalized from the strain of the project. "And even with the bust complete and at home over there at the Athenaeum, it's still not over for us. We'll be creating and delivering donor incentives for a long time."

But the biggest hurdle to the entire project was finding a home for old H. P. "In the creative community, nobody said no. They all donated items and volunteered their time and helped get the word out for us, but finding a home for the bust was an ordeal." According to Moore, what he found was that the people who signed the checks in Providence either didn't know who Lovecraft was, didn't want the burden of a memorial that would need upkeep, or just didn't want the Lovecraft fan attention. "I had one place where I was told I could put in a Coke machine, but no bust of Lovecraft."

But then Niels Hobbs stepped in and put him into contact with the staff at the Providence Athenaeum, which was more than willing to become the center of all things Lovecraftian in Providence. "People are going to turn this into a shrine," said Moore, "and I think the Athenaeum will benefit."

At the unveiling two nights earlier, Moore and Vuckovic flanked the still-shrouded bust. They were joined at the front by other members of the Lovecraft Bust team. Woodward was there. Also Mallory O'Meara, a small girl with long dark hair, glasses, and a massive green Cthulhu tattoo on her shoulder.

There was even a Sultan up there. Sultan Saeed Al Darmaki was from Abu Dhabi and was in his thirties. His website proclaims him as "Global Patron of the Cool Things," and he was a prominent supporter of the project, both financially and in other ways. "The Sultan helped me unload this thing from the truck when we pulled up here," Moore told me. I talked to the Sultan a little bit about growing up a horror fan in the Middle East.

"In Abu Dhabi, we always had access to all the best and most infamous horror movies." The two examples he relayed to me were *The Toxic Avenger* and *American Werewolf in London.* It was enough of a range to back up his statement. His favorite movies were those from the 1980s and any that used practical movie effects instead of CGI. He'd even started his own horror movie production company, Dark Dunes, and was president of the Bram Stoker film festival.

When I asked him about Lovecraft in particular, he said, "I found Lovecraft through movies. *The Unnamable* was one of my favorites, but his influence on movies was broader than just his own work. Like *The Creature from the Black Lagoon.* Totally influenced by Lovecraft."

Also up front was Alison Maxell, executive director of the Providence Athenaeum. It was Maxell who gave the bust a home when nobody else in Providence would. I asked her why. "If someone should do it, it should be us. Besides, it's not just about Lovecraft, it's about Providence."

"Did you know about Lovecraft before you talked to Bryan?"

"No, I'd never read any Lovecraft when I accepted the proposal. I still sleep with my covers around my neck when I hear a scary story. But after that, I did read *The Case of Charles Dexter Ward* because we're mentioned in it."

Finally, the last person at the front was S. T. Joshi, one of the Friends of H. P. Lovecraft behind the John Hay Library plaque. Joshi was born in Pune, India, in 1958, but has lived in the U.S. since he was five. He became fascinated with Lovecraft as a teenager, and it inspired him to attend college in Providence, at Brown University. Today, he is the leading Lovecraft scholar.

He was fresh from giving the keynote speech of the conference at the nearby First Baptist Church of America (which I had passed up due to its lack of air-conditioning and gin and tonics). He told me, "This is a huge part of the continued emergence of H. P. Lovecraft in his home city. He was a world figure, now he's a Providence figure. It's just going to keep going from here." Indeed, the new H. P. Lovecraft Square was certainly evidence of that. Joshi then leaned closer and almost whispered, "He's the reason I became an atheist, you know."

I didn't have a chance to pursue that further because it was time for his address, which was followed by some words from Maxell and then Moore. I spent the time half-listening, but mostly flitting around trying to get the best camera angles on everything. Had to earn that press pass, you know.

Finally, it was time for the culmination of months of work. Moore and Vuckovic whipped off the black tablecloth to reveal the gleaming head and shoulders of H. P. Lovecraft's first ever memorial bust. They shared an emotional hug as a couple of hundred people applauded.

The long face of Lovecraft was unmistakable, and the bust strongly showcased the fastidious look of the man. His features were slightly severe, his hair in a tight straight line across the top of his forehead, and he sported a tie and jacket on the part of the chest that made it into the bust. It also flattered him a bit by making him appear more masculine and confident than he does in many pictures. I assume that happens just by dint of being a sculpture. Always adds an air to the subject.

The most noticeable features were the eyes. Moore had carved them without pupils, giving him an eerie and almost evil cast, perfect for the memorial of a horror author. Later, Moore would show me the least noticeable feature, a series of numbers and letters carved into the back of the bust: 25152218520154189141 12515211822112209145.

It was a cryptogram, a secret code, hiding a message for the Lovecraft faithful. It was very Poe, actually. Poe made a name for himself in cryptography, using it in his story "The Gold-Bug," and challenged readers of the magazines he edited to send him any ciphers beyond his abilities to crack. Poe was no help to me now, but fortunately it only took a little cajoling for Moore to reveal the solution, on the condition that I didn't print it in this book, of course. Sorry.

*Bryan Moore and Jovanka Vuckovic unveil the H. P. Lovecraft bust*

Suffice it to say, it's a message he wants posterity to remember as long as the bust exists.

The plaque listing the project's team members also included major financial supporters, those who gave at least $500 to the Kickstarter project. The names ranged from big genre recognizables, like Guillermo del Toro, Peter Straub, Frank Darabont, Mike Mignola, and Stuart Gordon, all the way to everyday fans who just wanted to have a tangible part in Lovecraft's legacy. Like James Vargscarr.

I met James and his wife Karolya at some point that night. They had flown across the continent from Winnipeg to attend the event and to see James's name on the plaque in person. "When I found out about the plan for the bust, I wanted to do whatever I could to help the success of the project," he said. "Thankfully, as it turned out, more than enough others felt the same way. Having my name included on the plaque feels like the closest thing to signing a thank-you note to Lovecraft himself." He made me wish I'd forked over the chunk of cash to have my name on there, too.

After the unveiling, Brett Rutherford introduced a performance of a selection from his play *Night Gaunts,* based on the life of H. P. Lovecraft and starring Carl Johnson, one of the twin demonologists from the first season of the television show *Ghost Hunters.*

*H. P. Lovecraft bust, Providence Athenaeum*

But I didn't watch too much of that, as I ended up treating the event from that point onward more like a party than something to be covered, so the rest of the night was pretty much a swirl of wine for me. However, I always found myself, like everybody else that night, back at the bust, marveling at the bronze Lovecraft and Moore's craftsmanship. As will so many of Lovecraft's fans going forward.

I wondered if this is how it was at the beginning of Edgar Allan Poe's legacy.

After his death Poe went from a virtual unknown to a niche interest to universal acclaim. Today, there are Poe busts everywhere, but once upon a time, there was a first one.

The most compelling bit of context for me regarding Lovecraft happened when I exited the building after the evening was over. To do so, I went up the stairs and into the main library room. High above, set on pedestals around the ceiling, were the plaster busts of Greek gods, foundational philosophers, world leaders, and some of literature's greatest writers.

That's the party Lovecraft is now crashing, with his visions of old gods and tiny humans, of a terrifying, indifferent universe . . . the one that so many of us love.

And now we can go to Providence, look him right in the eyes, and tell him so.

## Poe at a Lovecraft Convention

NecronomiCon Providence was pretty much your conventional convention, as much as it could be, with such an outré focus. Most of it took place at the elegant Providence Biltmore, downtown. The schedule was filled with panels and talks about Lovecraft and related topics. There were some wacky bits, like a Cthulhu prayer breakfast, at which fans in druid robes sang hymns to the elder god, and nighttime revels, where people wore cephalopod headdresses and masks, but most of the conference was just people discussing Lovecraft. Oh, and buying Lovecraft.

Walking around the dealer rooms, I saw a lot of Lovecraft-inspired art—prints, T-shirts, sculptures. Mostly, the art focused on Lovecraft's creations, and predominantly that creation was Cthulhu, the ancient, tentacled giant that sleeps in a sunken city at the bottom of the ocean and torments mankind with its dreams, which is much more preferable to his waking up and quashing us out of existence.

In my experience, Poe seems to be bigger than Lovecraft everywhere except for one place: the Internet. There, the communities that would care about either one of those guys seem to gravitate more toward Lovecraft's vision than Poe's. It's one of the reasons the Lovecraft Bust Project found its audience so quickly, I think, as well as why there was a NecronomiCon 2013 in the first place, since it, too, was funded through Kickstarter.

I believe the Internet's greater interest in Lovecraft, if I'm not imagining it, is because the Web is primarily a visual medium. Post a 5,000-word essay that solves the world's largest problems and a picture of a kitten wearing a monocle, and the kitten will get more hits.

I'm no artist, but it seems Lovecraft's horrors are more fun to visualize than Poe's. Poe's horrors are madmen. Lovecraft gives us inter-dimensional monsters so terrifying that the very sight of them creates madmen. I mean, type in "Roderick Usher" into Google Image Search, and then type in Cthulhu and compare the results.

The interesting part of the idea is that Lovecraft is often poked fun at for relying too much on words like "indescribable," "unnamable," "amorphous," and "unutterable" to communicate his terrors. But that has the side effect of both challenging artists to make concrete the inconceivable while freeing them to really meld their own vision with that of Lovecraft's.

Like I said, it's a completely anecdote-based idea, but I wanted to test it a bit, so I picked an artist at a booth and approached him. I didn't pick him at random, though. I chose him because he was seated beside a full-sized mannequin with a corpse-pale face and mortician-black suit and tie. A square of paper safety-pinned to its lapel read, "I AM H. P. LOVECRAFT. CREATED BY TED DILUCIA."

"Is this your Lovecraft?"

The guy I directed the question to wore thick-framed glasses and a trilby. Turns out it wasn't his Lovecraft. His name was Nick Gucker, and the business cards on his table called him "Nick the Hat." They were illustrated on the back with an image of a mad scientist sorting through a pile of severed feet. Looking for a matching pair, I assume.

Nick had flown in from Seattle for NecronomiCon, and it was his first East Coast convention. Examples of his artwork were spread across the table and were hung behind him. They were highly detailed comic book–style illustrations of mostly Lovecraftian monsters, although he told me that his work was inspired by the complete gamut of literary and movie monsters.

Later, I would look Gucker up online and learn that he regularly illustrates Lovecraft's work for anthologies and e-zines and was even a featured artist in an issue of the revival run of *Weird Tales* magazine, whose predecessor published most of Lovecraft's published work during his lifetime. At one point, Lovecraft was offered editorship of the magazine. He declined because it would have meant moving from Providence to Chicago.

I introduced myself to Mr. the Hat, explained my book project, and then bounced the idea off him.

"Yeah, that might be true. Lovecraft is more bonkers with his cults and gods and everything. Poe is an incredible stylist, a word assassin. His work is rich and well thought-out. Lovecraft is not as rich, but has a similar effect. And he really pushes Poe's nihilism to the extreme."

That was a good way to put it. He meant philosophically, of course, but it worked on a much more tangible level, too. I mean, a guy robbing a grave to steal the teeth of a woman who has been buried alive is pretty extreme. A twisted spawn of an indifferent elder god trying to open the door to the apocalypse—well, we have nowhere to go after that, do we? The step from mad man to mad universe is simultaneously a small one and a large one.

"So why are you drawn to Lovecraft's work in particular?"

"I just want to explore Lovecraft's world, do my own take on it. It's hard to do, to keep the illustrations fresh, since so many artists are interpreting his stuff these days."

That's another reason, I think. Lovecraft created a mythology. Poe created a style. Both are fun playgrounds, but the former has a much bigger sandbox.

Satisfied with Nick Gucker as my First Witness in the idea of Lovecraft having at least that edge on Poe in the modern world, I continued through the dealer room. At one point I saw a zombified version of Edgar Allan Poe on a T-shirt being sold at one of the booths. When I asked the person behind it what that guy was doing here, he told me it was the official 2013 shirt for the New England Horror Writers Association.

It was the only place I saw Poe in the dealer rooms, but he appeared a couple more times in the panels and lectures.

The lectures were mostly of the academic variety, although the titles of the lectures by themselves seemed to promise a relatively non-academic experience: *It's Only Dark Because You Can't See: A Posthuman Look at Lovecraft's Cosmology; Xenophobia, Atheism, and Tentacles: The Slender Man Myth as Communal Lovecraftian Tale;* and *Poe, Lovecraft, and "The Uncanny": The Horror of the Self.*

The panels were more loose, with topics like *HPL Online, The Cinematic Lovecraft,* and *Why Cthulhu?—Is HPL Too Mainstream?,* the latter featuring Nick Gucker on the panel.

There was one panel, though, that I'd highlighted with triple asterisks, double underlines, and a mustard stain: *Lovecraft's Literary Influences.* On it were a group of writers in a variety of forms, all tied to weird fiction in one way or the other . . . S. T. Joshi, Joe Pulver, Faye Ringel, Robert Waugh, Dennis Paoli, and Darrell Schweitzer.

I found myself a seat in the Grand Ballroom, the main stage for the conference, just as the panel started. For the first part of the discussion, the word "Poe" wasn't spoken at all, like it was too obvious a thing to say and that it was much more interesting to talk about obscure influences and Gothic fiction as a whole. It felt like the panelists were playing a game, dancing around the poet to see who would be the first to trip and address the elephant in the influence.

Inevitably it was broached, and S. T. Joshi responded, "Poe's influence on Lovecraft is all-pervasive. We'd need a whole panel on that. He spent his life trying to shed Poe's influence, but never did." Joshi also listed a few examples of how Lovecraft mirrored Poe. "'The Tomb' and 'Dagon' was Lovecraft working in Poe. 'The Outsider' and 'Berenice' are really similar. 'Rats in the Walls' is his 'The Fall of the House of Usher.' Both are written in that first-person insane style that Poe perfected." First-person insane isn't a literary perspective I learned about in freshman lit, but Joshi was referring to the fact that many of the protagonists and narrators in Poe and Lovecraft's stories are trying to convince the reader they're not mad, especially if they are.

Going into the discussion I recognized only two of the panelists' names. The first was, of course, Joshi. The other was Dennis Paoli. Paoli's experience with Lovecraft and Poe was different from the others. He wasn't an anthologist. Not a novelist. Not a scholar or essayist. He wasn't known for being any of those things at least. He was on the panel for his work as a screenwriter. He was most famous for being part of a trinity of film makers that included director Stuart Gordon and actor Jeffrey Combs, who together have created most of our Lovecraft movie adaptations, and a few Poe adaptations, to boot.

On the Lovecraft side, Paoli helped pen the horror classic *Re-Animator* (1985), which was an adaptation of Lovecraft's story "Herbert West: Re-Animator." He also wrote *From Beyond* (1986), based on Lovecraft's short story of the same name; *Castle Freak* (1995), inspired by Lovecraft's *The Outsider; Dagon* (2001), which was a combination of Lovecraft's "Dagon" and "The Shadow Over Innsmouth" stories; and the Showtime *Masters of Horror* anthology episode *Dreams in the Witch-House* (2005). On the Poe side, his credits include *The Pit and the Pendulum* (1991) and another *Masters of Horror* episode, *The Black Cat* (2007). Stuart Gordon directed all of these, with Combs starring in all of them except *Dagon* and *Dreams in the Witch-House.*

The three also collaborated on a one-man stage play of Poe's life and works called *Nevermore* that has been running at venues across North America for the past few years.

Once Poe was a topic, Paoli jumped right in. "Both of the authors experimented with narrative, and both pushed the language and themes. You have to with horror for it to be affecting. Once something's written down, you've already domesticated it." Then he added, reflecting what Gucker had said earlier, "Of course, what Poe took to the edge, Lovecraft pushed over the cliff."

I tried to corner Paoli after the talk, but missed my window. Two months later, however, I randomly got the opportunity to talk to a different member of the trinity.

## *Jeffrey Combs . . . Poe's Mustache*

It was early October, and I had gotten wind that Gordon, Paoli, and Combs were looking to collaborate again, this time on a film version of their stage play about Poe, and that, like the H. P. Lovecraft Bust Project team, they were turning to

Kickstarter to help fund it. I had Bryan Moore's e-mail address, and I thought there might be a chance that he had a contact in the Lovecraft community who could put me in touch with Jeffrey Combs for an interview.

I already mentioned my burgeoning obsession with Poe actors in the Massachusetts chapter. I wanted to talk to Combs in particular because he's performed the poet on TV (in that Showtime *Masters of Horror* episode *The Black Cat*), on the stage in *Nevermore,* and would, if the Kickstarter got funded, on the big screen.

He had a Poe trifecta lined up, and if there's any actor with some unique Poe insight, it's gotta be him.

It turns out Moore and Combs knew each other from way back. Moore had done a life-sculpt of Combs for a statuette of his *Re-Animator* persona Herbert West. Hours after contacting Moore, I was on the phone with Combs. It was that fast. I mean, the previous night I had just introduced my wife, Lindsey, to *Re-Animator.* I had no idea that on the very next, I'd be talking to the star of the movie himself, Jeffrey Combs.

This was a pretty big deal for me. Watching Combs's movies was a non-elective part of my horror education back when I used to mainline horror movies in the attic of my parents' home on a tiny TV, thanks to a local video rental store that offered a deal of five movies for five days for five dollars. I'm talking VHS tapes here.

And that guy's phone number is now in my cell phone.

Calling people is usually hard for me to do, whether it's my mom or the dentist. Fortunately, calling a genre legend was too surreal to be a problem. Just ten digits later, I heard a "Hello?" on the other end.

"Mr. Combs?" I asked with feigned uncertainty. It was a formality. I recognized his voice right away, and not just because I'd heard it for an hour and a half the previous night. He's got a recognizable voice, and you can pick him out even when he's hidden under layers of makeup for *Star Trek* roles or doing voice-overs for cartoons like *Scooby-Doo! Mystery Incorporated* (in which he plays a Lovecraft parody character called Hatecraft).

We eased into the conversation by talking a bit about the app we were using to connect. He was filming his latest movie in Halifax, Nova Scotia, and even though I could've almost thrown a football to him from where I was in New Hampshire, the phone bill would have been like calling the Mars Rover since it crossed an international line. But Combs, with the knowledge of a man who travels frequently for location shooting, had suggested over e-mail we use an app to circumvent all that.

But then we quickly got down to black cats. (That was supposed to be a pun on brass tacks. I don't think it worked.)

"So tell me how this Poe thing got started for you. I mean, you've done him for TV, the stage, and now you're looking to do him on film. That sounds like more than just a passing interest or accepting a role."

"It's funny," he said. "I love history, and years and years ago, I was looking around for a historical character I could portray—not as a one-man show—but in whatever. Just something to really broaden my reputation beyond a horror and science fiction actor. I happened to be reading a biography of Poe at the time, although I was completely resistant to him as the character I was looking for—for obvious reasons.

"But after that biography I became fascinated by him—by his psychology, his contrasts, his character, the way he seemed to switch from genteel to raving in the gutter. It also helped that I'm his height, that we have the same eye color, so just physically he was a fit for me."

"What do you mean, 'his contrasts?'" I asked.

"I remember throwing down the book at one point and thinking, 'What a pathetic guy. You're begging people for money all the time, even asking for loans from the people whom you've written bad reviews about. He could be so beautifully poetic and then so crass."

"Yeah, I'm about halfway through his letters, and, honestly, he often comes off as unlikable."

"Exactly. You don't like him, and it's disappointing. But I see him as America's Van Gogh, a tortured soul and brilliant . . . I don't think he was steeped in Van Gogh's madness, but I think there are parallels, including the fact that neither had two nickels to rub together. Poe did get some notoriety, though, just not what he should have.

"And that's kind of another connection I made with Poe. He got his notoriety from stories that he kind of looked down on. We think they're genius, but he thought he was debasing himself to write them. He wanted to be poet. In a small way, it's like me and Lovecraft. People always come to me and ask if I read a lot of Lovecraft growing up, but I didn't live off of peanut butter sandwiches and spend six years learning the basics of my craft just so I could do Lovecraft. It found me. I didn't find it. I guess people like it, and it perpetuated itself."

"So you did the *Masters of Horror* episode, and that just turned into the stage show?"

"The one-man show is not actually something I'd ever have thought to do, but with the economic downturn, things really dried up. It was the Sahara out there. So I needed to do stuff that I could control, and after *The Black Cat*, Stuart really convinced me that it was something we should do."

That's Stuart Gordon, who is Tim Burton to Combs's Johnny Depp.

"Tell me more about *Nevermore.*"

"Did you see it?"

"Uh, no." I wondered if that's the worst thing you can tell an actor.

"Ok, I just wanted to know how much detail to go into. We deal a lot with those contrasts we were talking about."

Combs then went on to describe *Nevermore*'s take on Poe's story. The play, using minimal props and effects and basically just relying on Combs, shows Poe transmogrifying from the southern gentleman that Poe loved being to—as he gets drunker—a bolder, embittered, erratic man. It then ends with a sad redemption of sorts that sobers him up . . . the departure of Sarah Helen Whitman. Interspersed throughout the performance, Combs also performs a selection of Poe's works.

"About 90 percent of what I say comes directly from Poe, but we, of course, deviate from historical accounts to push the narrative to the salient points. Early in the night I read 'The Tell-Tale Heart,' pulling out the bottle while I'm doing it, and that's when the audience really reacts. That's when the party starts.

"I had an alcoholic uncle as a kid, a weekend alcoholic. Throughout the week he was uncolorful, mumbled a lot, but on the weekend, he was a bigger, more theatrical version of himself, free, entertaining . . . so I wanted to go on that kind of journey with Poe."

"So you performed Nevermore for three years in cities across the continent. What's it like to be Poe for so long?"

"I'm not the type of actor who has to be the character all the time, but it's Poe. There's a melancholia that you're steeped in with him and it gets to you. My wife actually told me at one point, "God, why don't you stop doing this play?"

I made a note: Jeffrey Combs's wife calls him God.

"But you know what was really intense about the show for me, was the one-man aspect of it on top of a relatively bleak character. I didn't realize what a lonely journey it is to have a one-man show. Nobody to commiserate with. Nobody to get drinks with afterward to blow off steam. Nobody to get into the moment with."

At this point, I assume Combs looked down at his phone, because he interjected, "Are you in Frederick, Maryland?" He pronounced the location like it was a foreign country.

"Ha. No, I'm in New England. I lived in the Frederick area for a few years and that's why I have that area code. I still have family there, actually." Frederick's about 50 minutes west of Poe's grave in Baltimore.

"I just shot a movie there not a year and a half ago or so."

"What? They do that in Frederick? What's the movie?"

"It's called *Elf-Man*."

I IMDB'd the movie right there, thinking it was a horror project. Turns out, it's a Christmas movie with Wee-Man from *Jackass.* I moved it into my mental Netflix queue for when the seasons rolls around.

"So obviously you're not done with Poe, even after all these years. Why the movie, and how do you translate a one-man show like yours to the screen?"

"Ever since I got into Poe, I've wondered why we don't have the great American movie about the great American writer. I kind of think of him as the human condition writ large—our highs and lows exaggerated in Poe."

"I'm not the definitive answer to Poe, but I'd love to give him a good shot. I have this experience with him and I love the poor guy, such an underdog.

"As for the movie, this will give us a chance to actually depict his stories and poems throughout this overarching story of Poe himself."

"And you're turning to Kickstarter to try to make it happen?"

"Yeah. I'm a little bit out of my depth with Kickstarter. I have trouble pushing myself onto people, 'Hey support me. I'm good.' It's out of my comfort zone. We got a good response to the Kickstarter at first, but we're to the point that the goal is the Andes and we only have one llama."

"So let me ask you this. If the Kickstarter doesn't fund, and if you can't get funding from elsewhere . . ."

Here he interrupted, "Which is probable. If the Kickstarter doesn't fund, people will use that as evidence for no public interest, no matter how much money gets pledged."

"So if it doesn't get funded, then do you still continue to do Poe or are you done with him?

"If it doesn't happen," here his tone became a little reluctant, but gradually firmed, "yeah, I'll hang up the costume and look for other challenges. An actor friend of mine once told me, 'All shows close.'"

Three weeks later, the Kickstarter closed, the $375,000 goal unmet, and while that might seem to hurt my thesis of Poe's place in modern culture (and that 2013 was a particularly good year for Poe), they did manage to raise $92,804 toward the movie from everyday fans. I threw in some myself. I was still smarting from missing out on having my name on the Lovecraft bust, but the real reason was that I wanted to see the movie they would've made about Poe. I also wanted to own Poe's nose. The reward for contributors at my level was one of the prosthetic noses Combs used during his lonely time as Poe on stage.

Of course, Kickstarter is an all or nothing thing, so technically they raised no money. And while a movie and a bust may be apples to oranges, they did outstrip the funding for the Lovecraft bust by close to $40,000.

Throughout the course of working on this book I was planning to get extremely close to Poe . . . as close as holding his handwritten poems in my hand, as close as kneeling by his wife's deathbed, as close as, well, six feet above his bones. And while that's pretty close, I'll never know what it's like to don the 'stache and really feel his work from inside.

So I rely on people like Combs to do that for me. Hopefully he's lying about hanging up the costume.

## Two Graves

My time in Providence was drawing to a close, but it was destined to have two different endings. The first was at Swan Point Cemetery.

Swan Point Cemetery has been around since 1846. It covers about two hundred acres on the Seekonk River and is still in use today. Some say it was one of the places that Whitman and Poe visited during their ill-fated relationship. The cemetery is at 585 Blackstone Boulevard and lies only two miles from Whitman's home on Benefit Street.

But the real reason to go to the cemetery is a bit more tangible. It's the site of H. P. Lovecraft's final resting place.

His grave is located at the intersection of Pond Avenue and Avenue B. There you'll find a tall obelisk marked with the name *Phillips*.

His name is engraved on the back of that obelisk, as Howard P. Lovecraft, right beneath the names of his parents, but there is also a small marker just for Lovecraft, directly behind the obelisk. Here we find another commonality with Poe, for both Poe and Lovecraft have headstones today because fans raised money and purchased them decades after the deaths of these authors.

I've been to Lovecraft's grave a few times in my life, and there are usually tokens of other visitations laid on and around the stone. This time, there was some sheet music, a small framed illustration of him, a nosegay of wilted flowers, and a 2009 Mardi Gras doubloon featuring an anthropomorphic crescent moon in a nightcap and a winged being above the word *Morpheus*.

Unlike the other times I've visited, there was also a security guard parked directly across from it. The guard was nice enough, but it's a reminder that the cemetery hasn't quite warmed up to the cold corpse of the famous horror author fertilizing its grass. But they might have good reason. On an October night in 1997 somebody made a half-assed attempt to dig up his bones. He/she/they/it gave up after digging up about three feet in the area near his gravestone. They dug in the wrong spot.

The gravestone was placed in 1977 near the obelisk under which Lovecraft was actually buried in 1937. So future Burkes and Hares should take note of that. Also that digging up the bones of a man who spent a life doing the same thing in his imagination seems like a much better tribute than it actually is.

Lovecraft's gravestone is a simple piece of granite, its face polished and angled like a book held for optimum reading. Its epitaph states:

HOWARD PHILLIPS
LOVECRAFT
AUGUST 20, 1880
MARCH 15, 1937


I AM PROVIDENCE


I've argued with a lot of epitaphs in my day, but defer to what's set in stone on Lovecraft's. The last line is a quote from one of his letters, and would have been a good title for his autobiography if it wasn't already headlined by the untoppable *Some Notes on a Non-Entity*.

And the beauty of what transpired at NecronomiCon is that Providence is finally becoming a lot more Lovecraft.

In many ways Lovecraft's legacy is an extension of Poe's. But before Love-craft, it had others to protect it. Like Sarah Helen Whitman. My second ending in Providence was at another cemetery, the North Burial Ground at 5 Branch Avenue, about 1.5 miles away from Swan Point. It's about half the size of Swan Point, but dates back further, to the year 1700. I arrived just as the caretaker was preparing to shut down the place for the night. I explained my purpose, and he told me I had until he returned to the front gate after his final cemetery check to visit the dead poet.

I rushed to Dahlia Path, which I knew from a visit years earlier was the loca-tion of the small loaf of a stone. It's on the left side of the path if you're coming

from the front of the cemetery, adjacent to an identical small block of stone that marks the body of her sister Susan Anna Power, which is, in turn, adjacent to a crumbling table monument.

Most gravestones give a name and a date range, but Whitman's plain stone, as does that of her sister, arranges that information a bit more true-to-life. It gives her birth year of 1803 first, then her name beneath that, and then, on the final line, her death year of 1878. All in all, a much better illustration of the birth, existence, and death of a human being. "Soft may the worms about her creep."

Whitman is the reason Poe had a presence in Providence that can be physically traced. The reason we have the "Ulalume" autograph and a couple of important daguerreotypes of the man. She was the reason we have his late-in-life poem, "To Helen," the second one he ever titled such. In it, he rhapsodizes about seeing her in the garden of 88 Benefit Street years before he ever met her. And even though things didn't end amicably, from the point of his death to the point of hers Whitman was one of Poe's staunchest supporters when his reputation was being disparaged.

During my time in Providence, I'd seen a portrait of her face, held a piece of her clothing, saw her autograph in a book, visited both her home in life and her home in death. She was a testament to the power of Poe. The few days total she spent with him gave her an immortality beyond anything she could have achieved otherwise.

And because she drew Poe to Providence, she could justly claim credit for some of the hold that he had over H. P. Lovecraft.

Providence is the crossroads of two of the founding fiends of horror literature. When I was talking to Kate Wodehouse at the Providence Athenaeum, we joked that the library should commission its own bust of Poe to keep its bust of Lovecraft company, not for the sake of the library, but for the sake of Providence.

Because Providence should embrace its dark side. It has a great one.

*Will Ryman's* Bird, *in front of the Flatiron Building*

# CHAPTER 3

# New York

## *This Home by Horror Haunted*

For just a few weeks in the early spring of 2013, the Flatiron District of Manhattan was dominated, as much as any district of that city can be, by a giant raven. I made a special trip to the city to see the bird. Had to. I was writing a book about Edgar Allan Poe, you know.

The twelve-foot-tall sculpture, called *Bird,* perched at the intersection of 5th Avenue and East 23rd Street, right at the tip of the cursor-shaped Flatiron Building that gives the area its name.

The bird was dark and ominous, like any of its species, and the massive size seemed to somehow fit the scale of the buildings better than the tiny people congregated around it.

Oh, and the whole thing was made out of giant nails. Because any sculptor worth his materials can make a big bird. But making one out of giant nails . . . that's art.

Small nails, too—the type you could buy at any hardware store, but mostly gigantic ones you'd have to either get specially made at a foundry or steal from the top of a magic beanstalk. The strange composition gave the metal bird a ruffled appearance, one that was simultaneously soft, like, well, feathers and hard, like, well, stainless steel nails. In the creature's beak was a red rose trailing a tentacular green stem.

The art installation was created by Will Ryman and, in just about every news article I'd read about the installation, was said to be "loosely inspired" by Edgar Allan Poe's poem of the same subject matter.

I'm not sure what that phrase in quotation marks means exactly, but I assume it's to protect the artist from appearing to encroach on Poe's own artistic use of that carrion fowl. The raven is Poe's. Kind of like white whales belong to Herman Melville and giant squids to Jules Verne. Except Poe made his irrevocable claim in less than 1,200 words. This is part of what we mean when we say this guy was a genius with words.

Actually, according to the original interview in the *Huffington Post,* what Ryman said when asked directly about whether Poe was his inspiration was, "The image of the bird, maybe, but very loosely. It's really more about the abstraction of the nail." Interpreted without all the graciousness, I think he meant, "Obviously you can't do anything with a raven without the ghost of Poe looking grumpily over your shoulder, but goddamn it, I just wanted to make a giant black bird out of nails."

Whether Ryman meant to or not, he picked a fitting city for a sculpture that may or may not have been a direct Poe reference. It was in New York City, just three or four miles away from the *Bird* installation, in fact, that Poe wrote "The Raven," a poem so well-known that over the years the title has almost evolved into "Poe's Famous Poem The Raven."

I say *wrote*, but it could just have been completed here. It's difficult to map the vicissitudes of the creative mind to the geography of the creative body. But it was certainly here that he finished it and here, in New York, where it was first published in 1845.

But we'll talk more specifically later about where Poe wrote "The Raven." The point here is that this single poem gave Poe the most recognition he'd gain as an artist during his lifetime. So, in a way, Poe made it big in New York.

And that's exactly why he came to the city. That's exactly why most people come to this city: to make it big. Of course, in Poe's case, he eventually had to lower that goal to just making do. And then further down to making ends meet. And, finally, to just making it at all.

In a way, the story of Edgar Allan Poe in New York fits the template for many New York stories. The Empire City can raise you to the heady spires of its skyscrapers and dash you to the disgusting tunnel floors of its subways. Poe's peak was a few stanzas about a croaking bird and a grieving man, while his pit was literary exile in what is today the Bronx. But that's just career-wise. His real New York nadir, the lead weight that held the raven earthbound, was the death of his wife.

Poe lived off and on in New York City and its surrounding areas for about seven and a half years, a sizeable chunk for a man who died at forty. The longest stretch was the last five and a half years of his life. His driver's license was a New York one when he died in Baltimore.

Also, it must, must, must be mentioned, that it was here where Edgar Allan Poe grew his trademark mustache. That's right. Poe was shorn and shaven most of his life. The image of Poe we all have burned into our collective consciousness is the New York Poe.

Poe, his wife, and his mother in law lived in a handful of places in New York City proper and in nearby locations that are today part of New York City, only three of which have been commemorated. The memorials vary widely in scope, from the mere perfunctory to the staggeringly impressive.

But we're going to start our New York Poe journey outside the city, where Poe's first foray into the Knickerbocker State started. Ingloriously, of course. The only way Poe knew how.

## An Officer and a Madman

In writing a book about Edgar Allan Poe, there were a few experiences I expected to have. I was pretty sure I'd find myself in a graveyard or two. That I'd get to see some rare artifacts under glass. That I'd get corrected on my pronunciation of Berenice and Eulalie. But I never thought I'd be passing through a military checkpoint while people with guns strapped to their hips scrutinized the old photo on my driver's license.

But that's what happens when you visit West Point.

Edgar Allan Poe spent two years in the Army as an artilleryman, and was stationed at three forts over that time: Fort Independence in Boston, Fort Moultrie in Charleston, and Fort Monroe in Richmond. By all accounts, he did pretty well, and was promoted to the highest rank he could attain as an enlisted man, sergeant major. But his time in the military was an escape plan, both from the foster father in his face and the hollow hunger in his gut.

However, he quickly realized that his escape plan needed an escape plan. He decided his new way out would be West Point.

The plan seemed to have potential. He wasn't soldier material, but maybe he was officer material. It at least appealed to the sense of aristocracy his upbringing in the South and wealthy foster father had imprinted upon him. More important, he had a year of college, two years of military experience, and a lineage that included a grandfather who was a respected quartermaster in the U.S. Army.

On top of it all, the move had the potential to put him back into the graces of that foster father. It would show John Allan that he'd grown up, grown serious, gotten a haircut, and gotten a real job.

So after some finagling himself out of his full five-year tour of duty, plus a year of sitting around waiting for all the money and red tape to align, he enrolled at West Point in July of 1830.

Seven months later, he got kicked out.

Apparently, Poe realized that a life in uniform, any uniform, wasn't the life he wanted, so he arranged to get himself dishonorably discharged. It would be great if this part of Poe's story turned into a screwball comedy (and indeed there's long been a false rumor that he did it by showing up to drill practice wearing nothing but a pair of pristine white gloves and an ammo belt), but in reality, he just kind of oozed his way out by not showing up to mandatory events and in general treating his Imp of the Perverse as a guiding light.

It was like that for Poe. His life would be a series of escape plans. From pits, from pendulums, from super-heated collapsing walls.

The only thing Poe really got out of his time at West Point was the coat with which he would cover his dying wife sixteen years later.

Oh, and a marble memorial, seventy-eight years later.

That's right. In yet another testament to the power of Poe, the place at which Poe spent only half a year and to which he presented his posterior for booting still wanted a piece of his legacy. And they did it with a doorway. That's what I was braving guns and guards to see.

The United States Military Academy at West Point is located on the Hudson River, about fifty miles north of New York City. It has a history that goes back to the Revolutionary War. General George Washington set up a fort there and made it his headquarters in 1779. Benedict Arnold's infamous treason was an attempt to turn it over to the British a decade later, when he was in command there. In 1802, President Thomas Jefferson turned it into an officer academy. Since that time it has graduated a string of famous names that we see in our heads back-dropped by either stars and stripes, stars and bars, or camouflage: Davis, Lee, Grant, Jackson, Custer, MacArthur, Patton, Eisenhower, Aldrin.

And Poe could have been one of them.

Before heading onto such storied (and secure) ground, my wife, Lindsey, and I stopped at the West Point Visitors Center, just outside of the USMA campus. I wandered the few displays, looking for any tell-tale sign that the world's most famous poet and horror writer once got kicked out of there, but I didn't see anything Poe-ish.

Behind the visitors center is the West Point Museum, an imposing four-story building full of artifacts from centuries of education in the art of war. By this time my appointment at the academy itself was looming, and I didn't have time to check it out, so I called the museum from its own parking lot.

"Do you have any exhibits on Edgar Allan Poe's time at West Point?"

"Negative."

"Roger that. Over and out."

So it was off to the Thayer Gate of West Point, just down the road. I was certain, even with our appointment, that we were about to be subjected to an intensive security check—opening my trunk, mirrors under the car, German Shepherds, the whole deal. Instead, upon pulling up, the woman looked at our licenses, stuttered out a few incomplete sentences, and finished with, "There's another checkpoint ahead." She waved us on with what seemed to me to be relief.

The second checkpoint was just as fast. The guard look at our licenses, asked what building I was headed for, as if the test was merely whether I knew the name of one, and then waved me through.

Then I realized why.

In my rearview mirror, I saw a long caravan of cars and motorcycles with lights flashing that were obviously escorting somebody of importance. The guards just wanted me out of the way.

It was mid-June and, other than that cavalcade, the campus was almost deserted. A few groups of cadets were doing training exercises. Some hard-hatted construction workers were doing their thing with back loaders. The sports fields were barren. And the hundred-year-old, castle-like Cadet Chapel perched silently on the hill as if it were actively guarding its souls.

We were there to meet Suzanne Christoff, the Associate Director for Special Collections and Archives at the USMA library. I had e-mailed her a couple years earlier, when doing research for another book and had enquired about what I'd heard referred to as the Poe Arch. At the time, it was inaccessible, due to a renovation project.

We met at the first-floor rotunda of Jefferson Hall, the academy's library. The polished stone floor bore the West Point crest: the gold helm of Pallas Athena (the favorite perch of a certain black bird) crossed by a sheathed sword against a red, white, and blue shield. Atop it a brown and white eagle perched, green leaves and golden arrows in its claws. Behind it a red banner showed the gold words DUTY, HONOR, COUNTRY on one side and WEST POINT, MDCCCII, USMA on the other.

Towering proudly over this, at the apex of the sigil, was a statue of Thomas Jefferson, the president who made this place an academy.

After talking to Suzanne for a bit, she handed us off to Casey Madrick, an archive technician. Madrick was a civilian, bearded and dressed casually, although he did sport a camouflage cap. The first thing he did was take us out of Jefferson Hall, and into the adjacent Bartlett Hall. Bartlett Hall was built in 1962 and was the campus library before the six-story Jefferson Hall was completed in 2008.

Bartlett Hall had been built using the stones from its predecessor library, the site of which it now occupies. That first library was built in 1841, and it was there that the Poe Arch was originally installed, almost seventy years later. So the Poe Arch never moved in space, just in time. And subject matter.

Today, Bartlett Hall is a science facility dedicated to dragging Diana from her car, driving the Hamadryad from the wood, and tearing the Naiad from her flood. It's apt for a pioneer in science fiction who capped his career with the strange treatise on the nature of the universe that is *Eureka*.

On the way to the fourth floor, where the Poe Arch arches, I asked Madrick if many people came around looking for the monument.

"People ask about Poe sometimes, but just in connection with his time here. They don't usually ask about the arch itself."

I apologized. He accepted graciously.

Eventually, we arrived at what looked like a large, cluttered meeting room, with rows of folding chairs facing a podium in what looked like a temporary arrangement. I asked Madrick what the purpose of the room was, and he gave a vague answer about board meetings or some such. Military secrets, man.

It took me a few seconds to find the ornamental doorway that is the Poe Arch. Like Poe himself at West Point, it fit awkwardly into its surroundings, off to the side as if they weren't sure what exactly to do with it. It formed half a corner, and through it and the open door it outlined a small section of hallway was visible.

In another context, it might have been grand. It was simple but elegant, like a soldier's grave in a national cemetery. The arch was at least ten feet high, made of white marble, and topped by a large tablet that read:

IN MEMORIAM EDGAR ALLAN POE
BORN MDCCCIX—DIED MDCCCXLIX
HOW DARK A WOE! YET HOW SUBLIME A HOPE!
HOW SILENTLY SERENE A SEA OF PRIDE!
HOW DARING AN AMBITION! YET HOW DEEP—
HOW FATHOMLESS A CAPACITY FOR LOVE!

The quote is from his poem "To Helen," the one inspired by a woman he met while still a boy in Richmond. Below it is another quote, from Francis Bacon:

THERE IS NO EXQUISITE BEAUTY WITHOUT
SOME STRANGENESS IN THE PROPORTION.

Poe used the Bacon quote in his story "Ligeia."

Of course, woe, beauty, love, and strangeness aren't usually the themes chosen for military monuments. I assume the Bacon quote kind of addresses that, but the excerpt from "To Helen" was chosen for a more relevant reason.

During the short time that Poe was at West Point, he amused his fellow cadets with rhymes making fun of the commanders at the academy. He then sold subscriptions for a collection of poetry his peers thought would be of the same hilarity. Instead, they got death, beautiful women, and ethereal angels. It was *Poems,* Poe's third volume of verse. He completed it after leaving West Point and dedicated it to the U.S. Corps of Cadets. It was a slim volume filled with recy-

*Poe Arch, West Point*

cled poetry from his previous collections, but it also featured some new poems, like "To Helen." Madrick mentioned that West Point has in its archives a canceled check one of the students made out to Poe for his work.

Later, I would see one of these volumes at the Poe Museum in Richmond, where it was on display and open to a random page. The museum curator told me they couldn't display the title page because the original owner, disappointed with the quality of the product, wrote an obscenity on it.

But all that backstory apparently didn't seem too strange to the faculty or donors who erected this monument to a seven-month stay. William Lyon Phelps, the famous essayist and professor at Yale called the combination of West Point and Poe a "superb combination" in a letter he wrote to the library faculty. I'd characterize it as a sarcastic statement, but it was accompanied by a donation from himself and his students.

It cost more than $2,500 to erect the monument and honor West Point's most famous dropout. It was paid for by contributions from "personal friends of the academy" that ranged from wealthy businessmen to students and faculty, and it was put up in time for the centenary of his birth, January 19, 1909.

There wasn't much more to do at the Poe Arch but walk back and forth through it a couple of times to say I did, while Lindsey struggled with photographing what's basically a back door.

Before we left the room, Madrick took us to a spot near the entrance. "We also have this." It looked like a large chair rack. He moved the large chair rack away from the wall. Behind it was another marble monument.

This one wasn't an arch, but a flat column of marble similar to the Poe Arch. It was the Whistler Memorial.

James Abbott McNeill Whistler was a nineteenth-century American painter from Lowell, Massachusetts, who is most famous these days for his mom. He painted the portrait of the black-clad, seated figure that has come to be called *Whistler's Mother* because, well, it was his dear old mom. Like Poe, he hated any type of moralizing in art and, like Poe, he was also a West Point dropout.

More accurately, he was a fail-out. He had gotten into West Point as the result of family connections and lasted about three years. However, he was constantly one demerit from expulsion due to a general non-soldierly attitude. But it was failing his chemistry exam that finally made his commanders put him on Poe Street right out of there. It is said that he liked to joke of his exit from West Point that if silicon had been a gas, he would have been a major-general.

Designed by Augustus Saint-Gaudens, Whistler's monument was installed the year before Poe's was. It's tall and thin, rather like the shape and size of a grandfather clock, and its inscription is bracketed between two torches and set beneath a crown of laurels:

TO
JAMES MCNEILL
WHISTLER

MDCCCXXXIV
MCMIII
THE STORY OF THE
BEAUTIFUL
IS ALREADY COMPLETE
HEWN IN THE MARBLES
OF THE PARTHENON
AND BROIDERED WITH
THE BIRDS UP ON THE
FAN OF HOKUSAI

The quote is the last line of Whistler's famous Ten O'Clock lecture, which he delivered in his adopted home city of London. In it, he defended art as a goal in itself, as opposed to a conduit for virtue. The monument makers left off the last five words, "at the foot of Fukushima."

The Whistler and Poe monuments are companion pieces, even if they're now across the room from each other. Originally, they shared a corner together, a corner to which I'd like to think bad cadets were sent to learn their lesson lest they get kicked out of West Point and achieve everlasting fame in the arts.

As we exited Bartlett Hall, Madrick had one more surprise for us. "Have you seen these yet?" he said as he motioned to three massive bronze plates set in a row in the outside wall of the building, right at the entrance. We had originally entered the building through a side door.

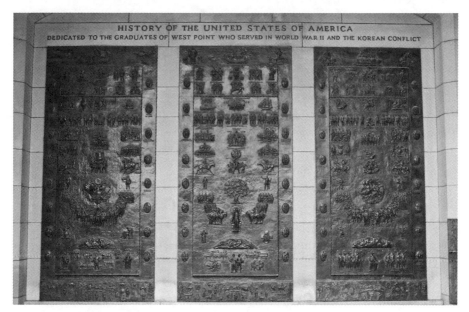

*Laura Gardin Fraser's American history reliefs, West Point*

When I say massive, I mean like the size of coffin lids for giants. The plates each measured maybe five or six feet wide by like twelve feet high and were covered with hundreds of small figures.

They were sculpted in 1964 by Laura Gardin Fraser, who mostly made medallion sculptures and who was the wife of James Earle Fraser. He basically sculpted the entire nation's capital.

But it wasn't so much the number of the reliefs on the panels that was staggering. It was the variety.

The triptych of bronze panels depicts the history of America, just in its own way. The three panels were roughly symmetrical in their arrangement of reliefs and told the story chronologically from the top of the first panel to the bottom of the third panel.

Some of the tiny figures were literal interpretations, like Lewis and Clark and Thomas Jefferson and the *Santa Maria*. Others were more fanciful, like Paul Bunyan. Others were symbolic, like the winged horse and gryphon that symbolized science and invention. The Four Horseman of the Apocalypse were there, as was the Jupiter rocket and a whale being killed for its oil. The Salem Witch Trials were represented by a classic Halloween witch on a broom. The Ku Klux Klan was signified by a single Klansmen in an oval, the same way Will Rogers and Sitting Bull were signified. There were animals and trees and machines, events and places and people, all labeled for either what they were or what they represented.

It's like she doodled her way through four years of high school American

History classes, and then had all of the notebooks bronzed. I want the triptych turned into a textbook for my kids to learn history from.

On a hunch, I played *Where's Waldo?* with the piece and soon found what I was looking for in the middle panel: a tiny Edgar Allan Poe standing in a group of his fellow literary contemporaries . . . Irving, Hawthorne, Longfellow, all the usual suspects. Emily Dickinson sat demurely in their midst.

So Poe finds himself twice memorialized in the same building at West Point.

Before we took our leave of Madrick, I asked him, "Are you guys scheduled to have a VIP on campus today?"

"Not that I've heard about."

It wouldn't be until weeks later that I learned who that caravan honored. I had inadvertently timed our visit for the burial of Lieutenant Colonel Jaimie Leonard. She had been killed two weeks earlier in Afghanistan. All this poet-chasing had made me forget what people mean when they talk about what it takes to be a soldier. The academy's annual report for 1909, in a section talking about the Poe and Whistler memorials, says of the two artists, "Neither of them was of the fiber that is required for a soldier, but each of them has left a name to be honored."

## *The Raven Hatches*

Poe spent some time in New York City after he left West Point, but it wasn't until six years later, in 1837, that he became an official New Yorker. By that time, he had a family and a career far removed from dress inspections and marching drills. Fresh off his awkwardly ended tenure as the editor for the *Southern Literary Messenger* in Richmond and with a young bride and mother-in-law on either arm, he was hoping to parlay his new magazine experience and the reputation he had earned as a sharp-edged critic into success on the New York literary scene and a secure home life. He was also harboring dreams of starting his own literary magazine.

A year later, he left the Rotten Apple for the Cracked Bell. He stayed in Philadelphia until 1844, when he returned to New York permanently, although he did move around within the city limits, or at least what would eventually become the limits of a city in the process of expanding to become the largest on the planet.

Only one of his New York residences remains intact, while the sites of two more are memorialized. One of these latter is the Brennan farmhouse, where he stayed from 1844 to 1845, and which is commemorated for reasons beyond its being the place where Poe lived. Even though he was only here about a year, it was in that farmhouse that "The Raven" hatched.

"The Raven" was published in January of 1845 in New York's *Evening Mirror*.

It was also published in the February issue of *The American Review,* another New York publication, in which it appeared under the byline "Quarles." Which rag actually hit the stands first is up for debate, and it makes more sense that it would have been first published under a pen name, but either way it debuted in New York. And then "The Raven" took flight. Everybody within spitting distance of a press wanted to publish it, even if they had to bundle it with other Poe works. The Year of the Raven saw both his *Tales* and his *The Raven and Other Poems* released to the public. It had been a decade and a half since he had published a book of poetry—his West Point volume, in fact.

Publishers wanted to get their hands on "The Raven" because there was a market. Everybody knew "The Raven." It was a hit, adored and parodied, discussed and criticized. He was invited to all the New York social gatherings and asked to recite it at lectures. Poe had finally made it onto the charts with his black bird, and it tenaciously dug its talons into the marble helm of the severed head of a goddess, just glaring from its roost and daring anybody to knock it off.

And that raven never flitting, still is sitting, still is sitting. Today, "The Raven" is unendingly recited, dramatized, performed, parodied, referenced, and reverenced across the multifarious tentacles of media that make up modern culture. It permeates our art and entertainment. His copyright might have officially expired, but he still owns it. You can't even make a black bird out of nails without referencing him.

However, unlike "The Raven," the place where the poem was originally incarnated is no more, swallowed up by the Upper West Side of Manhattan.

A surviving photo of the Brennan farmhouse shows a two-story edifice complemented by outbuildings. Its most prominent feature is where it sits, a large, rocky outcrop that makes it look like the house was marooned there after a flood. A rickety, wooden stairway curves down from the front of the house to the base of the rock, from where a sandy road, softly rutted with carriage wheel tracks, wends.

The farmhouse was torn down around 1888. Today, the area is West 84th Street, a busy residential-and-retail area bracketed between Central Park and Riverside Park. But Poe and his raven are still there.

The city named a block-long strip of West 84th Street between West End Avenue and Broadway after the horror author. Green signs proclaiming EDGAR ALLAN POE STREET to a massive and indifferent audience were at each end of the strip, high up on poles and sharing sign space with the street's numeric designation of West 84th.

But I wasn't strolling on the sidewalks of Manhattan just to see street signs. I'd heard there were two plaques commemorating the poem. That's right. "The Raven" is a two-plaquer.

The first one was easy to find, large and black and set a good ten feet above the sidewalk on the side of number 255, The Alameda, a thirteen-story apartment building built in 1914. The metal plaque states:

UPON THIS SITE
FORMERLY STOOD THE BRENNAN MANSION
IN WHICH RESIDED
FROM MARCH 1844 TO AUGUST 1845
EDGAR ALLAN POE
AND HERE DURING SUCH RESIDENCE HE PRODUCED
AND GAVE TO AMERICAN LITERATURE AND TO IMMORTALITY
THE RAVEN
IN COMMEMORATION OF THE POET AND OF THE POEM
THIS TABLET IS PLACED MCMXXII BY
THE NEW YORK SHAKESPEARE SOCIETY
DONORS

| APPLETON MORGAN | ALBERT R. FREY |
|---|---|
| OTTO H. KAHN | NATHAN D. BILL |

JOHN DREW

The donors were the president and secretary of the New York Shakespeare Society (Appleton Morgan and Albert R. Frey, respectively). Otto H. Kahn is the Filthy Rich Businessman Who Likes Art. John Drew was probably the actor John Drew, Jr. (uncle to the famous Barrymore actor siblings Ethel, John, and Lionel, making him great-great-uncle to actress Drew Barrymore). As for Nathan D. Bill, other than some unenlightening mentions in the society pages of the local newspapers, I wasn't able to dig up too much on him. Probably because he didn't have a Wikipedia entry.

If I'm remembering my Roman numerals right, this plaque went up about two years before the Boston Authors Club plaque at Poe's birth site in Boston, and has outlived it by ninety years. It's almost time for a commemoration of the commemoration.

What has really given the site some Poe flair for the past couple of decades, though, is a restaurant. For two decades, starting in 1990, the first-floor retail space at The Alameda was tenanted by a small European-style eatery called Edgar's Café. That place was, of course, named after the poet, and they touted the history of the site on the menus and with the general decor of the place. However, sometime in early 2011, the café was replaced by a salon . . . not called Edgar's.

*Menu from Edgar's Café*

The restaurant is still around; it just moved half a mile north, to 650 Amsterdam Avenue. It's still called Edgar's Cafe, so later I dropped by to see if they still used Poe as a brand-enabler.

The café is a tiny, cash-only place that fits about a dozen tables, with a couple more outside. Its walls are painted to look like plaster that has worn down to the brick in places, which may or may not be a soft reference to "The Black Cat" or "The Cask of Amontillado," depending on what's behind those walls. Various random bric-a-brac decorate the place, and its counter doubles as a dessert case.

And it is still lightly Poe-themed. A large oil painting of the man overlooks the place, and here and there on the walls is a raven or two. The painting is by Basmat Levin and looks to have been based on the Daly daguerreotype of Poe during his New York years. A sharp angle to the left side of his nose and mustache makes him look like he's sneering down on us for being hungry.

I patronized the place in October, and the Poe portrait was covered in cobwebs, with plenty of spiders and bats on the walls to keep the raven decorations company.

The back of the menu bears an image of the 1949 three-cent Edgar Allan Poe stamp, the one that commemorated the one hundredth anniversary of his death day, as well as a raven in flight. Above the imagery is the phrase "Edgar's Celebrates Edgar!," and it includes a short history on why you are eating tiramisu below a morose-looking man in a reading chair. I recommend the gnocchi.

Back on Edgar Allan Poe Street, the second plaque took me a bit longer to find than the first. I kept ending up at a plaque for Russian composer Sergei Rachmaninoff placed on the building where he lived for the last seventeen years of his life.

Finally, I ventured beyond the eastern boundary of Edgar Allan Poe Street at Broadway to 215 West 84th Street. There, set just three or four feet off the ground and almost hidden by a stone (and assumedly jealous) eagle was a modern-looking bronze plaque featuring a small bust relief of Edgar Allan Poe. His face was slightly weathered around the nose and mustache, giving the features a skull-like cast. Below were the words:

> EDGAR ALLAN POE
> AND HIS FAMILY LIVED IN A
> FARMHOUSE ON THIS SITE
> DURING 1844 WHERE HE
> FINISHED WRITING
> "THE RAVEN"

The eagle was one of two flanking the entrance to an apartment building called Eagle Court.

As a writer trying to keep you guys interested in the part of a story that is just me looking at two plaques with my hand on my chin, I was hoping for a bit of a Poe controversy. I mean, here we have two buildings less than a block apart from each other, both armed and armored with their own Poe plaques, vying to be the official site of a literary legend/legendary literature. It's probably a simple matter of taking advantage of not knowing the exact footprint of the Brennan farmhouse itself, but I thought I'd check into my imagined controversy a little. Very little.

Since those original New York Shakespeare Society members are long gone, I sent an e-mail to the folks at Eagle Court regarding their more recent tribute to the dark poet. I received a quick, unenlightening response from the general manager that read in total, "The local landmark society put the plaque up in 1986 when the building was renovated."

That's all I got. Further attempts to pull more of the story out of him or at least get the actual name of the society were met with the e-mail equivalent of a dial tone. Not every plaque has the backstory of the Boston Poe plaque, I guess.

But that disappointment in the lack of

*Eagle Court Poe plaque*

drama around the plaques only comes from my perspective as a storyteller. As a Poe fan, I dig that people want to be part and propagator of Poe's legacy, even if that part is more a ploy to sell sandwiches and rent apartments.

I imagine every building and business within three blocks of Edgar Allan Poe Street getting its own "The Raven Wuz Here" plaque, giving "keeping up with the Joneses" a whole new twist. I also imagine everybody realizing at the annual block party how silly that is and instead all chipping in to buy Will Ryman's *Bird* and installing it somewhere central to the area. From there, my fantasy just spirals out of control into an entire theme park dedicated to Poe and his works.

These tributes to Poe's most renowned poem are great, but they do seem a little scant for a work of such impact as "The Raven." Walking the street and staring at a couple of bronze rectangles on a congested city street Poe would not recognize as the site where his muse was at its kindest didn't really get me closer to Poe and his poem.

But there are other ways to do that.

## *Ghost upon the Floor*

Stepping onto the Morningside Heights campus of Columbia University, on the Upper West Side of Manhattan, was a familiar experience for me. Sure, I'd been there a couple of years earlier on another trek for another book, but that's not really why the place felt so familiar to me.

It's because I'd seen it in so many movies.

This is where the Ghostbusters worked before they were Ghostbusters. Where Peter Parker went to school when he wasn't slinging webs. Where the Marathon Man matriculated. Where William Hurt put the moves on a young anthropologist in *Altered States.* In *New York Ripper,* the protagonist comes to the college seeking advice to parse the twisted motivations of a serial killer. In *Q: The Winged Serpent,* the same thing happens, except replace serial killer with ancient Mexican god-pteranodon. Sometimes heroes need the help of academia, and in the moviescape of Manhattan, academia is more often than not symbolized by Columbia University. For good reason. The place looks goddamned erudite.

Columbia University started as King's College in 1754, making it one of the oldest colleges in the country. It jumped sites in Manhattan two different times before landing in 1897 at its present location in Morningside Heights. The main entrance is at 116th Street and Broadway, a pedestrian gate guarded by a pair of large stone figural statues representing art and science.

Inside those gates, it opens up into a large, grassy, rectangular space inspired by Grecian agoras, those ancient meeting sites where people gathered pre-social media. The space is made of a plaza, a promenade called the College Walk, and the south lawn. Its borders are formed by the various buildings of the campus, but it's the two buildings bracketing it to the north and south that really characterize both the space and the college.

To the north is the Low Memorial Library building, an elegant columned edifice that is now an administration building and on the steps of which is seated the Daniel Chester French sculpture, *Alma Mater.* To the South is the Butler Library, also columned, but broader and more blocky. Butler Library is the current main library of the college, and that's where I was heading.

But I didn't need to learn about the pathology of a serial killer or find some clue in mythology to take down an impossible creature. I was there to get as physically close to "The Raven" as I'd yet been. And I don't mean by checking it out from the library.

On approaching the entrance to the building, I saw that the façade was carved with names. A strip at the top of the columns listed in large letters the great poets, writers, orators, and philosophers of near and far antiquity: Virgil, Plato, Dante, Goethe, others. Near the bottom of each column, in smaller letters, was a selection of famous names in American literature.

By instinct I started looking for the triple name I misspelled in freshman lit and quickly spotted it. Just like at the Boston Public Library and the bronze plaques at West Point, Poe was enshrined with his contemporaries—Emerson, Hawthorne, Melville. The names were paired between the columns, and hilariously enough, Poe's was intimately inscribed with, and just below, that of his literary anathema, Longfellow.

*Butler Library, Columbia University*

Lindsey and I entered the imposing building, handed over our out-of-state IDs, and received a temporary library card ("reading only—no borrowing"). From there, we headed through the metal detectors and took the elevator to the sixth floor and the Rare Book and Manuscript Library.

I had e-mailed ahead to make sure I could get access to what I was there to see and, after being briefly and dutifully grilled by the librarian to make sure we didn't want to access any actual archive materials (else we would have to go through the full registration process), she directed us up a set of stairs behind us.

The Brennan farmhouse came down almost four decades after Poe's death, long enough for his posthumous fame to start to ascend. One appreciator of the poet's work, named William Hemstreet, learned of the imminent destruction of the house, knew of its place in Poe history, and was able to pull from it a memento, one with a probable direct connection to "The Raven."

We walked up the steps to a thin but bright and open hallway. On one side was a set of cluttered offices walled by glass. On the other, a white wall inset with a plain black fireplace.

Actually, it was only the mantel of a fireplace. The interior space formed by the three sides of the mantel, where the fireplace would have been, was just a black-painted sheet of plywood.

There wasn't much to it. The top was roughly carved with an oil lamp, a couple pineapples, and some leafy vines, and the black paint was chipped and dented and scratched. A pair of chairs and a small table were set cozily in front of it. Above it was a painting. But in looking more closely at the black mantel, we found a tiny brass plaque affixed to its side that read:

EDGAR A. POE
WROTE THE RAVEN
BEFORE THIS MANTEL

Holy crow.

This was the mantel that adorned the fireplace of the farmhouse where Poe wrote "The Raven" and probably the very fireplace in front of which he sat for warmth while he wrote it. More than that, we were looking at the mantel for the fireplace that more than likely inspired him to write the line, "It was in the bleak December and each separate dying ember wrought its ghost upon the floor."

At the very least, Edgar Allan Poe stood in front of this mantel while he warmed his bum.

Above the mantel was an unrelated-to-Poe picture of Charles Richard Crane, a wealthy businessman and politico from the late 1800s/early 1900s, and beside it a pair of similarly unrelated busts of Samuel and Bella Spewack, twentieth-century husband-and-wife playwrights. No ravens perched on the busts.

Paper placards atop the mantel told its story, as well as mentioning some of the other Poe treasures in the library archive, like a copy of "Annabel Lee" hand-written by Poe and the last known daguerreotype of the poet, taken in Richmond just weeks before his death in Baltimore.

One of the placards also relayed an interesting story about Poe and the mantelpiece:

> **A place upon the top of the mantel, where several layers of paint have been erased and afterward painted over, seems to confirm the story told by the late William Hand Brown, of Baltimore, that "Mrs. Brennan was never vexed with Poe except on one occasion, when he scratched his name on the mantelpiece in his room. On the day in question Poe was leaning against the mantelpiece, apparently in meditation; without thinking, he traced his name on the black mantel, and when Mrs. Brennan called his attention to what he was doing he smiled and asked her pardon."**

I looked cursorily at the top of the mantel, but didn't see the spot the write-up referred to. I wasn't in a very inspective mindset, though. I was too overwhelmed by the idea of Poe sitting in front of this piece of wood, chewing on the end of his quill, and trying to figure out how to make "laden" and "Eden" rhyme.

"The Raven" was my introduction to Poe. And, decades later and bearing all the tooth marks of an ever-gnawing culture, it's still this work that gets to me the most.

I came across "The Raven" as a young teenager, when my parents gave me a bunch of old college literature textbooks from the 1960s and '70s. When I discovered this poem in one of them, I had this immediate and strange impulse to memorize it. I wasn't one to memorize anything if I didn't have to, and especially not something as long as this poem, but for some reason I felt it needed to more than just exist on a page to be marveled at, but to be a part of me, inside the cytoplasm of my brain cells. If the future in Ray Bradbury's *Fahrenheit 451* came true, I wanted to be the one to preserve this piece of literature.

The story is simple. A bird hops into a room. That's it. The inciting incident. The climax. But the poem creates a mood and an image and a moment that we all recognize and fear, one that's identifiable to anyone who has ever been alone, vulnerable. Anyone who has ever fought wars in their heads. Anyone who has ever

*Poe Mantel, Butler Library, Columbia University*

been overwhelmed with loss, oppressed by existence. Anyone who has ever felt that talking aloud to no one in particular (or to a bird) is preferable to listening to the echoes in one's own soul. And yet, turn a degree to the left, and the poem is, well, funny. I mean, a man screaming at a bird in the middle of the night? "Take thy beak from out my heart"? Even the sad fancy of the narrator himself was beguiled into smiling at one point.

And, I know, I know. I've heard the criticisms . . . the mechanical nature of the rhyme scheme. The melodrama of screaming at a bird in the middle of the night (which I just acknowledged loving). That it's a poem obsessed with itself. I had all those teachers.

But the criticisms always seem like weak protests aimed more at its popularity. I mean, the rhyming structure is a marvel of wordcraft. The English language is such a sprawling, ungainly thing that nobody should be able to fit it together as Poe did in this poem. It's almost as if you could work out the mathematics of it like astronomers can with the inter-orbits of the planets. Indeed, Poe claimed in his essay *A Philosophy of Composition* that "the work proceeded, step by step, to its completion with the precision and rigid consequence of a mathematical problem." I think he's lying, but his pudding has enough proof to make me shut up about it.

Beyond all that, it's a pure physical pleasure to speak or hear the rhythm of the words. The poet Maya Angelou said in a 2013 interview in the *New York Times*,

> **I love Edgar Allan Poe. I didn't speak for almost six years when I was a young girl, and so I memorized Poe. I thought "The Raven" and his other poems sounded pretty much like rap because of the internal rhyme. When I was about fourteen, I heard Gregory Peck read "The Raven," but he read it without syncopation. I said out loud, "That's not the way that poem goes!" And the usher invited me out of the theater.**

She's so right. "The Raven" is rap. Add it to the list of genres that Poe invented.

And that's the way I naturally read it too, spit forth like a machine gun full of jewels. But even hearing it performed asymmetrically is a wonder of effect as well. It's like all those words found their best place in "The Raven." I discussed earlier in this chapter that Poe owns the raven as a symbol, but even individual words like "nevermore" and "Nepenthe" and the name "Lenore" can't be used again in a work of English language without getting Poe all over it.

Admittedly, such aspects of the poem are fuel for the criticism that it's showy. Literary acrobatics without force. But that's not true either. The word-play isn't what stuck in the collective consciousness. The effect of this story is palpable, dreadful. It's that image of a grieving man. You feel the loneliness of the night, the irrational anger at an animal. You feel the "stillness broken by reply so aptly spoken" and the dying fire beneath the very mantel I was standing in front of in the Butler Library.

Even Poe himself, in breaking down the construction of the poem in *The Philosophy of Composition,* could do little to damage it, as much as he inadvertently tried to. If the majority of what he says in the essay is true, we are let down by a magician explaining the mundane mechanism behind a trick. And, if it's wrong, he just comes off sounding like an ass. Actually, that's true either way.

Heck, I'll go further. I've long had a suspicion about poetry in general, and I assume many others do, based on the tininess of the poetry section at any book-store. An embarrassing part of me thinks poetry is a fraud. Or at least how much we value it. That it's not high art, that it's not at all difficult to craft. That it's merely, or at least often, just a collection of clever lines. Easy aphorisms. Vague images. It takes all the linguistic skill of a crossword puzzle. To me, "it has a certain poetry to it" should be backhanded praise.

But "The Raven" always bulwarked me against that cynicism. Redeemed the genre for me. Here is a work of obvious craftsmanship, something indelible, something difficult, something captivating, something inspired. This is what great poetry is capable of. Other Poe poems do that for me as well, but none so much as "The Raven."

And the inspiration happened right there in front of that mantel. As we stood there, a few staff members passed by, barely giving us a look. They were used to the thing I was treating like Moses's burning bush. Across the thin hallway were offices, a sheet of glass away from this amazing artifact. Nobody was in them at the time, but I couldn't help wondering what it felt like to fill a spreadsheet in front of something that witnessed the creation of "The Raven."

After taking as many photographs as we could from the awkward angles that the narrow hall provided, I sat down in one of the chairs, which creaked so loudly I was afraid it was only for show. On the way to the city, I'd pick up a book of Poe's poetry. It was an updated version of a 1912 collection, featuring some stunning illustrations by Edmund Dulac. I still have in my study that textbook where I discovered "The Raven," complete with the pencil marks of my past self, but I'd left it behind. It was big and bulky and would have been difficult to haul around the city and, most relevant, I'd plain forgotten it, so I stopped at a bookstore and picked this one up.

Because I had to read "The Raven" in front of the Poe Mantel.

I could argue that I never got closer to "The Raven" than reading it in front of the mantel where it was written . . . but I'd have to discount my trip to Philadelphia, where I got close to the poem in a totally different way. Two totally different ways, actually. But Philadelphia is later on our itinerary. Next, we hit up Greenwich Village.

## Greenwich Mean Village

When the Beatles sang, "You should have seen them kicking Edgar Allan Poe," in *I Am the Walrus,* they were, well, having fun with some nonsense from John Lennon. But there were quite a few people who treated Poe like a hacky sack, from his stepfather, John Allan, to his literary executor, Rufus Griswold, to the Three Fates themselves. As of 2000, we can retroactively include New York University in that group

New York University takes up a good chunk of the buildings around Washington Square Park in Greenwich Village, and it includes in its architectural holdings one of the houses where Poe lived. Or, at least it did. Now it includes something a bit weirder, Poe-wise.

Poe and his family moved to Lower Manhattan from the Brennan Farmhouse sometime around the fall of 1845, and lived there for about half a year, leaving in the winter of 1846. The four-story brick building he and his family lived in stood at 85 Amity Street. In 1862, the street was renamed to West 3rd Street, but would maintain the same house number. Poe would move only two more times in his life, both times to other houses in New York.

If I could speak in terms of playground equipment for the moment, if Poe's life overall were a downward slide, his time on Amity Street was a bit of a seesaw. On the one hand, his writing career seemed to be taking off thanks to the popularity of "The Raven." He also sort of realized another of his dreams, full ownership of a literary magazine, in this case the *Broadway Journal.* On the other hand, he was still broke and Virginia's health was getting worse.

It is believed that at this house he wrote "The Sphinx" and "The Facts in the Case of M. Valdemar," as well as starting "The Cask of Amontillado" and codifying a few of his poems in final form, including "The Raven." Oh, and this is the place where he supposedly got into a fistfight with another editor, after Poe was accused of crossing a line with a woman in his correspondence. Sorry that's so vague, but nobody seems to know exactly what indiscretion was committed, so they always use terms like "indiscretion." People do like to attribute that fight to fueling a certain plot he dreamed up around that time, about bricking up a rival inside a wall.

So as far as Poe sites go, while interesting, it's not the most pivotal, but it was Poe's last remaining residence in Manhattan and, even though it wasn't an official memorial, it was an important part of the rich literary heritage of Greenwich Village, which includes sites connected to Henry James, Edith Wharton, Dylan Thomas, Tennessee Williams, Louisa May Alcott, Jack Kerouac, F. Scott Fitzgerald, Ernest Hemingway, Robert Louis Stevenson, Mark Twain, Edna St. Vincent Millay, and, I think, every other writer on the planet.

In the 1990s, the juggernaut progress of the city clashed with the overwhelming legacy of the city. NYU decided that it needed to expand its legal school, and that meant tearing down Poe's house.

Naturally, a lot of people were appalled. Letters were written, injunctions were held, hundreds of people showed up for multiple protests, celebrities wrote letters, the ghost of Poe haunted the dreams of NYU's administration, but all to little avail. In 2001, at the dawn of our most enlightened millennium, NYU rubbled a bit more of Poe's physical legacy.

However, all the brouhaha did impel the University to create a memorial to appease Poe's vociferous fans. They offered to reconstruct the façade of the Poe house, using the original materials and setting it right in the side of the massive new Furman Hall, as a memorial to the poet.

And they did. Sort of. It's just down the street from the original site and looks like exactly what it is: a house that has been absorbed into a building. Unfortunately, in comparing pictures of the original to the reconstruction, the only thing they got right was its rectangular shape. The new memorial is only three stories tall, instead of four. The windows don't match, the doors don't match, and its bricks are glaringly new. The university claims that not enough bricks survived the demolition to reuse.

After the demolition, the bricks were parceled out to various Poe fans, and the Edgar Allan Poe Museum in Richmond received hundreds to incorporate into their own Poe shrine. Thanks to Robert Davis, the Calvin F. S. Thomas expert I met in Boston, I'd gotten to see brick number 204 sitting right beside my plate of sea scallops.

The memorial's backstory casts a bit of a shadow over it, making it seem sadder to me than it really is. In reality, the place is barely noticeable. The street is thin and surrounded by towering buildings, like most streets in New York are, so unless you're looking for it you'll probably walk past it without looking up. The

*Brick salvaged from original Greenwich Village Poe house*

only thing that tells passersby that it's a memorial is a plaque by the door that calls it an "interpretive reconstruction."

On the other side of the façade is a Poe Room that's open to the public. I tried to visit the room years ago, only to learn from the white painted letters in the window that it's only open to the public between 9 and 11 A.M. on Thursdays. I don't think there could be a more inconvenient time during the week, even if I lived in New York City. So I had to walk away, thinking the grapes were probably sour anyway.

For this book project, though, I was ready to make it work. After contorting my schedule in ways that involved a time machine and a severely out-of-date version of Microsoft Outlook's calendar, I ended up there right at 9 A.M. on a Thursday. I tried the door, but it was locked. I knocked, but received no answer. I paced a few times, stepping along a trio of in-flight ravens graffitied onto the sidewalk in front of the door.

Then I noticed another sign, a transparent one with black lettering, adhered to the window. It said that entry to the Poe Room was through the front entrance, around the corner, on Sullivan Street.

So that's where I went. I gave my license to the guard on duty, signed in, and got directions to Room 112, just a few doors down the hallway behind him.

The entire room is viewable from the hallway through a large picture window. When I walked in I found, well, a nice memorial to Poe. The room was a study lounge, and according to the plaque on the hallway wall on this side of the façade, named after somebody not Poe. In front of that picture window was a couch, some comfortable chairs, and a couple tables. An adjoining door led to a café.

But the rest of the room was dedicated to the poet whose house had been torn down so that the country could have more lawyers.

On the wall was a 2007 oil painting of Poe, a facsimile of "The Raven" in Poe's own handwriting, a framed timeline of his life, and an inset column of old bricks salvaged from the original house. A plaque explained that they were taken from the façade of the upper stories of the original building, the only part of the house that dated back to its construction in 1835. Two other plaques pointed out other features salvaged from the house: a laylight, which is a secondary skylight to relay light to a lower room, and the window frames.

On the opposite wall was a white bannister, also from the original house, while in the middle of the room was a large glass display case. It held a few modern editions of his books, as well as another of those brass-plated

*Interpretive reconstruction of Poe's Greenwich Village home, New York University School of Law*

bricks, although this one wasn't numbered and, like Davis's brick, didn't much look like the bricks in the column on the wall. The plaque explained that the sides and back of the building had been made of lower-quality bricks.

Filling the case were numerous artifacts excavated from this property and its two neighboring buildings: pottery, ceramic figures, metal pieces, glass bottles. The building at number 85 had been the home and restaurant of an Italian immigrant family named Bertolotti between 1904 and the 1940s.

I came into this memorial ready to consummate my frustration with it. The destruction of the original building, the badly interpreted façade, the ridiculously limited access to the room. But I left conflicted.

First, New York is not the first city to tear down a Poe house. Richmond did it. Boston did it. So did others. Sure, New York did it only thirteen years ago, long after they should have known better. But it's New York. When it comes to literary and historical riches, they've got enough that they can blow a few, I guess.

Second, the Poe Room is pretty cool. There's not a lot there, but the fact that it's a study lounge as well as a memorial makes me want to become a law student so I can hang out there.

Third, the original building never became a memorial until after its destruction. Before then, it just housed NYU offices and was a stop on literary walking tours. So it's kind of like Obi-Wan Kenobi—more powerful now than it was when it existed.

It's not an ideal way to treat the physical legacy of one of the world's most renowned writers, but I'm also not sure I can pretend John Lennon is singing about them anymore.

## *Pieces of Poe*

That there happened to be a major public exhibit of Poe artifacts just when I was writing a book about Poe seems like a great and happy coincidence for me. Truth is, come October of any year, Poe is everywhere, from cartoon shows to theater stages to the most urbane of institutions.

Poe is a bridge for sophisticated establishments like playhouses and museums that can't bring themselves to celebrate anything as crass as the spooky and the gory when everybody around them is celebrating the spooky and the gory. Poe salves the principled consciences of these respected organizations and gives them a pass to celebrate Halloween without losing their status as keepers of high culture.

But it's hard to call the Poe exhibition I saw at the Morgan Library and Museum a salve.

The Morgan Library and Museum started out as the private library of financial wizard J. P. Morgan. When you're rich, you buy cool, rare stuff. Then you die, and your kids give away everything you treasured.

In 1924, thanks to J. P. Jr., the Madison Avenue–located collection became a public institution dedicated to original manuscripts and Americana. But I didn't get much chance to explore the multiple buildings of its campus. I was only there for Poe.

Called *Edgar Allan Poe: Terror of the Soul*, the exhibition ran from October 2013 to January 2014 and included materials from its own collection, as well as pieces from the Berg Collection of the New York Public Library and private collectors.

I walked under a tall, thin doorway with the name of the exhibition overhead into a large, empty antechamber. Well, mostly empty. On one wall as a small display case containing a series of letters from J. D. Salinger to an aspiring writer in Canada named Marjorie Sheard.

On the opposite side of the room was the entry to the exhibition proper, but a few pieces spilled into the antechamber that were from the famous Poe collection of Susan Jaffe Tane. Like a dark bronze bust of Poe sculpted by Rudulph Evans in 1909. Also, a flat, trapezoidal fragment of wood the size of a fist that had been part of Poe's original coffin. Poe's bones were moved in 1875 from a barely marked grave to a large marble memorial, and when they dug him up they discovered that his original coffin was a decaying mess. So they gave him a new one, providing souvenir-seekers the chance to grab a few pieces of the death box of a death-obsessed poet. But that's a Baltimore story.

I assume the exhibit's curators placed such a fascinating artifact outside the exhibit proper to acknowledge it's what people really want to see and to get such ghoulishness out of the way so they could get to more sober and tasteful artifacts.

*Edgar Allan Poe: Terror of the Soul* took place in a spacious room with blood-red walls bearing a giant black outline of Poe's face and his autograph. I won't catalogue everything I found in that room of Prospero's abbey, but a few pieces really stood out for me, besides the chunk of coffin. They weren't going to top that.

First, they had three of the twelve known surviving copies of Poe's first published work, *Tamerlane and other Poems.* This was the one he self-published in an extremely limited run in Boston, the one of which a copy sold for $660,000 at the end of 2009. And here were three, or, as the market likes to call it, $1.98 million worth. Two were from the Berg Collection of the New York Public Library. The third was from the private collection of Susan Jaffe Tane, the foremost collector of Poe manuscripts and books. In her introduction to the exhibition catalog, she wrote, "It's doubtful that they've been this close together since they rolled off Calvin Thomas's printing press in 1827."

There were paintings, first editions of his works, daguerreotypes, a large French movie poster for the 1968 anthology *Histoires Extraordinaires* (*Spirits of the Dead*)—a movie with three stories based on Poe's works. Mostly, the exhibition was full of letters and manuscripts handwritten in that almost robotic cursive that Poe cultivated, some of the latter of which were written on long, thin scrolls he pasted together from fragments of paper.

The piece that arrested my attention the longest was the first page of his three-page unfinished work, *The Lighthouse,* written in his own hand. The last work he ever wrote, it purports to be the daily diary of a newly appointed lighthouse keeper who spends his days alone, save for his dog, Neptune, and his desire to write a book. Poe never made it to the good parts, but just the setup sounds modern. How many novels have started off with a guy who just wants to get away and write his book?

Like most things around Poe, it came off less as an exhibition and more as a shrine . . . reverential, strange, extremely well done, and almost completely, and probably purposefully, blind-eyed to what Poe has become in modern culture. All in all, it was very much fit for a classy Halloween outing.

## Fordham Tell-Tale Hearts Poe

I was driving down the Bronx's Grand Concourse. The day was rainy, dreary. Good weather for visiting a death bed. I didn't know it at the time, but it was also a day that would find me sprawled on my back on the hard planks of Edgar Allan Poe's last house and ascending to the roof of a ten-story bell tower via tiny iron rungs. My own micro version of enduring the highs and lows of New York City.

I was headed for Fordham, a neighborhood in the western part of the Bronx. Fordham is a place of contrasts. Much of the neighborhood has seen better days and not much worse; however, it's also the location of the grandiose New York Botanical Garden, the famous Bronx Zoo, and the handsome Fordham University.

Most important, it's a place that has done Edgar Allan Poe right.

Edgar Allan Poe lived in a cottage in Fordham from 1846 until his death in 1849. Back then, Fordham wasn't part of a borough of a gigantic city. It was just a rural village in Westchester County. Its most prominent feature was a small Jesuit school called St John's College, which would go on to become Fordham University.

My Poe hunt that day didn't get off to a good start. My first stop was a couple miles south of Fordham, at the Andrew Freedman Home on the Grand Concourse. The building was built in 1924 as a retirement home for the rich, and after some abandonment, has been repurposed over the years into a community center, bed and breakfast, and art exhibit space. My interest was in its front wall.

In 2009, the graffiti artist group TATS CRU was commissioned to paint a mural on that wall celebrating the Bronx. In a testament to Poe's standing in Fordham, a large section of the mural was dedicated to Poe. Images on the Internet show a pale white poet, barefoot and contorted, pointing at his Fordham cottage, which was set on a tree limb that transformed into a subway car.

Unfortunately, when I pulled up to the site, I discovered it had only been a temporary mural. The wall was now painted a solid beige, its only adornment a giant image of the face of Andre the Giant, not a famous resident of the Bronx, but instead the motif of choice for graffiti artist Shepard Fairey. Although the TATS CRU piece was gone, it isn't Poe's only appearance in the urban art scene. The calling card of Baltimore-based graffiti artist TOVEN is the striking image of Poe in an astronaut suit. Pretty cool.

My next stop was similarly unsuccessful. Apparently, Edgar Allan Poe School is only a name on paper for Public School 46 at 279 East 196 Street. The name didn't adorn the school building or the signs in front of it. There are schools all over the country named after Poe that I didn't try to visit. A quick Internet search yielded ones in Pennsylvania, Texas, Illinois, Virginia (Poe Middle School in Annandale, which claims Mark Hamill of Luke Skywalker fame as one of its alumni), and Maryland. The Fordham school just happened to be on my way.

Fortunately, the mural and the school were only meant to be hors d'oeuvres. I still had the main course and dessert.

And that main course was a meaty one. It is without a doubt the best Poe site in all of New York, and one of the top three Poe sites anywhere . . . Poe's Fordham cottage, the last home that he ever lived in.

At the time he, Virginia, and Maria moved into the cottage, Poe was still flying high off the reception to "The Raven," and by flying high I mean broke and struggling and still caring for a dying wife.

He was fresh off his failure at the *Broadway Journal* magazine, which he nabbed full ownership of just as it was about to go bankrupt. His years in Fordham marked the first time since his Baltimore days that he wasn't editing a magazine. Without a platform like that, he was basically in literary exile. He wrote in one letter, to Jane E. Locke, "Will you not remember that the hermit life which for the last three years I have led, buried in the woods of Fordham, has necessarily prevented me from learning anything of you?" In another letter, this one to Frederick W. Thomas, he writes about his plans to reenter the cultural sphere with a vengeance, "I have been quite out of the literary world for the last three years . . . living buried in the country makes a man a savage—wolfish. I am just in the humor for a fight."

But the thing about exile is it can be nice, too. Poe would walk the country-side around Fordham for miles, picnic with his little family, and just generally be a much less ambitious man than he was used to being.

But he was still writing. It was at the Fordham cottage that he wrote "Annabel Lee," "Ulalume," and "The Bells." Here he wrote *Eureka,* a philosophical science treatise that he thought would change humankind's entire understanding of the universe and reality. All right, maybe picnics and nature hikes did little to tamp his ambition.

It was also here that he wrote his last published piece of prose, "Landor's Cottage." It was about an idyllic little cottage in an impossibly majestic valley where lived a beautiful woman named Annie, probably patterned after Annie Richmond. Just like their relationship, nothing happens in the story.

Still, it came out in Boston's *The Flag of Our Union* in June of 1849, about four months before Poe's death and a couple years after Virginia's. It was published with the subtitle "A Pendant to 'The Domain of Arnheim'" since the story seemed

*Poe's Fordham Cottage*

to be a follow-up to one Poe wrote years earlier about an extremely wealthy man with artistic tendencies who decided to do more than paint landscapes; he created them, improving on the beauty of nature by taming its randomness and molding it according to conscious aesthetics.

Many believe Poe was inspired to populate this idealized world of Arnheim with his idyllic little Fordham cottage (and, of course, the idealized vision he had of Annie). And maybe Fordham was that for him. Or as close as he ever came.

Best way to find out, I thought, was to go see it, since his death house still lives.

Even more, not only does Poe's Fordham cottage still exist, it's the center-piece of a park named after him.

Poe Park is a Poe-asis in the middle of a crowded, ugly, urban, and histori-cally perilous area. Certainly no longer the landscape of "Landor's Cottage," the park itself is definitely an amazing memorial to Poe.

The park is small and thin enough that you could stand in the middle and still feel like you're in traffic. On one side is the Grand Concourse, on the other East Kingsbridge Road. Short black gates surround it, and here and there are small touches of Poe . . . metal plates on the fence bearing his autograph and a stone tile in the ground at three of the four entrances to the park. One bore an image of a raven, another of a gold bug, and a third . . . a tusked warthog.

That last one's a bit strange. Certainly hogs aren't one of the animals we usually throw in Poe Zoo, not like black cats and orangutans and homo-cameleopards, but it is a Poe reference. An obscure one, certainly, and probably the most obscure one I've seen committed to a memorial.

In script on the stone, below the wild pig, are the words HOG and EUREKA. The latter is a long work of philosophy, poetry, and science that Poe published in 1848. In it, he attempts to explain the principles that motivate the universe, including where it came from and where it's going. The work is dense, confusing, pompous, beautiful in places, interesting in others, uneven all the way through, possibly a joke, but mostly it's an oddity in an odd oeuvre. Poe believed it was the work on which his legacy rested . . . instead, it became one of his more avoided. Basically because nobody knows what to do with it.

Of course, that doesn't explain what the secrets of the universe have to do with a pig. The answer is . . . not much. Within the work, Poe cites a myth-ical letter dated a thousand years in the future found floating in a bottle on the sea. The letter references various thinkers and scientists of the far past, their names corrupted over the millennium. For instance, Aristotle becomes Aries Tottle, and is often referred to as the "Ram." The "Hog" is, quite naturally, Francis Bacon.

Two paragraphs to explain that reference, and I'm sure it's still confusing. That's *Eureka*. Although it still doesn't explain why just a black cat or an orang-utan isn't on that stone tile.

At one end of the park is a cement clearing with a circular bandstand. In the middle, a playground. Benches are scattered here and there. It was on a bench here in the late 1930s that Bob Kane and Bill Finger were hanging out when they came up with Batman. Ravenman just didn't have the same ring.

At the other end of the park is the cottage I came to see, but first I wanted to visit the newest building on the property. Situated across from the playground in the middle of the park is the Poe Park Visitor Center. I thought it was called the Poe Visitor Center, a subtle difference that hadn't really registered in my head yet.

Constructed in 2011, the small building is meant to evoke a raven, with its dark overlapping tiles and the wing-shaped angle of its roof. It's longer than it is wide, and at one end is a large picture window that faces and frames the Poe Cot-tage, as though the visitor center is a telescope. I walked in expecting a gift shop full of stuffed ravens and T-shirts. Instead, I found a large, open white space.

When I asked the woman about admission to the cottage, she told me I'd have to go to the cottage for that. Apparently the place isn't an extension of the Poe Cottage, but a community event and exhibition space. At the time of my visit, they were in the middle of prepping for an exhibition of high school

*Poe Park Visitor Center*

photography. The only interior acknowledgment of the park's namesake was a Halloween-decoration raven perched at the base of the picture window over-looking the cottage.

In the story, it took Poe more than eight hundred words to describe Landor's cottage. I could do the Poe Cottage in four: small, humble, white, two-story. Four-ish. Not only was this the simple residence of a famous author, it's also the last remaining residential structure from the old village of Fordham and the longest-established Poe museum in the country. Pretty auspicious for being so humble.

Around the time the visitor center was built, the house underwent a reno-vation, and it seemed to have done the place good. Older pictures show a more ramshackle place, while today it's neatly kept.

The first room I entered was the kitchen, a small corner of which was taken up by a tiny counter. Behind that tiny counter was Neil Ralley. His accent gave him away as British, but also because he used the word "dogsbody" when describing his role at the cottage. This entire project was worth taking up just for me to learn that term. Ralley was from Carlisle, a small city in England far enough north to almost be in Scotland, and was middle-aged, with thinning gray hair and a story of a trek to the States many years ago that he described as "a long and wending road involving a girl." He wore a light gray T-shirt that mismatched a Harry Clarke illustration of Poe's "The Pit and the Pendulum" with a quote from "The Tell-Tale Heart": "That which you mistake for madness is but an overacute-ness of the senses."

He introduced himself as a bit of an entrepreneur and, indeed, the business card he gave me bore five different websites, each selling something different, from stained glass window photography to tiles with poetry and Bible verses etched on them to Poe-themed T-shirts.

But on that day, as he was on most weekends, he was the Poe Cottage docent. Ralley didn't claim to be an expert on Poe. He told me that he only really learned about him as a result of taking the Poe Cottage gig, but I liked the way he told his stories.

Poe paid $100 a year to live in the cottage, which he did from 1846 until his death in 1849. It changed ownership a few times, at one point even being owned by William Fearing Gill, one of Poe's earlier biographers and somebody involved in a macabre story around the remains of Virginia that I'll save for the Maryland chapter. Eventually, the home ended up in the tooth-scarred hands of a dentist. A picture of the building from its time as a dental office shows its front porch jammed uselessly against a large neighboring house, with a sign at ground level advertising dental surgery. Above it, between two windows, a small sign with a raven on it noted Edgar Allan Poe had lived in the house.

Eventually, thanks to prompting from the Shakespeare Society (who, between their efforts here and with the plaque on Edgar Allan Poe Street, should really have changed their name), the city bought the house for $5,000. For that sum, they got only the house, not the land. According to Ralley, "The dentist who owned it basically had a gun to their head, said he'd just tear it down if they didn't buy it for that amount."

In 1913, the house was moved in one piece about half a block or so up Kingsbridge Road, from its original spot to its current resting place, where it's managed by the Bronx Historical Society.

All told, the homely home has only five rooms, plus a small basement that was added at its new site, which was the apartment of the caretaker back when Norman George stayed the night when he was touring as Poe. I dug up an old *New York Times* article where his overnight at the Poe Cottage was brought up. He said, "Outside, you could hear suitcase-sized radios blasting at 4 A.M. and motorcycles dragging down the concourse. And if you got up and went to the window you could see crack transactions."

Today, I can at least attest that the radios are smaller.

The first thing Ralley did when we started talking about the cottage was to lean out the front door and point to a tall building bristling with small satellite dishes down the road. "Just beyond that is where the house originally stood. There's a street named after him there." I had actually swung by it on my way to the cottage.

Called Poe Place, it's a dead-end residential street a little on the uninviting side. While I was there photographing the sign, a short man in a flat cap and smoking the dregs of a joint walked up to me. "What are you, getting ready for a movie?"

"No, writing a book." For some reason the explanation embarrassed me more than usual.

"About Poe Place?" He seemed incredulous, not that somebody would write about a street like Poe Place, but that somebody was in the know enough to realize that its residents should be written about.

"Well, about Edgar Allan Poe. The street's named after him."

"Oh, Edgar Allan Poe. Good guy, good guy. Well, you should write a book about me if you want a bestseller."

Back at the Poe Cottage, my conversation with Ralley was interrupted as three more people walked in, a pair of college students from Manhattan who had bicycled to the cottage and a young man who asked if the three-dollar student entrance fee was a suggested donation.

Ralley went official at that point, gave us all an introductory spiel about the place, and then invited us to tour it on our own.

The kitchen opened into the living room, which had been arranged with period furniture and, in the corner on a tall pedestal, a bronze bust of Poe, sculpted in 1909 by Edmund T. Quinn. Quinn's the guy who sculpted the statue in Gramercy Park of actor Edwin Booth as Hamlet and who would later commit suicide by jumping into New York Harbor. An image from the bust-unveiling event shows a lot of men in dark coats and matching bowlers and top hats. It's a strange image, like something out of *Doctor Who*. I would come across versions of this particular bust at three other Poe sites.

*Edmund T. Quinn bust of Poe, Fordham Cottage*

It was in this room that two of the three objects supposedly used by Poe and his family were on display: a rocking chair and a mirror. The third was a bed in the adjoining first-floor room. H. P. Lovecraft mentioned the same three artifacts in his *Homes and Shrines of Poe* more than eighty years ago.

As I stood in the room, Ralley popped his head in from the kitchen. "If you look

*Living room with rocking chair and mirror used by the Poes, Fordham
Cottage*

into that mirror, you can still see Poe's reflection." I got right up close to the dim,
tarnished mirror in its gilt frame on the wall and stared into it. All I saw was the
rest of the room reflected darkly through the mirror . . . including the Quinn bust
of Poe. I turned around and Ralley broke into a big smile that made me slightly
reinterpret the quotation on his shirt.

The last room on the first floor was a bedroom. An important one. It's the
room where Poe's wife died, and it contained her actual deathbed.

The room was tiny, with only that bed and a chair in it. On the chair was a
small book and a candle. The bed was dressed with a blue-and-white plaid cover.
It was a rope bed, meaning that instead of having planks or a box spring, it had
a rope wound about the frame, on which was tossed a straw-filled mattress. The
tops of two of the posts, one at the head and the corresponding one at the foot,
had been sawn off, possibly because it had once been in an upstairs room, both
of which had slanted ceilings.

When Poe and his wife moved to Fordham, Virginia had either just turned
twenty-four or was about to. She had been showing signs of tuberculosis since
living in Philadelphia five years earlier. They had come to the country hoping
she'd get better. Instead they buried her there, after about six months in Fordham.
She died in January 1847, at the age of twenty-four, possibly of the same disease
as Poe's mother. There's no way to be sure, of course, but after her death Poe did
remove a line from his first published story, "Metzengerstein," which said of
consumption, "I would wish all I love to perish of that gentle disease."

To me, this is one of the more powerful of Poe's remaining artifacts. If this is indeed her bed, here we have the source and symbol of Poe's most visited and most potent theme . . . the death of a beautiful woman. Poe talks about that theme in his "The Philosophy of Composition." In it he claims (not too convincingly) to have arrived at the theme logically, and it was written about a year before Virginia's death. However, for years he was daily buffeted by the imminent possibility. In a letter he wrote to George Eveleth a few weeks before the one-year anniversary of the death of his wife, he wrote,

> **Six years ago, a wife, whom I loved as no man ever loved before, ruptured a blood-vessel in singing. Her life was despaired of. I took leave of her forever & underwent all the agonies of her death. She recovered partially and I again hoped. At the end of a year the vessel broke again— I went through precisely the same scene. Again in about a year afterward. Then again—again—again & even once again at varying intervals. Each time I felt all the agonies of her death—and at each accession of the disorder I loved her more dearly & clung to her life with more desperate pertinacity . . . I had indeed nearly abandoned all hope of a permanent cure when I found one in the *death* of my wife.**

The ruptured blood vessel story is one he told multiple times, as if he didn't want to give even more credit to, again possibly, the same disease that took his mother away. But it was here, in this bed in this room in this house, where he found that permanent cure, where that theme reached its culmination in his life. To me, of all the moments in Poe's life, this one seems the easiest to visualize: Poe and Virginia's mother at her side, blood on her lips and handkerchiefs, wrapped in Poe's West Point cloak. Just the three of them, as it had been for more than a decade.

Virginia was buried in the yard of a nearby church, in a plot owned by their Fordham landlord, John Valentine. Poe would go there daily to mourn. Today the church and graveyard are no more, and Virginia's remains were long ago transferred to Baltimore to rest with her husband and mother.

The relationship between Poe and his wife is a bit of a mystery, as is Virginia Poe in general. She was his cousin, and he married her when she was thirteen and he twenty-seven. There may have been some mitigating factors to account for all that ickiness, mostly around the cultural norms of the time and the character of their relationship, but it was still icky.

Later I would visit their honeymoon suite in Virginia, and would think more about their life together, but standing beside that bed in that room in that house, my thoughts were consumed by her death and what was the worst in the series of tragedies that beset the tragic Poe.

As I headed for the tiny stairs, I tried to alleviate the heavy thoughts a bit by striking up a conversation with the young man who'd come in earlier. He didn't seem like somebody I'd peg as a Poe fan.

He didn't give me his name. Merely explained why he was there. "We're just the new poor family on the block. I mean, we're from New York, but just moved to the neighborhood. Wanted to see some of the history of the place."

That's about all I got out of him. I had no idea if he made the connection that the Poes were once the new poor family on the block . . . before it was a block, of course.

As I was about to make it up the stairs a piece of artwork on the wall caught my attention. It was a simple black-and-white print, and it depicted a solitary Poe crossing a bridge that stretched behind him. It was a winter scene, the trees stark and bare, and Poe was a dark blot covered in a cloak in the foreground. According to an adjacent placard, it was drawn in 1930 by Bernard Jacob Rosenmeyer and was called *Poe Walking High Bridge.*

I brought it up to Ralley afterward, and he told me the bridge was still standing, though closed. I had to see it, just because I was struck by that picture, but I wouldn't make it to the site for a few months.

High Bridge was completed in 1848 and was part of the Old Croton Aqueduct system that drew water from the Croton River, about forty miles north, to deliver

*High Bridge*

to a rapidly growing city. The series of Romanesque stone arches spanned some two thousand feet and crossed the Harlem River at the boundary between the Bronx and Manhattan. Today, it's the oldest bridge in the city.

But it was brand new construction when Poe used to walk it, which, according to Sarah Helen Whitman, he would do "at all times of day and night, often pacing the then solitary pathway for hours without meeting another human being." It was about a two-and-a-half-mile walk from the cottage to the bridge for Poe, but this was a man who, in his younger days, had walked from Baltimore to Washington, D.C., because he couldn't afford transportation and needed to meet with someone who could help get him into West Point.

Turns out, I'd actually seen the bridge many times over the years in passing through the city via I-95. The thing is surrounded by an ugly tangle of roads and highways, but eventually I found a spot beneath the bridge to take it all in.

It wasn't exactly at its grandest. The bridge had been closed since the 1970s, and some of it was covered with construction scaffolding. The half of the bridge that crossed the river had been replaced with metal, while the more elegant stone half crossed high above I-87, a noisy stream of cars speeding between its thick pylons.

My timing was slightly off for this site, as the bridge is supposed to open to foot traffic sometime in 2014, allowing people to once again walk in the lonely footsteps of Edgar Allan Poe.

Back at the Poe Cottage, I finally made it upstairs to discover there wasn't much there. Just two rooms, one that had a few pictures of Poe and the other that had been turned into a media room with metal folding chairs and a small TV that played a DVD about Poe and his cozy cottage.

His aunt/mother-in-law, Maria Clemm, whom Poe nicknamed "Muddy," lived here for only about a month after Poe's death. She couldn't pay the rent and would eventually travel around to wherever kind souls would give her a roof . . . Massachusetts, Connecticut, New York, Virginia, even Ohio, before finally returning to her home city of Baltimore. She died just shy of her eighty-second birthday, in 1871, outliving Edgar and Virginia by twenty years.

Before I left the house, I asked Ralley if he could take a picture of me kneeling beside Virginia's bed. Partly, it's because I just couldn't quite shake that spot and wanted to be able to say I knelt at Virginia Poe's death bed. Mostly, it's because getting my picture taken at the site is how all my visits for this book ended. I usually leave off my transformation from placid observer to excitable fan.

"Just don't lie on the bed," he told me. Excited, I took off for the bedroom, forgetting about the step up from the kitchen. I hit the wide painted planks of the floor hard on my back, right in Poe's living room. Above me, Poe's bronze face seemed to look down with impish delight. "How about if I lie on this?" I asked

*Room and bed where Virginia died, Fordham Cottage*

before getting up and leaving my pride to gloop between the cracks of the planks and into the basement.

Afterward, I exited the house to take some exterior pics and was interrupted twice when busloads of people were deposited outside the entrance to the park nearest the Poe Cottage. Each tour group only stayed a few minutes, long enough to walk up to the house to take pics with phones, cameras, and iPads. All of them took off without touring.

At one point, Ralley came out onto the porch and threw me another bon mot while I fiddled with a tripod. "Virginia wasn't the only Poe to die here, you know."

"You don't say."

"Catterina died here, too."

"Catterina Poe?" I asked a second before it sunk in. Catterina was Poe's cat. It had a tortoiseshell coat and had lived with Poe since at least Philadelphia. Naturally, its name was a pun.

"Maria Clemm found its body when she was moving out of here. Strange timing. Probably died soon after Poe did. Maybe the exact same time." Like a familiar, I thought, before remembering I knew nothing about familiars.

And thus ended my time at one of the more prominent sites in Poe's life. I'd actually tried to make it more central to this story. Taking a cue from Norman George, I contacted the Bronx Historical Society to see if I, too, could stay the night in Poe's house. I received an immediate "no" to that request. Fortunately, I was to get a unique experience at my next Poe site.

## Hell's Bells Bells Bells Bells Bells Bells Bells

Back in Poe's day, Fordham University was called St. John's. It opened in 1841 and was under control of the diocese until it was sold to the Jesuits in 1846, around the time Poe and his family moved to Fordham. The school was only about half a mile from his cottage, and he would visit it often. In one of his letters, he describes how he liked its faculty because they were "highly cultivated" men who "smoked, drank, and played cards like gentleman, and never said a word about religion."

Fordham University is a gorgeous place, with elegant stone buildings and an ambiance only slightly corrupted by the kids in tank tops and flip flops walking around. The atmosphere was placid and erudite, not counting the strains of Metallica's *Enter Sandman* that permeated the campus from the baseball field. The Fordham University Rams were about to face off against the Richmond Spiders. I wondered who Poe would've rooted for, having vested interests in both places.

I was there to see "Old Edgar Allan."

Old Edgar Allan is the nickname of the bell in the tower of the University Church. The story goes that the iron clanger, which Poe no doubt heard during his time there, was one of the bells that inspired him to write his famous poem "The Bells."

I'm going to be writing "bell" a lot in this section.

I arrived at the church early for my appointment and walked around its exterior. It was built in 1845 and had been expanded and updated over the years. The front part of the Gothic church was blocky and dominated by the square bell tower I'd come to see. Toward the back it got more ornate, with gargoyle gutters, spires, a dome, and other embellishments that I would need a vocabulary in ecclesiastical architecture to describe.

Of course, I wasn't appreciating its grandeur so much as I was, natch, looking for a plaque. Eventually I found it, in a recessed area to the side of the bell tower on the front of the church. It said:

THE UNIVERSITY CHURCH
"OUR LADY OF MERCY"         "OLD ST. JOHN'S"
THE REV. JAMES ROOSEVELT BAYLEY, THIRD PRESIDENT OF THE
COLLEGE, A NEPHEW OF THE VENERABLE ELIZABETH SETON AND
COUSIN OF TWO PRESIDENTS OF THE UNITED STATES, AFTERWARD
BISHOP OF NEWARK AND ARCHBISHOP OF BALTIMORE, ERECTED

THIS CHURCH IN 1845 AS A SEMINARY CHAPEL. THE WINDOWS OF
THE NAVE WERE PRESENTED BY LOUIS PHILIPPE, KING OF THE
FRENCH, IN 1846. THE BELL IN THE TOWER, KNOWN SINCE AS OLD
EDGAR ALLEN [SIC], IS SAID TO HAVE INSPIRED POE, A FRIEND AND
NEIGHBOR, TO WRITE HIS CELEBRATED POEM, "THE BELLS."

+     +     +

THIS TABLET WAS PLACED HERE BY THE FORDHAM UNIVERSITY
ALUMNI SODALITY—OCTOBER 1, 1939—AND UNVEILED BY MRS.
JAMES ROOSEVELT, THE MOTHER OF THE PRESIDENT

A + M + D + G

The beautiful thing about printing the entire text of the plaque is that it does all the explaining for me. Also, it shows how easy it is to misspell "Allan." Hopefully my copy-editor will double-check me throughout.

The four letters at the end of the plaque stand for *ad majorem Dei gloriam*. It's the Latin motto of the Jesuits and means "for the greater glory of God." After reading the plaque, I sat down on the steps and waited for my appointment. I was expecting a quick walk-through with a clergyman. He'd point up to the tower, make an excuse about saving some souls, and then leave me with a mostly empty notebook.

Instead, I met John Gownley. He was young, probably in his late twenties, and hailed from Scranton, Pennsylvania. His title was Assistant Director of Campus Ministry for Liturgy. "I'm not clergy," was the first thing he told me. "I live next to the church and help set it up for services and

*University Church, Fordham University*

such, but I'm studying for social work." He was currently sacrificing wedding ceremony preparations to tour me around.

He asked me if I wanted to see the plaque first. I told him I'd already seen it and pointed in the general direction of the one on the church.

"Oh, that one. No, I meant the other one."

He then led me to a rock about one hundred feet in front of the church. On it was a much newer plaque that read:

*View of the Bronx from University Church, Fordham University*

EDGAR ALLAN POE (1809–1849)
IN 1846, THE AMERICAN WRITER, POET AND LITERARY CRITIC
EDGAR ALLAN POE MOVED TO A COTTAGE IN THE BRONX AND
BEGAN A FRIENDSHIP WITH THE JESUITS AT FORDHAM (THEN
KNOWN AS ST. JOHN'S COLLEGE) THAT WOULD LAST FOR THE REST
OF HIS SHORT LIFE. LEGEND HAS IT THAT POE WAS INSPIRED BY
THE TOLLING OF THE UNIVERSITY CHURCH BELL TO PEN HIS
CELEBRATED POEM "THE BELLS," WHICH WAS PUBLISHED
POSTHUMOUSLY IN NOVEMBER 1849.
*HEAR THE TOLLING OF THE BELLS,*
*IRON BELLS!*
*WHAT A WORLD OF SOLEMN THOUGHT THEIR MONODY COMPELS!*

Like the spot where Poe wrote "The Raven," Old Edgar Allan was a two-plaquer.

Gownley took me into the church. "The first thing you should know is that we just recently digitized the bell." We entered the narthex at the entrance of the church, where I made him explain what the heck a narthex was. It's basically a small lobby.

This particular narthex featured a large wooden carving of a knight laying his sword at an altar and an angel slaying a dragon. Gownley pointed at the ceiling, which was a solid grid of woodwork and white paint. "The bell rope used to descend from here, and I'd have to pull it to ring the bell. The rope was massive, like an inch-and-a-quarter thick. Very tiring. It's kind of sad that's it digitized now, but not really."

In the auditorium, he showed me the series of stained-glass windows that had been originally donated to Old St. Patrick's Cathedral in Manhattan by King Louis Philippe I of France, but had come to the University Church when it was discovered they didn't fit St. Patrick's window frames. There was also an altar that had come from St. Patrick's, as well. So the place had some really cool hand-me-downs.

I asked him if many visitors ask about Poe. "Not really. It's mentioned on the tours, but people usually get interested in the church once they see it." I understood that. I kind of was myself.

"So do you want to go up and see the bell?"

This surprised me. From my various e-mail correspondence with the faculty, I didn't realize I'd get to go up in the actual tower. Had I known right then what it took to get to the top of the tower, I'd have been really surprised. And maybe trepidatious.

To get to the bell, we had to first ascend the steps to the balcony and clamber behind the pipes of a brand new, $2.5 million Schoenstein & Co. organ. As we were doing so, Gownley told me, "We were on the cover of *American Organist* for this thing. So that exists."

After that, it was three more ladders that consisted mostly of metal rungs anchored into the walls, as well as a few squeezes through tight spaces. Finally, we arrived at the bell room. I felt like Quasimodo.

The interior was empty, with blank white walls roughly plastered and long, slatted windows that looked more elegant from the outside. In the middle of the room was Old Edgar Allan. I thought.

It was smaller than I had imagined, just a few feet tall, maybe the size of a crouching person. But that meant it was still a big enough hunk of hollow iron. It was set close to the floor, so I had to get on my knees and elbows to sneak a glance up its skirt to see a massive clapper that was the size of a duckpin bowling ball. On the rim, at the top of the bell, was the name and location of the foundry: Clinton H. Meneely Bell Company, Troy, NY. Below that was the year it was made: A.D. 1881.

Uh-oh.

That was more than thirty years after Poe's death. Only his ghost had ever heard this thing clamor.

I was sort of prepared for this. Just a couple of hours earlier, while watching the video at the Poe Cottage, they had talked about Old Edgar Allan. The bell they showed was sitting on the floor of a storage closet.

*Administration building at Fordham University, dating back to Poe's time
and adjacent to Edgar Allan Poe Way*

I had rationalized that the bell was just being serviced, but I don't even know if bells get serviced. Now that I had firsthand proof that I'd come to see the wrong bell, I started to get the clammy feeling that I'd have to edit out this little adventure from the book project due to wild geese. But the feeling was quickly pushed from my mind when Gownley asked me,

"Want to go higher?"

Another set of vertiginous metal rungs later and I was on the roof of the bell tower, looking out over Fordham and the Bronx, forgetting all about Edgar Allan Poe.

Crazy Poe. He writes a semi-monotonous but lyrically brilliant poem about some bells, and more than a century and a half later, I'm on the roof of a church.

While there, Gownley and I talked about the new Jesuit pope, the fact that the school once erected a fake cemetery to keep the Bronx River Expressway from passing through the campus, and other things worth discussing when you're between a church and the Creator.

Eventually, we came back down to the floor of the church, and he took me back behind the altar and played the faux-Old Edgar Allan by pressing a couple of buttons on a stack of electronic gizmos in a closet. Inside, the bell sounded soft and muted, but as we stepped outside, its tone carried across the campus in a loud tolling. None of the students across the campus who heard it knew it was tolling for me.

And what a world of solemn thought its monody compelled.

Eventually, I would return to Fordham University to see the real Old Edgar Allan. Or the original Old Edgar Allan, as I guess the title could be passed down to each succeeding bell.

This time, I was headed across the campus from the University Church to the Walsh Library. My new bell-keeper was Patrice Kane. Kane is the Head of Archives and Special Collections at Fordham, and when I asked about the bell, she told me to come on over, and she'd take me to the vault.

The vault, it turns out, is a small closet full of old books, paintings, and esoteric ecclesiastical stuff. The bell was on a small wheeled dolly, close to the floor. It was much smaller than the current church bell.

I immediately dropped to my knees to look at the date on the bell. In a band around its top wound the words, "St. John's College"—that was promising—"Rose Hill, Westchester County, New York, 1840."

Bam. It was old enough to be Old Edgar Allan.

Kane told me the bell had a whole history that could be traced back to the founding of the college, one that the media often asks her about because of its fabled connection to Poe.

Apparently, the bell was never in the church. Back in Poe's day most of the school activities took place in a single building. That building had a cupola, where the bell was hung and rung to indicate it was time to change class.

*Original Old Edgar Allan, Walsh Library, Fordham University*

In the late 1800s, the school got a new bell, and the original one was given to a Jesuit summer home on Keyser Island in Connecticut, where it was promptly forgotten, until some sleuthing faculty member with an interest in Poe tracked it down.

In 1955, 115 years after it was cast and 85 years after it disappeared north, the bell was brought back to Fordham. Somehow, though, the original fervor over the bell was lost, and it found itself in an overgrown paddock that belonged to the school's mascot, a ram named Ramses, as all the live mascots of Fordham were named. Eventually, though, it ended up where I saw it . . . in a closet on a dolly.

When I asked Kane if she was sure

that this bell I was standing beside was the one Poe would have heard when visiting the campus, she said, "Positive. If someone wants to open it up for debate, I'm ready."

"So is the original building that it was in still around?"

"Yes, it's an administration building now, over by Edgar Allan Poe Way."

Naturally. On the way out, I made sure to pass by yet another place where Poe left his mark.

As to the legend of whether this bell, which he did certainly hear, possibly even while he was in his Fordham cottage, was one of Poe's Runic rhyme-keepers, who knows? The usual story is that the poem was started at the suggestion of his friend Marie Louise Shew, when Poe came to her house, suffering from writer's block.

Personally, I like the idea that Neil Ralley at the Poe Cottage gave me. He described Poe waking up on a Sunday morning in Manhattan hung over and hating life and covering his ears while all the bells from all the churches nearby were ringing and ringing and ringing. Kind of like the Grinch's "Noise, noise, noise, noise, noise." And then Poe took his vengeance with poetry.

In the state of New York, Edgar Allan Poe has been honored in just about every way a person can . . . with plaques, parks, monuments, museums, busts, preserved artifacts, school names, street names and, uh, interpretive façades. They've done almost everything they can for Poe except throw him into a hall of fame for cool people.

## Hall of Fame for Cool People

Bronx Community College was established in 1957 and moved to its present site in 1973, where it can now claim the honor of being the first community college campus designated a National Historic Landmark. That's because its current site is also the location of a much older campus for New York University that dates back to the 1890s.

As we walked up to its gates, we were immediately stopped by campus security because we didn't have college IDs. Six words later, they let us in anyway. The secret passcode was "Hall of Fame for Great Americans."

The campus is small and not singular—that is, until you approach the southwest corner. There, a trio of majestic buildings rise up that date back to the early days of the campus. Their auspicious names are inscribed in the stone of their lofty façades: Hall of Languages, Library of New York University, Hall of Philosophy.

The three buildings were designed by Stanford White, the famous architect who designed the second Madison Square Garden and was then murdered there by the jealous husband of a past lover. White also designed the structure that

*Hall of Fame for Great Americans, Bronx Community College*

wraps behind the three buildings: the Hall of Fame for Great Americans.

The Hall of Fame was established in 1900 to honor those citizens of the country who embodied the American spirit, advanced American culture . . . whatever, were great Americans. Enshrined there are ninety-eight bronzed heads of scientists, soldiers, artists, statesmen, and authors. That's it. There are fewer than one hundred great Americans.

Actually, the project ceased to be an active memorial sometime in the 1970s, so the Hall of Fame became more of a Hall of History.

The busts line an elegant 630-foot-long colonnade that arcs behind the buildings and commands a nice view of the Harlem River. We walked through the entrance beside the Hall of Philosophy, passing, as we meandered among the columns, such famous countenances and names as Thomas Edison, Abraham Lincoln, Alexander Graham Bell, Daniel Boone, Poe's West Point counterpart James Abbott McNeill Whistler, Augustus Saint-Gaudens (who both sculpted busts for the hall and is a bust himself), Edwin Booth (sculpted by Edmund T. Quinn, who did the Poe Cottage bust of Poe), Susan B. Anthony, Homer Simpson, and scores of other American greats.

Finally, toward the far end of the colonnade and right behind the Hall of Languages, we came to the authors' wing, where we were immediately drawn to the too-familiar mopey face of Edgar Allan Poe, flanked on one side by Samuel Langhorne Clemens and on the other by William Cullen Bryant.

Ballots were cast every five years. To be inducted, the historical person needed at least fifty-one votes out of one hundred. Poe was elected into the Hall of Fame in 1910, after missing the first two ballots. On that third ballot, he made it in with sixty-nine. Others who were inducted that year include James Fenimore Cooper and Harriet Beecher Stowe. Poe's bust wasn't installed until 1922, when it was unveiled with the likenesses of astronomer Maria Mitchell, artist Gilbert Stuart, educator Mark Hopkins, and some guy named George Washington.

The ceremony included an address by poet Edwin Markham, who also read Poe's poem "Israfel," and the honor of unveiling the bust went to the man who funded it, J. Sanford Saltus, an author and wealthy patron of the arts who died after confusing a glass of cyanide with a glass of ginger ale.

The bust was sculpted by Daniel Chester French, best known for sculpting the massive seated figure of Abraham Lincoln at the Lincoln Memorial in D.C. Below

*Daniel Chester French bust of Poe, Hall of Fame for Great Americans*

the bust of Poe is a Tiffany plaque with his birth and death dates and a line from his posthumously published essay, "The Poetic Principle": "A poem deserves its title only inasmuch as it excites by elevating the soul."

Even though Poe's face was just one of so many other famous faces, he still seemed to stand out to me. Part of the reason was the base of his bust. Most of the bases in the hall were plain, geometric affairs, but Poe's bust sits atop a base adorned with a raven and a cat, one on each side of a wreath encircling a book and lamp. So that bit was objective, but overall I just assumed that Poe stood out to me due to my own Poe bias.

However, campus historian Remo Cosentino, who was gracious enough to give me the information about the inauguration of Poe's bust, told me he believed French "managed to capture Poe's flamboyance and seriousness. Many of the busts appear heavy and lumpen, but Poe seems to want to flee."

I second that idea, and raise that it's also my favorite Poe bust of those I've seen in my treks for this book. It's also a fitting face-to-face farewell to the version of the poet who lived in New York, a state where he both lost and gained so much.

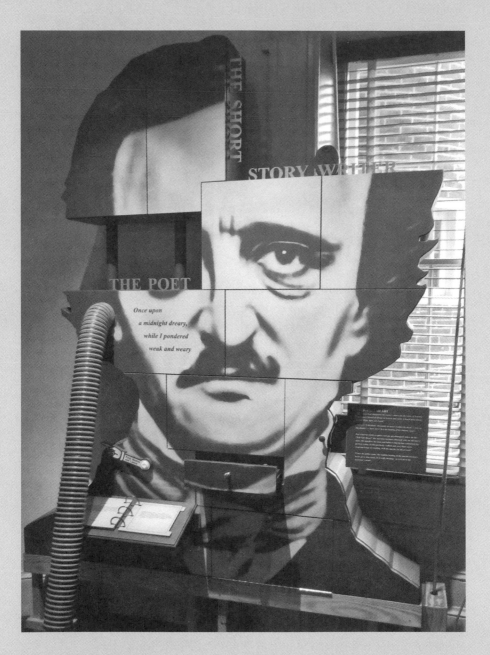

*Interactive Poe exhibit, Edgar Allan Poe National Historic Site*

CHAPTER 4

# Pennsylvania

*We Paused before the Heritage of Men, and Thy Star Trembled*

I WAS PARTICULARLY EXCITED about visiting Philadelphia for this book. Over the years, way before I conned a publisher into letting me do this, I'd had passing experiences with many of the major Poe sites. Obviously not to the degree or thoroughness that I was having now, but I'd at least some foreknowledge of them. For instance, I'd seen the Poe Cottage from the outside a couple years before I became so intimately acquainted with its floorboards. I had visited, just as a camera-handed fan, the Providence Athenaeum many years before I was given the opportunity to sift through its Poe artifacts.

But Philadelphia was a completely undiscovered country for me when it came to Poe. I'm not sure why I'd been to Philadelphia before. Heck, for a few years of my life, I lived less than an hour away from it.

If Philadelphia's place in Poe's physical legacy had been more like Boston's or Sullivan's Island in South Carolina, with very few tangible Poe traces, that oversight would've made some sense. But Philadelphia is the custodian of some major Poe-phernalia. I have no excuse for why it took me so long to get there.

This chapter is me righting a wrong in my life.

But, honestly, I kind of feel the same way about Philadelphia in general. It's one of the most populous cities in the United States, pivotal to the founding of the country and a major contributor to the culture. Yet somehow the city gets lost in the constant noise of civic clamoring that is the discourse of the major American cities.

I mean, yeah, we know about the Liberty Bell and Rocky and the Fresh Prince and that one Elton John song, but such a major city should defy easy characterization.

And I think that's part of the reason I overlooked Poe's place in the city. The other part is that, despite the fact that he lived about six years in the city (out of a mere forty, mind you), Poe's time in Philadelphia lacks the drama of his other homes.

145

I mean, it wasn't his birthplace and doesn't have the love/hate story of Boston. Or the body of Baltimore. He didn't spend his days in a doomed romance like in Providence. Didn't have the family problems he had in his adopted home state of Virginia. His wife didn't die there nor did he achieve his highest point of fame like in New York.

Basically, from about 1838 to 1844, he lived and he wrote. But, boy, did he write. Let me tell you what he wrote in Philadelphia (or at least first published when he lived in Philadelphia): "The Black Cat," "The Murders in the Rue Morgue," "The Pit and the Pendulum," "The Tell-Tale Heart," "The Gold-Bug," "The Fall of the House of Usher," "The Masque of the Red Death," "The Purloined Letter," "The Cask of Amontillado," "A Descent into the Maelstrom," "William Wilson," "The Man of the Crowd," and "The Oval Portrait."

Basically, Poe came into his own as a short-story writer in Philadelphia—although, strangely, none of them took place in this city that loves brothers.

Even long before he lived there, Philadelphia played a major role in his career by being the place where his first-ever weird tale, and first tale period, was published—*Metzengerstein,* about a possessed horse and vengeance from beyond the grave. Actually, his first five stories were published there, as they were part of a loosely tied together and incomplete collection called *Tales of the Folio Club.*

Anyway, that was his work in Philadelphia. In reviewing his life in the city, only two major things happened.

First, this is where he started in earnest his dream of owning a literary magazine. He was to name it *The Penn,* but after moving away from Philadelphia, the pun didn't work anymore and he changed the name to *The Stylus.* He would chase that dream without avail literally to his dying day. His last trip was a fundraiser for it.

Second, in Philadelphia, Poe's wife contracted the sickness that would eventually kill her in that little room on the first floor of that little New York cottage.

But the point of this whole introduction is that, even without a good Philadelphia story, Poe's time in Philadelphia is important to the story of Poe, first, for his stories . . . and, second, because it has preserved some top-tier parts of Poe's life that deserve more prominence in the Poescape.

More specific, there are two places you want to visit to experience Poe in Philadelphia: The Free Library of Philadelphia and the Edgar Allan Poe National Historic Site. My first stop? Neither.

## Poe in Prison

In 1849, Poe was living in New York, but he found himself back in Philadelphia in July of that last year of his life, for a short stop.

What we know of what transpired over the course of that strange week only comes from the stories recounted by those who heard them firsthand from Poe, as well as from some vague references in Poe's letters. Basically, there were no witnesses to the events, although there were witnesses to Poe's erratic behavior.

According to the story, Poe stopped in Philadelphia to avoid being murdered. He had caught wind of a plot on his life by two men on the train he was riding. After jumping off that train in Philly, he was thrown in jail for suspicion of passing a counterfeit $50 note . . . or for drunkenness . . . or for temporary insanity. Poe called it a "mania-a-potu" in his letters.

While in prison, he experienced a vision of a glowing woman who asked him questions and then turned into a black bird that called itself "Cholera" and flew him over the city. Later, he would see the guards mutilating his mother-in-law by cutting off her legs in sections. He was soon let go with just a fine, after being recognized for being that "Raven" guy. The whole thing ended with a bedraggled Poe fleeing in a state of paranoia to the home of John Sartain, the editor of the *Union Magazine,* to whom he told the story and from whom he demanded a razor, so that he could shave his mustache off. Sartain obliged by shaving the mustache for him, not trusting Poe with a blade in his present condition.

Poe's short trips to cities sometimes ended badly. For instance, his suicide attempt in Boston that ended in sickness and delirium. Or his trip to D.C. that turned into a drunken embarrassment and had him writing apology letters for days afterward. But the Philadelphia mania was out there even for Poe.

When you talk about old prisons in that city, Eastern State Penitentiary immediately comes to mind. The almost two-century-year-old castle of a prison on Fairmont Avenue had an enormous influence on prison architecture and prisoner treatment in this country. It is perhaps most known for holding Al Capone. The prison closed down in 1971—as an official prison, at least. Today, it's a major tourist attraction, where you can still see Capone's posh little cell.

But the place I was going to try to connect with the mania-a-Poe event was a tiny bit less interesting . . . a grocery store parking lot.

The prison where Poe claimed to be incarcerated wasn't Eastern State Penitentiary. It was Moyamensing, about three miles south of the famous prison.

Moyamensing Prison opened in 1835, just a few years after Eastern State, but was Danny DeVito to Eastern State's Arnold Schwarzenegger. It was a smaller building, although still impressively architected with castle-like adornments and an Egyptian-inspired wing. And, yeah, all those past tense verbs are correct. It was death-row'd in 1968 . . . all except for one innocuous stretch of low wall.

My wife and I pulled into the parking lot of the Acme supermarket on Reed Street, not knowing the exact location of this prison fragment that may or may not have been related to Poe.

However, we did immediately see a navy blue historic sign on the sidewalk at the far end of the parking lot. In yellow letters, it told this story:

MOYAMENSING PRISON
OPENED IN 1835, THOMAS U. WALTER DESIGNED IT WITH
ELEMENTS OF EGYPTIAN REVIVAL STYLE AND FOLLOWING THE
REVOLUTIONARY PRINCIPLE OF ISOLATED CONFINEMENT.
WITH LATER ADDITIONS, IT COULD HOUSE NEARLY 5000 INMATES—
AFRICAN AMERICANS AND WOMEN IN SEPARATE WINGS.
H. H. HOLMES, CONSIDERED AMERICA'S FIRST SERIAL KILLER,
WAS EXECUTED HERE. THE LAST HANGING IN PA. TOOK PLACE
HERE IN 1916, SOON REPLACED BY ELECTROCUTION.
CLOSED IN 1963, IT WAS RAZED IN 1968.

It was actually more interesting to me to see the name H. H. Holmes on the historic sign than to not see Edgar Allan Poe's.

H. H. Holmes was the more-distinguished pseudonym of serial killer Herman Mudgett. Mudgett was born in Gilmanton, New Hampshire, in 1861, and, like the sign said, is generally held to be the first modern serial killer in America. He was doing his thing on this side of the Atlantic Ocean at the same time that Jack the Ripper was doing his thing on the other side. In Mudgett's case, that thing was constructing an entire hotel purpose-built to be both a murder weapon and a body-disposal mechanism. It would come to be called the Murder Castle.

*Sign marking the site of Moyamensing Prison*

The Murder Castle was built in Chicago in 1893 to take advantage of the crowds of potential victims that were flocking there to visit the Chicago World's Fair. The building had gas chambers and body chutes and secret passageways and incinerators that Mudgett used to kill who-knows-how-many people. He confessed to more than two dozen.

The reason the name stuck out to me was that I had visited the site of his birth many years ago when I first moved to New Hampshire. The large, white house still stands in the middle of Gilmanton, and now here I was buying potato chips and looking for an obscure stone wall at the site of his death, 350 miles

*Surviving fragment of wall from Moyamensing Prison*

away, where he was hanged in 1896 for 15 minutes before finally expiring. His body was encased in cement and buried in an unmarked grave in Holy Cross Cemetery in Yeadon, Pennsylvania. In Chicago, the Murder Castle was burned down and replaced with a post office.

I know this is a tangent, but it is at least a Poesque one, as well as being another example of a how the life of a person can be told through physical sites. But to get this digression back on track, Mudgett's confession included the line, "I was born with the devil in me. I could not help the fact that I was a murderer, no more than a poet can help the inspiration to sing."

And, of course, it was for a poet that I was there.

The sign doesn't point out the remaining stretch of stone that is all that's left of Moyamensing in Philadelphia (I've heard it said that the Egyptian façade of one of its wards is in the vaults of the Smithsonian in D.C.). Eventually, we found it, though. It's behind the grocery store, around a small lot that serves as the employee parking and truck delivery area.

Reed Street runs both beside and behind the grocery store, and the low stone wall turns the corner with it. It's made of rough stones of varying sizes cemented together and is about four feet high. As the wall turns the corner with Reed Street, the stones become large rectangular blocks. The whole stretch is topped by a chain-link fence.

I'm not sure if that change in the stone depicts walls from different times or if it was all a part of Moyamensing. Either way, there is nothing at all noticeable about this masonry. No plaque. No sign. It doesn't look two hundred years old or like the ruins of a vast edifice. It looks like an ordinary wall of stone.

Still, it's all that's left of the site of Poe's imprisonment . . . or the focus of his delusion. Either way, it's a stop on the Poe tour. Just not an official stop. That was next for me.

## Gripping the Raven

The Philadelphia Free Library was built long after Poe lived in the city. The system was started in 1894, and its Parkway Central Library didn't open until 1927.

The Parkway Central Library is a massive, overwhelming stone building located downtown, on Vine Street. The library is adorned with the usual colonnades that signify important buildings.

Across the street from the entrance is the Shakespeare Memorial, which was proposed in 1892 by John Sartain . . . the same guy who clipped Poe's mustache to help him hide from phantom murderers . . . or from real ones who didn't catch up to him until Baltimore three months later. It was erected in 1926, though, decades after Sartain's death. The statue is a fourteen-foot-tall black tower of marble topped by a jester overcome with the giggles and a mopey Hamlet leaning his head against a knife . . . comedy and tragedy, respectively. On the base is the

*Free Library of Philadelphia*

Shakespeare quote "All the world's a stage, and all the men and women merely players."

The quote should be completed with "the play is the tragedy 'Man,' and its hero, the Conqueror Worm" because the Parkway Central Library isn't known for its Shakespeare collection, even though it does own editions of Shakespeare's first four folios. Parkway earned its columns with Edgar Allan Poe treasures . . . and other stuff.

There are actually a lot of libraries with Edgar Allan Poe collections, more than I'd realized before I started this project. Many of them are manuscript and book collections, although plenty have other kinds of artifacts, as well. The New York Public Library, the Boston Public Library, the University of Virginia Library, others. One of the most notable isn't even in a state where Poe ever lived or visited, the Harry Ransom Center of the University of Texas at Austin. It has a large collection of items and manuscripts, including Poe's desk from the *Southern Literary Messenger* and Poe's own 1845 copies of *The Raven and Other Poems* and *Tales,* marked up with his notes and corrections.

Not all of these collections were on my itinerary. I wasn't doing scholarly work and most of the collections are manuscripts and letters. I mean, I could probably goggle at his original pen strokes for the rest of my life, but it would be difficult to write about it after a while.

Over the course of this book, I would visit four of them—five counting the Morgan Library and Museum, which I visited only for a public exhibit—but each for very specific reasons. The first, I already told you about: the Providence Athenaeum. I really wanted to see that "Ulalume" autograph. The second was Columbia University's Butler Library. That was for the Poe Mantel. Another was the Enoch Pratt Free Library in Baltimore. We'll get to that story a little later. The fourth was the Free Library of Philadelphia.

Honestly, if I could have visited only one Poe-related library collection for this project, I'd, well, die with one more regret on my conscience. But I very well might have settled on what I found in the collection at Philadelphia.

However, since I didn't have to make that decision and had time to see more than one priceless cultural prize while I was at the library, I figured I'd check out a few manuscripts, too. The Free Library's Poe manuscript holdings are impressive, and include such items as full or partial autographed manuscripts of "Annabel Lee," "The Fall of the House of Usher," and "The Murders in the Rue Morgue." It features letters from Poe, as well as letters from his mother-in-law and sister dated after his death. It also has letters from various literary figures like Jules Verne, Charles Baudelaire, and Robert Frost that mention Poe.

The reason they have such a trove of original Poe-phernalia is mostly thanks to one man, Colonel Richard A. Gimbel. Gimbel was the son of the founder of the famous and now-defunct Gimbels department store. He was a collector of rare books and manuscripts and a Poe fan. He's the one who made the city such a Poe haven, both with his collection and because he's the one who originally preserved what's come to be elevated as the Edgar Allan Poe National Historic Site. We'll get to that.

At the library, Lindsey and I entered its massive foyer and then headed to the elevator. The Rare Book Department is on the third floor. Once there, we passed a small case of library souvenirs, including some related to Poe and some to Charles Dickens. Yes, Dickens is jumping into this story soon.

After ringing the buzzer for entry, I met Joseph Shemtov, a librarian from Montreal who led me through the alien process of viewing and handling irreplaceable things. He was also nice enough not to comment on the sunglasses I was still wearing. I had just undergone Lasik surgery, which meant that some of the first things I was going to see with my new eyes were priceless Poe artifacts. However, my surgery had gone a bit awry, and the whites of my eyes were filled with blood to the point that I looked like I should be in a Poe story instead of reading them.

He led us down a long hallway filled with cataloged wonders. At the end of the hallway, atop a tall cabinet in the corner, was a massive bust of Pallas, with a small black raven atop her ever-present helmet.

Lindsey opted to go on a tour of the Rare Book Department while I was led to a desk in a tiny niche of a room where I was surrounded by old-fashioned card cabinets, shelves, and books. Beside me was a window with a grand view of an exterior wall of the library. There, I filled out the official request cards for the items I had asked for in advance, and Shemtov laid down a green velvet mat in front of me like he was setting a place at a dinner table for me.

Actually, I should continue using that simile since, after that, like a waiter bringing out a range of exquisite courses at an exclusive restaurant, he presented me, one at a time, the series of manuscripts and artifacts I had requested.

The first course was a simple letter, written by Poe to a man named Eli Bowen, of Pottsville, Pennsylvania. It was framed in blue leather embossed with gold. On the reverse of the frame was the back of the letter, with Bowen's address, Poe's initials, and a five-cent postmark of October 19. A dark, circular stain that I would eventually see on other old letters, and which might have been sealing wax, marred the backside. Sometimes all you have to do to slip into history is be a stain on something significant.

I visited the Free Library of Philadelphia before my excursion to the Morgan Library, so this was the first time I saw Poe's painfully neat penmanship with my own bleeding eyeballs. His cursive was neat, almost a natural typeface, in ink aged so faint it looked like pencil.

What was really striking about the handwriting was his signature. It's the practiced signature of a famous person. Or at least a man who hopes for fame. All three initial caps of his name have loopy flourishes, and the whole thing was emphasized with a curvy underline.

Of course, Poe was interested in the signatures of famous men and women. In his *Autography* series of magazine articles, he analyzed the work and handwriting of "the most distinguished American *literati*," including with each entry the signature of that person. So it makes sense that he would pay particular attention to his own. Plus, it was a world where one's signature was as important an identifier as a mother's maiden name is today.

As to the content of the letter, there wasn't much. Bowen was a publisher of a magazine called the *Columbia Spy,* in which Poe had published some news ephemera. In this letter, as he did in so much of his correspondence, Poe's looking for help establishing his own literary magazine. The letter was written from Fordham on October 18, 1848, a year before his death. It says:

> **My Dear Sir,**
> **About three weeks ago I wrote you quite a long letter,**
> **enclosing a MS copy of "The Raven" and making you a**
> **proposition in regard to the establishment of a Magazine—**
> **but have received no reply.**
>     **In addition to what I then said I have now to say that I**
> **am willing to accept your offer about the Correspondence,**
> **and will commence whenever you think proper—*provided***
> **you decline the *tour* &c as I suggested. Please write & oblige**
>
> **Yours truly**
> **Edgar A Poe.**

Basically, I picked a very, very unimportant letter. I'd chosen it almost for the sole reason that he mentioned "The Raven" in it. But the letter was characteristic of the majority of Poe's correspondence, whether he was pushing his magazine or asking for money. But it was extremely relevant to the next item that Shemtov placed reverentially down on the green velvet in front of me.

Today, only one known complete copy of "The Raven" written in Poe's own hand exists in the entire world . . . and it resides in the Free Library of Philadelphia. That's what I held in my own stupid hands next.

It was the actual manuscript referenced in the letter to Bowen. The original of the copy I'd seen in the Greenwich Poe Room. It covered two sheets of paper, front and back, for a total of four pages. The pages had fold lines, like the previous letter, to fit into an envelope. The ink was faded, and the whole thing looked much less than the astounding literary treasure it was.

Unfortunately, what I was handed was also sealed in a clear Mylar sheath. Shemtov apologized and said that it must have been packaged that way for an exhibit and was never removed. His boss wasn't in that day, and he didn't have the authority to unseal it.

As a result, what I got to see was the first page and the last. On the first page, the title was underlined twice with a period at the end of the two words of the title. Even more than the letter I'd just seen, the poem was scribed so neatly it could be read like the best-designed typeface on a computer screen.

Still, I immediately looked for errors or penmanship quirks. Not because I was copyediting Poe, but because I thought that was how I could catch a glimpse of the man who had written the words. I wanted to see past the familiar phrases and the neat handwriting to the man who was sitting in his cottage in Fordham widowed and impoverished, but still somehow ambitious and hopeful.

I discovered "visitor" was spelled in the fourth line of the third stanza as "visiter," as it was often spelled before Microsoft Word codified the English language, with the cross of the "t" slightly missing its post to become an inadvertent accent mark over the "e." In the next line he writes the word the exact same way.

He was also obviously a very dashing man, that Poe. He used the horizontal punctuation eleven times just in the first five stanzas. Actually, Poe was a defender of the dash. In his "Marginalia" he wrote a few paragraphs on it: "The dash *cannot* be dispensed with."

And that's as far as the first page took me—the fifth stanza—so no stately raven making zero obeisances yet, just a lonely narrator whispering "Lenore" into the darkness outside his door.

Flipping the sheath over, it started right in with the histrionic shrieking of "'Prophet!' said I, 'thing of evil!—prophet still, if bird or devil!'" I had skipped about eight different emotional states between trepidatious hope and desperate anger.

It ends with his underlined signature, Edgar A. Poe, right under "Shall be lifted—nevermore.", on the right side of the page, with the dash in that phrase at least twice as long as the dashes anywhere else I could see. In the bottom left corner of the page, the poem is exuberantly inscribed to "Dr. S. A. Whittaker of Phoenixville," who is not, of course, Eli Bowen.

Another letter in the Gimbel collection clears that up. It's from Bowen to Whittaker and indicates that Bowen procured the copy from Poe on behalf of the Pennsylvania doctor, after showing it off to a few of his friends first, "somewhat ruff[ling]" it in the process.

The funny thing is, Poe tried to get "The Raven" published in Philadelphia first. He submitted it to *Graham's Magazine,* at which he had worked while living in Philly and to which he still contributed. George Graham, the owner and editor, turned it down, inadvertently giving New York the honor of playing Noah and sending "The Raven" out into the world. Graham did, however, kindly give him $15 since he knew of Poe's straits.

Unlike Graham, I had a hard time letting that manuscript go. Real hard. I knew this was a once-in-lifetime thing for me, and it was way worth leaving my wife stranded, my next appointment hanging, and the kind library staff awaiting nervously to close up for the day. Eventually I did, after taking about twenty selfies with it. Later, Shemtov would send me a digital scan of the manuscript so I could double-check my notes and peruse the portions I missed due to its plastic seal. It's now the only way I'll read the poem.

Next, following the order of the request cards I'd filled out, Shemtov brought me a thin, beat-up old pamphlet. Unlike the Bowen letter, and even "The Raven" manuscript, he couldn't leave me alone with this one. Wouldn't even let me hold it.

It was an original printing of Poe's first published work, *Tamerlane and Other Poems.*

As I've already mentioned, my visit to the Free Library of Philadelphia predated my visit to the Morgan Library. So this was actually my first time seeing what has been called the "black tulip of U.S. literature" due to its rarity. Still, between this one at the Free Library and the trio of them at the Morgan Library, I've seen just about a bouquet of black tulips, so I'm currently a bit jaded.

At the time, though, I wasn't, as Shemtov daintily handled what basically amounted to half a million dollars, taking excruciating pains in turning the pages as I, deeper into his personal space than I would have been allowed on any other occasion, stared at each page and took pictures.

I once worked in Boston for a couple of years just a block down the street from the still-unheralded spot where this book was printed almost two hundred years ago, and I couldn't help wondering now what parallel journey these torn, aged pages took while its creator went through a life of poverty, loss, and frustration, only to ascend to the highest perches of culture in the century and a half after his death.

The idea of this booklet is huge. The reality, not so much.

The front cover of this particular specimen had its upper left corner torn to reveal the beginning of a signature of one of its previous owners on the title page. However, the tear didn't affect what was on the age-browned and spattered cover:

TAMERLANE

AND

OTHER POEMS.

BY A BOSTONIAN.

YOUNG HEADS ARE GIDDY, AND YOUNG HEARTS ARE WARM,

AND MADE MISTAKES FOR MANHOOD TO REFORM. COWPER.

BOSTON:

CALVIN F. S. THOMAS. . . . . PRINTER

. . . . . . . . . . . .

1827.

It's only about forty pages long. The signature on the title page was revealed to be that of Joseph Bigelow, who was supposedly a carpenter from Maine, the state where this particular copy turned up in the 1930s.

After that was the introduction, where the eighteen-year-old Poe claimed the poems had been written when he was thirteen and includes this tragically prophetic statement, tragic for himself at least, not for those of us who love his work: "He will not say that he is indifferent as to the success of these Poems—it might stimulate him to other attempts—but he can safely assert that failure will not at all influence him in a resolution already adopted. This is challenging criticism—let it be so."

Then came the poem "Tamerlane," the deathbed confession of the fourteenth-century Turkish conqueror who chooses an empire over love. The four-hundred-plus-line poem takes up half the book. The rest of the poems are in a section labeled "Fugitive Pieces" and include none of his well-known poems. Those would take a much older, more world-weary poet to compose.

Shemtov also showed me a second copy of Tamerlane and Other Poems, this one relatively crisp, although only by comparison with the previous volume. It was one of the facsimile reprints put out in the late 1800s and early 1900s.

Shemtov took the Tamerlanes away, locking them, I like to think, in a series of vaults fit together like Russian nested dolls, but then returned with a pair of pictures.

Both were small cards that dated to 1878 and looked like they should come packaged with cheap chewing gum. One was a photographic print of the Mathew B. Brady portrait of Poe. The second was something the catalog called a "head-and-shoulders vignette" of Poe, this one based on the Daly daguerreotype.

I didn't stare at the images too long. I just wanted to look in the face the guy whose works I'd been marveling at that afternoon. And because I was excited about what I would see next, the real reason I came to the library, above wanting to see he handwritten copy of the most famous poem in Western literature, above wanting to see one of the rarest of American literary works. When Shemtov returned to retrieve the images from me, I had one last question. "Where's Grip?"

## A Tell-Tale of Two Authors

Charles Dickens's *A Christmas Carol* was published in England in December of 1843, less than six years before Poe's death in October of 1849, but the story wouldn't really take hold in America for many years later. I don't know if Poe ever read it, but I suspect he would have praised it for its moments of intense dread and tomahawk'd it for Scrooge's change of heart and the happily ever after of prize turkeys, business promotions, and second fathers.

Poe's Scrooge might have ended his tale by cracking his head on his own gravestone or strangling himself on his bed sheets or confessing maniacally to how he'd killed Tiny Tim, I guess.

And while it might seem juvenile to pretend how Poe would do Dickens, that's exactly what Poe did himself. Dickens was three years younger than Poe and hit fame at the age of twenty-four with his *The Pickwick Papers*. Dickens would quickly go on to become an international star of Western literature in his lifetime and was everything Poe wanted to be and the exact opposite of what he was. Poe finally caught up to him, of course. It just took a while.

But, by the time Dickens got big, Poe had at least found himself a comfortable chair at the helm of the *Southern Literary Messenger* in Virginia (a chair I would actually get to see during my Virginia trek), and the start of a magazine career. That career spanned multiple periodicals in multiple states, and Poe got to review Dickens's work, which he usually praised and criticized in the same review. During Poe's time in Philadelphia, while working at *Graham's Magazine*, he reviewed Dickens's *Barnaby Rudge*.

*Barnaby Rudge* is a historical novel set during the Gordon riots of the 1780s. It was released in serial form, as Dickens was wont to do, in 1840 and 1841. Poe took the opportunity to review it before the ending came out and, in his usual way of reducing (or elevating?) literature to a mathematical equation, predicted its ending based on a series of deductions culled from the first part of the story.

Unfortunately, his extrapolations turned out less than Dupin-like. Poe's clever riposte to that was, "We did not rightly prophesy yet, at least, our prophecy *should have been* right."

Even though Poe's fame didn't catch up to that of Dickens until after both were dead, he did catch up to him literally, and it happened in Philadelphia. In 1842, Dickens was on his first tour of the United States, the one that would produce his book *American Notes,* in which he was critical of the country and its citizens. Of course, while he was touring nobody realized he was secretly disgusted by them, so he was in high demand, mobbed in the streets, meeting the newly elected President Tyler and other famous Americans, and getting access to whatever places he wanted to see. Somehow, by corresponding with him, Poe managed to pique his interest enough to finagle an audience with the British author—two audiences if Poe's claims are true.

No real record of the meeting or meetings exists, but we do know that, based on the three letters that survive from the two men's correspondence (all from Dickens), Poe's real reason for wanting to meet Dickens was not to bask in his fame or literary acumen, but to get him to become his agent in London.

Poe had tried Boston. He'd tried New York. He'd tried Philadelphia. That was pretty much it as far as getting published in the U.S. back then. The only other option was overseas, and London, a city Poe had called home for five years as a young boy, seemed a good bet. And he was confident enough in his own work and ambitious enough in his own resolve to think Dickens would and could help him get published there.

Actually, the rendezvous could have been a true meeting of the minds, with the idea of Poe's work crossing the ocean rising naturally and through Dickens's own interest. The other interpretation of an ambitious Poe more interested in getting published in London than meeting Dickens is funnier, though, and I can't believe that Poe wouldn't at least have had that angle in his head going in to the meeting.

Either way, if Dickens is to be believed in the matter, the author gave it a go. But he was no Baudelaire and couldn't drum up any publisher interest for Poe in London. In a letter from November 1842 he wrote,

> **I am, however, unable to report any success. I have mentioned it to publishers with whom I have influence, but they have, one and all, declined the venture. And the only consolation I can give you is that I do not believe any collection of detached pieces by an unknown writer, even though he were an Englishman, would be at all likely to find a publisher in this metropolis just now.**

The coda on the Poe-Dickens relationship occurred twenty years after Poe's death. During his second and last tours of the United States, Dickens took the time while in Baltimore to meet up with Maria Clemm, Poe's mother-in-law, to provide financial support for her double poverty, as she was both without money (although used to that) and now Virginia and Edgar.

As interesting as that historical crossroads is, it is for a literary crossroads that I love the Poe-Dickens-Philadelphia connection.

As I walked to the end of the hall of the Rare Book Department, I approached a large glass case that was the size of a fifty-gallon aquarium. I was extremely excited, as I was about to see my favorite Poe-related artifact, one I had seen only in pictures on the Internet. The tank was set against the wall. Inside, and in the shadows cast by the wooden lid of the case, was another glass case, about half the size and framed in twisted lengths of tree branch. Inside that case, on a bed of fake ferns and grass, perched upon a fallen branch, was a large . . . black . . . taxidermied . . . raven.

I'm not sure what my next sentence should be. It could either go:

This was the pet raven of none other than Charles Dickens himself.

Or

This was the very raven that inspired Poe's "The Raven."

Either one works.

Let's start with Boz (Dickens's family nickname and a pseudonym he used for a time). Dickens loved his pets. I had once seen at the New York Public Library a letter opener that Dickens had made from the paw of his cat, Bob. The ivory blade that extended from the cat foot bore the inscription C.D. IN MEMORY OF BOB 1862. It was part of the same Berg collection that held two of Poe's *Tamerlanes*.

But I didn't have to travel that far to see Dickens's affinity for his animals. Directly across from the raven in the Free Library was a small wooden marker framed and hung on the wall—a grave marker. Its epitaph read:

THIS IS THE GRAVE OF
DICK
THE BEST OF BIRDS
*BORN AT BROADSTAIRS MIDS'R 1851*
*DIED AT GAD'S HILL PLACE 14TH OCT, 1866*

Dick was the Dickens family's canary, although technically it was his daughter's. Dickens had made the bird a gravestone. Of course, it was the other bird that interested me. The raven was large, in excellent condition, and thinner and more streamlined than the live ravens I've seen. It certainly didn't look like one of the more important literary muses of English literature.

The raven was Dickens's pet Grip, famously used as the inspiration for the talking raven companion of the titular simpleton character of *Barnaby Rudge*. You see where this is going, but it gets better. Actually, the raven in the book was based on two of Dickens's pets, one that had died after eating lead paint and the other having vociferous reactions to drunken men. I assume the stuffed corpse I was witnessing was the second one, which died of unknown causes in front of the fire, "his eye to the last upon the meat as it roasted," because Dickens didn't get another raven. "Since then I have been ravenless," he wrote in the preface to the book.

That's right. The raven character was important enough that he spent half the preface talking about the two pets that inspired it. In the story, Grip had a much bigger "stock and store" than Poe's raven, although along similar lines, as it crawked such phrases as "I'm a devil, I'm a devil, I'm a devil" and "Grip the clever, Grip the wicked, Grip the knowing."

In Poe's review of the novel, he singled out Rudge's avian companion specifically, opining that Dickens missed a great opportunity with the bird:

> **The raven, too, intensely amusing as it is, might have been made, more than we now see it, a portion of the conception of the fantastic Barnaby. Its croakings might have been *prophetically* heard in the course of the drama. Its character might have performed, in regard to that of the idiot, much the same part as does, in music, the accompaniment in respect to the air.**

The italicization of "prophetically" is Poe's own, and it takes zero imagination to see that idea tinder, four years later, into a "prophet, thing of evil, prophet still, if bird or devil." I mean, we have no actual admission from Poe on the matter, not even in his "The Philosophy of Composition," where he straps the bird to a dissecting table. He does open the essay with a reference to a letter Dickens wrote to him that mentions an observation Poe had made about *Barnaby Rudge*. That might be evidence enough.

Regardless, I love that this raven still exists, almost two hundred years later. That Dickens first immortalized it in one of his works and then immortalized it again with a gut full of sawdust. That it caused Poe, an ocean away, to create his ultimate work. And the thing is right there in a library in Philadelphia for anybody to see. Talk about never flitting.

So Philadelphia might have passed on the first go at "The Raven," but they ended up with it just the same.

Of all my "The Raven" experiences in this book—the spot where it was written, the mantel piece that witnessed and helped inspire it, the actual copy of it painstakingly scribed in the poet's own hand, all the various original printings of it in exhibitions and museums—Grip is by far my favorite.

By the time I'd gotten to him, Lindsey had rejoined me after a personal tour through the Rare Book exhibits. While I had been lost in a world of Poe, she was fresh from seeing ancient Egyptian papyruses, cuneiform tablets, antique illustrations, and all the other wonders of the collection. After we finished getting our nose and forehead prints all over Grip's glass, she told me, "You should really see what's in the next room."

There, set at the end of the hall beside Grip's case was a door. It was locked, but we found Shemtov again and asked if we could go inside. He took us in and showed as a gorgeous private library right in the middle of that public library.

The room was large and paneled completely in wood. Red curtains matched luxurious red couches and rugs and hung from tall windows artificially lit from behind. Rare prints and paintings adorned the walls; in one wall was a white fireplace. Ancient-looking books filled shelves floor to ceiling, and simple chandeliers descended from above. This was the private library of William McIntire Elkins.

Elkins was a wealthy businessman who was also a collector of books and Americana. He died in 1947, and his heirs donated his collection to the library per his directions. But they donated it with a stipulation—that the library put it together exactly as it was in his home. So they did, even down to blowing up photographs of the original views from his library to set in the false windows.

But the most remarkable piece to me in the entire Elkins Room turned out to be a small, innocuous—at least in that luxuriant setting—desk of polished mahogany wood. Lindsey pointed to a spot on its surface. I bent closer and saw two faint letters carved into it: CD.

It was the desk of Charles Dickens. The chair was his, too. A small portrait of the author hung above the desk.

The souvenir table I'd passed on the way into this department was making more sense. Not only did the library boast one of the greatest collections of Poe-phernalia in the world, it also boasted the same for Dickensia. In addition to wooden tombstones and dead ravens and graffitied desks, the library had quite a few other Charles Dickens artifacts, mostly letters and rare books, much of it from William Elkins.

Interestingly enough, Grip is not included with the Charles Dickens stuff, but came from Gimbel's collection, making it technically a part of the library's Edgar Allan Poe holdings.

Finally and unfortunately, it was time to leave this rare Rare Book Department. However, as we gathered our things and neared the exit, we found a man waiting for us.

He looked like Charles Dickens.

## *Ed and Edgar*

When I was trying to find somebody to talk to about Edgar Allan Poe in Philadelphia, I typed two words into Google: Philadelphia and Poe. It came back with the Philly Poe Guy.

His real name is Edward G. Pettit. He's a writer and a part-time teacher at La Salle University . . . and he just happens to have a beard that's a foot long.

Pettit entered the public Poe-sphere in October of 2007 with a single article, a cover story for the *City Paper,* a local Philadelphia alt-weekly. It was called "We're Taking Poe Back" and the cover was a photo of an actor playing Edgar Allan Poe bound in rope and shoved into the trunk of a black Lincoln Town Car with a Philadelphia bumper sticker and a license plate reading 2HELEN.

The piece begins, "This is a literary grave-robbing," continues through "Poe is ours. He belongs to Philadelphia," and ends with an exhortation to Philadelphians to truck on down I-95 and exhume Poe's body from Baltimore to return it to Poe's rightful home. "Edgar Allan Poe is a Philadelphian. Richmond? Baltimore? New York City? Please. Poe is ours . . . evermore."

The three-thousand-word piece from an unknown author in a local paper somehow blew up. The mayor of Baltimore released a statement, as did the curator of the Edgar Allan Poe House in Baltimore. There were op-ed responses in the *Baltimore Sun.* Newspapers across the country ran stories about a "custody battle" over the remains of the poet. Pettit was interviewed by *The New York Times,* and at one point, a Japanese television crew invaded his home. The article launched two public debates on the topic, one in Philadelphia and one in Boston, with Dr. Paul Lewis representing Boston, Jeff Jerome (then-curator of the Edgar Allan Poe House in Baltimore), and, of course, Pettit in Philadelphia's corner. Basically, it was a great opportunity to put Poe into the headlines, and a good number of good-humored people jumped at the chance.

The most interesting part of the *City Paper* article, I think, wasn't the colorful and Poesque exhumation angle. It was the actual case Pettit put together, which was three-pronged. The first is one I've already mentioned—that the bulk of the work we associate with Poe was written in Philadelphia. So no real argument there.

But Pettit goes further, saying much of what Poe wrote was written because of the city's character at that time. Basically, the shining city of Ben Franklin was a crime-ridden, dirty, chaotic place during Poe's residence there, and that gave him a model to paint. All he had to do was set his easel by his upstairs window. I like the idea of having pride in an author for being inspired by the worst parts of one's home city, or, more accurately, its past.

But mostly, and most interestingly, Pettit's point rests on the literary tradition of Philadelphia, something he described to me, when we finally met, with a phrase he didn't actually use in the article: "Philadelphia Gothic."

We had originally planned to visit the Edgar Allan Poe National Historic Site together after the dizzying and surreal traipse I took with Lindsey through the Free Library of Philadelphia's Rare Book Department, but the house was closed for a renovation at the time, so our Plan B was TGI Fridays. It was across the street from the Free Library, and the sky was raining iron bolts. Heck, it was pouring so hard we didn't even so much as pause when he walked right over one of those mysterious Toynbee tiles in the crosswalk as we rushed sodden to the restaurant.

We settled in, Pettit ordering something simple after explaining that due to his beard he could only decorously eat certain foods in public, and I explained my project to him.

He said, "I was born and raised in Philly, so I grew up with the idea that the places where the Founding Fathers walked and where they worked and lived, that they're important. I don't know if it's true . . . maybe you just bulldoze everything and keep rebuilding since life is about the living, but I can't shake the feeling that it needs to be preserved."

"Tell me your Poe story. How did you get introduced to him?"

"Everybody I know has this great first experience with Poe: 'Oh, I was eleven and this book was on the shelf and I was sick.' I have nothing like that. I kind of always knew who Poe was. I'm a horror guy and into all that and always knew his strong Philadelphia connection. I never thought it would be a specialty for me, but he's always been around me."

"Why hasn't Philadelphia made a stronger pass at Poe's legacy? I mean, they have all the materials. I just saw some of the best Poe stuff in country, and the city has one of his only three remaining homes."

"Philly's got the whole Rocky-underdog thing. That goes way back to the nineteenth century, where the feeling in Philadelphia culture was, 'We were great, and now we're not.' I mean, we shouldn't be that way. We're a major city."

"I know you said you're into horror, but your interest in Poe seems to spring more from your love for your home city."

"It's a big part of it for me. My dad worked at City Hall for like twenty years, and I've always been into the city and aware of its history. I was nine years old at the United States Bicentennial, and collected all the souvenirs that came out at the time."

I admitted to him that I was having trouble coming up with an angle on Poe's story in Philadelphia, one I hoped I would solve by the time you read this.

"Well, Poe was so in tune with the literary culture, and Boston, New York, and Philadelphia were the literary centers of the country at the time. Boston was all about poetry, and if you want to be a great poet, you needed to go there. That's where the poets are in America in the 1830s and 1840s. New York was becoming a big publishing center, but was still not as big a one as Philadelphia. In the late 1850s and beyond, New York becomes the place, but Philadelphia was the magazine capital at the time in the country. That's why Poe came here, to be in that culture and have a better chance at success.

"Philadelphia literary history is just absolutely ignored in any literary history written now. It's all about Boston transcendentalists and the growth of New York. That's become the entire literary history story for the nineteenth century. Philadelphia gets ignored. It's crazy because what was being published during Poe's time was immensely important for what people were reading at the time. And you could say for the works that shaped all of culture because Poe wrote most of his big stuff here."

"You seem to be skipping over the southern chapters of his work."

"Poe is not a southern writer at all. People talk about Southern Gothic all the time, which is ridiculous. There is no such thing as Southern Gothic before the Civil War. There are gothic writers in the south at the time, but their writing is European-style Gothicism that has nothing to do with the South.

"The primary thing about Southern Gothic is that sense of lost culture, of a past curse, and that only comes out after the Civil War. Southern Gothic is really a twentieth-century thing, I think. O'Connor, that's Southern Gothic. Faulkner, that's Southern Gothic. It's then that the South really starts discovering this sense that something has been lost and that it is cursed by its past . . . the slave culture, of course.

"But there is a Philadelphia Gothic back then. Few, maybe even no literary historians recognize it and only recently have academics, only a few of them, started to write about it as a kind of genre or movement. But Gothic . . . you could even say horror literature in America . . . starts in Philadelphia."

"That's a big statement. I can't even name a Philadelphia horror writer off the top of my head . . ." and then I interject before he could correct me, "besides Poe."

"Charles Brockden Brown. He was from Philadelphia, from a Quaker family back in the late 1700s, early 1800s. He does live for a time in New York, but even then, when he's writing his early Gothic novels, they were all set in Philadelphia or just outside it. That's the American Gothic, and it starts with Charles Brockden Brown. Poe knows this. Poe reveres the guy. Wanted to write a history of American literature, and Brockden Brown would've been his first chapter.

"Brockden Brown's novels are the first gothic novels different from the European novels. European Gothic almost always involves the supernatural, or if it's not supernatural, you think it is until the very end—like a Scooby Doo ending. It's about curses, sins of the father, sins of the past coming down and hurting you. The aristocracy and the religious orders are the villains against the common man.

"That all changes in America. We don't have an aristocracy, and we're against that idea. And the past is no more. Literally, we got to start over, so we don't have a past to hurt us anymore."

He then told me about Brockden Brown's 1798 novel *Wieland,* generally considered the first American Gothic novel. It's about a guy who thinks God is talking to him, tells him to kill his wife and kids, which, of course, Abraham and Isaac set the precedent for. So he takes an axe and butchers his family. "That's a very American horror, and the ending makes it more so. I'll give it away." That last statement was a spoiler alert in the moment for me concerning that two-century-old book, and now it's one for you before you read the next sentence. "By the end he discovers it was a guy playing a trick, somebody who could throw his voice." I'd find out later that the story was actually based on a real-life event in New York.

Another Brockden Brown novel Pettit described to me was *Arthur Mervyn,* which came out the year after *Wieland.* This one was set in Philadelphia during the yellow fever epidemic of 1793 and tells the story of a country boy who comes to the city and ends up trapped by its horrors. "It's a murder mystery with a half-deserted, disease-ridden city. Very Gothic. But it's in a city, not in a castle or out in the countryside. We're talking about an urban environment in the New World. This is all new stuff."

"So what you're saying is when people talk about American Gothic, they're really talking about something that started as Philadelphia Gothic."

"That's right. It's not really American, it's Philadelphia-based. What drives a lot of Brockden Brown's work are his experiences in what was at the time the most important city in the country. It was the capital of the country at the time, and all the big stuff was happening here. Brockden Brown was very political in his books. He sent a copy of *Wieland* to Jefferson, who had just been elected president. He didn't like Jefferson's politics, and it was almost a statement of 'This is what your country is like or going to become. We're going to have nightmares here, just different nightmares than we had in the past.'

"Brockden died at thirty-nine, but really influenced American literature and writers in the nineteenth century. And he changed Gothicism. It's no longer about the supernatural. It's about the madman with the axe."

That sounded like Poe's own story, almost to the death.

"And then you've got George Lippard, who writes the most important and popular American Gothic novel in antebellum America, *The Quaker City, or the Monks of Monk Hall.* That's everything about American Gothic crammed into one massive, weird book, all set in Philadelphia. It came out in 1845, and was the biggest selling novel in America until *Uncle Tom's Cabin,* seven years later."

Lippard's name I recognized. I had come across it before, but not for his writing. He was a friend of Poe's, one of the fellows who helped him out after the weirdness of his Moyamensing incident. In a letter to Maria Clemm, Poe names

Lippard (*L* in the letter) as one of the friends he was "indebted for more than life" who "comforted me and aided me in coming to my senses."

*The Monks of Monk Hall* is, like *Wieland,* based on a true and strange crime, this one happening on a ferry between Philadelphia and Camden, New Jersey. In that case, a man named Singleton Mercer shoots another man for trapping his sixteen-year-old sister in a brothel and having his way with her. Mercer is then acquitted on an insanity defense. Lippard spins that story through a larger, chaotic one that involves an entire corrupt enclave of city leaders and gutter creepers who nightly commit murder and torture and sexual depravity in a labyrinthine old mansion in South Philadelphia that sounds eerily similar to the Murder Castle of H. H. Holmes.

"What Lippard really introduces to the general public is not only this new kind of Gothic novel that is specific to America, but also that Philadelphia is the place where that kind of stuff comes from. I mean, Boston and New York publish Gothic novels, but they're more the European-style Gothic. Philadelphia will publish those, but also this new American Gothic. Philadelphia becomes so well known for it that some of the bylines from the time are 'by a Philadelphian' because publishers recognize the value of these things coming from a citizen of Philadelphia. Philadelphia becomes like the horror capital of the country for at least the antebellum years. "

"And that's the city E. A. P. comes to."

"That's it. All his Gothic tales prior to Philadelphia are European—'Ligeia,' 'Morella,' 'Metzengerstein'—and then he comes to Philly and, well, first gets 'The Fall of the House of Usher' out of his system, but then his work changes. We get 'The Tell-Tale Heart,' 'The Black Cat,' even the 'Masque of the Red Death,' which does have a European setting, but is about the plague . . . and Philadelphia had cholera epidemics all the time." Again, I was reminded of the Moyamensing incident and the hallucinated black bird named Cholera. "But his horror works change from supernatural to the guy with the axe who kills you for no reason. Because your eye bothered him. That's American Gothic. That's American horror.

"And that change happens, I think, because Poe is in Philadelphia. If he'd been in New York instead of Philly for those years, he would've continued writing European Gothic."

"And now you want his corpse. Or you did six years ago. I listened to an audio recording of one of the debates, actually, the one in Philadelphia. Sounded like a great time. How come there were only three of you?"

"When I started the whole Poe War, Jeff Jerome immediately jumped in, and we wanted to get all five Poe cities involved." Yes, "Poe cities" was the exact phrase he used. "Paul Lewis got involved, so that was great. I sent copies of the *City Paper* article to the Richmond Poe Museum and to the people who run the New York Poe Cottage . . . not a peep."

"Why do you think that was?"

"Well, New York, that's just because it's New York. They've got enough to do. 'There's an old writer's house here? So what? We have a million.' With Richmond, it's because they're snobs. They're like, 'We have the Poe Museum. He was raised here.' They know they're the center of the Poe universe. They won't even engage a fun argument in the press. They do a great job with Poe, but they don't seem to want to engage in anything else. Jerome wasn't like that. Lewis wasn't like that. We all saw it as this great opportunity to talk about Poe, while genuinely disagreeing with each other and having fun."

And Pettit did seem to be having a lot of fun with claiming Poe for Philadelphia. But, in getting to know him, I think the secret of Edward G. Pettit, the Philly Poe Guy, is that, given the chance, he would actually dig Poe up, or the "dark earth" that is left of him, and inter his remains in Philadelphia.

Of course, if Pettit ever did, there's a great spot for it right on 7th Street.

## *Any Friend of Poe*

When the Philadelphia Poe house finally reopened a few months later, I couldn't imagine visiting it without Pettit, so I arranged to pick him up at his home in Jenkintown, about ten miles north of the city.

That's right . . . he doesn't live anymore in the city he defends so vigorously. "Jenkintown reminds me of an old Philadelphia neighborhood, so I'm all right with it," he told me. The place was technically an independent borough instead of a town, and only covered a little more than half a square mile of land. It did, however, boast two fire departments down the street from each other due to a bit of nineteenth-century squabbling between the local Protestants and Catholics. There are stories everywhere.

Pettit moved to the borough for his wife, Kate, whose family had lived there for three generations before her birth. She runs a small toy shop in the town, and they have five daughters, ranging from elementary school age to off-and-married. He invited me into his old, vertiginous house, where we walked through green streamers and hand-drawn wanted posters in a room labeled SHERWOOD FOREST, a sign left over from a recent Robin Hood–themed birthday party for one of his daughters.

He led me upstairs to his study. It was tiny, like a space capsule, and probably had more cubic feet of books than of air. I loved it. Everything was within arm's reach and stuff was stacked on stacks of stacks, meaning every find was a hard-wrought jewel instead of a coldly catalogued item. Still, he told me, he longed for when enough of his daughters would move out that he could annex a room and expand his study.

He lit up a pipe from a rack of about a dozen or so, and smoked by a small window fan while we talked about literature and Philadelphia and Philadelphia literature. Mostly we talked about George Lippard.

The longhaired author of *The Monks of Monks Hall*, and Poe's friend and defender, was Pettit's long-time obsession, dating back to even before his interest in Poe. He'd written a piece on Lippard for the *City Paper* six months before his Poe piece. "Being the Philly Lippard Guy wasn't going to get me into *The New York Times*," he told me. At the time that I met him, Pettit was working on a book about Lippard.

Eventually, the tobacco in Pettit's bowl crisped to white ash, and it was time for our jaunt into the city to see the house that inspired one of the most well-known uxoricides in all literature.

"So do you want to go straight to the Poe house or see something else first?"

"What else you got?"

"How about Lippard's grave?"

I want to see everybody's grave. So we headed to Lawnview Cemetery in Rockledge, just three miles from Pettit's house.

This wasn't Lippard's first death site. Like Poe, he had been reinterred, although unlike Poe his remains had been carted to a completely new cemetery. He died in 1854 of tuberculosis, just shy of his thirty-second year and after out-living his wife and two children by only a few years. His last words were supposedly, "Is this death?"

He was buried at Odd Fellows Cemetery in the city, but when that plot of land was reclaimed for the living about a hundred years later, he was moved to Lawnview, an eighty-two-acre cemetery instituted in 1904.

As we entered the gates, passing a pair of patrol cars parked inside, it didn't seem at first like a cemetery. It took us a little bit of driving to even get to any tombstones.

Pettit directed me to Lippard's current address, in a crowded group of what, judging by the names on the epitaphs, appeared to be old Greek Orthodox stones.

Behind those stones was Lippard's incongruous death weight. He'd brought it with him from Odd Fellows, and it was more memorial than grave marker. Sculpted to look like it was made of rough rock, the monument was about four feet tall, five counting the stone embellishments atop it. Those included a book, a small, plain Ark of the Covenant, and an urn. Curiously, someone else had recently visited and placed a red candle on top of the memorial.

On the side of the stone was a cross above a globe and on the front, below his name and dates of life, was a scroll with a selection from the fourth chapter of the book of Luke:

> THE SPIRIT OF THE LORD IS UPON ME
> BECAUSE HE HATH ANOINTED ME TO
> PREACH THE GOSPEL TO THE POOR;
> HE HATH SENT ME TO HEAL THE
> BROKENHEARTED, TO PREACH DELIVERANCE
> TO THE CAPTIVES, AND RECOVERING OF
> SIGHT TO THE BLIND, TO SET AT
> LIBERTY, THEM THAT ARE BRUISED,
> TO PREACH THE ACCEPTABLE
> YEAR OF THE LORD.

It seemed more the grave marker of a religious leader than a man accused of salacious book-writing. Truth is, Lippard was as much a social activist as he was a novelist. He organized a secret society/proto labor union called the Brother-hood of the Union, which lasted until the 1990s. It was this group that erected the monument to its founder.

Pettit brought a cigar to leave on Lippard's grave as a token to the avid smoker. While we hung out, waiting for Pettit to smoke it down to a length worth parting with, we wandered among the surrounding stones, looking at the small, oval photographic portraits on graves that dated back decades.

But then it was time to take our leave of Poe's friend and catch back up with Poe.

## If These Walls Could Scream

The most arresting thing about the Edgar Allan Poe National Historic Site is, well, what's across the street from it . . . a two-story mural of the face of Edgar Allan Poe.

Philadelphia is a city of murals, thanks to a social initiative that began in the 1980s that put artists and at-risk youths

*Grave of George Lippard*

and criminals to work making the drabbest parts of the city bright and colorful and worth taking a picture of. There are hundreds of murals across the city, and not just generic civic ones, but quirky, pop culture–ridden things, as well. I saw a massive three-story mural of basketball star Dr. J in a suit and a smaller tribute to David Lynch's 1977 weirdfest *Eraserhead*.

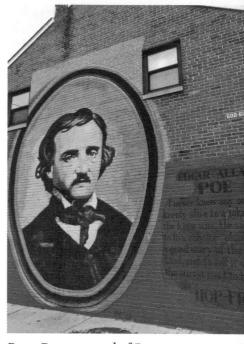

*Peter Pagast mural of Poe*

The mural of Poe on the side of the red-brick building at Green and North 7th Street was painted by an artist named Peter Pagast in 1999. It features Poe's face framed in an oval beside the opening lines of his story "Hop-Frog": "I never knew anyone so keenly alive to a joke as the king was. He seemed to live only for joking. To tell a good story of the joke kind, and to tell it well, was the surest road to his favor."

The likeness was a good one, and depicted him more stately than the usual care-worn Poe we're used to seeing. The quote was a strange one to choose, but I liked it just for that fact and, after about my fiftieth picture of the mural, Pettit observed, "I just wish it was the Philadelphia version of Poe. No mustache, you know?"

Not only did Poe not have a mustache while he lived in Philadelphia, but during his infamous Moyamensing moment on his return years later, he had it shaved off. According to Pettit, "He wanted it shaved to be in disguise, but anybody in Philly who would have known him wouldn't have recognized him with a mustache anyway."

Poe lived in quite a few places during his six years in the city, but only one still stands, at 532 North 7th Street, in the Spring Garden neighborhood. He only lived there about a year in 1843, and the building has changed a bit since that time, but mostly through accretion. Today, it's actually three buildings in one. A large, newer brick duplex faces the street, while the smaller brick house that Poe would have known extends out the back. What would have been his front door is now the side door of the whole complex.

For its preservation, we can once again thank Richard Gimbel. In 1933, he bought the place, filled it with furniture he claimed to be Poe's, painted HERE POE WROTE THE RAVEN or some such marketing fluff on the side of it, and turned it into a museum.

He willed it to the city, and in the late 1970s, it became a National Historic Site—as in a place run by the United States National Park Service, the same guys in charge of Mount Rushmore and Yosemite and, well, Philadelphia's Independence Hall, about a mile away. That means it's run by the federal government and staffed by park rangers in Smokey the Bear hats. It's also why I (mostly) keep calling it by its full name, "Edgar Allan Poe National Historic Site," instead of merely "Poe House."

Pettit spun it this way in his *City Paper* piece: "If you are a law-abiding citizen, then my arguments for a Philadelphian Poe are unnecessary. Congress has already legislated that Poe belongs to the city. In 1978, the Poe House at Seventh and Spring Garden was added to the National Park Service as a National Historic Site. Congress had to pass a law granting the interpretation of Poe's life and legacy to the management of the NPS at the Philadelphia Poe site. Poe is a Philadelphian by law."

The site has no admission fee, and the entrance is through the newer parts of the building. The space inside the duplex has been turned into a small gift shop and exhibit area.

"I was hoping Helen would be here," Pettit told me after being greeted by the park ranger on duty. "I really wanted you to meet her."

He meant Helen McKenna-Uff, a tall woman in her fifties who is also a Poe

*What would have been the front of Poe's house in his day, Edgar Allan Poe National Historic Site*

performer when she's not wearing the park ranger badge, the only female Poe performer I'd hear of on this trek. "She's pretty good. She also does Sarah Helen Whitman." McKenna-Uff was also the Edgar Allan Poe tied up in the back of the town car on the *City Paper* cover.

In the small exhibit, there was a miniature model that highlighted the part of the building that was the house where Poe lived, a plaster cast of the Edgar Allan Poe bust at the Poe Cottage in the Bronx, and an original 1843 copy of the first issue of James Russell Lowell's short-lived magazine *The Pioneer,* opened to the first-ever printing of "The Tell-Tale Heart." There were piles of Junior Ranger Guides with Poe on the cover and paintings on the wall. George Lippard's now-familiar-to-me countenance made a small appearance on an exhibit with a bon mot about his literary works and relationship with Poe.

There was also a large interactive Poe head, black and white and two-dimensional, where children could solve a cipher, crank a hot-air balloon out of his noggin, listen to recordings of his work, open pieces to view items from his stories, and generally just enjoy interacting with a big black-and-white, two-dimensional Edgar Allan Poe head.

In the adjacent viewing room, visitors can watch an introductory movie about Poe and the Poe National Historic Site. On our visit, the walls of that room happened to be covered with crayon drawings from children illustrating "The Black Cat" . . . and doing a decent grisly job of it too, with the black felines hanging by the neck from tree limbs and human hands reaching out from crevices in brick walls. The site also features a reading room in that part of the house, decorated according to Poe's "Philosophy of Furniture," even down to the crimson-tinted window glass.

Even without a red sign admonishing people to watch their steps and the black and yellow caution stripes laid down on the floor of the doorway, the transition from exhibit space to Poe house was an obvious one. The actual building where Poe lived was empty, and the walls had been scraped down to a gray, patterned strangeness. It looked like the decaying house where the harried detective finds and faces off with the serial killer at the end of the movie.

It was far removed from how H. P. Lovecraft described it in 1935, soon after the house opened and with all of Gimbel's set dressing: "Of the Poe houses still standing, none comes to life more vividly as a typical home than this unpretentious cottage." In fact, of all the Poe sites Lovecraft visited and wrote about, he seemed particularly taken with the Philadelphia site, ending an otherwise chronological journey through the world of Poe with a prediction about the house in which I was now standing: "This shrine is likely to become, as time passes, a leading place of pilgrimage for those who revere genius and admire one of the greatest and unhappiest of its exemplars."

And while that latter statement may well have ended up being true, the former one is a bit off, thanks to the NPS. One of the requirements of an NPS site is that it not be cheesy about things. Restorations can be performed only if there's genuine proof it's being restored to appear as it did at the time period for which it's preserved. Since we don't have any of that, they couldn't pull a Gimbel. They got rid of everything that wasn't original to it, down to the paint and paper on the walls.

As a result, each room looked like it was covered in old television static or the claw marks of a trapped man or Rorschach tests that you can stare at for hours to see if you're crazy. I said as much to Pettit.

"Yeah, it's a cool effect. The downside is it can reinforce the stereotype of Poe wandering crumbling halls, bemoaning his existence," he replied. Admittedly, that's my favorite version of Poe.

Nevertheless, Pettit told me that the best time to come see the house is during the nighttime tours they conduct in October, the busiest month for the site. "There's no electricity in the Poe house itself, just in the front part, so it makes it really atmospheric and creepy."

The house has three floors and a cellar, with two rooms on each floor. . . . all more or less empty. Every once in a while something was stashed in a closet . . . a plush orangutan or pamphlets for the house. In one empty room, Pettit walked

*Bedroom, Edgar Allan Poe National Historic Site*

to the corner and lifted up a floorboard. Hidden beneath it was a severed hand. "It was a heart the last time I was here," he explained.

It was a reminder that here Poe had written "The Tell-Tale Heart," the original printing of which we had just seen a few floors below. The story of a psycho crazy enough to kill for no reason but not crazy enough to be protected from his own conscience is said to have been inspired by a famous murder in Salem, MA, as well as a Charles Dickens story. "The Tell-Tale Heart" is probably his second most famous work today, after "The Raven."

There was plenty of light in the house since one whole side of it, what would have been the front wall back in Poe's day, had plenty of windows, but the rooms still seemed dingy, thanks to that wonderful and inadvertent wall texture. The gloominess of the rooms was broken here and there with scrims—stretches of cloth painted with household furniture—a fireplace, a desk. In one room, a scrim filled a window that faced an interior wall with a scene as Poe might have seen it in his day. In another, we walked in on Poe himself. The scrim depicts him seated at his desk, facing away from the room so that we only see his back, one hand on his quill, the other either holding down the paper or reaching out to pet a lolling Catterina.

Poe and his family moved to this house because it was more rural and wholesome-seeming than their previous Philadelphia residence. They felt the need for a better environment because a year earlier, Virginia suffered what Poe termed a "ruptured blood-vessel." In a letter dated February 3, 1842, to his friend Frederick W. Thomas, Poe wrote, "My dear little wife has been dangerously ill. About a fortnight since, in singing, she ruptured a blood-vessel, and it was only on yesterday that the physicians gave me any hope of her recovery."

Whether his reference to a "ruptured blood-vessel" was denial, a mistake, a doctor diagnosis, or just what he called it is unknown. Certainly, consumption wasn't an alien thing to anybody living back then and especially not to one whose mother had died from it. In addition, in a letter he wrote a year after Virginia's death, he still referenced it as such, even in the context of her five-year illness, an illness that worsened in one of these rooms and ended in that small room at the Poe Cottage in New York.

Moving on to grim topics of a fictional nature, next was the cellar.

It's as empty as any of the rooms are, but its floor is brick, and its walls are rough stone, covered in places with chipped cement plaster. Cobwebs bestrew the low rafters almost as if they were purposely put there by human hands. The central stairway extends down to the middle of the cellar, although a sign forbade using the steps, and a large crack in its post seemed to justify it.

As a result, we had to backtrack to enter at a side door that connected the cellar to the front part of the house. To get there we descended a stairway and

*Scrim of Poe, Edgar Allan Poe National Historic Site*

went through a small landing that bore a grand total of four bronze plaques designating the house as historic. And you know how much I love Poe plaques.

One was undated and merely labeled the house as what it was. Another harkened from 1966 and referenced the rejuvenation of a park around the house. And then there were two matching plaques dating to 1971 that greedily claimed Poe's authorship of "The Raven" to place it atop the largess of works Poe wrote in this city.

It's easy to roll one's eyes at how many places claim to be the birthplace of "The Raven," but Philadelphia has a somewhat legitimate claim since it was here where he read *Barnaby Rudge,* and here where he published the tell-tale observation about Rudge's raven. Maybe the fireplace on the second floor was the actual place where "each separate, dying ember wrought its ghost upon the floor." I still hold with New York, since Poe wasn't one to sit on works, and he generally tried to get them published as early and as often as possible to bring in the slim amount of cash that he could, but there is probably a slight case to be made for the raven speaking "nevermore" with a Philly accent.

A yellow paper sign on a metal door bore a cat and the words ENTRANCE TO THE CELLAR. We opened it and immediately espied a fake black cat set in a niche in one wall. The simple Halloween decoration further revealed why the cellar of the Poe National Historic Site was so interesting . . . it was this cellar that almost certainly helped inspire Poe to write "The Black Cat."

*Cellar, Edgar Allan Poe National Historic Site*

"The Black Cat" is almost a companion story to "The Tell-Tale Heart." It was published around the same time and deals with the same idea of inhuman murder and human conscience. It's another one of those "I'm not crazy, and listen to me prove it" kind of stories, where the narrator grows to loathe a pet black cat that may or may not actually be his wife and then does actually kill his wife. It climaxes in the cellar, where he fixes some masonry, admires his handi-work, and then is revealed to the police by a mewing of the black cat that had been trapped behind the wall when the narrator inadvertently bricked it in with the bludgeoned corpse of his wife. Such a great story.

It was published in Philadelphia in August 1843 in the *United States Saturday Evening Post,* months before he left the house, and one can't help but imagine Poe coming down here and staring at the walls, testing out the story. Maria, upstairs caring for an ill Virginia, calls down to him, "Eddie, dear, where are you?"

"I'm in the cellar."

"What are you doing?"

"Planning the murder of a wife."

"Okay. Could you bring the towels when you come up?"

The inspiration for his story might be even more apparent thanks to a wife-sized, give or take a cat, brick chimney jutting out from one wall. Had you not known that Poe lived and wrote "The Black Cat" there, you'd have still imme-

*David Caccia raven statue, Edgar Allan Poe National Historic Site*

diately seen it as the hiding place for a body. At some point the front of the hollow column collapsed, leaving it even more obviously ready for a victim. I immediately clambered in and made Pettit take my picture.

The cellar is the highlight of the tour because of that direct connection to the story, making it an artifact like Grip the Raven or the Poe Mantel or the Fordham bell. Even though it seems little has been preserved from Poe's life, it's still pretty amazing what is.

Finally, after hanging out in the "Philosophy of Furniture" room for a while and leafing through old maps and pictures, we exited to the fenced-in lawn beside the house. This was the park referenced in the 1966 plaque outside the basement door. It was large and open and with regularly spaced trees. Closer to the blank brick wall that had once born Gimbel's museum marketing about "The Raven" was a massive black metal raven sculpture by David Caccia atop a ten- or fifteen-foot-tall matching black beam.

The wings of the bronze bird were spread dramatically and it seemed to be two-to-three times the size of a real raven, but it was hard to tell because it was so high above us. However, it is big enough that its open beak often shelters nests from other birds. The shadow of that massive black raven has been floating on the blank brick wall and courtyard since 1979, and it has become one of the icons of the site, along with the mural of Poe.

While I stood breaking my neck to admire the raven, Pettit was looking elsewhere, out across the lawn. He pointed out a vague spot in the middle and said, "That's where we would put a statue of Poe."

It's the only thing Philly's really missing when it comes to the author.

Besides the body.

*Grave of Edgar Allan Poe, Westminster Burying Ground*

# CHAPTER 5

# Maryland

*The Play Is the Tragedy, "Man"*

A MAN IN A PURPLE-AND-BLACK JESTER'S COSTUME and mask waved around an enormous bottle of fire-red liquid as he drunkenly capered and welcomed us into the hall. Suddenly, a tall, thin man wearing a top hat and purple-and-red eye mask and brandishing a silver-topped walking stick leaned in behind him and whispered something about a cask of amontillado and the family crypt.

We weren't in Venice. We were in Baltimore.

Of all the places Poe lived, it is the city of Baltimore with which he has historically been the most associated, even though he lived there for only about five years. One reason overshadows them all for this association, and we'll get six feet deep into that one shortly, but it's bolstered by a few other salient points. Let's start with those.

When Poe lived in Baltimore, he was in his twenties, spending almost a year in the city, before his West Point woes and then four more not too long after.

His father's family, the Poes, were from Baltimore by way of Ireland. It was here that his brother Henry was sent after the death of their mother, and here where Henry died at the age of twenty-four.

It was in this city that Poe met the two people who were the closest to him in his entire life: Virginia, his wife, and her mother, Maria "Muddy" Clemm, who were both, of course, also his relatives.

It was here that he met John Pendleton Kennedy, the man who took an interest in him and his work and not only helped him out financially when he was past the brink of despair, but also helped him get the gig at the *Southern Literary Messenger* that was his first decent job and the start of his magazine career.

It was also while he was living in this city that his fiction career really began. Even though his first published stories, the *Tales of the Folio Club* pieces, were published in Philadelphia, he was living in Baltimore at the time they came out. These were "Metzengerstein," "The Duke de L'Omelette," "A Tale of Jerusalem,"

"A Decided Loss," and "The Bargain Lost." (These last two were later called "Loss of Breath" and "Bon-Bon," as Poe continued to refine and add to the *Tales of the Folio Club* throughout the 1830s).

The stories were published anonymously, and he didn't get paid for them, so it was more like a false start to that career. However, it was also here that he got his first income from a short story, winning $50 in a *Baltimore Saturday Visiter* contest for his "MS. Found in a Bottle." He also more than likely wrote key stories such as "Berenice"—the first real Poesque story—as well as "King Pest," "Morella," and "The Unparalleled Adventure of One Hans Pfaall" in this city; all these stories would get published in the *Southern Literary Messenger* soon after he moved to Richmond.

He never lived in Baltimore again after moving in the summer of 1835 . . . and I mean that in more than one way. Baltimore is where he died. And that death has yielded more interest than his entire life. Heck, his life and death have separate Wikipedia entries.

He wasn't supposed to be in Baltimore on that night in October 1849, and no one really knows what happened to Poe in the mysterious few days before he was found and taken to the hospital, but Baltimore is where his merry-go-round stopped. So this is where he is buried.

If, as many postulate, the mystery of his death is the most important contributor to our interest in his life and work, that makes Baltimore extremely important to both his literary and physical legacy.

Did I mention I'm from Maryland?

As I write this, I've been a New Englander, living just forty-five minutes from the site of Poe's birth for a good six years. But my first quarter century of this fever called "Living," give or take a detour for college, was spent an hour from his grave. I might be guilty of favoritism toward Poe's physical legacy in this state.

But honestly, factually, historically—of all the Poe cities, Baltimore was the first to really start embracing him as their own. The people of Baltimore preserved the house he lived in, commissioned a magnificent statue of him, erected a grand monument above his bones, and, in 1996, named their brand-new and brand-important National Football League team after his most famous poem.

However, in 2013, a year when most of the Poe cities have pushed his physical legacy far forward, the legacy of Poe in Baltimore is shakier. That's for a few reasons, but the most important of them is that for almost the entire year of 2013, the Baltimore Poe House was shut down.

That's why I was at a party with Fortunato and Montresor in an ex-church whose yard bore the very last earthly remnants of Edgar Allan Poe, give or take a lock of hair. It was a fundraiser for the Poe House.

## Pigskin Poe

Driving into the city, one of the first things you see in the distance is the massive M&T Bank Stadium, known colloquially as the "Bank." Technically, it's the largest monument to Edgar Allan Poe in the universe.

In 1996, Baltimore got its first NFL team since the Baltimore Colts moved to Indianapolis under the cover of night in 1984. The Colts are still around, so Baltimore needed a new name for this new team. It had to be fierce. Something that could be respected on the field. It had to match up in a division full of Steelers and Bengals and Jaguars and, uh, Oilers. An entire state needed to be proud of it. It had to look good on clothes and merchandise. More than that, it had to make money. Tons of money. It was, after all, to be the brand of a company worth hundreds of millions of dollars.

According to an article in the *Baltimore Sun,* some of the names under consideration on a list of about a hundred were the Rhinos, Bombers, Steamers, Mustangs, Railers, Marauders, and Americans. The corporate machine went into action, taking surveys and polls, analyzing market data, and spending massive amounts of money to make sure the most profitable name would be chosen.

In the end, the biggest data point was a large poll of the residents of Baltimore. After all the above work, the team's stakeholders narrowed the potential names down to three finalists: Ravens, Marauders, and Americans. A phone election was then conducted by the *Baltimore Sun* that pulled in more than 33,000 votes. The winning name nabbed more than 21,000, while the two also-rans garnered just over five thousand votes each.

And Baltimore named its professional football team . . . after a nineteenth-century poem written by a man whose popular reputation is that of a depressed alcoholic obsessed with death. The system works.

More likely, that's the power of Poe.

The fact that that Baltimore named its identity-forming football team after Poe's "The Raven" is pretty much the only point I need for the central thesis of this book. This one fact is enough to prove the oddity of Poe and his influence. If this were a trial, I'd throw a Baltimore Raven helmet, with its purple raven head and gold "B," into the jury box as Exhibit A, and then walk out of the courtroom for a Big Mac.

I mean, how do you reference poetry in NFL football and not get laughed out of the league? Could New England have pulled off naming its football team after anything Longfellow wrote? Maybe the New England Birds of Passage or the New England Village Blacksmiths? No. And that's because, in Baltimore's case, it's not just poetry. It's Poe.

Of course, Baltimore is no stranger to black birds. During baseball season, the black and orange of the oriole, also the state bird, has adorned the banners on its lampposts for half a century. These days, during football season, it's the black and purple of the raven.

The year 2013 was an up-and-down one for the team. In February, the Ravens won the Super Bowl for the second time in the team's short life. They found themselves and, by extension, Poe found himself in the brightest spotlight of modern sports. Well, other than during the infamous and spooky half-hour blackout that occurred in the middle of the event. Later that year, as I drove past the bird banners and the stadium, all was just as empty and quiet as the blackout. The very next season, this championship team didn't even make the playoffs.

I'd been to M&T Bank Stadium years before, but didn't remember anything especially Poesque there. I searched the Ravens website and online shop, but found no images of a forlorn, mustachioed poet. The closest I got to a direct Poe reference was the name of the Ravens mascot. Originally, there were three Ravens mascots, each one, naturally, named Edgar, Allan, and Poe. At some point they ditched the other two and just kept Poe. Otherwise, the lack of Poe references made it seem as if they were doing their best to divorce the bird from the poet.

Thinking this was kind of weird, I e-mailed the team to see if anything on the grounds of the stadium directly referenced the poet instead of just the bird. It made sense to me that the history of the name would somehow be represented . . . maybe with a plaque or a restaurant named after him. Surprisingly, my e-mail received a response. It was from the vice president of stadium operations. Here was the answer I received in full: "There aren't any references to Edgar Allan Poe in M&T Bank Stadium."

There was no "I'm not sure" or "Let me check" or "You can eat at the BBQ Pit and Pendulum." It's almost as if the line were boilerplate, taken directly from an internal document that mandated that the team try to push Poe as far away from the bird as they could. Thinking through it again, it made sense. To maximize the benefit of the brand, the bird has to be the property of the Baltimore Ravens, Inc., and not that of a dead poet. When somebody says "raven," they want "Baltimore Ravens" to be the first thing they think of, not Edgar Allan Poe.

Certainly, driving around the city these days, it's impossible to know whether the ravens you see in the graffiti are references to the poet who is buried there or the team that plays there. Either way, though, it's still all because of Poe.

## Party for Poe

The fundraiser Lindsey and I were attending was called The Cask of Amontillado Wine Tasting Among the Bones. It was themed according to the titular Poe story, with actors in Fortunato and Montresor costumes wandering around and performing snippets of the story, but it also had a bit of "Hop-Frog" to it. Maybe even a pinch of "The Masque of the Red Death" thrown in.

It was being held at Westminster Hall, which was built in 1852 as a Presbyterian church. In 1977, the building lost its religion and became a function hall. It's now owned by the surrounding University of Maryland School of Law and run by a nonprofit trust. On its grounds is the tall white pillar that marks the grave of Edgar Allan Poe. He was only about seventy-five feet from his own party.

On the stage at the front of the space, backed by the massive, colorful pipes of an 1882 Johnson pipe organ, a range of entertainment was going on, including goth belly dancers, an Irish band, and a performance of "The Raven" by veteran actor Tony Tsendeas.

*Westminster Hall*

Elsewhere in the main hall, they were holding the wine-tasting that included a limited edition batch of Poe-themed wine. Tour guides were taking groups into the catacombs below the hall. A palm reader measured out fates in the balcony. A silent auction was under way that included an old paving stone from Poe's grave during a prior landscaping design and a piece of horsehair plaster from the Baltimore Poe home that had been salvaged during a restoration. Somebody beat my bid for the latter.

They even had a noted Poe scholar "on display": Jeff Savoye, secretary and treasurer of the Edgar Allan Poe Society of Baltimore, who was one of the editors of the latest edition of *The Collected Letters of Edgar Allan Poe* and who runs the end-all Edgar Allan Poe resource, eapoe.org. He was on a dais off to the side, thumbing obliviously through some quaint and curious volume of forgotten lore. I didn't know who he was at the time, but those two resources ended up being invaluable to me beyond any others in this book project. In front of him was a small display case containing various pop culture items related to Poe, as well as a piece of Poe's coffin fashioned into a pen holder and a lock of Virginia's hair, both part of the holdings of the Edgar Allan Poe Society of Baltimore.

If I'm not making a big enough deal about those latter two artifacts it's because somehow, despite my senses having been sharpened to anything Poe . . . I completely missed them. I vaguely remember the case having a DVD copy of Roger Corman's and Vincent Price's 1963 film *The Raven,* though. I learned about the artifacts later because my wife brought it up after the event was over.

"That coffin piece and lock of hair were pretty cool."

"What?"

"Oh, you didn't see that?"

"No. No I didn't. I guess I was too busy looking at the orangutan on the tightrope."

"They had an orangutan there? And a tightrope?"

"No."

And while missing those artifacts might seem like reason enough to scrap this whole book project, I was able to make up for the botch later in my Maryland trek . . . with a totally different piece of Poe coffin and totally different locks of hair.

At one point during the event, I wandered through some of the hallways outside the auditorium, winding up at an area that a sign on the wall called Poe's Proscenium. It was a stretch of hallway that connected Westminster Hall to the rest of the Maryland School of Law.

The walls were decorated with images from Baltimore history, like an ancient map of the city and an image of a painting by Maryland-born artist Charles Willson Peale called *Rachel Weeping,* in which his wife cries above the body of their dead child. Another image depicted General Sam Smith, a Revolutionary War hero and United States senator buried on the Westminster grounds.

Most of what adorned the walls was about Poe, or, rather, his grave. A series of black-and-white pictures showed visitors and ceremonies at his grave throughout the twentieth century. Painted in large letters above the photos were quotes from various newspaper accounts about the unveiling of his grave monument. Except for one quote that stood out from the rest. It was from Vincent Price, dated 1977: "This place gives me the creeps."

It wasn't a reference to Westminster Hall, nor to anything in its graveyard. He said it upon his visit to Poe's Baltimore digs.

The people who organized the wine-tasting event had held similar events over the years, but this particular one had more urgency than past ones. The Poe House for which they were fundraising was closed to tourists for the first time in its seventy-year history.

At the time of the event, they weren't sure whether the house was ever going to permanently open again. In all of 2013, it opened for a grand total of eight days. I found myself there on one of them.

## Evicting Poe

The welcome signs for the city of Baltimore always seem to have warning labels attached. Just about every year, good old Charm City makes the top-ten list for most dangerous cities in the country. Poe himself didn't even make it out alive. When tourists visit, they mostly stick to the Inner Harbor, which was specially designed by NASA scientists in nearby D.C. to be as different and separated from the rest of the city as the laws of planetary engineering would allow.

But the area around the Baltimore Poe House and Museum, in particular, gets a lot of negative attention. It's part of the oldest housing project in the city, called Poe Homes, dating back to the end of 1940. I don't think I've ever read an account of the attraction that didn't include a caution about the area. "It's cool, but wear Kevlar."

The area is certainly not a welcoming one, but is it outright hostile under ordinary conditions? Let's just say you don't have to be Snake Plissken to visit. Based on my experience, it's no more dangerous a spot than the neighborhoods in the Bronx and Philadelphia where its counterpart houses are located. Or many spots in any city, I guess. Same rules apply: Be smart. Don't be unlucky. It's just that the Poe House in Baltimore has always received more press than the other Poe sites, so the bodies in its walls get aired out more often.

If you drive there, it's an easy visit. There's on-street parking right in front of the house. And even the most ardent Poe fan will find it hard to stay longer than an hour or two. It's also only open during the brightly lit non-mugging hours and is regularly patrolled by police.

The actual downside of the house is that it's about a mile and a half away from the Inner Harbor, meaning that only the diehard make it to the house. The Baltimore Poe House receives only about five thousand people a year, which is a good number of diehards, but that doesn't bring in enough revenue to run the house without a subsidy from the city . . . a subsidy which was recently yanked.

I hate starting the section on one of the most important Poe sites on such a downer note, but the fact is 2013 wasn't a great year for Edgar Allan Poe in his death city of Baltimore, despite starting off with a Ravens Super Bowl win.

In 2010, the year after the invigorating Edgar Allan Poe Bicentennial, the city of Baltimore decided that the measly $85,000 dollars they were dedicating to it was too big a slice of the annual budget for something that helped define its international reputation and cultural heritage. With that money gone and assumedly invested into filling a few potholes somewhere, the house fumed along on reserve funds until the end of 2012, when it closed.

A group called Poe Baltimore was formed as a result of the closing to figure out how to run the house privately. However, in 2013, they did make an exception, since barring entry to anything Poe-related in October is a crime against nature and humanity. After taking advantage of the closing to renovate the house, Poe Baltimore opened it during the October busy season on the weekends for four hours each day.

I have to admit, even though I lived in the small, oddly shaped state of Maryland for twenty-five years, I had never made it inside the Poe House. I don't know why. That confession might invalidate this entire book . . . or validate it. I don't know.

The day I finally rectified that omission was October 26, a week before Halloween. For me to fit the visit into my schedule, I had to fly in and fly out the same day, the first time I'd ever pulled off that aerial feat, while my parents, who still live in the state, chauffeured me around for the few hours that I was on Maryland soil. I'm not sure whether they suddenly regretted giving me the college textbook that introduced me to Poe two decades ago.

We pulled up in front of 203 Amity Street at 11:30, half an hour before its noon opening time. Already, about a dozen people were milling around on the sidewalk in front of the entrance, waiting for the house to open. At this point, the place had been closed for almost an entire year.

The Baltimore Poe House and Museum is a thin, two-story brick house at the end of a row of connecting brick houses whose architecture mismatches the Poe House in every way except the brick building materials. The other houses don't have the green shutters or the sloping red roof or chimney or the Cyclopean gable window. You could see the jagged scar down the side of the house where the new bricks overlapped with old ones. The housing project extended behind it, while across the street was an empty lot that stretched for blocks. Plans are currently underway to build a pair of new apartment buildings and a park on that lot, as part of a massive project to revitalize the area.

Poe lived here in the early to mid-1830s. Back then, the area was outside the city limits, in the countryside, and it was half of a freestanding duplex. A brick archway at the side of the house today was once the entrance to a narrow alley between the halves of the duplex. The house's address at the time was 3 Amity Street.

It was a cold day, so I sat in the shelter of the car instead of getting in line. My parents weren't going to join me in the Poe House due to some mobility problems. You pretty much have to be able to climb monkey bars to navigate the tiny, twisty interior of the place.

While we sat there, a patrol car pulled up, singled out a local who was walking down the sidewalk, made him sit on the curb, and started questioning him. I couldn't hear the whole story, but the man being questioned was definitely agitated and defensive. And it all happened right behind our bumper. Eventually, the officer let the man go, but it was enough of an altercation that it forced me to include the first few paragraphs of this section after planning to skip the whole issue.

Eventually the line started growing long enough that I realized I needed to jump in. Once in line, I counted about sixty people waiting to enter. Soon, a different cop pulled up and parked across from the house. He got out and leaned against his patrol car, fiddling with his cell phone and just hanging out. I got the feeling he wasn't there for fear of the sedate line of bookish people waiting to enter the literary land-mark.

Somehow, the guy behind me mistook my chattering teeth for a hello, and we started talking. He was visiting with his family from northern Virginia. They had tried to enter the house the weekend before. Despite arriving an hour before closing time, the line was too long, and

*Edgar Allan Poe House*

they didn't make it in before the cut-off. So they were trying again that week.

While I waited in line, jotting down notes like "cop questions guy behind our bumper, cold day, sixty people, fiction writers don't have to worry about lines and weather," a woman approached me.

"You're busy writing. Are you a journalist?"

"No, worse . . . travel writer." I then explained my project to her.

She handed me a card and introduced herself. Her name was Kristen Har-beson, and she was the president of Poe Baltimore. Because I was unprepared to interview her, and she was busy making sure everybody was having a good experience, we didn't talk too much. Months later, though, I called her up to discuss the organization and the future of the Baltimore Poe House and Museum.

When Poe Baltimore was formed in mid-2012, they found themselves in an unenviable situation. An extremely important national and local cultural land-mark had been defunded and was about to close, and they were smack dab in the middle of some bad PR around the circumstances of that closure. Certainly, they were sharing that bad PR with the city of Baltimore, but the city, being used to that kind of thing, merely shrugged, balled it up, and threw it atop their already massive pile of bad PR (third largest peak in the eastern United States).

In this case, rumors were rampant that the house would never open again or would be subsumed by another museum or be closed to walk-up visitors. None of the rumors were true, or at least they didn't turn out to be true, but the one unavoidable reality was that, much like Edgar Allan Poe himself, there was no way his house would ever be self-sustaining. This was 100 percent because of its size and location.

"The situation wasn't actually as bad as the rumors," explained Harbeson to me. "Sure, it wasn't great that the city was pulling the funding, and, yes, keeping the house open is a huge financial problem, but long before the house was closed, the plans for Poe Baltimore were in place and reopening was always part of the plan. The city unfortunately didn't communicate that plan very well."

She went on to explain that the rumor of the Poe House becoming accessible on only a limited basis through scheduled tours bussed from another museum came out because of the role that Baltimore's B&O Railroad Museum played in transitioning the Poe House to a private entity. "The B&O Museum acted as the midwife for the process. It's a very well-run museum, and the city signed a year-long contract with it to help build this brand-new organization. We also invited its director of grants to be on the Poe House board, because that kind of experience is invaluable to running a small museum. The director of the B&O also came on board after the contract was over because he was extremely committed to the success of Poe Baltimore."

Harbeson is no slouch when it comes to small museums. She grew up in New York's Hudson Valley, where she worked at Sunnyside, the home-turned-museum of none other than author Washington Irving. Sunnyside is a photographic negative of the Baltimore Poe House. The picturesque ivy-covered cottage sits right on the banks of the Hudson in a touristy part of the state, just a mile from the author's beloved Sleepy Hollow. If Poe had just thought to give the horse in "Metzengerstein" a headless rider.

Her experiences there inspired her to pursue a master's of history and a certificate in museum studies at the University of Delaware. She came to Baltimore to work on some of the ship museums permanently anchored in the harbor—such as the nineteenth-century U.S.S. *Constellation* and the USCGC *Taney*, the last surviving warship from the Pearl Harbor bombing—and she got involved with the board of the Small Museum Association, as well as with various preservation societies.

She has lived in the city for the past fourteen years and, today, she lives less than a mile from the Poe House. Despite all that museum experience, the Poe House isn't the job that buys her bread and milk. She's the chief of staff for an incumbent in the Maryland House of Delegates.

All in all, with her small museum and political experience, she sounds perfect for the gig. But, more important, is she a Poe fan?

"I'm a big reader. I love the mystery genre and the gothic sensibility, so I do love Poe. I'm not as single-mindedly obsessed with him as some are." Translation: I would never undertake this project you're on. "But I also have that hometown pride in him. I see Poe as a very Baltimore writer. And what I mean by that is when I find myself describing him, it's the same way I describe the city—gritty, dark, fantastical, wonderful, flawed."

"So what is the actual future of the Poe House? Right now, while we're talking, it's February of 2014, and it's still closed."

"Right. So our target date has always been spring of 2014. We're planning a big event for it. Now, with the funding the way it is, it'll probably only be open on weekends at first, which is when the majority of people visit anyway, and it won't be open year-round. Hopefully we'll be able to expand those hours in the future, though." Since you're holding this book when you are, you'll be able to test most of those predictions right away.

She continued "Keep in mind, Poe Baltimore is more than the Poe House. The official charter of the organization is beyond the house and is dedicated to preserving and expanding Poe's legacy in the city overall. That said, everything we do supports the house in some way."

To me, all that sounds like good news. Sure, it's currently a step back from what the Poe House was in the past, but maybe that step back is to gather room for a running start to give one of the most important Poe sites we have better times than it has ever known. It's a big maybe, but it's still a maybe. I do know that the Bronx figured out how to do it with its Poe home. So did Philadelphia. And neither of those houses is in a touristy location, either, so there's no reason Baltimore shouldn't be able to figure out how to keep this piece of Poe alive and accessible.

However, when I was in line that October weekend, waiting to get into the Poe House, I didn't have that context and everything looked pretty bleak to me. Mostly, though, I was wondering how long before I made it inside and whether my fate would be that of the Virginia family behind me. Soon, I noticed the people who entered were coming out pretty fast. Turns out, most of the holdup was the size of the house. They could let in only fifteen people at a time.

It's hard to gauge the size of its interior from the outside, but the house is made up of a total of only five rooms spanning two floors and an attic. When Poe lived here, he had four roommates, Virginia, Maria Clemm, his grandmother, and Virginia's brother, Henry (not to be confused with Poe's own brother, Henry). That's extremely close quarters.

Outside the front door are a couple plaques. A metal one dating from 1972 calls the site out as a registered National Historic Landmark and explains, THIS SITE POSSESSES EXCEPTIONAL VALUE IN COMMEMORATING OR ILLUSTRATING

THE HISTORY OF THE UNITED STATES. Small print at the bottom further clarifies that "exceptional value" is defined as much less than $85,000 per annum.

Another, more modern placard showed images of Poe and Virginia Clemm and tells the history of the house in three paragraphs.

A few short, green wooden steps led to the front door. This particular set of stairs was new and had, at one point, become symbolic of the sudden vulnerability of Poe's legacy in Baltimore. Within a month of the house closing down, its previous set of front steps were stolen and the door graffitied.

Today, the house looked pristine, and those steps led up into a parlor small enough that one couldn't spin a child around without doing damage to both the walls and the child. The room's only architectural feature was a fireplace, but it had a few informational placards on the walls and some artifacts on display. These included porcelain Rockingham dinnerware and some glasses etched with an "A" that had belonged to the Allans in Richmond. EDGAR WOULD HAVE DINED ON THESE PLATES AND DRUNK FROM THIS CRYSTAL read the informational placard above it. There was also a long bronze plaque that looked like it was at one time affixed to the house: IN THIS HOUSE LIVED EDGAR ALLAN POE. Finally, a white copy of the Edmund Quinn bust from the Fordham cottage, similar to the one I saw at the Edgar Allan Poe National Historic Site in Philadelphia, welcomed visitors into the house.

From there, it was two steps down into a similarly sized room with another fireplace. This room would have been the kitchen. It was empty of furniture, but the walls were covered with information. There was a map of Poe-related places in the city and a painting of the house as it looked in Poe's day. Bracketing the fireplace were placards listing the works he is "presumed" to have written within these walls. To the left of the fireplace were the stories: "MS. Found in a Bottle," "The Visionary," "Lion-izing: A Tale," "Shadow: A Parable," "Siope: A Fable," "Berenice," "Morella," "King Pest," and "The Unparalleled Adventure of One Hans Pfaall." To the right, a much less impressive selection of his poems: "Latin Hymn," "Enigma (On Shakespeare)," "Serenade," "To—[Sleep On]," "Fanny," "The Coliseum, "To Elizabeth," and "To Mary [Winfree]."

Despite there being nothing in the room, it was relatively crowded. Thanks to a volunteer with an arm like a metal gate, I quickly found out it was because we had to be staged for ascending the thin stairs to the next level.

When enough people had exited from their visit upstairs, it was finally my turn. I sucked in my breath and walked up the winding staircase to find two rooms, one on either side of a small landing that's probably more accurately described as just the top of the stairs. The rooms were two of the three bedrooms in the house. Nobody really knows who slept where, though.

The room on the left was empty and featured three windows. On one wall was the Poe family tree, going all the way back to his forebears in Ireland. On another, it had, like at Westminster Hall, quotes painted on it. This time they were from Poe's famous admirers and included, among others:

> **Stephen King:** "Poe was the first writer to write about main characters who were bad guys or mad guys and those are some of my favorite stories."
>
> **Charles Baudelaire:** "I do not need to add, I presume, that American critics have often disparaged his poetry. We are familiar with that kind of sparring. The reproaches critics heap upon good poets are the same in all countries."
>
> **Jules Verne:** "You might call him 'The Leader of the Cult of the Unusual.'"
>
> **Alfred Hitchcock:** "It's because I liked Edgar Allan Poe's stories so much that I began to make suspense films."
>
> **Russell Baker:** "Few of us can make paper speak as vividly as Poe could."
>
> **H. L. Mencken:** "The poems of Poe are lovely things, indeed, but they are as devoid of logical content as so many college yells."
>
> **Arthur Conan Doyle:** "Where was the detective story until Poe breathed the breath of life into it?"

*Foyer, Edgar Allan Poe House*

The other room on the second floor had a fireplace, and a small closet underneath a set of stairs that went to the attic. But it was the three artifacts on display that immediately arrested my attention.

One was a plain wooden chair that was unremarkable, other than that it belonged to Poe. According to information included in the exhibit (I'm tired of writing "placard" in this book), the chair was preserved by the family of Henry Herring, who was Poe's uncle. Herring lived in Baltimore and played an important role in the final scenes of Poe's life and death

The second artifact was a small mahogany telescope with brass fittings and a short stand. It belonged to the Allans, and the way-cool idea behind this artifact is that Poe probably spent many hours of his life with his eye pressed against its lens. It might have been this exact instrument that helped first kindle his interest in space, an interest that later showed itself in stories where he sent a man to the moon in a balloon, killed off humanity with a comet, dramatized a supernova, and tried to solve the fundamental mysteries of the universe.

The final item was a portable writing desk—basically a hinged wooden case with felt-lined compartments for paper and ink and writing utensils. According to the exhibit, this also belonged to the Allans, and was probably used by Poe while attending the University of Virginia.

While I gazed at these great pieces, the people around me merely milled. Most had preceded me upstairs and had already marveled at the exhibits and were now just waiting their turn to go up the small flight of stairs beside the fireplace.

Only one person at a time was allowed up the steps, which were steep and narrow enough that I pulled myself up by the ceiling and walls more than climbing the steps themselves to get up there. At the top, a glass partition rose a couple of feet from the floor, barring actual entrance to, but not the view of, the last of the three bedrooms.

Inside, the room was furnished with period pieces that included a bed and chest. A chair beside the bed had a black coat thrown over the back and a pair of black boots on the floor in front of it. Against the wall was a stand with a wash basin and pitcher.

The room didn't really have a ceiling. The walls were so slanted on both sides since they were also the inside of the roof that they just met at the top. The single dormer window that I had seen from the sidewalk outside belonged to this room.

From the way it was furnished and detailed, and the fact that all the other rooms literally led up to this one, it was easy to come away with the impression that it was Poe's actual room. Again, though, there's no record of which rooms were whose in the crowded house. Still, it felt like the right way to end a tour of the house.

*Attic Bedroom, Edgar Allan Poe House*

Because, with that room, I was done, leaving the building so that the next person in line outside could join the fourteen other people inside.

Poe himself left the house in the late summer of 1835 for Richmond and a job at the *Southern Literary Messenger*. Somewhere around the same time, his grandmother died, and her pension went with her, forcing the Clemms to move. Poe quickly returned to Baltimore to take Virginia and Maria back to Richmond with him and to marry Virginia.

In fact, it was Virginia and Maria Clemm that really make this house such a fascinating one on the Poescape. It was, after all, in those very rooms I had just left that the bond he had with those two women, a bond that so thoroughly defined and fulfilled his life (as far as his life could be, at least), was first formed.

All in all, it was a great visit to the Poe House. I wasn't disappointed and wasn't shot, but I also didn't get the creeps like Vincent Price . . . although I see how under the appropriate circumstances, the tiny, creaky, empty house would probably produce that exact sensation.

Still, I left the Baltimore Poe House and Museum slightly unsatisfied . . . as if there was something missing from this experience that I had looked forward to for so many years.

## The Face of Poe in Balto

For more than thirty years, Jeff Jerome was the face of Edgar Allan Poe in Baltimore. He even had the mustache to back it up. But he wasn't a Poe performer. He was the manager, curator, and sole employee of the Baltimore Poe House and Museum and—by extension as the Poe guy in the city most associated with him— the custodian of the poet's popular reputation for all those decades.

He was also one of the organizers of The Cask of Amontillado Wine Tasting Among the Bones. It was there that I first met him, only briefly and just to introduce myself. The event had him drawn in multiple directions and almost quartered, so I merely explained my book project and asked if I could look him up some time when he wasn't coordinating goth belly dancers and palm readers and journeys to the center of the catacombs.

Ten months later, on the day after Edgar Allan Poe's 205th birthday, we found ourselves in a Thai joint on Federal Hill.

"Tell me your Poe story."

"Oh, my interest in Poe goes back to the 1960s, when the Vincent Price /Roger Corman films came out. Up to then, the only horror films being released were science fiction films, giant tarantulas and ants, black-and-white stuff. I was eight or nine, something like that, and at that time they had a rating system—it was before the MPAA—but they had a rating system. I have this poster from *The Fall of the House of Usher* that has four bloody X's on it. That meant no one under sixteen could see the movie. These days, it means porno, I guess.

"But my older brother would let me in the side door to see these films, or sometimes the ticket seller wouldn't care and let me in. So here I was, this little kid, looking up and seeing Vincent Price's face and Edgar Allan Poe's name, and that got me interested in Poe—Vincent Price on the big screen."

Now it's probably become apparent over the course of this book, and the next chapter will even better emphasize it, but the 1960s Vincent Price/Roger Corman movies kindled the interest of an entire generation for Edgar Allan Poe. I was part of a later generation of horror fans, but we still felt the reverberations of those films decades later.

I way dig Vincent Price, although Price and Poe were actually separate tracks in my horror development. My discovery of Price was through the *Dr. Phibes* movies of the 1970s. My discovery of their convergence later was more a consummation than anything else. But, really, for most horror fans by that time, the Vincent Price/Roger Corman movies were more a chapter in Horror Cinema 101 than an original revelation. Regardless, the big difference between Jerome's Poe origin story and many others in this book is that it has a really big payoff.

"It must have been crazy meeting Price, then?"

That 1977 quote about the creeps, painted in the hallway of Westminster Hall, from Vincent Price? That came about because of Jeff Jerome, who had recently started volunteering at Westminster Hall and knew his way around the Poe House. I didn't really know his Vincent Price story going in, but I had seen the great black-and-white picture of Price standing beside the grave of Poe and knew Jerome had taken it.

"Oh, yeah. He was my idol. I originally met him because he invited me to the Morris A. Mechanic Theatre here in Baltimore." The Mechanic was built in the 1960s, went derelict in the 2000s, and has been on the brink of demolition since then. There's a good chance it's gone as you read this.

"How did you swing that?"

"Well, I knew Price was performing there, he was doing his one-man Oscar Wilde show, so I called the PR guy at the theater, told him what my job was and that I wanted to invite Mr. Price to see the Poe grave and house. He thought it was a good idea, passed along the message, and I got the invite."

"You used Poe as your in to meet Vincent Price."

"Right. And I felt so stupid. I went backstage there with two of my friends, and shook his hand, and I'm just standing there not saying anything. He sensed the awkwardness, and said, 'Do you like homemade bread?' Strange question, but, of course, I said yes. And then he said, 'It's good for the hands, you know, kneading it,' and just like that he had me relaxed and we started talking. It was great."

"So he came to the grave and the house and what happened?"

"Well, unbeknownst to me, the PR guy at the Mechanic invited the media. There were TV cameras and photographers following him around. But it was fun. It really was."

"Who else famous have you toured through the house or Westminster Hall? Must be quite a few." I was about to learn that Jerome was the opposite of a name dropper.

"There was that French actor who was popular in the 1950s. He was a bad guy in a James Bond movie, and then he was in *Swamp Thing*." He was referring to Louis Jourdan. Also *Octopussy*.

"And that guy who was in that movie with Kevin Costner and Gene Hackman about the Russian spy. He was the aide to Gene Hackman. He stopped by." Will Patton. *No Way Out* was the movie.

"I'm leaving out people . . . Jack Palance, Ossie Davis, a few others. I'm terrible with names. Oh, Danny DeVito was at the cemetery once. There was an event at Westminster, and he was there, and we gave him a tour. He had an entourage, all these babes hanging on to him and fawning all over him."

The obvious question at this point is how does a person get such an awesome gig where you're hanging out in Poe's house all day and ushering through stars who want to experience a legend? For Jerome, it started at a fish store.

In 1976, he was working as a writer and photographer for a trade newspaper and was assigned to interview one of its advertisers, who ran a fish store. As they talked, the fishmonger mentioned he was also the historian for what was at the time the historic building that was shifting from being Westminster Church to Westminster Hall, and he needed volunteers. So Jerome checked it out one night.

"I went there and got hooked . . . open crypts, bones, all dark and spooky. It didn't look the way it does today. Now, they have plexiglass and lights and it's well kept. Back then, it was like walking into a Vincent Price movie. And I got hooked. Boy, did I get hooked."

It was around the same time that he became a volunteer at Westminster that the Edgar Allan Poe Society of Baltimore transferred its ownership of the Edgar Allan Poe House and Museum to the city. The city approached Jerome to develop the site interpretation and a job description for a manager of the house. When he completed it, he was also asked to apply for the job. "Now, I tried to play it cool when they asked, but inside I was so excited. This was 1978. In 1979 the city took it over, and that's when I started officially working there."

"How has the attitude toward Poe changed in the thirty-plus years you were curator?"

"Well, Poe has never been bigger, in my time at least, than the 2009 Poe Bicentennial. Before then, we were pretty much the only Poe site organizing events and getting into the press a lot. Some of the other sites in the country were historically less apt to really push Poe, usually because they were run by staid boards or just didn't have the dedicated personnel to take an interest in the site or didn't see Poe as a way to draw people to the area.

"It happens a lot with small museums, especially in the past. I used to be the curator at the Babe Ruth Museum right around the time I started at the Poe House . . ."

"I totally forgot about the Babe Ruth Museum. I went there when I was a kid. Is that still around?"

"Oh, yes."

"He's kind of like Poe in Boston. Not many people know that Ruth was a Marylander."

"My first meeting there, I put out the idea of bringing in school groups and expanding the hours. The board was horrified. They treated the Babe Ruth birthplace more like a shrine than as a community resource. Everything I wanted to do they shut down."

"So what did you do about it?"

"I waited for them to die. I mean, those people were old enough to actually know Babe Ruth himself. You have to outlive those people. Once they were gone, young people got involved and things changed. I've seen that at other historic sites, as well."

"What was your average day at the Poe House like?"

"Oh, there was no average day. You never knew who was going to walk through that door. Each person was different. You'd have people come in with no questions. They paid their admission fee, walked around, and then left. When I was there, we had more exhibits and we had a video presentation. They don't have that anymore. But each person was different."

"But I assume they all had in common an interest in Poe, right? Because of where the house is you weren't getting random tourists who just happened to be walking by looking for something to do. These were people consciously coming to see Poe."

"That's right. One of my favorite encounters happened just a few years ago. It was a young lady, sixteen years old, from China, who came in with her father. Neither one spoke a lot of English, but it was enough that we could have somewhat of a conversation. When they came in, the father told me, 'Daughter, Chinese, wants to be a poet. Loves Poe.' They went through the house, and when they came back down, I asked her to sit in a chair we had there, which she did. I told her, 'I'm impressed that you want to be a poet. Guess what? You're sitting in Poe's chair.' And she looked at me in surprise, jumped up, and tears started to show up in her eyes."

"Is this the same chair that's on exhibit in the house these days?"

"Yes, that's the one. When she started tearing up, I thought, 'Oh, what did I do? Did I just start an international incident?' But she said, 'I am not worthy to sit in his chair.' And I argued with her about it. 'Yes you are. I'm sure Edgar would appreciate having a fellow poet sit in his chair.' After minutes of cajoling, she finally sat back down in it, and she was just holding on to the arms real tight. Then she got up and gave me a hug, and I told her, 'The next time you come back here, I want you to be a published poet.' On the way out, her father said to me, 'You do so much for my daughter. Thank you.'

"I really enjoyed talking to different people every day about Poe. I got paid for that job, but it was never really a job for me."

He was talking in the past tense because, as a result of the whole debacle between the city and the Poe House, Jerome had also lost the job he had been faithfully performing since about the time I was born. That's what I had been missing from my visit to the Baltimore Poe House and Museum. Jeff Jerome wasn't there. I asked him about the whole messy situation.

"The city really bungled the house. I mean, they're bureaucrats, so that's what usually happens. And I don't say that as a guy who lost his job as a result of it. I had over $380,000 in the Poe House account from pure fundraising efforts. They could've kept the Poe House open for five more years and really had the time to set up Poe Baltimore before they got out of the Poe business if that's what they wanted."

At the time, I hadn't yet talked to Harbeson, but I had met her, so I brought her up.

"Oh, I've known Kristen for years. They at least picked the right person for that job. She has an uphill climb, though. Fundraising was always hard for the Poe House. When you go to somebody with money and say, 'Poe House,' in their mind they're weighing children with cancer or abused dogs against this poet who wrote about murderers and grave robbers. Still, if the city had kept the house open for the past year until Poe Baltimore was fully up and running, things would have been a lot better for them."

I didn't want the conversation to be too much of a downer, so I switched to another topic, one in which Jeff Jerome is the preeminent expert: the Poe Toaster.

Every year on Poe's birthday, after midnight on the freshly turned January 19, a cloaked man with a walking stick steals into the back of the cemetery to Poe's original gravesite. (His remains were moved in 1875 to the front part of the cemetery under a new monument.) He raises a toast of cognac to Poe, deposits the partially emptied bottle and three roses (which has been supposed to represent the three people interred in Poe's grave . . . more on that later), and then leaves as quietly as he came. Nobody knows the identity of the man, just that he's been doing it for a very long time. And we know that because of Jeff Jerome.

When Jerome first started working at the grave and the house, he spent his free time doing research at the Maryland Historical Society. He came across an item in a 1950 edition of the *Baltimore Sun*. In it, the pastor at the Westminster Church, a Reverend Bruce H. McDonald, is paraphrased as saying, "The anonymous citizen who creeps in annually to place an empty bottle (of excellent label) against the tomb of Poe, on the anniversary of his death, is a jokester."

In looking closely at the dates, Jerome figured that the reverend meant Poe's birthday, instead of death day, especially as it was just past the centenary of his birth. So, as January 19 wasn't too far off, he decided to stake out the grave to see if that annual tradition was still happening.

He parked his car on the corner across the street from the graveyard and waited. Nothing happened. And then nothing happened. And then nothing happened. Eventually, Jerome left his car and walked to the nearby hospital to use the restroom. When he returned, there was a bottle of cognac and three red roses on the original grave site. "I got goose bumps. It was still going on after all these decades."

He talked to some of the older members of the church, and some of them remembered idly hearing about the offering as far back as the 1930s. When he asked what happened to the bottles of cognac, he was told that the caretaker always took them home to finish them off.

And that began an annual vigil for the mysterious man who would come to be called the Poe Toaster, a vigil that has gone on for three decades.

"And you could never tell what he looked like or who he was at all?"

"He had a coat, hat, and scarf, and back then the cemetery didn't have the lights it has now, so it was darker. At some point I started inviting people to watch for him with me, and it's funny—I can sympathize with the police department, when they have ten witnesses to a crime and everyone has a different story. That's exactly what happened with the Poe Toaster. 'He had a mustache.' 'No, he didn't have a mustache.' 'He definitely had light hair.' 'No, it looked dark to me.' We all saw the same thing but each saw somebody different . . . which added to the fun of the evening."

Most relevant, Jerome just never tried to find out who he was. "I was careful not to interfere with him. That would have been inappropriate. I even tried to help him out as much as I could once the story got out and the crowds started getting big."

The crowds started getting big thanks to *LIFE* magazine, which ran an article on the event in 1990 and included a grainy black-and-white photo of the cloaked form of the Poe Toaster kneeling in front of the headstone, his cane propped against it.

Suddenly, instead of just Jerome's small party in Westminster Hall, they were joined outside the gates by crowds of people . . . sometimes more than one hundred braving the late cold winter night to catch a glimpse of one of Poe's most secretive fans as he crept swiftly through the back of the cemetery.

But these weren't people looking to solve a mystery. They were mostly looking for an excuse to party. Many times the Poe Toaster would come and go, with nobody on the sidewalks the wiser and the only witnesses to his passing being Jerome and his friends, warm in Westminster Hall.

Sometimes, the Poe Toaster would leave notes. In 1993, one read, "Some traditions must end, while others take their place. The torch will be passed." The next year they had a blizzard, and the man didn't show, although somebody else did. The year after that it was yet another, different person.

That's when another note appeared, filling in a few of the gaps. From Jerome's interpretation of the cryptic notes, the original Poe Toaster seems to have died, while his two sons had continued the tradition in his honor, each one alternating years.

But apparently these apples fell a bit farther from the tree, as 2009 was the last time any Poe Toaster appeared.

"I always thought that if the Poe Toaster didn't appear one year, I'd still have the vigil the next year. What if he was sick that year or his car broke down? But in 2010, he didn't show up. 2011, he didn't show up. After 2012 and another no show, I had to call it. We've had lots of Poe Toaster wannabees since then, though."

Faux-toasters, they're often called, and they had three at the most recent anniversary. "Real easy to pick those guys out, huh?"

"Oh, yeah, very obvious after all these years."

"Even though you 'called' it, you did another vigil for his 2014 birthday. How long are you going to continue?"

"Well, I've been doing it since 1977. Haven't missed a year. It's hard to stop. And they're fun."

"So, on the topic of Poe's grave . . . when I first searched you online to get some background, the image that kept popping up was you fixing the drapery on a casket that held a dummy of a deceased Edgar Allan Poe."

"Yeah, the Poe Funeral. The crowning achievement of my Poe career, I think . . . other than keeping the Poe House open all these years, of course."

"How did that come about?"

"I'd been thinking about redoing Poe's funeral for years. Obviously, he was buried without any ceremony and only a handful of people came to it. I thought it would be cool to rectify that, and 2009, the Poe Bicentennial, seemed the perfect time for it. But I knew it would be a big job and I didn't have a staff. So I talked to Mark Redfield."

Mark Redfield was a local actor whom Jerome met in 2006 when Redfield was promoting his movie *The Death of Poe*. Redfield wrote, directed, and starred in the film, which chronicled Poe's last days. The two eventually hit it off and in recent years have been organizing events together, including the Wine Tasting Among the Bones. Redfield is active with Poe on his own, as well. He produced the East Coast premiere of *Nevermore*, starring Jeffrey Combs, runs a magazine called *Poe Forevermore,* and has been producing a ten-hour audio-drama biography of Poe called *Alone: The Life of Poe.*

Once Jerome broached the idea to Redfield, the two took off with it. They started hiring actors to play people from Poe's life, with Tony Tsendeas as George Lippard and Philadelphia Poe performer Helen McKenna-Uff as Sarah Helen Whitman. They got somebody to play Walt Whitman and Poe's deathbed physician John Joseph Moran. They also found actors to portray later artists whom Poe influenced, like Alfred Hitchcock and H. P. Lovecraft, and a few present ones, like actor John Astin and artist Gris Grimly, attended. The body of Edgar Allan Poe itself was played by a mannequin with a head created by a local sculptor.

The whole thing started as a twenty-four-hour viewing, with the fake Poe body in the back bedroom of the Poe House. Jerome and Redfield sent out a press release treating it as a real viewing and funeral. "We made sure to include hours limited to family only."

To further the effect, they made sure the tour guides asked all visitors to be respectful and keep their voices down. "People came nonstop the entire time. Some would kneel and cross themselves on entering. I'm not sure if that was creepy or evidence that it worked perfectly. There were these three ladies in their twenties who left the viewing extremely agitated. I asked one of the tour guides what happened, and she told me that the girls had come down from New York and thought they were going to see the real remains of Edgar Allan Poe. So I guess it worked."

It all sounded very William Castle to me.

They then had a funeral procession to the gravesite. The faux-Poe was loaded into a horse-drawn hearse escorted by local police and a band of bagpipers. The character actors, the paying funeral attendees, and the curious brought up the rear.

"I think we had three hundred people follow us from the house to the grave- yard. It's on YouTube, check it out. People in the neighborhood were asking, 'Who died? Who died? I thought Poe was already dead.' We did the funeral twice and it sold out both times. Television crews from all over the world filmed it. It was unbelievable. I still have the Poe corpse at my house."

The event had both spectacle for the uninitiated and in-jokes for the entan- gled. At one point Jerome spontaneously asked the actor who played George Lip- pard, Poe's staunch friend and defender from Philadelphia, to throw a cup of water in the face of Rufus Griswold during his anti-Poe eulogy.

"People were already booing and hissing Griswold, but when that happened, they clapped and cheered. Of course, the actor who played Griswold went along with it. I knew the guy. He was a good sport."

Jerome's nostalgia was palpable. His years invested in Poe had obviously been great and well worth it, even if, in the end, a bureaucratic "bungle" had forced him out. However, from what I'd seen, he was far from over Poe.

"So now that you're free of Poe, if you wanted to be at least, why . . ."

" . . . am I so bothered with Poe? Is that what you're going to say?"

"Yeah, exactly. If anybody's earned their retirement from Poe, it's you. I mean, I've done this book for about a year, and I'm almost Poe'd out."

"I always thought, when I retired from the Poe House, that I wasn't going to be that guy who hung outside and held on too tightly to the past. But, honestly, the Poe fans won't let me go away. The media won't let me go away. So I thought to myself, just because the city of Baltimore dumped me, why should I stop doing what I love? It's been so much a part of my life since 1977, and I'm just having a good time. So I gave myself the title curator emeritus . . . I earned it, you know."

## Poe at the Pratt

As you could probably tell, tracing Poe's story through Baltimore is less an exploration of his five years living in the city and more an exploration of his five days dying there. It's a strange thing to be proud of—killing one of our greatest poets—but Baltimore has done pretty well with it.

So it was no surprise to me that when I visited the Edgar Allan Poe collection at the Enoch Pratt Free Library, I found many of its most notable holdings were directly related to Poe's death. No surprise, but still astounding stuff.

The Enoch Pratt Free Library is the public library system in Baltimore, named after the businessman who financed it in the 1880s. Its main branch, Central Library, was built in the early 1930s on Cathedral Street. It's one of those large, regal, civic structures, like most city libraries, the type I always feel I'm trespassing in, purely due to my own inadequacies as a literary person.

Fortunately, I didn't have to find my own way through its daunting stacks and floors and corridors.

I was met at the front desk by Michael Johnson, the manager of the Special Collections Department. I'd had extremely good luck with the many helpful librarians over the course of this project, and at the Pratt, I got really lucky, as Johnson seemed the kind of guy you'd meet browsing the stacks as opposed to having to set up an appointment with.

He got into library sciences by a "circuitous route," studying philosophy at the Catholic University of America in D.C., where he fell in love with rare books. Somehow that turned into having an office a few floors away from a vault that held incredible pieces of the life and death of Edgar Allan Poe.

As he led me over to the Special Collections Department, in the back of the first floor of the library, we talked a bit about Poe.

"So are you into him, or do you think it's weird what I'm asking to see?"

"I like Poe. I wasn't a fanatic, but he did have an impact on me growing up. I remember watching this hour-long Saturday morning special that was a live-action version of 'The Gold-Bug.' That's kind of my first experience with Poe, and it always stuck with me. When I got the job here, I knew we had all these letters written by him, and after reading those, you see that he has this artistic, volatile, highly emotional personality that makes him intriguing. But if my eleven-year-old self knew that in a few decades I'd have Poe's handwriting sitting in front of me, I don't know, it would have been ridiculous."

He ushered me into a room, where he had already laid out a series of folders and boxes on a table that took me through the story of Edgar Allan Poe in Baltimore, as told through the Pratt holdings. Most of the items came into the collection from a descendant of Amelia Poe, who was the daughter of one of Edgar Allan Poe's cousins, Neilson Poe. Neilson Poe figures prominently in both Poe's life and death.

Johnson started my tour by showing me a series of original letters. The first one was written by Poe himself, although it wasn't written in Baltimore, but in Richmond, Virginia.

The letter is the most important one we have from Edgar Allan Poe, the one where we most clearly see that "highly emotional" personality. In it, which he's writing after securing a position at the *Southern Literary Messenger,* he tells Maria and Virginia how desperate he was to have them both in his life. At the time, the two were only related to him by blood and had just received an offer to join the household of Neilson Poe in Baltimore.

The letter deserves some delving into, but I'm going to save it for the next chapter, as that's where I cover Poe's re-acclimatization to Richmond and visit Poe and Virginia's honeymoon suite in Petersburg. Same with the next piece Johnson showed me, which was the original Valentine poem Virginia wrote to Poe, the only known correspondence from her to her husband.

Next, was a pair of manuscript poems. The first, "To Elizabeth," was originally dedicated to his Baltimore cousin, Elizabeth Herring. Over the years the title would change depending on which girl Poe wanted to impress, which was something he did with more than a few of his poems. Poe wrote in his essay "The Poetic Principle" that the purpose of poetry was to incite "an elevating excitement of the Soul," but he also knew it came in handy with the ladies.

The second was a Valentine poem Poe wrote to Frances Sargent Osgood, a poet he met in New York and with whom he had a literary dalliance. The interesting part of this poem is that he hid her name in it, but not in the usual acrostic way. In this poem, the first letter of the first line, the second letter of the second line, the third letter of the third line, and so on, spell out her full name. Mostly. In the original manuscript that I was looking at, he misspelled her middle name "Sergeant" and had to fix it in later versions. I could also see that somebody, assumedly Osgood, connected the letters throughout the lines with a light pencil. It's a good trick, although it makes it a little harder to repurpose the poem for other muses.

One of the vague points about the end of Poe's life was whether he was, at that time, engaged to his childhood sweetheart, Sarah Elmira Royster Shelton, who lived in Richmond. Actually, reengaged. He had been engaged to her as a teenager, but it was broken up by her father while he was in college. For the two months prior to his death, he was in Richmond, and he rekindled at least a close friendship with Shelton, although it seems the two might have taken the relationship further than that. Shelton denied it, though, in later, post-Poe years. The next folder that Johnson slid in front of me seemed to back up Shelton's position. In it was one of Poe's last letters, dated September 18, 1849, and in it he opened and closed the letter with information that seemed to put his new relationship with Shelton into context:

> **I think she loves me more devotedly than any one I ever**
> **knew & I cannot help loving her in return. Nothing is as yet**
> **definitely settled—and it will not do to hurry matters . . .**
> **If possible I will get married before I start—but there is**
> **no telling.**

Still, while distraught and delirious in his last few days, Poe mentioned to the physician attending him that he had a wife in Richmond. That obviously could have been a regression to his life with Virginia Poe in that city, but the next letter that Johnson handed me seemed pretty solid proof that plans for marriage were, in fact, underway.

In the folder was the letter from Shelton to Poe's mother-in-law, Maria Clemm. It was a relatively long letter, especially since it was coming from somebody, as Shelton phrased it, "whom you have never seen." She says she's writing at Poe's insistence, but far from it being a letter of obligation, writes, "I am fully prepared to love you, and I do sincerely hope that our spirits may be congenial." The whole letter sounds like groundwork for a relationship with Clemm, one which Shelton would have to form with the woman Poe considered "more than mother" if she was to marry him. Most important, it was dated three days after Poe's own, so it sounds like Poe had made progress.

And then we got to an extraordinary letter, one which kind of transformed Maria Clemm into a real person to me, as opposed to just an important character in the story of Edgar Allan Poe. It was the very letter she wrote to Neilson Poe as soon as she heard about Poe's death, a day later and from the newspaper:

> **Dear Neilson,**
> **I have heard this moment of the death of my dear son**
> **Edgar—I cannot believe it, [I at] once have written to you,**
> **to try and ascertain the fact and particulars—he has been**
> **at the South for the last three months, and was on his way**
> **home—the paper states he died in Baltimore yesterday—**
> **If it is true God have mercy on me, for he was the last I had**
> **to cling to and love, will you write the *instant* you receive**
> **this, and relieve this dreadful uncertainty—My mind is**

prepared to *bear all*—conceal nothing from me.
**Your afflicted friend,**
**Maria Clemm**

Holding that letter in my hands, I couldn't help but imagine her alone in her house in Fordham, first reading the newspaper, then sitting there momentarily numbed before dashing off this quick missive in a desperate panic to the man Poe had once called "the bitterest enemy I have in the world." *Afflicted* seems far too inadequate a word to describe her state of mind. Edgar Allan Poe was the last possible loved one she could have lost in her life, having already lost her husband and all her children, including Virginia. Then she had to sit there waiting days for a response from Neilson Poe . . . which the Pratt Library also has.

I looked at that letter as well. It includes a firsthand account of Poe's sad, short, little funeral. I could only imagine Clemm's heart dropping at the first line, "I would to God I could console you with the information that your dear son Edgar A. Poe is still among the living."

Later in the letter, Neilson Poe writes, "Edgar has seen so much of sorrow—had so little reason to be satisfied with life—that, to him, the change can scarcely be said to be a misfortune." Goddamn—what an epitaph that is.

The next, and last, letter I looked at was from Dr. John Joseph Moran to Maria Clemm, dated the month after Poe's death. In it, as one of the few firsthand witnesses, he describes Poe's last days. Unfortunately, his testimony would prove relatively unreliable due to the deviations in his stories over time. But it's still pretty much all we have. I'll get into that more later, because the truly exciting artifacts were next.

Through sheer perversity, Johnson was holding off showing me the two items I wanted to see the most. Even now that we were done with the letters, he still found a way to put it off, by first showing me a pair of items that, while extremely interesting, still weren't the crowning jewels of the Pratt's Poe collection . . . to me, at least.

The first was a bill of sale for the slave owned by Maria Clemm, whom she sold out of financial need in 1829, shortly before Poe entered West Point. Poe acted as the agent for his not-yet mother-in-law in the sale. The slave's name was Edwin, and he was twenty-one years old. Poe's abject poverty throughout his life meant that the issue of slavery is a virtually nonexistent one in his story, although hailing from Richmond more than likely meant he had at least southern leanings and probably southern fallings on the issue. We do know that the Allans kept slaves when Poe was growing up in their house. In Poe's "break-up" letter to John Allan that had him heading up to Boston to eventually join the Army, he wrote, "You suffer me to be subjected to the whims & caprice, not only of your white family, but the complete authority of the blacks."

The other item was a marbled green memorandum book that Poe used to keep track of subscribers to *The Stylus*, his unrealized dream magazine that never became more than that short list of names in the memorandum book.

Finally, Johnson pulled out a small gold frame, about the size of a 3x5 card. In it, were two locks of hair. One was about an inch long, while the other was more a ringlet, curled in on itself and much longer than the other. Both were the same dark brown color.

I was holding in my hands the very hair of Poe and his wife, Virginia . . . actual pieces of the person whose physical legacy I was tracing across the world. Simply amazing.

*Entrance to Poe Room, Enoch Pratt Free Library*

Keeping them together in the same intimate case like that was beautiful, and somehow seemed a more fitting tribute to their relationship than matching tombstones or a family portrait. I don't know how. I can only describe the sense I got from it.

Next, Johnson handed me a small container holding a sliver of polished wood . . . a piece of Poe's original coffin, the one that disintegrated when they moved his remains to a more prominent part of the cemetery, under a new memorial. It was the second piece of Poe's coffin I'd seen in my trek, but that first decaying fragment of flat wood was the depth of an exhibit case away from me. This one, though a tinier piece at about an inch or so long, was in my hands. The surfaces of the fragment were smooth, with a beveled edge, confirming it was a piece of definite woodwork. Maybe a coffin. Possibly a coffee table.

As I was holding these astonishing, irreplaceable artifacts, I suddenly wondered why I was able to. After all, it wasn't my first time ogling unique Poe artifacts in the archives of a prestigious library. I realized I had no idea whether I was given access because I claimed a book project or if anybody could randomly request to see pieces of the hair and coffin of one of the most influential writers of all time. I put the question to Johnson.

"One of the things we take pride in here is that we're a public library, and while we certainly take care of these materials, they're still here for everybody to benefit from, so, no, you don't need to be writing a book or doing research to see these. You just need to set up an appointment. Maybe one day we'll get together a permanent exhibit." Until that time, they go back in the vault.

But I wasn't quite done with the Pratt. "How about the Poe Room? Is that open?"

"We can find out."

Johnson led me to the second floor to a large glass door marked "Edgar Allan Poe Room." While he went to retrieve they key to open it, I bent close to the bust of Poe that guarded the door. It was cast from an original and larger bust created by George Julian Zolnay in 1898, and was generally one of the more interesting sculptures of the poet's likeness, due to its texture and the way Poe leans his head on his fist. I would come across versions of this bust, as well as the original at the University of Virginia, throughout my Poe trek. A miniature version of it had been sitting on the table where I pawed the Pratt Poe treasures.

Finally, Johnson returned and opened the door. A flick of the light switch revealed a gorgeous room walled with shelves of books. The Edgar Allan Poe Room was dedicated in January 19, 1934, and has been used as a meeting and event space ever since.

A large portrait of Poe hung above a fireplace at the front of the room, and a small collection of minor artifacts were displayed in a glass case inset into a section of shelves filled with Poe books. The room had couches and comfortable chairs, but was mostly set up for presentations. Rows of chairs filled the center space, and a podium was set off-center at the front. I immediately imagined myself giving a Poe talk based on this book here at some point that would consist of me saying "I'm in the Edgar Allan Poe Room" over and over.

As I left, expressing my appreciation for the afternoon to Johnson, I threw one last look at the Zolnay bust, a great work of art, but still a distant second to Baltimore's signature Poe sculpture.

## How Statue-Like I See Thee Sit

I don't know whether there's a more ultimate way to honor somebody than with a statue. Sure, you can name giant things after them: buildings, cities, stars (Poe has a crater on the planet Mercury named after him), but after a while they're just names. You can build massive, impersonal memorials to them, too, I guess, but those are just structures in the end. I mean, the Washington Monument was erected to honor a man, but it's come to symbolize a city. There's just something about casting the physical body and face of a person in a permanent material that seems the epitome of veneration. And a little clingy.

We're deep into this Poe trek, and despite how revered Edgar Allan Poe is, we haven't seen one statue of this poet. Lots of busts, but no life-sized stone or metal Poe. And we won't see many by the time it's over. We've talked to a bunch of people in Boston who are erecting a pretty cool one, and, when we travel a little farther south, we'll see a sedate affair set prominently on official grounds.

But, to me, Baltimore's excellent statue of Poe makes up for the general lack of Poe statues anywhere else.

Now, there are quite a few obvious ways Edgar Allan Poe could have been enstatuated. Seated in a velvet reading chair, pondering over a quaint and curious volume of forgotten lore. Struggling with an orangutan that has its hands wrapped around his throat. Reaching out desperately from a hole in a bricked-in wall.

However, Moses Jacob Ezekiel, the sculptor of Poe's Baltimore statue, chose to petrify Poe by enthroning him . . . against his will.

Moses Jacob Ezekiel was a Jewish, Richmond-born, Berlin-educated Confederate army veteran with an Italian knighthood. The last commission of his life was from the Edgar Allan Poe Memorial Association to sculpt the Poe statue for Baltimore. After a fire, an earthquake, two broken sculptures, a world war, and the death of Ezekiel, the Poe statue was unveiled in 1921.

*Poe Room interior, Enoch Pratt Free Library*

Ezekiel sculpted Poe in bronze, depicting him in his usual coat, cravat, and misbuttoned vest, semi-seated in a small throne-like chair. A long greatcoat is thrown over the back of the chair, from under which an unknown book peeks out. The sides of the throne are adorned with reliefs of angel-like muses, one holding a harp and walking into a thistle bush, the other lifting a leafy garland. The statue is black with a green patina and is set on a concrete pedestal.

The plaque at the foot gives Poe's name, dates of existence, and the snippet "Dreaming dreams no mortal ever dared to dream before." A previous pedestal had the inscription inscribed directly on it, although it left the *i* out of dreaming and pluralized mortal. A local was so incensed by the latter, he brazenly walked up to the statue and chiseled the *s* off. He was promptly arrested for it. The current plaque comes with no good story.

If you look closely at the base of the throne,

you can see inscribed on it at various places the year and city in which it was sculpted, ROME, 1915, the signature of the sculptor, and the foundry mark CORINTHIA FOND. ART. ROMA.

I love that there's not a raven or black cat to be seen in the design (although I would also have loved to see them . . . I'm conflicted about those two Poe icons that have become both integral to and clichés about him). The muses are a nice touch to shake things up. Poe's work is resplendent with angels and ethereal beings, more so than madmen and the undead: Israfel, Oinos, Agathos, Ligeia, Ianthe, Angelo . . . um . . . the Angel of the Odd.

Poe seems to be half-rising from the throne of which he's permanently a part. Like he's uncomfortable. With what? Fame? Existence? Life? His art? Doesn't

*Moses Jacob Ezekiel statue of Poe*

matter. I adore the sentiment as is. It's like he wants to get up and be elsewhere. Or, at the very least is asking for an easier chair.

This interpretation is, of course, not at all what the sculptor intended.

According to Ezekiel, the statue is meant to give the following impression: "As Edgar Poe was the one poet we have whose poetry does not seem to be based on anything that existed before his own, I conceived the idea of representing him as seated listening in rapt attention to a divine melody and a new rhythm in his art."

At least I didn't share H. L. Mencken's impression of the statue . . . he thought it made Poe look drunk. Ezekiel's explanation does remind me of the section in Daniel Hoffman's *Poe Poe Poe Poe Poe Poe Poe* where he talks about the poem "Israfel":

> **Israfel's lyre! Poe would, if he could, have always smitten those angelic strings. Poetry, to him, is *song;* and this one option bends his verses on its stave, making inaccessible to Edgarpoe all those other marvellous effects attained by Romantic poets from Wordsworth to Williams, the poets for whom poetry is *speech* . . . Ideality, that perfect beauty on which Poe gazed with such longing, that perfect beauty**

**he attempted to imitate and enshrine in his verses, is for
him attainable, if at all, through the effects of musicality of
sound and indefiniteness of meaning.**

The statue was placed in Wyman Park, where it sat for decades (and where its
original pedestal was vandalized into accuracy). In 1983, it was moved to its
present location in Gordon Plaza, at the University of Baltimore School of Law,
a little more than a mile from his grave at the Westminster Burying Ground.

For some reason, in my mind, I always compare Ezekiel's statue of Poe to
Daniel Chester French's statue of Abraham Lincoln at the Lincoln Memorial in
D.C. Like Poe, Lincoln's enthroned in a squarish chair. However, the two statues
couldn't be more opposite. Lincoln is depicted regally, stately, gigantically, in
expensive white marble, calmly overseeing his realm. He's been sculpted to be
worshipped, and the Greek temple that surrounds him supports this idea. Ezekiel's Poe is small, black, bronze, and adorned to a point, and instead of sitting
peacefully, he shifts in his seat.

One statue makes us want to idolize, the other makes us want to apologize
for putting the subject through anything. It's as if we're pretty confident how to
honor a man like Lincoln, but we're still uncertain how to adequately honor a
man whose gifts were such as Poe's. Ezekiel gave it a superb go, though. Personally, I just want to stick a poker table between the two statues.

## Balti-Nevermore

My evening with David Keltz was supposed to be a sedate affair at an Indian
restaurant on North Charles Street in Baltimore. And it did start out that way,
until the restaurant owner walked over to us with appetizers and a question for
me: "Is that your car in front of the restaurant that's being towed?"

It was.

So Keltz put a call in to his wife, Teresa, who was home sick in bed but who
was still nice enough to pick us up and take us to the impound lot, where I paid
the city of Baltimore a hefty sum made all the more bitter since none of it was
going to the Poe House.

We turned the interruption to our advantage, putting off the interview and
dinner for an impromptu driving tour of some of the more obscure Poe sites in
Baltimore.

David Keltz has been portraying Poe in the city of his death and other places
for twenty-two years, more than half of the time that Poe was Poe. Growing up,
having an Army father meant Keltz lived all over the country, but he discovered Poe as thirteen-year-old in Alabama while his father was stationed at Fort
Rucker for flight school.

"I remember the day so well. All the short stories we'd read to that point hadn't been that interesting. That day, the teacher assigned us a story and then left the room. Of course, anytime a teacher leaves, it's a free-for-all. But for some reason, I read the story. I mean, I almost didn't. I started socializing with everybody, and then I looked down and read those first lines: 'TRUE!—nervous—very, very dreadfully nervous I had been and am; but why will you say that I am mad?' I got pulled into 'The Tell-Tale Heart' and was just mesmerized. Later that night, when I went to bed, my door was partly open, and the story was so much in my mind that I kept imagining it swinging open just a little more as I watched."

Acting was always the path Keltz wanted to take and, in 1973, a few years after a stint in the Army that included a tour of Vietnam and then a degree from Florida Atlantic University in Boca Raton, he decided to head up to New York, where stage actors are supposed to go. But then, like Poe himself, he got waylaid in Baltimore and never left.

"I decided to stop over in Baltimore to see the Poe House and a couple of friends. I liked the city so much that I wound up staying here."

Sometime in the late 1980s, he realized he was getting work only about four months out of the year. That gave him plenty of time and motivation to put together a one-man show. Although he wanted to try Poe, he started with a few other historic personages: D. H. Lawrence, H. L. Mencken, Captain John Smith. Even Orson Squire Fowler, the nineteenth-century phrenologist and sexologist, which had Keltz reading the bumps on the skulls of the audience after every performance.

Then he finally got around to the one he really wanted to do. Jeff Jerome had been looking for someone to do Poe, so on Halloween night in 1991, at the gravesite, Keltz did a twenty-minute show, performing "The Tell-Tale Heart" and "Annabel Lee."

"I got into Poe more than any of the characters I had been doing and so did the audience, so I realized I needed to do more. I added some more stories, a few of his opinions from his letters and essays, and started a full-length show. I've got over five hours of his work committed to memory now."

And that was the veteran of Baltimore and Edgar Allan Poe who was touring me around the dark, snowy streets of the city in his car, since mine was still smarting from the tow hook. I had already seen the major Poe sites in Baltimore, so we decided to check out some of the more obscure ones. Some of the sites were based on rumors, some were downright dubitable, others were dead-on, but they were all part of a network that Edgar Allan Poe cast across the city.

For the past couple years in October, Keltz has been doing a unique twist on a bus tour of Baltimore Poe sites. He would jump on the back of a motorcycle in full Poe costume, which would lead the bus around the city while someone aboard the bus narrated the tour. At certain points, like at the Poe statue or at Poe's grave, Keltz would hop off the bike and perform. "Hopefully I can find most of the sites. I'm not usually the one driving, and we don't go to everything on the tour because of time and the fact that it's hard to get a bus near some of these places."

We drove past an old house on Front Street that some swear Poe stayed at for eight months when he was an infant. Also a garage on Eastern Avenue that was the former site of the house where Poe lived before moving to the Amity Street house. On Essex Street, we saw the site of the house of Mary Starr, known as "Baltimore Mary," who claimed she had a turbulent relationship with Poe while he lived there.

We drove past the site of the Holliday Street Theatre, where Poe's mother had performed. It was now a courtyard in front of Baltimore City Hall. We saw the former site of the home of Poe's uncle Henry Herring, who paid for Poe's original coffin, a piece of which I had just held. Also the former site of the High Street office of Dr. Joseph Snodgrass, who took Poe to the hospital where he died. It was now a post office. We drove past 30 North Gay Street, where Poe had lectured in the Egyptian Saloon at an Odd Fellows Hall that is no longer there.

Keltz told me a certainly apocryphal story of Poe visiting a brothel at 1 Tripolet Alley in the city the year before his death. It was run by a woman named Mary Nelson. According to the tale, Poe went there with a friend and, being too poor to afford any of the house's services, spent the night talking to a sixteen-year-old girl coincidentally named Lenore, whom he tried to talk out of the life she was living. Keltz pointed out where he thought it was . . . at the back of what is now Larry Flynt's Hustler Club.

He took me to the former sites of bars that Poe was supposed to have frequented, the Seven Stars Tavern, which is known more as the place where the American Odd Fellows was established. Widow Meagher's Oyster Parlor, where the proprietress supposedly called him "The Bard." The most interesting spot, mentally anyway, that Keltz took me to was where Poe was found "in need of immediate assistance" after mysteriously being off the grid for days and before being taken to the hospital where he died. Back then the site was a tavern called Gunner's Hall that was doubling at the time as an election polling site.

The address of Gunner's Hall was 44 East Lombard Street. Today that part of the street is lined with row homes. Poe was apparently found on the north side of East Lombard, between Exeter and High Streets, somewhere around numbers 900–904.

"The road has been widened since then, so we probably drove right over the spot."

This site is where lore gives us the image of a blasted Poe, face-down in a gutter, insane and dying. The truth of it isn't too far from that. We know that a man named Joseph W. Walker found Poe on the night of October 3, 1849, at Gunner's Hall and, at the request of a delirious Poe, contacted Snodgrass with this note:

> **Dear Sir,**
> **There is a gentleman, rather the worse for wear, at Ryan's**
> **4th ward polls, who goes under the cognomen of Edgar**
> **A. Poe, and who appears in great distress, & he says he**
> **is acquainted with you, and I assure you, he is in need of**
> **immediate assistance.**
> **Yours, in haste,**
> **Jos. W. Walker**

Snodgrass and Herring found Poe in a state of terrible mental and physical disarray and wearing clothes that didn't seem to be his, including a straw hat. They believed him to be drunk and sent him by carriage to Washington College Hospital. He died there four days later, after varying periods of consciousness and coherence.

The place of Poe's discovery has given rise to two prevailing theories for his condition. Since the site was a tavern, that he drank himself into that bad spot. After all, it wouldn't be the first time Poe followed the bottom of a glass around, even if his drinking problem has been extremely exaggerated as part of his myth. However, his death-bed physician John Joseph Moran claimed that he saw no evidence of Poe being inebriated. Since the site was also a polling station, the other theory goes that he was the victim of cooping, a practice in which gangs in the employ of a political candidate would kidnap victims, drug them or make them drink by beating them, and then take those victims to the polls and force them to vote for a particular candidate over and over again, changing their clothes each time to disguise them. It fits nicely with the description of the strange outfit that Poe was wearing when he was found, but is, of course, only one of many scenarios that do. In addition, none of the newspapers from that election mention anything about a cooping problem.

Basically, there is circumstantial evidence for and solid evidence against either scenario. Other theories for his condition range from a mugging to any number of health afflictions, including epilepsy, heart problems, brain disease, or even rabies.

The one thing that all these sites that Keltz had taken me had in common was that none of them was marked. In fact, the only place that had a Poe plaque was the Latrobe House. In that still-standing, three-story brick residence at 11 East Mulberry Street, John Pendleton Kennedy, James H. Miller, and John

H. B. Latrobe met in October of 1833 to choose the winners of a short story and poetry contest for the *Baltimore Saturday Visiter.* They unanimously awarded Poe's "MS. Found in a Bottle" the $50 prize, in effect starting his fiction career.

That's the gist of the plaque bearing Poe's face on the front of the Latrobe House. However, the story goes further. Apparently, Poe also submitted works for a concurrent poetry contest for the newspaper. The three men thought Poe should win that contest, as well, with his "The Coliseum." However, John Hewitt, the editor of the *Visiter,* overrode their judgment and decided that the poetry prize should go to an entrant named Henry Wilton . . . a pen name for himself.

Later, Kennedy became one of Poe's best friends and supporters in Baltimore, helping him get the gig at the *Southern Literary Messenger* in Richmond. He told Poe he should have received both prizes. This incensed Poe so much that he tracked down Hewitt and had a physical altercation with him in front of the *Baltimore Saturday Visiter* office. Keltz showed me that spot, too, at the corner of Baltimore and Gay Streets.

Honestly, I didn't take good notes of our trek through Baltimore, so keep that in mind if you ever try to follow the above itinerary without the help of a distinguished Poe actor. It just seemed not in the spirit of what we were doing. We got lost a few times, were stuck in snow once, found ourselves confused on more than one occasion, and just generally had a great phantasmagoria of a night in the virtually empty city, which was still digging itself out from a snowstorm the day before. It felt almost like the beginning scenes of a *Twilight Zone* episode, as if at any moment we'd come around a corner and see a black-clad man in a mustache retracing his steps from those last, mysterious nights.

Finally, hours later than we had intended, we ended right back at the same table at the same Indian restaurant on North Charles Street. The waitress even remembered our order.

The first thing Keltz told me was that one of the jobs he'd gotten in the past was a part as Poe in commercials for the Baltimore Ravens when they became a team.

"So in the beginning the Ravens did play up the Poe connection?"

"Well, when they started they didn't have any footage of the team, so I played Poe coming up out of his grave, recommending to fans to come see the team."

"Man, I really wish they were still doing that. By the way, I've been meaning to ask you, 'Do you always wear a mustache, or is that left over from your performance the other night?'" It was jet black and trimmed to a neat and angular geometry.

"Oh, I've liked mustaches all my life. I started wearing one way back in my early twenties. Some people tell me I shouldn't wear one because it's so out of style, but I like it, and I get to use it in my Poe show."

The performance I had referenced was for Poe's 205th birthday party at the Annabel Lee Tavern, a small Poe-themed restaurant at 601 South Clinton Street.

I'd eaten at the place months before. It's a nice place, but is small, with maybe a half dozen tables and a short bar, all of which are constantly in demand. Lindsey and I had early dinner reservations, but we showed up about fifteen minutes late and lost our table. Fortunately, we found spare room at the bar, but only by seconds.

This demand seemed strange to me because the Annabel Lee Tavern is kind of out of the way. It's not near the tourist area. It's not even near any of the Poe sites. But it has managed to do a lively business since it opened in December of 2007.

The most striking aspect of the restaurant is its exterior. The corner building that houses the restaurant was constructed in 1905 and is painted white with black, Poe-themed accents on its façade. A black gate leading up to it on one street has a framed image of Poe beside a quote from the apocryphal "Some Lines on Ale": "I am drinking ale today." Elsewhere on the building it says, "The happiest day, the happiest hour," which are the first few words of "The Happiest Day," one of Poe's early poems. Ravens are in every window and a raven weather vane perches atop the two-story building.

A side door is painted black with a white, leafless tree. Above it is Poe's signature, as well as a few lines from "To One in Paradise": "And all my days are trances / And all my nightly dreams / Are where thy dark eye glances." The front door had a modified quote from "Annabel Lee": "A wind blew out of a cloud,

chilling my beautiful Annabel Lee."
(The restaurant owners left off the
"and killing" part.) And then in
smaller print below that: "Please be
careful when opening the door. The
wind pulls the door open."

Inside, its dark walls are
painted with the words of Poe in
large, white letters. Poe's picture
was above the fireplace and here
and there throughout, including on
the cover of the menu that we were
handed.

The only part of that menu that's
really Edgar Allan Poe–themed is
the cocktail list, with everything
from a Morella and a Masque of the
Red Death to an Auguste Dupin and
a Manhattintinnabulation. I can't
remember what I ate there, probably because of that cocktail menu,
but I do remember ordering the
Edgar Allan Pâté for dessert, which

*The tavern menu*

the menu described as "tri-chocolate Pâté served with Madeira raspberry sauce
and whipped cream." It was awesome.

I asked Keltz what it was like to perform there on Poe's birthday. "It was a
packed house. As soon as a table emptied, people filled it up. I walked around
and did requests, so I performed 'The Raven' about a million times. 'Annabel
Lee' about fifty."

"Speaking of that, you've been doing Poe for a long time now. Do you get
tired of him?"

"No, I've never gotten tired of doing Poe. I just love it."

"Have the audiences' reactions to Poe changed over the time that you've
been performing him?"

"Well, I think the biggest change I saw happened around 2001 and 2002. The
Twin Towers had fallen and the Beltway Sniper had the area under siege." The
attacks on 9/11 need no comment, but I remembered the October of the Beltway
Sniper vividly, as I lived in the area at the time. Over the course of about three
weeks in the fall of 2002, ten people were shot and killed and three injured randomly in the D.C. Metro area: at a gas station, a Home Depot, and the mall. I had

friends who missed some of the attacks by mere hours, and I would see white vans pulled over by police outside my office as they looked for a killer they thought was driving around in such a vehicle. The killer, of course, ended up being killers, John Allen Muhammad and Lee Boyd Malvo, who would shoot random victims in crowded areas from the modified trunk of a blue 1990 Chevy Caprice.

"I was still getting requests for Poe, but people didn't want to hear the usual Poe stuff. I kept being asked if Poe had anything funny, so I started doing his short story 'The Spectacles.' Also 'Three Sundays in a Week.'"

These comedic stories are probably more representative of Poe's fiction work than his horror stories. Both play out like a single setup and punch line, with the former being a case of mistaken identity that ends up with a man marrying his great-great-grandmother, and the latter being a story of calendar quirks and date lines that might have inspired the ending of Jules Verne's *Around the World in 80 Days*.

"But really, the answer to your question is that every audience is already different, whether it's a literary event or a social event or a corporate event."

"You do Poe for corporate events?"

"Yes, quite a few. Those are often very stiff, you know, and everybody's worried so much about how well the event's going that they have a hard time enjoying it. What they really want is entertainment about them, not a writer from another time, and they certainly don't want serious things as much, but they do want something local or representative of the city, which is Poe."

Right. Edgar Allan Poe is Baltimore's local color, especially now with the purple and black of the Ravens.

"I had this one really interesting conversation with a guy who was planning a corporate event for an ultrasound group that was in town, and they wanted me to perform my Poe show." Keltz then acted out the conversation between himself and the event planner for me:

> **"Do you have any favorite Poe works that I should do?"**
> **"Well," the guy said, "I don't know too much about it,**
> **but the funny stuff, we want the funny stuff."**
> **About the only thing I'd got at that time was maybe**
> **"The Cask of Amontillado." This is before I'd worked in**
> **"The Spectacles" or "Three Sundays in a Week."**
> **"What's that about?" he asked me, and I told him about**
> **the catacombs.**
> **"Catacombs. Does he talk about bones in that?"**
> **"Yes, as a matter of fact, it refers to bones a great deal,**
> **mounds of bones, bones stacked to the ceiling."**

**"That's great, that's great, that's wonderful, that's exactly what we want. We're an ultrasound group and we deal with bones. Can you mention bones in there?"**
**"Of course, I'll mention bones anywhere."**
**"Great, great, that's great. I'll tell you, though, we study one particular bone in the human body, the tibia. Can you say something about the tibia?"**
**"Of course."**
**"Great. As soon as they hear that, they'll love it. There's one other thing, do you know what cortical bone is?"**
**"No."**
**"Well that's the outer layer of the bone, and that's more specifically what we study, the cortical bone in the tibia. Do you think you could mention something about that?"**

Continuing, Keltz told me how it ended up. "'This is getting so far from Poe,' I thought, but I did it. At the point in the story where Montresor sits on a pile of bones to listen to Fortunato scream behind the wall, he says, 'I ceased my labors and sat down upon the bones,'" but I said, 'I ceased my labors and sat down upon a pile of tibia, crunching the cortical bone as I did so.' And sure enough, they laughed."

I next tried to tease out what he thought of other Poe performers, either stage actors or screen actors. "I liked a lot of what Jeffrey Combs did and Norman George. But I have my own set idea of Poe, obviously, or I wouldn't do it the way I do it. But in movies, most of what I saw—Roger Corman, for example—just didn't do it for me."

"I was going to bring that up. You're one of the few people in this book who hasn't brought up Roger Corman and Vincent Price."

"I just wasn't into them, personally. Vincent Price never gave me the feeling that I get when I read or see Poe. There was one, *The Premature Burial,* that I liked, although I never finished it. Price wasn't in it, but Roger Corman directed it."

"Ray Milland was the guy in that one."

"I really liked what he did. His voice was great, the character is Poesque. But like I said, I never finished the movie. Do you know who Steven Berkoff is?"

His name didn't ring any bells for me, but after looking him up later, I recognized him. He's an English actor that we know best in the States from his 1980s villain roles in *Rambo II, Beverly Hills Cop,* and *Octopussy.* He's also done a little bit of time in Poe-Land, writing and starring in a TV short based on "The Tell-Tale Heart."

"I've seen some of his live shows, and I find them interesting and entertaining. What he would sometimes do with his Poe stage performances, he would come out and talk as himself, about his opinions and thoughts on Poe, and then he performs the story.

"I always thought, if I ever got to the age where I was too old to pull off Poe— right now I feel like I could perform him into my nineties, you know . . ."

"John Astin didn't start his Poe show until he was almost seventy."

"Right, but if I ever look too old, I'd like to shift to doing what Berkoff did."

"So what do you think about the phenomenon that actors would rather play Poe over any of Poe's characters?"

"He might've liked that, I think. When I perform the stories in middle schools, I tell the students beforehand, these stories are not autobiographical, but they still want to know after, 'Why did you kill the cat? How did you not go to jail for murdering your wife?'"

"How much of your career is Poe these days?"

"Most of it. It's always been that way. I used to do theater acting a lot, you know, with a whole cast." In fact, he'd met his wife, Teresa, when they were both performing in a stage version of Akira Kurosawa's *Rashomon.* "I did that until about 1988, but then I found out firsthand that I can do one night in a Poe show and earn more than a whole run in a theater play with other characters."

"Is that the nature of the one-man show or Poe?"

"I get more money for Poe than for anybody else I do. One time I was asked to do a Christmas show, but they still wanted Poe. So I took his meeting with Dickens at that hotel in Philadelphia and pretended that Dickens told Poe about a new story he was writing about Christmas. I would say, 'And in the hotel room, he acted it out for me, and his rendition of the story as I recall was very nearly if not accurately, thus . . .' and I turned around and launched into a British accent and 'A Christmas Carol.'"

Made me wonder what our Christmases today would be like if Poe had set a single story during that holiday.

## *Crypt-ography*

Back at The Cask of Amontillado Wine Tasting Among the Bones, we were descending into the depths of Westminster Hall's catacombs. That's the "Among the Bones" part.

Westminster Burying Ground dates back to 1789. It's a small cemetery, but it's where the founding fathers of Baltimore and quite a few heroes of the Revolutionary War are laid to rest, famous and important historic personages whom it's easy to forget while you're there because of somebody who was quickly and with little ceremony dropped into a hole there in 1849: Edgar Allan Poe.

When you place a man like Poe in your rot garden, you need to holy it up real fast, so three years after Poe was buried, they built a church in the graveyard. Actually, they built a church on top of the graveyard.

Westminster Hall roosts above almost half of the cemetery. To avoid disturbing the dead, they erected the church on brick piers that raised the structure above the tombs and ensured that they'd never be able to store stuff in a basement. Meanwhile, the dead in that section of the cemetery found their sky view exchanged for the undercarriage of a church.

And, of course, these days it's the undercarriage of a rental facility. Death is sometimes not the last humiliation.

So, going down into the depths of the church with my tour group, I had no idea what to expect. I knew very well that what I was about to see could be pretty cheesy, since they weren't real catacombs. However, I was hopeful.

I'd been down in a catacomb like this before, in Connecticut. Center Church-on-the-Green in New Haven was built in 1813 above a portion of a graveyard. In fact, all of New Haven Green, where the church stood, was once a cemetery, but they moved the tombstones and added six feet of dirt. All the human remains stayed in place, but were just shorn of their headstones and buried deeper. The only clue that you're having your lunch break above Connecticut's ancient dead is what's protected in the basement of the church itself.

That crypt in New Haven was fascinating and looked exactly like what it is: a section of graveyard under a church. It was well lit and paved in brick, and table graves and traditional headstones stuck out of the floor in normal graveyard configurations.

But the geometry of the Westminster catacombs in Baltimore is harder to grasp. Large, squat tombs dominated the space. Here and there a gravestone stuck up from the packed dirt floor with its recessed lighting. Loose gravestones leaned against walls and tombs. The place had great atmosphere, even with large windows and doors that faced the day, since technically, literally, and metaphorically, this was the Hall's ground floor.

It was a small space, but all the nooks and crannies and general dimness made it seem as if it had more to explore than it did. Despite the plexiglass and lights Jeff Jerome had mentioned at our dinner on Federal Hill, the place certainly was creepy, even with my tour group milling around and checking things out as though it were a department store.

Our tour guide, an older woman named Lucy, a lifelong Marylander who had lived in Baltimore for the past fourteen years, had us all sit down in rows of short church pews that had been set up in an open space. She then regaled us with a range of absolutely lurid stories. She told us that the graveyard was infamous in its day for being the haunt of grave robbers for the nearby medical college. She brandished a meat hook and told us how they would open the graves, and jab

*Westminster Hall catacombs*

implements like it beneath the soft space in the jaw beneath the chin to drag the corpses out of their holes. She told us of a church caretaker who would hide bodies in casks of rum and sell the former to the medical school and then the latter to the local taverns. She told the story of two morticians who had been wedded right there in the gloom of the tombs. It was one of the better tour spiels I've heard, both ghastly and believable.

However, she left out a single grisly story that Jeff Jerome would later fill me in on. George Spence was the graveyard caretaker who originally buried Poe and dug him up and reburied him again, when he was moved to his monument at a different spot twenty-five years later. Apparently, he lived in the catacombs . . . and died there, committing suicide "among the bones."

The tale naturally segued into the topic of ghost stories. Jerome told me that psychics and ghost hunters would regularly come to the cemetery, drawn by both Poe and the catacombs. He never heard anybody bring up the suicide of George Spence until he mentioned it during one of the many television interviews he had over the years. Not long after that, a psychic came in and felt the presence of a ghost who had killed himself, someone with the initials "G. S." "Ghosts appear after I talk about them," Jerome laughed.

"Whenever a psychic would start doing his or her thing, I would know after the second sentence what website they went to or what television show they watched." He told me that once a show called *Creepy Canada* was filmed at the Poe House. (Apparently the place fitting only half of the premise for the show was good enough.) The show dramatized what it presented as real-life ghost stories. I caught the episode on YouTube and saw that it incorporated footage from Redfield's *The Death of Poe*. According to Jerome, "They were really good ghost stories, they just never happened. But sure enough after that we would regularly hear a psychic tell one of the tales that *Creepy Canada* made up."

After Lucy finished her stories, we wandered around on our own, taking in the graves and the informational signs. The thing I bee-lined for, though, was something that had caught my attention during Lucy's talk. Leaning against a wall, on its end, was an empty, open, child-sized coffin with a perforated bottom. It was an ice coffin, used to keep the dead fresh for the funeral in those pre-embalming days.

At the front of the catacombs were some spectacular Poe artifacts. Like about half a dozen bottles of unfinished cognac and a few dried roses, actual offerings from the Poe Toaster. "Well, that's what Jeff tells us anyway, but I'm pretty sure they are from his own private stash," Lucy joked.

In front of the Poe Toaster artifacts was a large marble medallion of Poe's face, the features worn down enough to make him look scarred and ghoulish. It was the original bas-relief from his grave monument that had been replaced with a more durable bronze version.

There was also a large bronze plaque from Edgar Allan Poe School. It told his Baltimore story and included what I assume to be the school motto: MALO MORI QUAM FOEDARI, or "Death Rather than Disgrace." It also includes the

*Original marble medallion from Poe's grave and cognac bottles from the Poe Toaster, Westminster Hall catacombs*

*Ice casket, Westminster Hall catacombs*

quote "Poetry is the rhythmical creation of beauty," from Poe's "The Poetic Principle." The school was erected in 1880 and named after Poe in 1913. It was actually near Westminster Hall, and, according to an old tour program of the Poe House that I found online, people who attended the school remembered playing with skulls and bones from the catacombs at recess. The school's no longer around, having taken its motto literally, I assume.

The fact that there are catacombs at the cemetery where the man who wrote "The Cask of Amontillado" is buried is perfect and shows the universe had a plan for Poe, if one that Poe obviously didn't get a vote on. The only thing that would make the catacombs better would be if the remains of Poe himself were sheltered there behind some brick wall, but they're not. He's outside, about twenty feet away from the entrance to the catacombs, in the most prominent part of the cemetery.

## Edgar Allan Poe Is Dead

The entire point of any journey to a Poe site, and certainly one of the purposes of this book overall, is to get closer to Edgar Allan Poe. And you can't get any closer to the man than six feet above his bones. Poe's grave is the one site you have to visit if you can visit only one Poe site. It's the reason Poe is the figurehead of Baltimore culture . . . possession is, after all, nine-tenths of the law.

In many ways, the history of Poe's grave is a microcosm of Poe's own life and legacy. Before it got grand, it started out sucky.

The exterior graveyard—how great is it that I have to use that modifier?—is a thin strip of land that wraps around Westminster Hall. Like the catacombs, the geometry is a bit hard to fully fathom at first glance. It's mostly made of large, low tombs of varying designs, with a scattering of classic gravestones. It also has a pyramid, and at one place a raised connecting structure between Westminster Hall and the law school crosses over the cemetery so that you have to duck under to see the graves there. It's quite the wonder for a tiny urban cemetery, and would be interesting for its aesthetics even without Poe's remains hallowing its plots.

The story of Poe's after-death begins at what was once the Washington University Hospital. It was here that Poe was taken after he was found in that dismal state on East Lombard Street. Here he raved and swooned for three days. Here he cried out for some unknown but much guessed-at person named "Reynolds" throughout the night. Here he talked to imaginary beings in the room. Here where, in response to a bit of hopeful cheer that he would soon be well and with friends, he replied, "The best thing my best friend could do would be to blow out my brains with a pistol." Here where he breathed "Lord, help my poor soul" before dying.

Or at least that's the story. The facts of those four hazy days were handed down by only one witness, Poe's attending physician, John Joseph Moran. Poe's cousin Neilson Poe almost became a witness, but was turned back from visiting the author at the hospital because of Poe's wretched state and need for rest. Moran's first written version of the account that we know of was that original letter I had seen at the Enoch Pratt Free Library, the one in which he filled in Maria Clemm on her son-in-law's final hours.

The letter is a strange one. At points it's so flowery that it seems the doctor is attempting to sugarcoat the poet's demise so as not to disturb Clemm's feelings, with the twist being that the exaggerated platitudes he offered inadvertently turned into fulfilled prophecy: "How many thousands will yet, and for years to come, lament the premature demise of this truly great man!" He also gave such comforts as, "Those who had previously known him pronounced his corpse the most natural they had ever seen" and offered her Poe's oddly redemptive final words.

And while that seems to be reason enough to discount it, he's also pretty brutal in his account of the hours that led up to the death. Everything I listed happening in that hospital room three paragraphs back comes from that letter, as well.

To further complicate the account, in the last decade of his life, Moran went on the lecture circuit, discussing Poe's last days, giving contradictory accounts, and dramatizing his tale to hold his audiences.

And, of course, despite the doctor taking such an interest in Poe . . . we still don't know what the hell Poe died of.

Everything has been put forward, of course—heart problems, drunkenness, rabies, injuries sustained during an attack, drug overdose, congestion of the brain, cholera (which would make his Moyamensing delusion prophetic), exposure, betting the devil his head. If a man can die of it, it's been ascribed to Poe.

But regardless of the truth, the outcome is the same: Edgar Allan Poe died.

Today, the five-story brick building where it happened still stands. In fact, other than some architectural additions that relegated the building to a mere

*100 North Broadway, formerly Washington College Hospital*

wing, the exterior at 100 North Broadway is still recognizable from Poe's day. It has that same cupola on the roof (one of them, at least) and the same tower-like extrusions on either side of the door.

It's no longer a hospital, though. Sometime in the 1850s, it closed (after multiple attempts to burn it down due to its association with grave-robbing). It was then bought by the Episcopalians and turned into the Church Home and Hospital. That lasted until the new millennium, when it and its additions were turned into a mixture of public housing and middle- and upper-class town-homes.

The tower that held Poe's room was supposedly gutted for a stairwell, although that's not known for sure, as there is no conclusive proof of where in the building Poe spent his last breaths. Inside are supposed to be, or once were, two plaques, one in the lobby and one in that stairwell, each dating back more than a century and attesting to the soul that flew there.

But I wasn't able to enter and find out about the plaques due to the threatening NO TRESPASSING signs and severed heads impaled on spikes at the gates. That was dumb of me. I should have trespassed.

However, just outside those gates, the Maryland Historical Society marked the spot with a historic sign. Its header proclaims SITE OF POE'S DEATH, and it gives a brief account of the building and its significance. It does not end with, SORRY, WE KILLED POE.

*Poe's grandfather's headstone, Westminster Burying Ground*

Perhaps the only thing crazier about this being the building where Poe died so mysteriously is that it's also the building where his beloved Muddy died twenty -two years later, when it was the Church Home and Hospital. It's unknown whether Maria Clemm was aware of that strange layering of reality.

Poe's next stop was the grave.

Poe was given the saddest funeral service ever. It was October 8, a gloomy, damp, cold day that didn't even provide him the dignity of a rain shower. Only a few people were in attendance, despite the fact that Moran told Clemm in his letter, "His remains were visited by some of the first individuals of the city, many of them anxious to have a lock of his hair." Those in attendance were three of his Herring relatives, his cousin Neilson Poe, Dr. Snodgrass, a University of Virginia classmate named Zaccheus Collins Lee, and Joseph Clarke, who was one of Poe's past schoolmasters. It was presided over by Reverend W. T. D. Clemm, a relative of Virginia and Maria's. All told, that's eight people to see Poe off into the afterlife/oblivion.

Three minutes later, he was in the dirt, beside the grave of his grandfather, his grandmother, and his brother, in a cheap coffin that was little more than polished planks of wood nailed together. He got no headstone. Neilson Poe would purchase one about a decade later, but it was hit by a derailed train that ran crazy through the stone carver's yard. Of course. Its epitaph was supposed to have read in Latin HERE, AT LAST, HE IS HAPPY. The universe could not have a happy Poe.

For more than a quarter of a century, Edgar Allan Poe moldered, unheralded, in that Baltimore plot, except for a small sandstone block inexplicably marked "80" that George Spence, the man who buried Poe multiple times and then killed himself, placed.

But he is not there, for he is risen.

The location of Poe's original plot is behind Westminster Hall, in the Poe family plot. It sits right beside a gravestone erected for his grandfather, David Poe, Sr. (1743–1816), which notes him as a "patriot" and "grandfather of Edgar Allan Poe" as well as giving his birthplace as Londonderry, Ireland.

The plot is deep enough into the cemetery that you could see how the Poe Toaster could sneak in and out, despite the crowds of recent years looking out for him. In 1913, a man named Orin C. Painter decided to mark the spot officially, even though Poe's remains weren't there anymore. So he bought a stone marker for Poe's ex-plot that still stands today.

It's shaped like a gravestone, rectangular with a semicircle atop it that encloses a relief of a very tame-looking raven that these days is missing the tip of its beak. The "epitaph" reads:

ORIGINAL BURIAL PLACE OF
EDGAR ALLAN POE
FROM
OCTOBER 9, 1849
UNTIL
NOVEMBER 17, 1875

———————————

MRS. MARIA CLEMM, HIS MOTHER-IN-LAW
LIES UPON HIS RIGHT AND VIRGINIA POE,
HIS WIFE, UPON HIS LEFT UNDER THE
MONUMENT ERECTED TO HIM IN THIS
CEMETERY.

By the way, this is exactly how I want my tombstone to read: JUST KIDDING . . . BURIED ELSEWHERE.

Today, as it has been for about 140 years, Poe's dust is at the front gates of the cemetery. It's an interesting story. One night, before the flesh had completely dropped off his bones, Poe pushed his way through the loam and shambled wearily over to a new spot in the cemetery, much like someone would switch positions in bed. The nearby residents of Baltimore didn't want him doing that again because it was, well, damned spooky, so they stuck a larger and heavier grave marker on top of the new spot to stop him from getting up anymore.

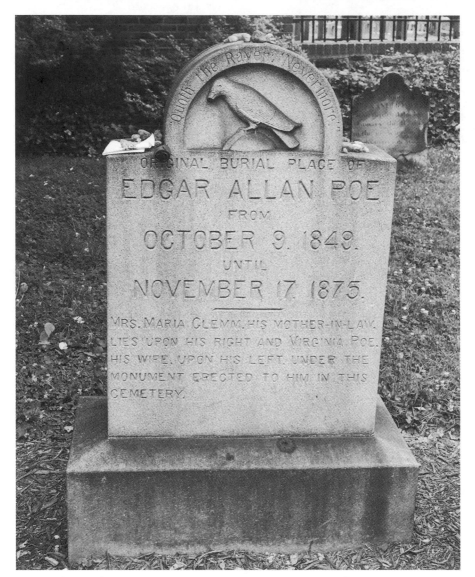

*Original site of Poe's grave, Westminster Burying Ground*

Actually, the bones were moved as part of a new memorial to him, which was unveiled on November 17, 1875. It was on that date that Baltimore really, officially claimed Edgar Allan Poe.

About ten years earlier, when Sara Sigourney Rich, a local teacher, decided to raise money for a proper Poe monument, Poe still sat under the sandstone 80. Students started a penny campaign, various people donated, and half the cost was covered by Philadelphia publisher George W. Childs, who was born in Baltimore.

The monument was designed by George A. Frederick, who also designed

Baltimore's City Hall. It turned out it was too big to fit the original plot, so it was placed over the site of Maria Clemm's grave, who had died just a few years previously. That meant Poe had to be dug up. An article in Baltimore's *Evening News* described the exhumation, which was led by a Mr. Tuder, who apparently was the guy people called when they needed coffins pulled from the earth:

> He set about his task early in the afternoon, and the sun was just setting behind the western horizon when his spade sounded on the coffin lid of the poet. It lay about five feet from the surface, and at first sight appeared as sound as when first put into the earth. On carefully raising it to the brink of the grave Mr. Tuder discovered that it was partially broken in at the sides, and that the lid near the head was so much decayed that it fell to pieces on the ground. On looking through the aperture thus created Messrs. Spence, Tuder, their assistants, and the News man beheld the skeleton of Poe. The flesh and funeral robes of course had crumbled into dust, and there was nothing left but the bare bones and a few clumps of hair attached to the skull, to tell that a body had once been there. The skeleton was in perfect condition, the arms lying as they were arranged in death, and the back and leg bones were in a natural position. The ribs had fallen out, but lay in order on either side of the coffin, and the skull had not moved in the least from its proper place. The teeth of the upper jaw must have been shaken out in the lifting of the coffin, for they lay scattered about the skull, but those of the lower jaw, which had fallen from the rest of the "face," were perfect, not one being missing from either side. The teeth looked pearly white, and were in excellent preservation. Without loss of time Mr. Spence had the coffin placed within a wooden case and lowered to the grave prepared for it, and before the darkness set in the clay was dashed for the second time on the hollow sounding casket, and the remains of the poet were covered up, never, it is to [*sic*] hoped, to be disturbed again.

As in life, Poe couldn't stay in just one place. And that's how Susan Jaffe Tane, the Enoch Pratt Free Library, and the Edgar Allan Poe Society of Baltimore attained their pieces of Poe's box.

But then the monument and the remains it marked were moved again to a more prominent part of the cemetery: the front corner at Fayette and Greene Streets. Maria Clemm came along with Poe, as she did so many times in life. Ten years later, Virginia Poe was reunited in what is the closest to a happy ending the three ever had . . . although how Virginia came from her New York plot to Baltimore is, as so many Poe-related ones are, a strange story.

Her remains were brought courtesy of William Fearing Gill, the early Poe biographer and one-time owner of the Poe Cottage in Fordham. The church lot where Virginia was buried was being razed, and according to Gill's story, he just happened to be there to rescue Virginia's bones from the shovel as they were about to toss them out. He put them into a box and placed them under his bed, where they sat for years, until a

*Grave of Edgar Allan Poe,*
*Westminster Burying Ground*

raven came into his room and rebuked him. He immediately sent them down to Neilson Poe to have them buried with Poe and Maria Clemm.

Obviously, it's hard to tell how much of the story is fanciful, a joke, or what, but it's generally held that it's not a hoax or a mistake, that the remains are at least those of Virginia Poe, although whether they were pilfered early, watched over carefully, or rescued just in the nick of time by that ardent Poe fan is unclear.

The unveiling of the monument in 1875 was a grand occasion. John Latrobe was there. Neilson Poe was there. Walt Whitman was there. Poe's send-off was a quarter of a century late, but it was done in style.

I have visited Poe's grave more than any other site in this book. It's a tall, white rectangular marble column, more stately than spooky. Not counting the granite pedestal on which it sits, the monument is about six and a half feet tall. In the center of its front side is Poe's face in a circle of dark bronze, the one that replaced the weathered marble version I saw in the catacombs. Actually it replaced a previous bronze medallion, as the one that replaced the marble one was stolen, probably for scrap, as opposed to unscrupulously zealous Poe fans.

Poe's name is the only other thing that adorns the front of the monument, while the other three sides give merely the names and dates of the three sets of remains beneath it. It's as if nobody felt up to the task of composing the epitaph of the man who wrote with such genius about death and eternity. Still, Poe couldn't escape unscathed. His birthday is mis-engraven as January 20 instead of January 19, but at least his middle name is correctly spelled.

Poe's grave is always visible to passersby, even when the front gates are locked, as it's almost within arms distance of the wrought-iron fence at the front of the property.

In some ways, I like the marker on his original grave better. It's more Poesque and benefits from a more secluded spot, as opposed to being adjacent to a busy city street. I can't really imagine Poe's current grave monument fitting in the middle of "Ulalume." Obviously, I want Poe's grave to be eerie. But thanks to the size of his monument and the bronze plaque of his face right in its center, it really does feel like you're squaring off with the massive legacy of the man.

The last time I cast a shadow on that grave in the course of writing this book was the evening of January 19, 2014, Poe's 205th birthday. It was at another one of those celebrations thrown by Jeff Jerome in his self-appointed capacity as curator emeritus. About a hundred people showed up on that cold January evening, as light turned to dusk and dusk turned to night, to listen to actors in period costume read Poe above Poe.

This one site is almost more biographical than any book could be. It's the death site of America's great morbidist, yet its dignified design shows a legacy beyond his famous work in the macabre; it honors him as America's most venerated author and poet. Finally, it marks the eternal reunion of the three people who were all the world to each other in life.

It's hard for me to say goodbye to Edgar Allan Poe in this book, which is why I'm happy to say I'm not going to . . . yet.

*Tower of London raven cage with the Shard in the distance*

CHAPTER 6

# Great Britain

*Some Enchanted Far-Off Isle in Some Tumultuous Sea*

I HAD TO CROSS AN OCEAN FOR THIS BOOK, and it was John Allan's fault. Also Peter Fawn's. I'll get to both of these guys here in a bit.

The case can be made that Edgar Allan Poe—the Tomahawk Man, the Yankee-born southerner, America's most influential writer—was actually a European author. His tales were frequently set across the ocean. "The Cask of Amontillado" takes place at, or rather under, the Carnival of Venice. "The Oval Portrait" is painted in the mountains of Italy. "A Man of the Crowd" and "King Pest" cover the streets and alleys of London. "William Wilson" takes place mostly in England and ends in Rome. All three of his Dupin mysteries are Parisian. "The Pit and the Pendulum" happens in Spain, "Metzengerstein" in Hungary. Even those tales that aren't given an actual place still feel European, what with their castles and abbeys and aristocracies—"The Fall of the House of Usher," "The Masque of the Red Death," "Hop-Frog," "Ligeia."

His work also resonated more and resonated more quickly with audiences in Europe, where his popularity started to take off before the end of his life and whose influence on the Old World is probably rivaled by no other New World author. It was the French who really first discovered his value, and the poet Charles Baudelaire, in particular, who evangelized him. That's generally the way things go. The States has cool stuff, but we don't know it until Europe clues us in. Like the blues.

But this book isn't an analysis of geography in Poe's fiction. I'm bringing up the European quality of his works because for five years, Poe really was European—specifically, he was British.

Poe died in the previous chapter of this book, but if in his delirium, his life flashed before his eyes, some of his first memories may have come from a place on the far side of the Atlantic Ocean.

In the summer of 1815, Edgar Allan Poe was six years old. He had been living with his foster parents, John and Frances Allan, in Richmond for four years at that point. Allan was a merchant in a partnership with a man named Charles Ellis, and business was good. So good that they decided to open a satellite office in London. Allan, who was from Scotland anyway, was to be the one to run it.

A month-long sea voyage later, Poe stepped a tiny foot onto the motherland of his birth mother. For the next five years, Poe would receive his early schooling in London. Maybe pick up a slight accent, I don't know.

Eventually, Allan's business tanked, and in the summer of 1820, he took his family back to Richmond, where he would have to settle for his dreams of wealth being fulfilled by the death of a rich uncle.

Had Allan's fortune went otherwise in London, the family might have stayed. In that case, who knows what would have happened to Poe. Maybe he would have found a more receptive audience during his lifetime. Maybe he would've gotten famous without having to die first. He and Charles Dickens could've toured America together as a double bill and joked heartily over a ruby port about how Poe came this close to growing up American. Or maybe the shift in environment would have been just enough to tweak his personality to make him more amenable to joining the foster-family business. But that's not how it happened, and his childhood across the ocean usually merits only a few pages in his biographies.

In addition, very little of Poe's time in London is publically memorialized. But there is one place. Whether it was worth crossing an ocean for, I was about to find out.

## Kilts and Crowns

The first thing the Allans and Poe did upon landing on the island is spend some time in Scotland, visiting relatives and just generally stretching their legs after more than thirty days at sea.

Their time in Scotland was only one to two months, although some say it was long enough for Poe to attend school for a little while in John Allan's hometown of Irvine, but a residue of little Eddie still exists from that short, boyhood trip to the southwest area of the country. Unfortunately, I couldn't fit Scotland into my book itinerary. It helps quiet my completist soul to know that Poe's most regarded biographer, Arthur Hobson Quinn, described Poe's time in Scotland as "overemphasized" and doubts whether he even went to school there. But some cursory research revealed a few Poe spots that, had I all the money, time, and interest in the world, I might've checked out.

Like the Flowerbank Guest House bed and breakfast in the town of Newton Stewart, which advertises that Edgar Allan Poe visited the house during the trip.

Or the North Ayrshire Heritage Centre in Saltcoats, which displays a gravestone of a husband and wife named David Poe and Ann Allan, whom they deem to be relatives of the poet.

Or the city of Kilmarnock, where people claim that Poe copied gravestone inscriptions in the yard of the New Laigh Kirk and where, elsewhere in the city, the local council has installed a plaque that reads:

> THIS PLAQUE HAS BEEN ERECTED NEAR
> THE SITE OF THE HOME OF ALLAN FOWLDS WHO
> WAS A SEED MERCHANT IN EARLY 19TH CENTURY
> KILMARNOCK. HIS WIFE WAS THE SISTER OF
> JOHN ALLAN, WHO WENT TO THE UNITED STATES
> OF AMERICA AND WAS THE GUARDIAN OF
> EDGAR ALLAN POE (1809–1849),
> PICTURED LEFT.
> EDDIE, AS HIS FAMILY CALLED HIM,
> SPENT SOME MONTHS IN 1815 LIVING WITH
> RELATIVES IN IRVINE AND OFTEN VISITED THE
> FOWLDS IN KILMARNOCK. SEVERAL AYRSHIRE
> INFLUENCES ARE THOUGHT TO HAVE LATER
> EMERGED IN POE'S WORKS.

The image of Poe "pictured left" shows a full-length figure holding a hat in his hands.

Although Poe's Scotland connection is tenuous, the London one certainly isn't. We know a good bit of the specifics of Poe's stay in the Big Smoke. For instance, the young Poe boarded for two years at 146 Sloane Street in Chelsea at the school of Miss Dubourg, a name he would remember and recycle into his "The Murders in the Rue Morgue." His family, meanwhile, lived at 47 Southampton Row in Camden and then later a few houses down at number 39. He used the latter address in his story "Why the Little Frenchman Wears His Hand in a Sling."

Unfortunately, nothing survives of his time at those addresses, the buildings long since replaced and the landscape long since changed, nor do any memorials mark the time here of the boy Poe. The one place in London that does memorialize Poe is in the district of Stoke Newington.

But I had all day to check out Stokie, so in the morning of my only day in London, I decided to kill some time and shake some jet lag by hitting up the Tower of London. This eighteen-acre castle complex on the Thames was begun in the eleventh century by William the Conqueror. Over the centuries, the place has been expanded and its main purpose changed, from a royal residence to a zoo

*Tower of London grounds*

to a treasury to a prison and execution site; the last is its most famous phase, and it was a prison for much of its pre-tourism existence, up until the 1950s, in fact.

Poe might have visited here during his childhood. His parents' Southampton Row address was only a little more than two miles away. One of Allan's surviving letters from right before they left England for good even mentions "the Tower" in regard to the political soap opera that was the entire marriage of Queen Charlotte and King George IV:

> **The arrival of the Queen produced an unexpected sensation. Few thought she would return, but the bold & courageous manner by which she effected it has induced a vast number to think her not guilty. She was received with immense acclamations & the Populace displaced her horses, drew her past Carlton House & thence to Alderman Wood's House, South Audley. The Same day the King made a Communication to the House of Lords charging her with High Treason (adultery). Some said she had been arrested on Wednesday & sent to the Tower but I think this report *then* premature though equally certain in a few days.**

Today, the Tower of London is a carnival for those who love English history. You can see the lawn where Henry VIII had Anne Boleyn beheaded and the Bloody Tower, where Sir Walter Raleigh was imprisoned. The crown jewels are there. I also saw a two-story-tall dragon made out of armor and some actor in medieval rags roasting a rabbit. You enter the walls of the Tower of London a mere tourist and come out a tea-sipping Anglophile.

And I did all this. I darted through the castle's many towers, saw an exhibit on torture devices (no pits, no pendulums), marveled at the armor of famous kings, took pictures of the Tower Bridge looming just outside the gates and all those guys dressed like that dude on the gin bottle. But, in the spirit of my trip, I was really there to see the ravens.

The Tower of London keeps a domesticated unkindness of ravens, officially six of them, cared for by a full-time ravenmaster from its ranks of Yeoman Warders. Unlike the Tower's past prisoners, the birds are given free reign of the tower grounds, although their wings are clipped to keep them from getting into trouble.

The original reason that ravens are kept at the Tower is somewhat unclear, but these days they are part of the lore and tradition of the place. The legend goes that if the six ravens ever flee the Tower, the kingdom will fall. That's a lot of pressure to put on the birds, so the tower helps them out by keeping more than six birds at any given time.

When the tower became a raven sanctuary is also unclear. Legend again says that it dates back to Charles II in the 1600s. Some say it goes back even further, that ravens have been amassing there since the early executions, awaiting their turn at the condemned. Most think it started more recently, in the Victorian Era, and one of those ideas attributes their famous presence at the Tower to a certain American poem in the 1840s that made ravens popular. If ravens are around, Poe's in the story somewhere.

In another, less direct Poe connection, it was discovered in May of 2013 that a fox had taken down two of the ravens. One of the darkly departed was named Grip, after, of course, the pet raven of Charles Dickens who would inspire Poe's poem and whose carcass I saw at the Free Library of Philadelphia.

During my visit, most of the ravens

*A Tower of London raven*

stayed in a cage on the lawn near the White Tower, which is the central and oldest part of the castle, but a few of them were hopping the lawn and posing for the tourists. I got within two feet of one of the large black birds, although I was wary of the CAUTION! RAVENS MAY BITE signs that were prominently posted.

The entire time I was there, their croaks reverberated among the various towers, even above the din of the extremely large crowd. I spent much of my time there following the ravens around and ignoring the important history of the place. But, eventually I was done chasing ravens. Next on my itinerary was a fox.

## A Bit of a Bust

After Poe's time at Miss Dubourg's in Chelsea, John Allan enrolled his ward at the Manor House School in Stoke Newington. Poe would have been eight years old at the time he started there, and Stoke Newington was farther away from his family, about four miles outside of London at the time. The next couple of years were a tumultuous period for his parents back in London, as John faced financial ruin and Frances health issues, but nothing much of consequence happened to Poe . . . except that the school stuck with him enough to flavor the first part of his story "William Wilson."

In that story, a boy away at school discovers he has a doppelganger, one who thwarts him every time he attempts mischief. As he becomes an adult and travels the world, the mischief metastasizes into crime and immorality, but his strange twin always mysteriously appears to frustrate him. For the beginning school scenes, Poe worked in details of the Manor House School and the area and buildings surrounding it. Even named the headmaster after his old Manor House School headmaster, John Bransby.

To get to Stoke Newington, I took the Piccadilly line in the direction of Cockfosters. When Poe attended school there, the town was on its way to changing from a rural village to the more urban outer edge of London. But even today, as a district of that city, it's still not the most accessible. The crowds that had packed the Tube to riding-on-shoulders-room-only at the

*St. Mary's old church (foreground) and St. Mary's new church (background)*

central London stops had thinned to just a few people in each car by the time I got to Arsenal. From there, I had to walk a mile, cutting through Clissold Park at the end.

Poe had me expecting the below from his story:

> **A misty-looking village of England, where were a vast number of gigantic and gnarled trees, and where all the houses were excessively ancient. In truth, it was a dream-like and spirit-soothing place, that venerable old town. At this moment, in fancy, I feel the refreshing chilliness of its deeply-shadowed avenues, inhale the fragrance of its thousand shrubberies, and thrill anew with undefinable delight, at the deep hollow note of the church-bell, breaking, each hour, with sullen and sudden roar, upon the stillness of the dusky atmosphere in which the fretted Gothic steeple lay imbedded and asleep.**

Stoke Newington still maintains its quaintness, but it's that of a bustling town in the borough of Hackney now instead of the rural village Poe described.

I was headed to Stoke Newington Church Street, a nice little stretch of the district populated with unique shops and restaurants, and which replaced the general area that was the domain of the young Poe and later that of the fictional young Wilson.

The Manor House School was a plain, rustic, two-story building with a pair of pyramidal roofs. It no longer stands, but the old church, with its "Gothic steeple" that Poe uses in his story as one of the few places outside the school the pupils are allowed to visit, is still there, so close to the new church across the street that they almost cross steeples. Both are called St. Mary's, but the one Poe would have known was built in 1563. It's smaller, darker, and barely showing the damage it sustained in World War II. It also has a gloriously unkempt and crumbling graveyard. The "new" church dates back merely to the 1850s.

Another place on the street I wanted to check out was Stoke Newington Library. Unfortunately, it was a few days after Christmas. While that gave a festive air to the window displays in the stores and the decorations on the light poles, it also meant that the library was closed for the holiday break. Had I been able to enter its foyer area, I would have found a plaque that states:

EDGAR ALLAN POE
BORN 1809 DIED 1849
AMERICAN ROMANCER, POET & CRITIC

WAS A PUPIL
AT THE MANOR HOUSE SCHOOL
WHICH STOOD NEAR THIS SPOT
DURING HIS BOYHOOD 1817–1820
ERECTED 1949 THE CENTENARY OF HIS DEATH

Fortunately, I was in England for a better reason and in Stoke Newington, particularly, for a better memorial. Just down the road, I could see the glowing severed head of Edgar Allan Poe floating high above the street.

The Fox Reformed is a wine bar stuck between a small electronics shops and what was once a small café, but which was being remodeled into who-knows-what. The wine bar's sign is a large, flat fox jutting out perpendicular above the red-painted wood of its façade. It was about here that the Manor House School stood.

Testifying to that fact, above the restaurant and attached to the pale brick of the second story, high above vandal height, was a white bust of Edgar Allan Poe.

*The Fox Reformed restaurant*

It was set on a white pedestal marked with the simple black letters P-O-E.

It wasn't a bust of the poet as a nine-year-old boy, as we have no clue what that kid looked like, but the New York Poe with the iconic mustache, which is the only way we recognize the poet. Actually, the bust somehow made the author look older than the forty years he lived. I don't know if it was a trick of the white stone, or the pronounced bags under his eyes, or the squarish, protruding forehead with tamer hair than I'm used to seeing on the poet, but the bust just seemed to depict a Poe who lived beyond that tragic stop in Baltimore.

Not that it was a bad bust. I liked it. Had a nuance to it and wasn't just a carbon copy of the countenance we're all familiar with. And it was immediately recognizable as Poe, even without the black letters, and even though it was three thousand miles away from his homeland.

Directly below the bust, closer to my

own head's height was a pair of plaques. The top one was circular, colored brown, and stated:

LONDON BOROUGH OF HACKNEY
EDGAR ALLAN POE
1809–1849
WRITER AND POET
WAS A PUPIL AT THE
MANOR HOUSE SCHOOL (1817–1820),
WHICH STOOD ON THIS SITE.

The plaque below this was rectangular and slate-colored. It read:

POE
UNVEILED BY STEVEN BERKOFF
ON 4 JUNE 2011
THE FLICKER CLUB

THE EDGAR ALLAN POE SOCIETY

The first plaque is the historical one. The latter plaque commemorated the event

*Poe bust, The Fox Reformed restaurant*

where the white bust directly above it was unveiled. YouTube footage of the event shows a packed street and a black cloth over the bust that was removed by a rope to much applause. The man at the other end of that rope was Steven Berkoff, the '80s movie baddy whom I had discussed with David Keltz in Baltimore.

The bust, which was sculpted by Ralph Perrott (who for some reason didn't get his name on the plaque when the guy who pulled the rope did), was unveiled during the Stoke Newington Literary Festival with help from the Flicker Club, a group that celebrates and organizes events around movies based on literature.

After I stared up at Poe long enough

for my neck to ache, I was ready to move on. However, what I had planned to do next was rendered moot for two reasons. I wanted to walk into the restaurant, sidle up to the bar (if sidling is something they allow in England), order up something extremely British-sounding off the menu, and ask the bartender how often people drop by because of Poe.

The first reason this question would have been irrelevant is that as I, deep into that darkness peering, stared through the window of the restaurant, I could see from the small portion visible to me that the interior of The Fox Reformed was Poe-themed.

A large placard affixed to the wall by the bar bore an old photograph of the Manor House School, an image of Poe's face, and some text I assume was an explanation of why there was a floating ghost head outside. I also spied a large poster from the 1964 Roger Corman–Vincent Price movie *The Tomb of Ligeia*.

Second, and more relevant, the restaurant was closed, meaning this is going to be a much shorter section of the book than I had hoped. The sign on the window advertised that it was open from noon to midnight, and I was there at the thoroughly respectable hour of four o'clock. This was a big bummer less because of Poe and more because the menu in the window advertised duck confit and mulled wine.

The place seemed worthwhile enough that I decided to stick around for a few hours to see if it opened after dusk. After hanging out in the park for a bit, and then the old church cemetery, I jumped into a pub just down the street called Ryan's Bar, where I learned what a bacon butty is and watched more English football in an hour than I had in my entire life until then.

Eventually, an hour after dusk, when the place still hadn't opened, I had to give up and return downtown. I stood outside the wine bar and looked up at Poe one last time, almost glowing in the night by the light of the Christmas decorations, a pallid bust just waiting for its own raven.

I finished that night at the top of the Shard, the brand-new giant glass splinter of an office tower that is the tallest building in the European Union. I was there to take in London in a single, 360-degree panorama, just so I could say I saw all of London in a day. However, despite my adventure in London, it was the next day that was the big one.

## The Man Who Collected Poe

I won't say I was driving the highways out of London at Withnail speeds, but I was in a hurry. At the end of my road was the largest collection of Poe memorabilia on the planet.

This was the real reason I crossed the ocean. Not to see a bust on a wine bar, not to chase ravens across execution sites, not even to learn first-tongue what a bacon butty is. I was there to meet Peter Fawn and sift my oily fingers through his Amazing Collection of Poe.

That meant I was headed toward one of the suburbs of Brighton, on the southern coast of the island, where Fawn lives . . . sometimes.

Let me tell you what I expected Peter Fawn to be like, based on the little I knew of him prior to shaking his hand. I knew he was a high-tier collector of items connected to one of the most famous authors in history. I knew he worked in the lucrative payments industry. And I knew he spent most of his time abroad on business. I had corresponded with him over e-mail while he was stationed in Kenya. He had only a brief window, when he would be back in England for Christmas (and he very graciously agreed to sacrifice one of those days for me), but would then be off for his next assignment, in Nigeria. "In the past five years, I've probably spent a year and half here in England," he would later tell me.

So I expected someone with a salesmen's personality, a boisterous wheeler and dealer. Someone who tromps across the world doing big business, regaling important clients at expensive dinners, signing and getting people to sign contracts filled with zeroes. Someone who knew how to make big bucks and how to spend them with over-the-top aplomb.

And maybe he can be that way, but the man who answered the door for me was soft-spoken, deferential, and as I got to know him over the course of the day, an easy-going guy who happens to be obsessed with an American author whose works involved ripping the teeth out of victim's mouths with pliers or severing their heads with clock hands or—and sorry to be so graphic on this one—ruminating on the proper way to furnish a room.

Fawn led me through his house and out to the small backyard. As we walked he asked me how I was faring in London. Since the phrase Stoke Newington is one of the code words of the Poe community, I mentioned that I'd been there the previous evening.

"Oh? Did you see my bust?" He raised his hand high into the air.

"You were behind that?"

"Yes, that's mine. My friend Clive Perrott and I wanted to do something to commemorate his life there, so I got somebody to make the bust. What did you think of all the stuff inside?"

I told him about my unfortunate timing, which was apparently more unfortunate than I realized. According to Fawn, the place had more Poe than just the placard and poster I'd been able to snatch a glimpse of between the wine bottles stacked in the window . . . and it was all from his collection.

We ended up at a small, single-car garage adjacent to the house. Well, at one time it was a garage. Fawn had turned it into an Edgar Allan Poe shrine.

As he flipped a switch for the fluorescents, I walked into the room, where an overwhelming crowd of black mustaches and beaks stared back at me in the cold light of what looked to be a relatively disorganized suburban home office. "I, uh, guess we should start at the beginning."

Peter Fawn was from the Brighton area. When he was sixteen, American Express opened an office downtown, and he got a job there, a job he turned into a thirty-two-year career with the company, overseeing projects in Eastern Europe and the Middle East. Recently, he had left American Express to become a partner in a new venture in the same industry and had been working on the African continent.

But his Poe collection was not really an expression of his financial success. Not directly, anyway. It had started when he was ten years old.

"I was reading this book called *Supernatural Stories for Boys*. I still have it, actually, in my warehouse. But it had 'The Black Cat' in it, and I just stopped there. I was fascinated. It was so different." His next Poe memory was a single scene from a documentary or biopic of Poe's life, in which Virginia's mouth starts gushing blood while singing at the piano. "I'm about twelve years old at this point, and I'm like, whoa, this is crazy."

After that, he chose Poe as a topic for a school assignment, the type where most of his classmates chose what they did over the school break. "Nobody had heard of him in my class, even some of the teachers maybe, because he's not taught in school here until university or maybe A-level. I just went overboard. I wrote to all the museums in America. I did all these illustrations for it. I got an A.

"But this, more than anything, changed my life." He pulled out a tall, thin hard-back book with a garish collage of what seemed like Poe or Poesque references—a curved blade, an aristocrat with a bloody face, an old castle, a veiny hand with broken nails, a skull with an eyeball in its socket. They were actually repurposed images from the posters of contemporary 1970s British horror movies . . . *Demons of the Mind, Tales from the Crypt, From Beyond the Grave, The Wicker Man*. It was called *The Edgar Allan Poe Scrapbook* and was edited by Peter Haining. Dominating all the images on the cover was the face of Poe in lurid green and yellow.

"I was walking from Brighton Station with my mum, and we passed this anti-quarian bookshop. I glanced in the window and said, 'That looks like Poe.' The book cost ten pounds, and when you're that young, and especially in the family situation I was in, where I didn't have a father and my mum had to work, ten pounds was an awful lot of money to spend. But she bought it for me, and I just treasured it, and it became my inspiration. That really was the turning point. After that I bought a film poster for ten pounds in London . . . *Tales of Terror*."

His first paycheck from American Express, at the age of 16, was 160 pounds. He spent 130 of it on a first edition Poe, and he just never stopped.

*The Edgar Allan Poe Scrapbook* wasn't the first artifact from the Peter Fawn

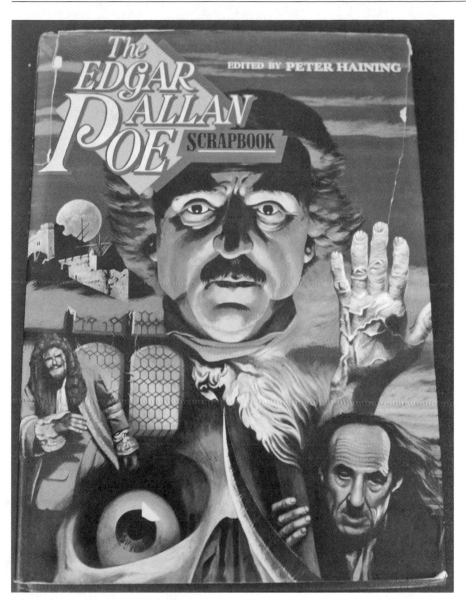

*The Edgar Allan Poe Scrapbook*

Poe Collection I'd seen. At the Morgan Library exhibit in Manhattan, I'd noticed his name under a painting of Poe. I'd thought the piece of art was just another of the million paintings of Poe that exist, but Fawn disabused me. "No, that one's unique. That was the painting created by Micheal Deas for the 2009 U.S. Postal Service stamp." Deas is a well-known painter based in New Orleans. He's painted portraits of famous Americans for more than twenty U.S. stamps, and is the guy who painted the iconic woman-with-torch Columbia Pictures movie

*Vincent Price autograph on a first-day cover of the 1949 three-cent Poe stamp*

studio logo. He is also the author of the 1989 book *The Portraits & Daguerreotypes of Edgar Allan Poe,* which has become the standard reference work on the topic.

"Normally, the Postal Service keeps the paintings it commissions, but since Michael painted two of its most profitable stamps, James Dean and Marilyn Monroe, they made an exception and let him have Poe. And now I have Poe."

Most of the items weren't really displayed so much as they were kept. As a result, we didn't just view them; we dug into them. He immediately started pulling items out for me to look at. "Just tell me when to stop." I didn't.

There was a signed letter from President Theodore Roosevelt discussing Poe. A Grolier Club medallion, the same kind as the one affixed to the Fayette Street house in Boston. An original street sign from Edgar Allan Poe Street in Manhattan, bright yellow instead of green, leaning against a filing cabinet. Poe's middle name had been misspelled

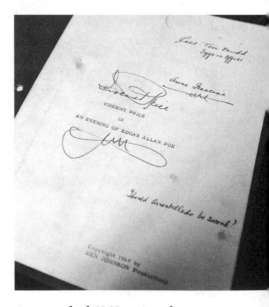

*Autographed 1969 script of Vincent Price's* **An Evening of Edgar Allan Poe**

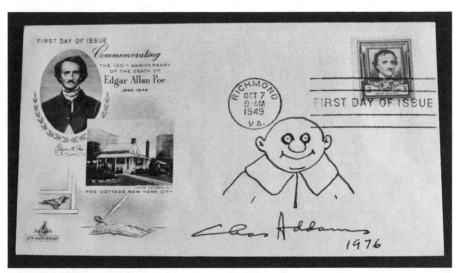

*Charles Addams autograph on a first-day cover of the 1949 three-cent*
*Poe stamp*

on the sign in the usual way and then corrected by overlaying an *a* over the *e*. Fawn had an original, autographed script from 1969 used by Vincent Price for his *An Evening of Edgar Allan Poe,* covered in Price's notes. On the front page Price had inked, "Should Amontillado be second?" and "Eggs in office."

He had an original doorknob from the Edgar Allan Poe National Historic Site in Philadelphia from a previous renovation. "Poe's hand touched this. Great, right?" He had an original playbill from an 1808 play that starred both of Poe's parents, as well as another from *Cinderella* that Poe's mother performed in 1807 at the Boston Theatre. He had a first-day cover of the 1949 three-cent Poe stamp with an autographed doodle of Uncle Fester from Charles Addams and another one autographed by Alfred Hitchcock. He had an original ticket for an appearance by Poe himself in 1845 at New York University.

At one point, he motioned up to the shelf where one of Poe's actual letters was framed. I had just finished reading the two-volume set of his correspondence put together by Ostrom, Pollin, and Savoye on the plane flight over and

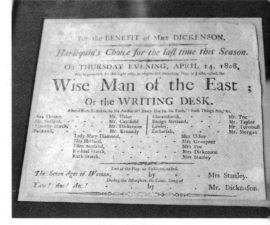

*Original playbill featuring Poe's biological parents nine months before Poe was born*

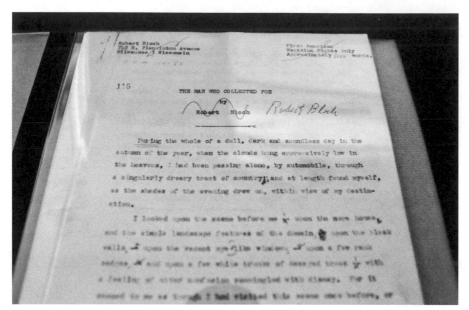

*Original manuscript for Robert Bloch short story "The Man Who Collected Poe"*

was curious which one he nabbed. "It's a response to a collector asking for his autograph." He smiled. "Naturally."

Then he pulled out a manuscript. "I've never showed this to anybody before, but I think it's relevant to what you're looking for."

It was an original typed draft of the 1951 short story "The Man Who Collected Poe" by Robert Bloch, author of *Psycho.* The manuscript was covered in Bloch's edits and, curiously, someone, assumedly Bloch, had crossed out the typed byline with red ink and then rewrote it exactly the same way in pen.

I didn't know anything about the story, but when I returned home, I immediately looked it up and watched the film version that was included in the 1967 Amicus Productions anthology horror film, *Torture Garden,* all the segments of which were Bloch stories. The Poe segment starred a black-mustachioed Jack Palance and, in the titular roll, Peter Cushing.

Both tell the story of a visit to a third-generation collector named Lancelot Canning (Launcelot Canning in the book), who lives in Maryland and is the world's greatest collector of Edgar Allan Poe memorabilia. In one scene in the film, Cushing tells Palance, "My whole life is centered around Edgar Allan Poe in every respect."

It was eerily reminiscent of my situation, except that Fawn and I were in England, and instead of the luxurious Amicus-style mansion, we were in what would have passed for somebody's home office. Also, our visit didn't end with me hitting him over the head with a candlestick and breaking into the deepest, darkest secrets of his collection, like in the movie.

"There was no way I wasn't going to have this. If there's anything that sums me up, I am the man who collected Poe." Interestingly enough, Robert Bloch also wrote the forward to *The Edgar Allan Poe Scrapbook*. The script cost Fawn $3,500. He would tell me the prices he paid for numerous pieces (sometimes in dollars and sometimes in pounds), not to brag, and not even really in that way that most collectors need validation that they picked up a good deal. It was to prove a point on how he valued his collection.

"I've got some stuff that I've paid 30–40,000 pounds for, and other stuff that I've paid two pounds for and, to be honest, I treasure the cheap stuff just as much as the others. Like this." Here he pulled out a small, illustrated bit of bound paper in a plastic bag. "You asked me about some of my favorites. This is a calendar put out by an Italian cologne maker. Why they'd do Poe, God knows. I paid ten dollars for this. I love these illustrations."

In fact, the first thing I noticed in his collection was that there was a lot of recent, mass market Poe memorabilia, the cheesy stuff, some of which I had in my own study back home—Living Dead Dolls of Poe and Annabel Lee, the Edgar Allan Poe action figure, a twelve-inch-tall Vincent Price doll from the 1963 film *The Raven*. I asked him how he could have, say, an original 1898 miniature bust of Poe by George Zolnay right beside a six pack of Poe-themed beer?

"Listen, I know a lot of my collection would be seen by many purist collectors as rubbish, but to me it's essential to show Poe's relevance to popular culture. The stuff makes me happy because it reminds me that just about everyone, even if they don't know it, has seen, read, watched, or heard something directly relating to Poe—whether that's comics, film, TV, theater, opera, paintings, cartoons, whatever. It's not all about first editions, and I think it makes other people happy, as well, that they can relate to many of these items."

To better explain the tenor of his collection, he compared it to the renowned Edgar Allan Poe collection of Susan Jaffe Tane, with whom he was friends. "I have—reputedly—the biggest collection in the world. Susan has the best. She may have far less items that I do, but it's the kind of pieces that museums and libraries covet. Not like raven poop." He pointed to a small plastic jar of orange, purple, and black jelly beans that he had purchased from the online store of the Baltimore Ravens NFL team.

I had seen a good selection of Tane's collection at the Morgan Library. Her copy of *Tamerlane and Other Poems* was there, as well as a few of her manuscripts. As I mentioned in that section, the bust and the coffin piece were hers, as well.

"I guess I could skip all the small things I collect and save up for the big things, but it's not what I want to do. Susan's and my collections really complement each other, I think. Hers is the best quality, but it's mostly old books and manuscripts, which is appealing to scholars and people who are really into old books, but, sadly, it's not exciting enough to attract the masses at an exhibition. What I usually do for exhibits I put together is to use some of Susan's key items as center-pieces and then complement them with a lot of my pieces, the things that people of this generation can relate to. That way I have something for everybody.

"If you want to get people into Poe, you need to show them stuff like this." He dug behind a shelf of books and pulled out a massive, severed arm. It was about four feet long, made of latex, and—despite its size—highly lifelike. It had fingerprints the size of half dollars and individual hairs that sprouted from realistic-feeling skin covered in veins and pores. It looked like it had been ripped off of a monster. "Have you ever seen *The League of Extraordinary Gentleman?*"

As soon as he mentioned the movie, I knew exactly who that arm belonged to.

*Prosthetic Mr. Hyde arm from the film* The League of Extraordinary Gentlemen

The 2003 film was based on an Alan Moore comic book where a group of characters from classic novels—Captain Nemo, the Invisible Man, Tom Sawyer, Allan Quatermain, Dorian Gray, Mina Harker from *Dracula*, and others—come together to fight evil as some sort of literary superhero team. And one of those characters, or two of them, is Dr. Jekyll and Mr. Hyde.

In the movie, Hyde is a gigantic brute, a sort of Incredible Hulk figure. The reason his arm is in the Peter Fawn Poe Collection is because when the brute is introduced in the film, he's done so with a Poe reference. He's tracked down at Paris's most famous fictional street, Rue Morgue, and is mistaken for a giant ape. In the comic book, the Poe connection is stronger and even features C. Auguste Dupin himself as a character.

That was enough for Fawn to add it to his Poe collection, but it was a great piece in general. I immediately asked if I could put it on and, barely waiting for an answer, found the mechanical controls halfway down the inside of the arm for clenching and unclenching the fist. It took everything in my power not to swing it around and destroy the nearest $150,000 dollars in irreplaceable (and replaceable) Poe memorabilia.

Fawn pointed at a framed film cell on the wall from the first Halloween special for *The Simpsons,* in 1990. In it, the main characters from the show act out "The Raven," which is narrated by James Earl Jones. "To find something from 'The Raven' episode like that is almost impossible. Over the past 20 years, I've only seen two come up, and I've got them."

He then pulls out a poster from the 2004 Tom Hanks movie *The Ladykillers,* about a bunch of thieves and an off-the-wall plan to break into a casino. Hank's character, who dresses like the KFC's Colonel Sanders, quotes Poe throughout the movie.

"I have his costume," Fawn said, referring to the cream-colored cloak, "because there are so many references to Poe in it, and his costume was such a prominent part of the movie, I wanted it." He imagined putting his poster, costume, and autographed Tom Hanks photo together as part of an exhibit on Poe's influence on culture.

He didn't need to convince me. He had me at Mr. Hyde's arm. I mean, at this point in my trek through Poe-Land, I'd seen amazing handwritten letters and rare books, but I often viewed them with a reverence reserved for holy artifacts, safely kept by some unseen priest in a holy of holies somewhere. And I find it strange to admit it, but I may, may, may have been more excited to see Fawn's 1979 original script of a Poe biopic written by Sylvester Stallone for Sylvester Stallone as I was to see most of what was in the Morgan.

And here's the funny thing. In that little garage, with a giant latex arm over one of my hands and a sixty-year-old ceramic Poe-shaped Mystery Writers of America award in the other, I was seeing (and wearing) only a mere fragment of his collection. When I asked him to quantify "biggest collection in the world," he answered, "At least 20,000 . . . but to be honest, I've given up counting." Most of what was in his garage was what he had collected while living in Bahrain for twelve years. He just needed something close to him when he's in town because the

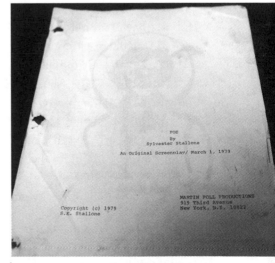

*1979 script for Sylvester Stallone's unproduced movie,* Poe

*A pair of Edgar Awards from the Mystery Writers of America*

warehouse space where he keeps the bulk of his collection is packed floor to ceiling and not easily accessible.

But even though he's away from the collection most of the time, he's extremely active with it, both privately and publicly. Just that morning he had bought a series of twenty movie stills from the 1942 film *The Loves of Edgar Allan Poe*. Fawn is an avid eBay-er and knows the market inside and out, thanks to decades of collecting.

I've already mentioned what he did at The Fox Reformed and his contribution to the Morgan Library exhibit. He's even looking into having a version of Poe translated into Swahili because the Poe landscape in Africa, where his life is centered currently, is "very sparse." He frequently talked to me in terms of exhibits he can show people. In that regard, his crowning moment was in 1999, when he singlehandedly organized and financed the world's largest Poe celebration, the International Edgar Allan Poe Festival.

It was in Prague and lasted three months. He took over three cinemas, seven theaters. He got them to open up the ancient cellars of Prague Castle for the first time in one hundred years and put on an opera there. He hired the Prague equivalent of the Royal Albert Hall and put on the biggest concert there since World War II. It was Rachmaninoff's "The Bells." He owns the original sheet music for the piece. He put on an exhibition at the 650-year-old University of Prague that covered twenty-two huge rooms. He imported Poe performers and hired a guy to walk around with a large papier-mâché Poe head. He sponsored the raven and orangutan cages at the local zoo. He commissioned a large, gorgeous mosaic of Poe, leaving the design up to the artist, Jindrich Vydra. What Fawn got from Vydra was the head of Poe surrounded by black ravens and red tongues of flame, like the poet was in a hell of his own making. As Fawn was telling me all this, he was slapping down glossy 5 x 7-inch personal photos showing everything.

"Why did you put this on in Prague? Why not one of the major Poe cities?"

"Well, I was living there at the time. I was in Prague for six years. But there's also a big Poe fan base in Eastern Europe. Under Communism, Poe was on the okay list because his work was inoffensive . . . politically, at least, so he was widely translated and illustrated in the Eastern Bloc."

Obviously Fawn's collection is extremely versatile. He could cut it into a

*Poe mosaic commissioned by Peter Fawn and created by Jindrich Vydra*

thousand different themes for an exhibition—stamps, music, film, history, presidential memorabilia, advertising, parody, comics, TV. In some ways, it was impossible to characterize it overall. He would often stop mid-sentence and show me something astounding. Like a set of correspondence from the 1800s between noted Poe biographer and collector John Ingram and literary critic R. H. Stoddard arguing over the authenticity of the poem "Alone," or a ticket to an 1882 lecture on Poe delivered by none other than Poe's physician, John Joseph Moran, MD. Or he'd pull out the original, autographed comic art from the 2003 Batman comic *Nevermore* that teamed the Dark Knight with Edgar Allan Poe himself. It was a beautiful pencil image—Batman wrestling a giant black cat while Poe rushes, cane in hand, to help him. Poe as Robin instead of Raven.

But in another way, most of the collection had a unique personality that was easy to identify: the intersection of Poe and pop culture. I tried to nail him down on one iconic piece that summed up his collection, but he always brushed it off. Maybe Buddy Holly's high school homework assignment on Poe? "I have tons of things like that." The film cell of the first-season *SpongeBob SquarePants* episode "Squeaky Boots"? Just kidding. Although he does have that. The episode was a takeoff of Poe's "The Tell-Tale Heart." "The further it is, the stranger it is, the better it is," he told me.

More than tons, I was starting to believe he had everything. When I told him I'd gotten the 1963 comic book adaptation of the Roger Corman Film *The Raven* for

‌‌‌‌‌

‌‌‌‌‌‌‌‌‌‌‌‌‌‌‌‌‌‌‌‌‌‌‌‌‌‌‌‌‌‌‌‌‌‌‌‌‌‌‌‌‌‌‌‌‌‌‌‌‌‌‌‌‌‌‌‌‌‌‌‌‌‌‌‌‌‌‌‌‌‌‌‌‌‌‌‌‌‌‌‌‌‌‌‌‌‌‌‌‌‌‌‌‌‌‌‌‌‌‌‌‌‌‌‌‌‌‌‌‌‌‌‌‌‌‌‌‌‌‌‌‌‌‌‌‌‌‌‌‌‌‌‌‌‌‌‌‌‌‌‌‌‌‌‌‌‌‌‌‌‌‌‌‌‌‌‌‌‌‌‌‌‌‌‌‌‌‌‌‌‌‌‌‌‌‌‌‌‌‌‌‌‌‌‌‌‌‌‌‌‌‌‌‌‌‌‌‌‌‌‌‌‌‌‌‌‌‌‌‌‌‌‌‌‌‌‌‌‌‌‌‌‌‌‌‌‌‌‌‌‌‌‌‌‌‌‌‌‌‌‌‌‌‌‌‌‌‌‌‌‌‌‌‌‌‌‌‌‌‌‌‌‌‌‌‌‌‌‌‌‌‌‌‌‌‌‌‌‌‌‌‌‌‌‌‌‌‌‌‌‌‌‌‌‌‌‌‌‌‌‌‌‌‌‌‌‌‌‌‌‌‌‌‌‌‌‌‌‌‌‌‌‌‌‌‌‌‌‌‌‌‌‌‌‌‌‌‌‌‌‌‌‌‌‌‌‌‌‌‌‌‌‌‌‌‌‌‌‌‌‌‌‌‌‌‌‌‌‌‌‌‌‌‌‌‌‌‌‌‌‌‌‌‌‌‌‌‌‌‌‌‌‌‌‌‌‌‌‌‌‌‌‌‌‌‌‌‌‌‌‌‌‌‌‌‌‌‌‌‌‌‌‌‌‌‌‌‌

‌‌‌‌‌‌‌‌‌‌‌‌‌‌‌‌‌‌‌‌‌‌‌‌‌‌‌‌‌‌‌‌‌‌‌‌‌‌‌‌‌‌‌‌‌‌‌‌‌‌‌‌‌‌‌‌‌‌‌‌‌‌‌‌‌‌‌‌‌‌‌‌‌‌‌‌‌‌‌‌‌‌‌‌‌‌‌‌‌‌‌‌‌‌‌‌‌‌‌‌‌‌‌‌‌‌‌‌‌‌‌‌‌‌‌‌‌‌‌‌‌‌‌‌‌‌‌‌‌‌‌‌‌‌‌‌‌‌‌‌‌‌‌‌‌‌‌‌‌‌‌‌‌‌‌‌‌‌‌‌‌‌‌‌‌‌‌‌‌‌‌‌‌‌‌‌‌‌‌‌‌‌‌‌‌‌‌‌‌‌‌‌‌‌‌‌‌‌‌‌‌‌‌‌‌‌‌‌‌‌‌‌‌‌‌‌‌‌‌‌‌‌‌‌‌‌‌‌‌‌‌‌‌‌‌‌‌‌‌‌‌‌‌‌‌‌‌‌‌‌‌‌‌‌‌‌‌‌‌‌‌‌‌‌‌‌‌‌‌‌‌‌‌‌‌‌‌‌‌‌‌‌‌‌‌‌‌‌‌‌‌‌‌‌‌‌‌‌‌‌‌‌‌‌‌‌‌‌‌‌‌‌‌‌‌‌‌‌‌‌‌‌‌‌‌‌‌‌‌‌‌‌‌‌‌‌‌‌‌‌‌‌‌‌‌‌‌‌‌‌‌‌‌‌‌‌‌‌‌‌‌‌‌‌‌‌‌‌‌‌‌‌‌‌‌‌‌‌‌‌‌‌‌‌‌‌‌‌‌‌‌‌‌‌‌‌‌‌‌‌‌‌‌‌‌‌‌‌‌‌‌‌‌‌‌‌‌‌‌‌‌‌‌‌‌‌‌‌‌‌‌‌‌‌‌‌‌‌‌‌‌‌‌‌‌‌‌‌‌‌‌‌‌‌‌‌‌‌‌‌‌‌‌‌‌‌‌‌‌‌‌‌‌‌‌‌‌‌‌‌‌‌‌‌‌‌‌‌‌‌‌‌‌‌‌‌‌‌‌‌‌‌‌‌‌‌‌‌‌‌‌‌‌‌‌‌‌‌‌‌‌‌‌‌‌‌‌‌‌‌‌‌‌‌‌‌‌‌‌‌‌‌‌‌‌‌‌‌‌‌‌‌‌‌‌‌‌‌‌‌‌‌‌‌‌‌‌‌‌‌‌‌‌‌‌‌‌‌‌‌‌‌‌‌‌‌‌‌‌‌‌‌‌‌‌‌‌‌‌‌‌‌‌‌‌‌‌‌‌‌‌‌‌‌‌‌‌‌‌‌‌‌‌‌‌‌‌‌‌‌‌‌‌‌‌‌‌‌‌‌‌‌‌‌‌‌‌‌‌‌‌‌‌‌‌‌‌‌‌‌‌‌‌‌‌‌‌‌‌‌‌‌‌‌‌‌‌‌‌‌‌‌‌‌‌‌‌‌‌‌‌‌‌‌‌‌‌‌‌‌‌‌‌‌‌‌‌‌‌‌‌‌‌‌‌‌‌‌‌‌‌‌‌‌‌‌‌‌‌‌‌‌‌‌‌‌‌‌‌‌‌‌‌‌‍

‍‍‍‍‍‍‍‍‍‍‍‍‍‍‌‌‌‌‌‌‌‌‌‌‌‌‌‌‌‌‌‌‌‌‌‌‌‌‌‌‌‌‌‌‍‌‍‌‍‌‌‍‌‌‍‌‌‌‍‌‌‌‍‌‌‌‌‍‌‌‌‌‍‌‌‌‌‌‍‌‌‌‌‌‍‍‍‍‍‍‌‍‍‌‍‍‌‌‍‍‌‌‍‍‌‌‌‍‍‌‌‌‍‍‌‌‌‌‍‍‌‌‌‌‍‍‌‌‌‌‌‍‍‌‌‌‌‌‍‍‍‍‍‍‍‍‍‌‍‍‍‌‍‍‍‌‌‍‍‍‌‌‍‍‍‌‌‌‍‍‍‌‌‌‍‍‍‌‌‌‌‍‍‍‌‌‌‌‍‍‍‌‌‌‌‌‍‍‍‌‌‌‌‌‍‍‍‍‍‍‍‍‍‍‍‍‌‍‍‍‍‌‍‍‍‍‌‌‍‍‍‍‌‌‍‍‍‍‌‌‌‍‍‍‍‌‌‌‍‍‍‍‌‌‌‌‍‍‍‍‌‌‌‌‍‍‍‍‌‌‌‌‌‍‍‍‍‌‌‌‌‌‍‍‍‍‍‍‍‍‍‍‍‍‍‍‍‌‍‍‍‍‍‌‍‍‍‍‍‌‌‍‍‍‍‍‌‌‍‍‍‍‍‌‌‌‍‍‍‍‍‌‌‌‍‍‍‍‍‌‌‌‌‍‍‍‍‍‌‌‌‌‍‍‍‍‍‌‌‌‌‌‍‍‍‍‍‌‌‌‌‌‌‌‌‌‌‌‌‌‌‌‌‌‌‌‌‌‌‌‌‌‌‌‌‌‌‌‌‌‌‌‍‍‍‌‍‌‍‌‌‍‌‌‍‌‌‌‍‌‌‌‍‌‌‌‌‍‌‌‌‌‍‌‌‌‌‌‍‌‌‌‌‌‍‍‍‍‍‍‌‍‍‌‍‍‌‌‍‍‌‌‍‍‌‌‌‍‍‌‌‌‍‍‌‌‌‌‍‍‌‌‌‌‍‍‌‌‌‌‌‍‍‌‌‌‌‌‍‍‍‍‍‍‍‍‍‌‍‍‍‌‍‍‍‌‌‍‍‍‍‍‍

*Original artwork for the comic book series,* Batman: Nevermore

Christmas from my in-laws, he pulled out all the original artwork for it. "Just bought this last year."

Most telling to me, I think, were pictures he had personally gotten from Disney animators. They were doodles of Mickey Mouse and Donald Duck, the type of thing they would do for children who met them. Fawn had convinced them to draw the characters quoting lines from Poe. He was making his own Poe pop-culture crossovers. "They seemed uncomfortable with that for some reason."

If that sounds like a Poesque crack in his psyche, he had better tell-tales. Besides investing millions of dollars into a dead poet, of course. Both his children received middle names related to Poe: Vincent for his son and Ligeia for his daughter. Oh, and he'd had Vydra construct for him a fully functional pendulum, also for the Prague Poe festival. It was one of the first artifacts he mentioned to me and the only one he expressed regret over for not being able to show me. It was packed away in the warehouse—but he had pictures.

The nine-foot-tall contraption was made from the four-hundred-year-old wood of a Prague mill. The bed had a twisted skeleton painted on it. The pendulum blade was razor-sharp and connected to a series of gears that lowered it as it swung. A pale green ceramic skull was attached to it, just above the blade. When a golf ball was placed inside the skull, the white sphere looked like a single vulture eye rolling back and forth between the sockets, clicking out a metronome of doom as it hit the sides of the cranium. It took an inexorable eight minutes to drop. Except for that one random time it took six.

Fawn had been showing some press around, and they wanted pictures of the pendulum. A Poe performer Fawn had brought over from the States offered to lay on the table below the pendulum for a few dramatic shots. The performer posed for a good five minutes as the journalists took their photos. Meanwhile, the pendulum slowly swung and lowered. Finally, the performer got off the table with what he thought were minutes to spare, but no sooner had he moved out from under the blade than it dropped straight down, narrowly missing giving him a wide smile, two feet below where he should have had one. "It was the only time it ever did that," Fawn told me. An engraved cane, given to Fawn by the per-

*Tiny portion of the Peter Fawn Poe Collection*

former, was leaning against a shelf and cited him as the "World's Best Poe Event Organiser." Apparently the Poe performer didn't harbor any ill feelings over the matter. His name was David Keltz.

Besides his penchant for almost splitting friends in half, I think what endeared me most to Fawn was his easygoing attitude toward the collection. The items in it are not insured, not catalogued, not even really organized, and most of them are stored while he's a continent away. He had no problem letting me pull anything I wanted out of cabinets and protective sleeves, even bringing me tea, mince pies, and Christmas chocolates while I did it, regardless of the danger my sugary fingers posed to his treasures.

And he showed it all to me in a manner that wasn't the least bit braggadocious. In fact, he had the enthusiasm of a newcomer to the hobby instead of one who had been doing it for decades and could pretty much afford anything he wanted. At one point, he was sitting on the floor, pulling out comic book art and spreading it around him, looking like a teenager in the 1960s surrounded by vinyl rock records in a bedroom. And, of course, he had a vinyl collection of Poe-related music, too, some of the oldest ones, which dated back to the early 1900s, as thick as a dinner plate.

Toward the end of my time surrounded by his collection, he asked me if I liked old movies. It's the kind of question you always say yes to even if you don't, and when I nodded my head he opened a cabinet with stacks of thousands of movie stills and behind-the-scene photographs. "That's my pension."

This was another insight for me into his Poe collection. I'd asked him earlier if he collected things besides Poe-phernalia. He told me, no, just Poe. But now I was learning that he also had more than 100,000 movie photographs and more than 400,000 movie posters, few of which were related to Poe. They were economic investments, items he sold regularly. He'd recently unloaded a still from the 1927 Fritz Lang silent *Metropolis* for $8,000. But he hated parting with anything in his Poe collection.

He told me that at one point he'd been forced to sell a couple of original Poe illustrations, one by Harry Clarke and another by Edmund Dulac. It was during the eighteen-month financial blank spot between his exit from American Express and his new business. He'd done it just to keep liquid and had sold it to a friend so that it was "still in the family," but I could tell it was a tender spot for him. He brought it up three different times throughout the day.

Finally, about five hours of a stranger shuffling greedily through some of his most prized possessions, we were ready to head out to dinner. As we walked out, I made sure I had on me the small black booklet that he had gifted to me earlier, saying, "That's for you to have. It's over one hundred years old. Quite a rare one." It was an elaborately lettered and decorated printing of *The Raven* done by the Stone Printing and Manufacturing Co. of Roanoke, Virginia, in 1909. Even had the business card of the president of the company inside, meaning it was a promotional item for the company as opposed to a commercial one, more than likely for the company to show off its printing chops.

What was probably the 19,978th coolest thing in his collection is now one of my favorite things I own. I mean, I'm sure he had twenty of them, but for a man who doesn't like to part with his pieces of Poe, it meant a lot to me. But it might end up biting him. Next time he's on eBay, he may have some more competition.

## Kingdom by the Sea

I don't know whether Poe ever made it to the southern coast of Great Britain as a child, but back in those days, Brighton was already well on its way to transforming from a small fishing village into a seaside resort town. In 2000, it finally achieved city status (the city's name is officially Brighton and Hove, after the two ex-towns that form it), and today it's one of the most popular places on the island.

As we drove my rental into the city, Fawn pointed out the location of the warehouse where most of his Poe collection was entombed, a nondescript site that made me want to write a story about a couple of twelve-year-old boys who break into the local warehouse and discover things that change their lives forever.

After that, we passed the picturesquely decaying skeleton of the West Pier, built in 1866, abandoned since 1975, and subjected to collapse, arson, and safety demolition in the intervening decades. Today, it's just a large metal latticework marooned in the water as a perch for gulls and a subject for photographers. Its nearby counterpart, Brighton Pier, dates from 1899 and was alive with the lights of its carnival.

Once we'd parked, we settled into a restaurant called Little Bay, where I finally got my duck confit and I could concentrate on grilling Fawn without getting distracted by the wonders of his collection. But even there, we couldn't escape the baleful gaze of Edgar Allan Poe. The place was part of a UK chain, all set up to look like old theaters, with plenty of red curtains and gilding; it even had balcony seating. Each of the gold-painted boxes was wrapped with paintings. One such theater box held images of Poe himself, an image inspired by the poem "Annabel Lee," and the raven atop its favorite pallid perch. A fourth image looked like a Caspar David Friedrich painting of a crumbling wall that might have been standing in for the House of Usher.

"So do you have a white whale piece?"

It took him a while to decide, but he finally came up with, "Probably a piece of Poe himself . . . his hair, clothes. Also one of Vincent Price's costumes from his Poe movies. I'd love to have one of those."

"Do you ever get frustrated that there's so much out there to collect with Poe?"

"To me, that's the beauty of collecting. Every day I can find something. If you were a collector and had a complete collection, what the hell would you do?" I imagined Scrooge McDuck swimming through a vault of coins.

"Every day, huh? What is your longest dry spell of buying Poe stuff? Do you have any?"

"The year after I did the festival, because it killed me, honestly. I did it all while still working full-time for American Express and, and even though we had some great sponsors, I still put a lot of money into the event."

"What would you collect if you didn't collect Poe?"

"I'm a big fan of Laurel and Hardy. Also really interested in the Anglo-Zulu War."

"What about non-collectors? Can you empathize with them at all?"

"Oh, I admire them. They spend more time with their family, collecting that kind of stuff, I guess."

"So would you steer people away from collecting?"

"Oh, no, but I would advise that they focus their collection. Obviously mine is all over the place, I have to have everything. It gets ridiculous. I would say to my wife, 'Do you need anything?' and if she said no, I'd go and drop a thousand pounds on Poe. I never deny her or the kids anything, but if she doesn't want it, I spend it. I'm not really a saver, at least not of money."

"So at this stage, are you even interested in Poe as a writer or as a historical figure, or is it now Poe as a cultural icon?"

"I'm fascinated with his life more than anything. There are some of his writings that I actually don't like. Sometimes he's up his own ass, to be honest." He might have said arse, I don't remember.

"So why do you think his first printings and original manuscripts are commanding such huge sums these days, more than even the estimates?" In 2009, a copy of his *Tamerlane and Other Poems* set an American literature record by going for $662,500. Poe dethroned himself. The previous record holder was the same book for a fraction (although still a large one) of that amount, two decades earlier. As I mentioned in the introduction, just in July of 2013, a version of "The Conqueror Worm" handwritten by Poe went for $300,000 at an auction in Massachusetts—$280,000 more than its estimate.

"Well, the 2009 bicentennial of his birth inflated prices somewhat, so they'll come down again. Mostly, I think it was the 2008 stock crash." Back at his house, he had shown me a framed print of a striking October 2008 cover of *The New Yorker* that depicted the stock market crash in terms of the "Masque of the Red Death" via the red costume in the 1925 Lon Chaney film *The Phantom of the Opera.* "People can't trust their money to stocks. That's just a hole, so they invest it in rarities and antiques, stuff that keeps its value. There are entire companies and consortiums that you have to bid against these days, not just private collectors."

Eventually, we started talking about Poe sites in the States. Fawn had visited most of the major ones for the first time on a solo trip in the early 1980s. It wasn't a great time to visit Poe sites, especially not by oneself. He had more than one story of police escorting him out of areas where a young, naive British guy didn't need to be.

Another time, he had seen the Poe Cottage in New York, the Edgar Allan Poe National Historic Site in Philadelphia, and the Poe House in Baltimore—all over the course of six hours. "I was in Baltimore, and suddenly realized how doable that was, what with the trains and all, so I just did it."

We talked about some of the possible outlets for his collection once he had the time to do it. He had dreams of a comprehensive website, and he wanted to do a series of coffee table–style books, each one about Poe's influence on a different medium—film, theater, illustration.

Then I asked him the big question. "What happens to it all when it's over?"

"When it's over? Well, the ideal is to start my own museum that could go on after I'm gone. I mean, I could give my collection to another museum or library, and the collection will be named after me, but they'll store it away, pull out a few pieces every important Poe anniversary date, but most of it would never be seen again, and they'll probably sell some of it to raise money to buy something else.

"Honestly, if I don't get my own museum, I'm okay if all this floods back out on the market. I'd do a massive catalog, send it all out into the market at one go."

I've interviewed my share of people with collections, many of them extremely unique collections. I've learned that coming to terms with death for a massive collector means something much bigger than it does to most of us. Heck, even the idea of loss is much more troublesome. Fawn had said something similar earlier that day.

"The things I love to collect around Poe are the things that could so easily get lost. I just recently bought about 150 photos from the newspaper archives in Boston, Baltimore, and Philadelphia, dating from 1924 through the 1950s. They haven't been digitized, and could easily just be gone." It also fit with his interest in culture, so much of which is ephemeral . . . popped culture and all that. As he put away the calendar from the Italian cologne company, he had observed, "How many of these would have survived?" He left the "if I hadn't preserved them" unsaid.

Later, after dinner, he toured me through Brighton in the cold, late December night, the Christmas lights strung above us across its thin streets and spaces, past pubs that dated back almost half a millennium, through the alley where they filmed the sex scene between Jimmy and Steph in the 1979 movie version of The Who rock opera *Quadrophenia,* and to the massive and incongruous Indian palace built in the eighteenth century by King George IV before he was king.

We parted at the train station. He had to get back to his family and enjoy what was left of his holiday before heading to the Dark Continent. I had a long drive ahead of me of whispering notes into my cellphone and then an ocean flight back home the next morning. It was a much more genteel ending than "The Man Who Collected Poe."

I think one of my most daunting tasks of this book has been explaining my experience with the Peter Fawn Poe Collection. Here is somebody who is single-handedly attempting to do what entire organizations and institutions and cities are trying to do . . . preserve the physical legacy of Edgar Allan Poe. And he's doing it in his own house and could not care less whether that legacy is silly or serious. As long as it's not lost.

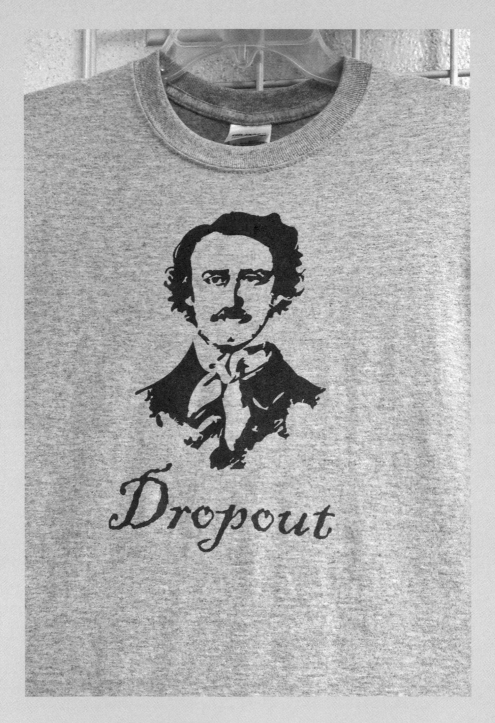

*Shirt in a store in Charlottesville*

CHAPTER 7

# Virginia

*From Childhood's Hour I Have Not Been*

IT WAS LUNCHTIME ON A FRIDAY, and I was sitting in an empty strip club in downtown Richmond, talking to the man beside me about Edgar Allan Poe, while a thin, naked, black coed called Sparkle danced two feet away.

We're going to have to start at the beginning for this one. Like 1811.

Even though Poe was born in Massachusetts and died in Maryland, it's the state of Virginia that really bookends his life. On one end, it's where he lost his mother as a young child, where he was taken in by the Allans, where he grew up (minus his five-year stay in England, of course), and where he attended college. At the other end, he spent the last two months of his life here, reconnecting with his sister Rosalie Mackenzie and his first fiancée, Sarah Royster, lecturing and performing his poems to interested audiences and friends, before embarking on his final trip.

Virginia is also a major volume in between. It was in Richmond where he started his literary career as editor of the *Southern Literary Messenger,* and where he married his wife Virginia. The state, and the city of Richmond in particular, influenced his manners, his self-opinion, heck, even his disdain for Northern literature. Virginia is why some Poe performers play him with a southern accent and why early drafts of "The Raven" feature the line "and so gently y'all came rapping/And so faintly y'all came tapping."

Most important, it's the state that Poe himself, of all the places he lived, considered home. He claims Old Dominion in an 1841 letter to his friend Frederick W. Thomas in Washington, D.C. The letter was an attempt to get a cozy government position in the John Tyler administration, one that didn't take up too much of his time and allowed him to write whatever he wanted while still providing a life for his family. In it, he writes, "My claims, to be sure, are few. I am a Virginian—at least I call myself one, for I have resided all my life, until within the last few years, in Richmond."

At the time Poe was living in Philadelphia, hence the caveat, but he had lived in all the states that he was to live in at that point and could take his pick. His only other move after Philadelphia was a return to New York a couple of years later.

With so much of his life having been spent in Virginia, there are a lot of interesting Poe sites to see there. Most of it, of course, is focused in the collection of buildings in Richmond that is the famous Edgar Allan Poe Museum, and we'll end up there eventually in this chapter.

But I want to start this tour of Poe's Virginia legacy at a few finish lines first.

## A Family of Graves

The little white church on East Broad Street in Richmond didn't look like much, but it had a line 50 people long waiting to get in. That's because this church, St. John's Church, is one of the more famous in American history.

Built in 1741, it's the oldest church in the city. It was the site of two different political conventions where those men who would go on to become Founding Fathers plotted the start of a new country. It was during the first convention, in March of 1775, that the fame of the small Episcopal church was secured. There, in front of such future presidents as George Washington and Thomas Jefferson, Patrick Henry gave his "Give me liberty or give me death!" speech. Across the street is a park named after the guy, with a large etched glass pane in a white frame memorializing the words.

But I was taking a figurative and literal left at the front of the church. Its graveyard wraps all the way around the building, but against the wall that borders North 25th Street stands a tall stone marker, set apart from the others. A brick path leads past a magnolia tree directly to it, and a single bench keeps it company.

This is the grave of Poe's birth mom. Probably.

As with most things, Richmond started badly for Poe. His mother had moved south in the summer of 1810 for the theater season and had been hitting stages in Charleston, Norfolk, and Richmond. At the end of that year, while in Richmond, Poe's sister, Rosalie, was born. By that time, David Poe had disappeared, dead or off fathering some other eventually famous author. David and Eliza Poe had been married in that city just five years earlier. Now, it was just Eliza Poe and her three children. And then, a year later, it was just her three children.

On December 10, 1811, she died of consumption in Richmond. Edgar was two years old.

Eliza Poe's gravestone is six feet tall. The only words on the front are ELIZ-ABETH ARNOLD POE, and they are engraved beneath a large bronze medallion inset into the stone. On the medallion is the face of a woman, her eyes closed and holding an urn against her forehead. Out of that urn peeks a raven. I don't know if symbolism is better or worse when you get it right away. A wide swath of the marker, from the bottom of the medallion all the way to the ground, was scoured back to its original whiteness from whatever corrosive substance leaches from the medallion during the rain.

On the back of the tall stone is a matching bronze circle, this time filled with a thousand words instead of a picture. It reads:

TO THE

MOTHER OF

EDGAR ALLAN POE

ELIZABETH ARNOLD

BORN IN ENGLAND 1787

DIED IN RICHMOND 1811

BURIED HERE

"THE ACTOR OF TALENT IS POOR AT HEART,
INDEED, IF WE DO NOT LOOK WITH CONTEMPT UPON
THE MEDIOCRITY EVEN OF A KING. THE WRITER OF
THIS ARTICLE IS HIMSELF THE SON OF AN ACTRESS—
HAS INVARIABLY MADE IT HIS BOAST—AND NO EARL
WAS EVER PROUDER OF HIS EARLDOM THAN HE
OF THE DESCENT FROM A WOMAN WHO, ALTHOUGH
WELL-BORN, HESITATED NOT TO CONSECRATE TO
THE DRAMA HER BRIEF CAREER OF GENIUS AND
OF BEAUTY."

POE IN "THE BROADWAY JOURNAL" JULY 19, 1845
THIS TESTIMONIAL IS ERECTED BY THE RAVEN
SOCIETY, UNIVERSITY OF VIRGINIA, WITH THE
GENEROUS COOPERATION OF THE ACTORS'
EQUITY ASSOCIATION OF NEW YORK
AND THE EDGAR ALLAN POE
SHRINE OF RICHMOND.

1927

The date at the bottom is no lie. Her deadstone was erected more than a century after her death. The BURIED HERE part? That might be. She died in poverty and her grave was unmarked, so no real record survived of its location. An educated guess had to be taken by the Raven Society, an organization within the University of Virginia with which I would eventually become much more familiar.

Still, what remains of her on this earth is in that historic churchyard some-where. And it seems proper to honor the woman who gave us Edgar Allan Poe

*Grave of Elizabeth Arnold Poe*

twice . . . first by bringing him into the world and second by becoming his first tragedy in a life defined by it.

What happened next to the young Edgar Allan Poe can be traced to another graveyard, about two miles away in a far less touristy area of the city.

Shockoe Hill Cemetery was established in 1822, when the churchyard at St. John's ran out of space to plant bodies. (It's not necessarily an either/or thing with liberty and death.) It's a small cemetery with no real funeral statuary, no grandiose gates, and a total of only four paths. Most of it is sparsely treed.

However, it is filled with notable locals that include state governors and Revolutionary War soldiers. It's the final resting place of Elizabeth Van Lew, who was a spy for the Union during the Civil War, and John Marshall, the fourth Chief Justice of the United States. His plot is the most prominent in the grave-yard, right in the middle and surrounded by a low metal gate with a sign tacked on it.

And, even though it's not even hinted at on the historic sign outside the cemetery's red brick wall, this humble-looking cemetery is a major Poe site.

Shockoe Hill can boast the bones of four major players in Edgar Allan Poe's life, including two of the most important ones, John and Frances Allan. The hus-band and wife were Poe's guardians after the death of his mother, the reason for his middle name, and—one of them, at least—big contributors to the harshness of his life.

After the death of Eliza Poe, her three children went separate ways. The oldest, Henry, ended up with the Poe side of the family in Baltimore. Edgar and his sister Rosalie were welcomed into two local Richmond families. Rosalie was adopted by the Mackenzie family, while Poe ended up with the Allans, although he was never officially adopted.

And it's easy to read into that fact after the fact. The relationship between John Allan and Poe is kind of hard to encapsulate, but it's usually done so with such words as "contentious" and "combative." Allan did give Poe a good upbringing, and fed him, housed him, provided for most of his schooling, but somewhere around Poe's time in college, when he was seventeen, things went south.

In reading through the surviving letters and reading the synopses of Poe's biographers, the problems the two had don't sound far off from many father-son relationships. John Allan often disapproved of Poe's choices and attitude, thought him to be ungrateful, and even called him in one letter "miserable, sulky & ill-tempered." The young Poe seemed to react strongly to Allan, assert his independence in childish ways, and say many things he regretted later. The gripes were often over money. Allan was rich, thanks to the death of a wealthy uncle, but seemed rather miserly with the funds when it came to Poe, sending him off to college without providing him enough to afford what he needed. Meanwhile, Poe was unable to write a single letter to him without coming off as whiny and begging for something. Most of the time it was for money, but it was also often for affection.

After college, where Poe racked up large gambling debts that Allan refused to alleviate, Poe exacerbated the situation by taking off from home, leaving the South for Boston, and joining the military. From that point on, their relationship would be a mere letter-writing one, although it would lose little of the venom.

Poe's last known letter to Allan was written in April of 1833 from Baltimore, where Poe was living in that small, cramped house with his aunt, grandmother, and two cousins on Amity Street. It states:

> **It has now been more than two years since you have assisted
> me, and more than three since you have spoken to me.
> I feel little hope that you will pay any regard to this letter,
> but still I cannot refrain from making one more attempt to
> interest you in my behalf. If you will only consider in what
> a situation I am placed you will surely pity me—without
> friends, without any means, consequently of obtaining
> employment, I am perishing—absolutely perishing for**

**want of aid. And yet I am not idle—nor addicted to any vice—nor have I committed any offence against society which would render me deserving of so hard a fate. For God's sake pity me, and save me from destruction.**

We don't know if Allan responded to this letter, but we know he died a year later. It's said that when Poe went to see Allan on his death bed in 1834, the weakened man threatened to strike him with his cane if he didn't leave.

When Allan died, he left none of his large estate to Poe, although he did leave something to the illegitimate children that he fathered during an affair he had. The next year, that chapter in his life closed, Poe would return to Richmond to start work at the *Southern Literary Messenger* with a family of his own.

The effect of this caustic relationship on Poe's life is incalculable, and not just because he missed out on a life of comfort that Allan's money could have provided him. In an 1835 letter, he said, "I have many occasional dealings with Adversity—but the want of parental affection has been the heaviest of my trials."

I had approached Eliza Poe's grave with reverence. With Allan's grave there at Shockoe Hill Cemetery, it was more like confliction. The grave is located on Avenue A in the cemetery, close to where it intersects with Avenue C. It's a rectangular column topped by a simple urn, but the inscription is almost book-length:

SACRED TO THE MEMORY OF
JOHN ALLAN
WHO DEPARTED THIS LIFE
MARCH 27, 1834
IN THE 54TH YEAR OF HIS AGE.
HE WHOSE REMAINS LIE BURIED BENEATH
THIS TOMB WAS A NATIVE OF AYRSHIRE, SCOTLAND.
BLESSED WITH EVERY SOCIAL AND BENEVOLENT
FEELING, HE FULFILLED THE DUTIES OF HUSBAND,
FATHER, BROTHER, AND FRIEND, WITH SURPASSING
KINDNESS, SUPPORTED THE ILLS OF LIFE WITH
FORTITUDE, AND HIS PROSPERITY WITH MEEKNESS.
A FIRM BELIEVER IN CHRIST, AND RESIGNED TO
THE DECREES OF ALMIGHTY GOD, HE GAVE UP
LIFE WITH ALL ITS ENJOYMENTS, WITHOUT A MURMUR.
WHILE AFFECTION MOURNS THE GREAT LOSS IT
HAS SUSTAINED, THE REMEMBRANCE OF HIS
VIRTUES AND THE HOPE OF A REUNION HEREAFTER

ARE THE ONLY SOURCES OF CONSOLATION TO
THE BEREFT HEART.
HE HATED EDGAR ALLAN POE.

Okay, that last line isn't on the grave, but the words that are etched there certainly don't come off as the epitaph for a villain. Perhaps the epitaph was born out of the usual tradition of canonizing the dead, regardless of what they were like in life. Or maybe it is a clue to a much bigger picture of the man than we usually get looking at it through the lens of his relationship with Poe. Or maybe Allan was just right in his opinion of his ward.

The memorial is flanked on its left by a similar, but smaller, version dedicated to Frances Allan. Hers also bears a long epitaph:

SACRED
TO THE MEMORY OF
FRANCES KEELING ALLAN
WHO DEPARTED
THIS TRANSITORY LIFE ON THE MORNING OF THE 28TH OF
FEBRUARY 1829.
THIS MONUMENT IS ERECTED BY JOHN ALLAN, HER HUSBAND.
IN TESTIMONY OF HIS GRATITUDE
FOR HER UNABATED AFFECTION TO HIM
THE ZEAL TO DISCHARGE HER DOMESTIC
DUTIES AND THE FERVOR SHE MANIFESTED
BOTH BY PRECEPT AND EXAMPLE
IN PERSUADING ALL TO TRUST IN THE
PROMISES OF THE GOSPEL.
BELIEVE IN THE LORD JESUS CHRIST
AND YE SHALL BE SAVED.

Poe's relationship with his foster mother is less plumbed than that with his foster father. It's generally held that it was an affectionate relationship, and perhaps the best evidence of this happened after her death. Poe was stationed at Fort Monroe in Hampton, Virginia, when she died. For a period after that, Poe's relationship with Allan softened, as shown by the letters to Allan during that time, which were much warmer, and in which he addressed him as "Pa" . . . although he still begged for money.

On the other side of Allan's marker was the grave of Louisa G. Allan, the woman Allan married after Frances died. She was another complicating factor in Poe and Allan's relationship.

*Graves of (left to right) Louisa Allan, John Allan, and Frances Allan*

She bore Allan three children and basically created a new life from which it was easier to dismiss Poe. She certainly had no connection to Poe, and other than a random story about her seeing him approach and not answering the door, there is no real documentation of them ever interacting during his *Southern Literary Messenger* years in the city.

In reading through the materials and playing with the situation a bit in my imagination, I feel like I sometimes side with Allan and sometimes side with Poe, but mostly I think that the ill-will between the two wasn't insurmountable. Perhaps what seems typical of many quarrelsome father-son relationships was worsened for them not being an actual father and son. Why Poe was never adopted by the Allans has always been one of the mysteries of his life for us, and probably one of the burdens of his life for him.

Still, this was a monument to a man who quite possibly could have changed the direction of Poe's miserable life, but didn't. Even if Allan did provide for Poe earlier in life and set him on a good path, he eventually gave up on him. Of course, if he hadn't turned his back, we might not have gotten the Edgar Allan Poe that fascinates the world. Phrased another way, it's either because of this guy that we have Poe's tormented genius or because of this guy that we don't have more of it. Either way, it's hard to know which side to come down on: reverence or vandalism.

To top the feeling off, Poe visited this spot more than a few times in his life, so he stood right there where I was standing, thinking thoughts about Allan that must have been full of regret and anger and confusion and sadness.

He also visited the cemetery long before either John or Frances died, to pay his respects at a different grave, that of one of the earliest muses of his life.

Jane Stith Stanard was the mother of his childhood friend Robert Stanard. He met her when he was fourteen and she thirty and was apparently infatuated with her. She died about a year after he met her, though, in 1824, after going insane. His memory of her stuck with him enough that she inspired his original poem "To Helen" (giving her a new name, as he seemed to like doing), and which is, of course, a better thing to have than any epitaph:

> Helen, thy beauty is to me
> Like those Nicean barks of yore
> That gently, o'er a perfumed sea,
> The weary, way-worn wanderer bore
> To his own native shore.
> On desperate seas long wont to roam,
> Thy hyacinth hair, thy classic face,
> Thy Naiad airs have brought me home
> To the glory that was Greece,
> And the grandeur that was Rome.
> Lo, in yon brilliant window-niche
> How statue-like I see thee stand,
> The agate lamp within thy hand,
> Ah! Psyche, from the regions which
> Are Holy Land!

Her grave is near the Allan plot, across the path and at the intersection with Avenue C. Hers is another urn-topped rectangular column with a massive epitaph of platitudes. Inset into the ground at its base is a plaque that reads:

> POE'S HELEN
> HELEN, LIKE THY HUMAN EYE
> THERE TH' UNEASY VIOLETS LIE—
> THERE THE REEDY GRASS DOTH WAVE
> OVER THE OLD FORGOTTEN GRAVE—
> ONE BY ONE FROM THE TREE TOP
> THERE THE ETERNAL DEWS DO DROP—

It's not a quote from the most famous mention of his woman in literature, but from Poe's poem "The Valley of Nis," about the grave of a woman, perhaps this grave of this woman, in a valley far away. A much older Poe would call Jane Stith Stanard "the first, purely ideal love of my soul."

The last grave marker on the Shockoe Poe tour was certainly never seen by Poe, having been installed some 160 years after his death. It's not too far away from the Allans and Stanard, in the same general area outlined by Avenue A and Avenue C, but closer to the wall on 2nd Street. In that area is a table grave, a large slab mounted horizontally on six pillars. The inscription on the slab has worn just about to illegibility, but a small, recent plaque set into the ground beside it gives this information:

SARAH ELMIRA ROYSTER SHELTON
1810–1888
FIRST AND LAST FIANCEE OF THE POET EDGAR ALLAN POE
"SHE WAS A CHILD AND I WAS A CHILD,
IN THIS KINGDOM BY THE SEA.
BUT WE LOVED WITH A LOVE THAT WAS MORE THAN LOVE—
I AND MY ANNABEL LEE—"
EDGAR A. POE

The plaque was placed there by Richmond's Poe Museum (we'll get there, I promise) in October of 2012. The museum also was involved with the plaque on Stanard's grave, as well as Eliza Poe's memorial marker. The weathered table grave beside Shelton's plaque is that of her husband, Alexander Shelton, who died in 1844.

The choice of the poem on the plaque is interesting, especially since Poe wrote other poems more likely inspired by her. The problem with Shelton being Annabel Lee is, well, Annabel Lee dies in the poem. I mean, Poe outlived a string of his muses, but Shelton wasn't one of them. On the other hand, poetic license is pretty broad in 48 out of 50 states.

And they were both children in love. Poe met her as a teenager, back when she was just Sarah Elmira Royster, and the two got engaged. As cliché as it sounds, the relationship ended when Poe went off to college, which is strange because it was an all-male college. Actually, Poe wrote her many letters during that time, but she never received them, as they were intercepted by her disapproving father. Poe thought she was ignoring him, Shelton thought he was ignoring her, and apparently that love that they loved with more than love wasn't worth pursuing after that.

*Grave of Jane Stith Stanard*          *Grave of Sarah Elmira Royster Shelton*

Shelton got married at the age of 17. Poe dropped out of college and headed for Boston. And one of them lived happily ever after.

Poe would see Shelton again, of course, when he came back with the young Virginia on his arm, but Shelton doesn't really enter his story again until the end of his life.

On that last trip to Richmond, he would find her widowed and well off, and since he himself was one of those things, the two got engaged. This time, instead of her father disapproving, it was the entire universe, and Poe died in Baltimore weeks later. Not a break could Poe catch.

That's it for Shockoe Hill Cemetery, but I think I'm going to shoehorn one more Poe grave into this section. It's not in Richmond, not even in Virginia, but it's not too far away, and now seems to be the most relevant point to mention it.

When we last saw Poe's sister Rosalie, she was adopted by the Mackenzie family. She lived in Richmond for much of her life and, honestly, isn't treated too

*Grave of Rosalie Mackenzie Poe*

well by biographers and anecdotists. She's called a simpleton and an annoyance and a half-sister and other things you usually only jokingly call kid sisters.

She apparently didn't have much of a place in Poe's life, and eventually left Richmond sometime after her brother's death to head for family in Baltimore. She outlived Poe by a quarter of a century, dying in 1874, a little more than a year before his stately grave monument was unveiled in Baltimore. It ended sadly, in poverty in a shelter for the destitute in Washington, D.C. She tried to fend off that poverty by cashing in on the growing fame of her brother, selling photos of him and items that she claimed were his, but it wasn't enough.

However, she at least ended stylishly. She's buried in D.C.'s Rock Creek Cemetery. It's the home to a wide range of amazing sculptures, including the famous Adams Memorial sculpted by Augustus Saint-Gaudens. It's also the final resting place of Upton Sinclair, Gore Vidal, and a host of famous people of the type that would be drawn to a place like D.C.

Rosalie Mackenzie Poe's grave isn't as impressive as any of theirs; it's just a stone plaque in a row of them in the middle of Section D. On it, her birth year is given as 1812, the year after her mother died. I guess she couldn't let her brother have all the death-mystery.

## Edgar Allan Poe, Rich . . . monder

Obviously, there are many sites in Richmond that are connected directly, indirectly or other-directly to Poe, some still standing, some not. Technically anything that was around during his time was probably visited by him or somebody relevant to him. The ex-capital of the Confederacy is a spider-web of degrees of Poe. The major sites, though, are few and can be done in a casual couple of hours if you are semi-efficient and not counting the Poe Museum itself (we'll get there, I promise). Also, it depends on how you define *major*. Judging from the following itinerary that my wife and I followed on one of my visits, I defined it sweatpants-loose.

We went past the house where Elmira Shelton lived when she got engaged to Poe. It's a beautiful red brick edifice with white trim at 2407 East Grace Street, just behind St. John's and the grave of Poe's mother. A blue placard on a quaint lamp-post labels the site as Shelton's. And I say "went past," because it's a private residence, and that's pretty much all we could do without testing the city's tres passing laws.

*Home of Sarah Elmira Royster Shelton*

We also, because it was easy, checked out the childhood home of Jane Stith Stanard, which is also private. It's at 1812 East Grace Street. A historical sign outside its white fence calls out the large, white house as the Craig House, Craig being Stanard's maiden name. The sign doesn't point out the vague Poe connection because it, well, doesn't exist at this place. Poe wouldn't have visited her here, but where she lived later with her husband, Robert Stanard. The sign does point out, however, that it was built in the 1780s, making it possibly Richmond's second oldest structure.

None of the Richmond houses that Poe actually lived in himself are standing, unfortunately, and the only public clue to any of his residences is a plaque on the side of a teal building at the intersection of 5th and Main Streets. The ornate plaque bears three sailing ships at the top and says simply:

NEAR THIS SPOT
STOOD THE HOME OF JOHN ALLAN
WHERE ONCE LIVED
EDGAR ALLAN POE.

*Plaque denoting the location of John Allan's Moldavia, where Poe lived*

Below the beautifully succinct sentence is the name of the group that placed it, the Association for the Preservation of Virginia Antiquities, and the year it got bolted to the brick, 1907. What it doesn't let on in the slightest was that the "home" it refers to was Moldavia, the mansion Allan purchased upon receiving the inheritance that set him up for life and helped set him at odds with his broody ward.

At lunchtime, we stopped by the closest thing Richmond currently has to a Poe-themed restaurant. The conclusion that it was Poe-themed was drawn solely on the name of the place, Poe's Pub. The sign had an unpromisingly placed shamrock in place of the apostrophe and included, also unpromisingly, a cartoon raven in sunglasses holding a pool cue. Inside, it wasn't Poe-themed. It looked like a biker bar in the throes of transforming into a family eatery. Still, I can attest that it served food.

We also checked out Monumental Church at 1224 East Broad Street. The Allans rented a pew here, number 80, and Poe attended as a child. But the reason I wanted to visit was for a much more interesting story connected other-directly to Poe.

If Monument Church is a strange name for a place of worship, it's an even stranger-looking church. From the outside, it looks like it belongs somewhere in D.C. Like there's a marble statue of a Founding Father in there. The building is completely white, topped by a dome instead of a steeple, and shaped somewhat like an octagon. Part of that is because its designer was Robert Mills, who also designed the Washington Monument. But the bigger reason is because it's as much a memorial and a mausoleum as it is a church. The church was built to house the remains of seventy-two people, who are buried beneath it in a crypt, all victims of the same tragedy and reposing on the very dirt where it happened.

The church sits on what was once the site of the Richmond Theatre, which burned down on December 26, 1811, killing the people who now make up its foundation. The theater fire, as so many of them are, was the result of an accident that involved a candle and some flammable scenery. It happened during a performance attended by some 600 people on that day after Christmas.

*Monument Church*

We walked up to its grand portico and tested the doors. They were locked, as expected.

The place is owned by the Historic Richmond Foundation and is more of a venue these days than an attraction. Above the doors was the year the place was finished, 1814, and taking up much of the portico was a large urn-topped block, inscribed with the names of the victims of the theater fire. It's a replica of the original monument that stood there.

I went around back and climbed up on a bench to peer into a window. The interior was filled with parallel rows of white, box-like wooden benches with doors at their ends. A balcony with more benches surrounded the upper parts of the auditorium. I didn't know which one was pew number 80. From my vantage, I couldn't see the front of the church, but images online show it to be a blue dais and podium flanked by two blue pillars stretching to the ceiling.

The real interesting angle on this building as far as the life of Poe is concerned is that had his mother not gotten sick and then died two and half weeks earlier, she very well might have been on that stage, as it was her company that was performing. That also meant her children might well have been in attendance, hanging out backstage where the fire started. Even with her death helping the young Poe siblings avoid a smoky, burning fate, the Allans might still have been in attendance with Poe had they not been out of town for Christmas that year. In an alternate universe things went awry for Poe in a totally different way.

Next, we were on to the Masons. Richmond is home to the oldest continuously operating Masonic lodge in the country, Randolph Lodge No. 19. It was built in 1787, and can be found on East Franklin Street. In 1824, when Poe was fifteen, he acted as a member of the honor guard who escorted General Lafayette, beloved hero of the Revolutionary War, around town during his grand tour of the United States. At one point, they followed Lafayette to the lodge, standing watch outside while he was entertained inside.

Today the building's a bit worse for wear on a street almost unwearable. It is surrounded by abandoned brick buildings, and the white paint on the wooden slats that covered its façade is peeling. However, with its colonnaded entrance and the cupola atop its lofty roof, it still maintains the look of a once-important place. I just wanted a quick picture of it, so Lindsey stayed in the car up the street while I jumped out.

However, a young man was standing directly in front of it. He was dressed about five decades older than his age, with thick white glasses, a bow tie, and blue blazer. I waited awkwardly across the street for him to move. When I realized he wasn't going to anytime soon, I went ahead and snapped the picture.

"Did you really just take a picture of this place?" he called to me across the street.

"Uh . . . yeah."

*Randolph Lodge No. 19*

"Like, you drove over here specifically to see the lodge."

"Uh . . . yeah."

"Do you want to see inside it?"

"Uh . . . totally."

I ran back to the car and told Lindsey hurriedly, "We're going inside the lodge."

"Wait, what?"

"There's a guy out there in a bow tie. He says we can come in."

"Well, as long as he has a bow tie."

When we returned, he asked me my interest in the place. I explained the Poe connection and my project.

"Oh, yeah, his mother used to perform here. I'll show you where."

According to the business card he handed me, his name was Michael Cain Seay III. He took us inside, where we were immediately struck by a strong smell of mildew. He explained they'd just had some water damage and were in the process of cleaning things up.

Passing through the foyer, we saw a large portrait of General Lafayette himself.

He first took us to what looked like a cafeteria. It was a large room with white walls and folding tables and chairs. The floor was an alternating pattern of black and white tiles, and an old Weber grand piano stood to one side. "This is where she would have performed," Seay III informed us. Back in the day, the large building often acted as an entertainment venue, and it's generally held that Eliza Poe performed there on at least two occasions.

Next, he took us to the second floor and the Royal Arch Room, the space dedicated to a chapter of practitioners who have achieved the degree of Holy Royal Arch. The room was carpeted in red, with three ornate chairs at one end and a series of curtains spaced through the center, like the tabernacle of the Israelites. It was certainly a room for rituals. On the walls were paintings of various Old Testament scenes: Moses at the burning bush, the Levites carrying the Ark of the Covenant. Oh, I went to Sunday School.

The third floor contained the Lodge Room, which was also carpeted in red. Its walls were painted pale blue, and it seemed less esoteric than the Royal Arch Room. It had chairs set into ornate wall niches labeled with virtues such as wisdom and strength.

I'm not sure if that was the end of the interesting rooms in the lodge or if Seay III got bored with us at that point, but that was pretty much the extent of the tour. On the way out, I asked about a room I saw that seemed to be a jumble of artifacts and glass cases. "Yeah, that's our exhibit room. We're in the process of moving that, so it's a bit of a mess in there."

*Charles Rudy statue of Poe*

Our impromptu tour through the lodge was a random but well-worth-it experience. It might be the only surviving stage that Poe's mother performed on.

Actually, all the sites in this section have been pretty random. If you come to Richmond looking for Poe, and you skipped everything in this section, I wouldn't blame you. After all, if you come to Richmond for Poe and only visit the Poe Museum (we'll get to that, I promise), you'll have done all right. But you really should also at least see the Poe statue.

And that's because there aren't that many full-size Poe statues. Richmond's is probably the most humble of them, but also the most honored. I'll explain.

This bronze statue of Poe was created in the mid-1950s by sculptor Charles Rudy at the funding of a doctor named George Edward Barksdale, who gave it to the "people of Virginia," according to the inscription on its pink granite base.

The sculpture is about five feet tall (the base adds another four feet) and depicts Poe in a seated position, with a manuscript in one hand and a quill in the other. However, because of the somewhat odd angle of the neck and hands, it almost looks more like the statue of a lifeless Poe marionette than of Poe himself.

As a result, there's no real aggrandizement of him in the pose, so in some ways it's one of the more honest depictions of him. But the one thing that elevates it above the other statuary of Poe is where it resides . . . on the grounds of Richmond's 225-year-old Capitol building.

You can find it in the southwest corner of Capitol Square, near the intersection of 9th and Franklin Streets, within eye- and ear-shot of the ceremonial tintinnabulation of Richmond's almost 190-year-old Bell Tower, which these days is a visitor center. The spot is just across the street from the site of the house of Jane Stith Stanard, the one Poe certainly visited.

But seeing Poe in black bronze wasn't the end of my time in Richmond. I still had two more sites to see, not counting the Poe Museum (we'll get to that, I promise). Like Poe himself, it was necessary for me to leave Richmond for a while before returning, if I was going to follow his chronology. You see, next on our itinerary was Edgar Allan Poe: The College Years . . . or year, to be exact.

## *Thomas Jefferson, Side of Poe*

As I walked the grounds of the University of Virginia, with its serpentine brick walls and stately buildings, it was nothing like the lawless frontier Poe described to John Allan in his letters. In those he talked about the pistols everyone wore and how "a common fight is so trifling an occurrence that no notice is taken of it." And how one of those fights in front of his dorm room door was so bad that one man left "bitten from the shoulder to the elbow—and it is likely that pieces of flesh as large as my hand will be obliged to be cut out."

Granted, I was there in the summer time, so most of the students were assumedly raising hell back at their homes instead of throughout the grounds.

Poe started at the college on February 14, 1826. It was only the second year of this brand-new Charlottesville institution, and parts of it were still under construction. He joined some two hundred other students in this college established by ex-president Thomas Jefferson, whose Monticello was within telescope distance of the place.

Despite the chaos, Poe did well at the university, studying languages like Latin and French. Unfortunately, his time at the university marked the second major left turn in his life, after the death of his mother.

The story goes that John Allan sent Poe to the college without enough money to actually attend. This was after Allan struck it dead-uncle rich. Poe eventually went into debt buying books and clothes and then turned to gambling to try to meet those debts. Or, he just might have turned to gambling.

After all, gambling at the university was as big as violence, so the whole place had basically a "William Wilson" atmosphere. One particular gambling scandal, Poe tells his foster father in a letter, scared about fifty students into hiding from the law in the woods of the surrounding Ragged Mountains, making the college close to the ghost town I discovered.

When Allan found out about the debts, which some say amounted to $2,000, he ripped Poe from school ten months into his coursework and refused to pay the outstanding debts. That was the beginning of the rift that sent Poe off on his own and prompted the T-shirts I would see in stores in downtown Charlottesville that bore Poe's visage above the word DROPOUT.

It wouldn't be the first Jeffersonian institution Poe would parachute out of. Years later, he'd leave of his own free will from West Point in New York, which was made an academy by then—President Jefferson.

The University of Virginia today is certainly Jefferson-Land, with Poe being mere Donald Duck to Jefferson's Mickey Mouse. Traces of the founder and

Founding Father are everywhere, from the buildings he designed to the statues that honor him. In fact, it was the story and activities of two of the college's societies, the Jefferson and the Raven, that brought me to this place, and why it was that I was meeting Thomas L. Howard III.

The distinguished name belonged to a guy in his early twenties, who was a fifth-year student at the university. Not in the *Animal House* Bluto kind of way. He'd graduated the previous year with a major in history and a minor in urban planning. He was currently pursuing a Master's in Higher Education Administration.

And he way dug the college. He was from the area, so there was local pride involved, but his enthusiasm for the place was more because his history focus was on the early America/Constitution period. He was all-in at UVA.

The reason I was meeting him out of the more than twenty thousand students at the university was that, at the time of our meeting, he was president of the Jefferson Literary and Debating Society and secretary of the Raven Society, so he was head of a society that once included Edgar Allan Poe as an officer and another whose name is inspired by Edgar Allan Poe. More on this in a bit.

Howard was going to take us to a few sites on the grounds. As we walked to our first stop, I asked him what it's like to attend such a historic place.

"It's amazing. In many ways it's completely different from those days, and in others, it hasn't changed at all. It's still similar enough that you can see we're treading the same ground both geographically and intellectually. Like I said, amazing."

The first place he took us was to the dorm room of Edgar Allan Poe. Right, Poe's dorm room. This is pretty cool. They've preserved Poe's room at the University of Virginia. We're going to need to know the layout of the school a bit for this one.

The center of the campus (or "the Grounds," as I've been corrected by more than one person involved with the college) is a quadrangle called the Lawn. It's bookended on the north side by the Rotunda, the dome-toped flagship building of the university, and on the south side by Old Cabell Hall, which is mostly an auditorium. The east and west sides of the Lawn are lined with brick dorm rooms reserved for certain eligible seniors (or fourth-years, as terms like freshman, sophomore, junior, and senior aren't officially used on the campus, er, Grounds). Outside of those dorms are garden areas, outside of which are more brick dorms. Now, all of these dorms date back to the beginning of the college. Jefferson himself designed them, and the whole community there is referred to as the Academic Village. The outside rows of dorms are called the East and West Ranges, and they're only available to grad students.

The front doors of these small, single-occupancy rooms all face outside.

Poe's room can be found at 13 West Range. It was the second dorm room he stayed in during his short collegiate career, with the first being somewhere on the West Lawn. So his preserved room is in a row now reserved for grad students, which I guess is kind of funny.

Later, Howard would show us his own room, which was on the East Range, to give us an idea of the typical living conditions in the Ranges. It was small, cozy, with almost everything within reach from the bed. A fireplace was the room's most notable feature, and even with his beer bottle collection and iMac, it still felt like a historic site.

The exterior of Poe's room sticks out slightly from its neighbors. All of the doors in the Ranges are lined by black shutters, except for Poe's, which has historically accurate green shutters. It's also topped by a plaque that gives his name, the year he attended in Roman numerals, and the Latin phrase DOMVS PARVA MAGNI POETAE, which, translated, means either "Stay in School" or "Small Home of a Great Poet." Latin is tricky.

At the side of the door is a doorbell-like button labeled with a brass plaque that misspells Poe's middle name and tells you to press the button for a narration. The narration lasts about a minute and a half, much to the consternation, I was told, of Poe's neighbors on either side, who have to listen to that spiel from feet away every time somebody pushes a button. I pushed it like ten times while I was there.

A state historic sign on the grass in front of the dorm, close to McCormick Road, explains why one less grad student a year can get into the Ranges.

*Poe's dorm room at the University of Virginia, Charlottesville*

A glass door blocks entry to the room while allowing a full view of its interior. Inside is nothing that belonged to Poe, but there is period furniture. A bed with a heavy, green jacket thrown over it, a chest, a writing desk, a mirror. The mantel above the fireplace had some books and a raven statue on it.

I could only think that the American literature classes must have a blast here. Maybe they'd spread out on the grass in front of his dorm and read "A Tale of the Ragged Mountains," Poe's only story set in Charlottesville. Actually and strangely enough, it's the only one really set in Virginia, although his "The Premature Burial" does end on the James River, near Richmond. "A Tale of the Ragged Mountains" is the story of a man who hikes off into the mountains and then either time travels, hallucinates, or has a memory of a previous incarnation fighting a battle in Calcutta. Hardly southern literature.

Honestly, at this point, I wasn't too interested in checking out the room. Later on, we were to meet with a man who had the key to the glass door and who was going to allow us actual entry.

However, while we stood there, an older man with a camera around his neck shouted to us from down the Range a bit, "Is that Poe?" When we answered in the affirmative, he shouted, "Good!" and made his way to join us. After introducing ourselves, we found out his name was Dwayne Preston, and he was a retired English teacher from Illinois. He was on a road trip with his brother-in-law. They were there to see Jefferson's Monticello, but being an English teacher, he wanted to detour to the Poe Room. When I asked him why he was going out of his way to see a sparsely furnished room under glass, he merely said, "I think Poe was brilliant."

Next, Howard took us to the meeting room of the Jefferson Society. Called Jefferson Hall, it's located just a few steps down the West Range (and across Poe Alley) from Poe's dorm room. The Jefferson Society is the oldest student union currently at the university, beginning mere months after the students first arrived. It splintered from another merits group, the Patrick Henry Society, which is no longer extant.

Poe was a member of the Jefferson Society during his time at the college and even served as secretary pro tem for at least two meetings. His signature is on the minutes of the meeting, and, interestingly enough, only his signature remains of those minutes. In 1895, most of the Rotunda burned due to faulty electrical wiring, taking all of its books and records with it. However, fortunately (in this instance at least), years before, somebody had defaced the minutes, cutting out and stealing the signature and inadvertently saving it for posterity. It's now in the collection of the school library.

Today's Jefferson Room wasn't the one Poe went to for meetings. It moved there in 1837. The room was large and yellow, and at its front was a dais. Jefferson's portrait dominated the room, with another of Edgar Allan Poe on his left and Woodrow Wilson, another UVA dropout, on his right.

A bannister delineated the dais, over which were hung two ties, for speakers that forget to bring their own. One had purple stripes. The other, cartoon sheep. Every Friday the organization meets here, drinking, talking, debating, reading, and performing classic and original works until two or three in the morning. Poe himself is supposed to have read an essay at the meeting called, "Heat and Cold." Every year they host Poe readings in his honor.

Howard pointed out a worn, but ornate chair off to the side of the dais. "That's called the Poe chair. It's where the secretary sits."

"So, explain to me . . . this is the Jefferson Society, but from what you've told me it doesn't seem to be so much about, I don't know, political discourse. Poe and Jefferson don't really appear to be kinsman enough to have such an overlap in this society."

"But they are. We place a high value on the written word of any kind, not just political speeches, so we don't think it's weird to talk about these guys in the same breath. They both had masterful control of the language. To us, history is as much literature as poetry."

Finally, Howard took us to the Rotunda itself. The Rotunda was designed by Jefferson and based on Rome's Parthenon. The building is made of red brick, domed, and fronted by a white, columned portico. Originally, the Rotunda acted as the school library. Poe himself was on campus toward the end of its construction and, in the same letter to John Allan where he talks about guys biting guys, he writes: "They have nearly finished the Rotunda—The pillars of the Portico are completed and it greatly improves the appearance of the whole—The books are removed into the library—and we have a very fine collection."

As I've already mentioned, much of the original Rotunda went down in a fire in 1895 and had to be restored and rebuilt. In doing so it, the design was changed a bit, but restoration work in the 1970s brought it back to Jefferson's original design.

Today, it's a place where meetings and events are held, and it's open daily for the public to tour on their own or as part of an official group. As we walked through it, we arrived at the inevitable marble statue of Thomas Jefferson. A bronze version of him stands atop a bell outside the north entrance to the Rotunda, as well. The latter was sculpted by Moses Jacob Ezekiel—the same guy who did Baltimore's Poe statue.

At the marble statue, Howard pointed out a chip in the robe and told us that during the fire, the students and faculty had tried to save the statue but it had wedged in a staircase. One professor tried to cut off the fire from the main building with dynamite (the fire had started in a connecting structure) . . . and while that made the fire worse, the blast did inadvertently dislodge marble Jefferson so that he could be salvaged for the new Rotunda.

After a quick jaunt through the Rotunda, Howard left us to go overachieve elsewhere. We had a few minutes until our next appointment, so we made our way to the Alderman Library.

There in the front room near the check-out desk was a bust of Poe commissioned by the university and sculpted by Romanian sculptor George Julian Zolnay in 1898. This was the same sculptor who created the Jefferson Davis statue that tops the president of the Confederacy's grave in Hollywood Cemetery in Richmond.

I'd seen casts of this particular bust in other places—a small one in Peter Fawn's collection, a couple at the Enoch Pratt Library, even one at the Richmond Poe Museum (we'll get there, I promise)—but here was the original. The bust is highly textured, from his hair to his jacket, and the way he holds his fist near his face and the large-eyed expression implies a sadly contemplating figure . . . that is often ridiculously adorned in this library, depending on the holiday. On our visit it still wore the white boater with red and blue band from the recently passed Independence Day.

Finally, we made our way to the office of Alexander Gilliam, whom we were introduced to as "Sandy." Gilliam was from Virginia and was an alumnus of the university. He also worked there starting in 1975 as an assistant to the president. He retired from that position in 2009 and now acts as the university historian.

He told me a bit about his time as a student back in the day. He'd entered majoring in biology since both his father and grandfather were doctors. But he had a tough time with organic chemistry due to his own inclinations and a particularly cantankerous teacher. "I went to his funeral, actually, just because I felt bad. I was one of the few people there. His daughter gave me a hug and said, 'You must have been one of his favorite students.'" Gilliam let out a laugh at the memory. "I switched majors because of that guy."

He approached his father and asked if he could become a history major. His father agreed, only on the condition that he see a psychiatrist friend once a week since, in his father's view, one had to be crazy to trade the life of a doctor for one of a historian.

After one session, the doctor told him, "Boy, you ain't crazy," and then made a deal that he wouldn't have to come back as long as they both kept it from Gilliam's father. At the end of the semester, the psychiatrist wrote a letter certifying his sanity. Gilliam found the letter in his father's papers after his death. "I think it was one of the prouder moments for my dad: My son is sane."

Besides being sane, Gilliam was also a member of the Raven Society . . . and he was the guy who was supposed to get us into Poe's dorm room.

On a shelf there, in his office, was a small bust of Poe, a Raven Award he received in 2009. This award is bestowed by the Raven Society upon certain students, alums, and faculty for, he told me, "ill-defined reasons."

The Raven Society was established in 1904. At the time, the university didn't have a Phi Beta Kappa chapter and needed something similar. They named it after Poe's poem, and it has continued to this day. Out of about 3,500 in each freshmen class, 25 get elected.

These days they do have a Phi Beta Kappa chapter. Gilliam told me that a great academic record could get you into Phi Beta Kappa, but it took that and a record of service to the community to get into the Raven Society.

"So what are your feelings toward Poe himself?"

"Because of the way he uses language, he's a lot of fun to read out loud. Start doing that and you tend to get caught up in him." Then he recounted to me that one year the Jefferson Society celebrated Poe's birthday with a three-day non-stop Poe reading. Gilliam got the honor of closing out the marathon with a reading of the "The Raven." When he arrived, there were people passed out on the floor, draped dazedly over chairs, and leaning unsteadily against walls, all of them overwhelmed by a general feeling of Poe-verdose.

Gilliam got up on the dais—Jefferson, Poe, and Wilson at his back—and before he knew it he was treading the boards with such gusto that the videographer kept tripping over prostrate forms in his efforts to keep up.

But it wasn't just the campus family that dug Poe. In his role as university historian, Gillian regularly takes visitors on tours of the college. "I've seen firsthand how much he's loved overseas. People from other countries visit here to get a sense of American history, but just about everybody that I tour around, no matter what country, immediately perks up at Room 13."

I perked up, too. "So can we see the room now?"

"Unfortunately, and I'm sorry for this, I don't know where the key is." Apparently there was a bad hand-off of the key to Gilliam and, since it was summer, none of the relevant officers were around to remedy it.

We said our goodbyes, and dragged our feet dejectedly back to Poe's dorm.

It was now dusk, and the light in the room had automatically switched on. I decided I needed to at least see it from the other side, as there was a large open window. I went around the Range, squeezed through some of the construction scaffolding that's always hanging off historic places, and took a look. I could see some Raven Society stuff stashed in a corner behind the open door—a banner, a bust of Pallas, some boxes—but the perspective didn't give me much more perspective. Beneath the window, carved haphazardly into the brick, was "R. J. Price, 1886."

The window I was looking through reminded me of another bit of lore about the poet. The story goes that he etched a verse into the pane of the window in his dorm that read:

> **O Thou timid one, do not let thy**
> **Form rest in slumber within these**
> **Unhallowed walls,**
> **For herein lies**
> **The ghost of an awful crime.**

The pane was removed and supposedly kept somewhere on campus. I'd originally heard that it was on display at the Rotunda, but didn't see it on my visit and was told by the building's manager of operations that they had no such thing there. I later contacted some of the staff at the special collections library—Director Nicole Bouche and Heather Riser—who dug around and discovered that they did, in fact, have such an artifact in their archives.

Whether it was Poe's handiwork or not, who knows? Maybe it was R. J. Price's.

When I came back around to the front door of the room, two women were taking pictures of it and talking excitedly in Russian, as if Gilliam sent them himself to prove his point.

After my visit to the University of Virginia, I still couldn't shake the fact that I was a pane of glass and a lost key away from entering Poe's dorm room. That's why, about six months later, I found myself driving through a January snow storm and pulling Ryan Bugas, the president of the Raven Society, out of bed . . . all so I could clomp snow around a tiny space that I could see in its entirety from the doorway and which was full of nothing Poe owned.

What makes me even a little more ridiculous is that the university is not even positive that this was Poe's dorm. The powers that decide such stuff are confident that Poe lived in either 13 or 17 West Range for most of his college career. Of course, given those two choices, you certainly pick number 13 for Edgar Allan Poe.

## Fortified in Virginia

After Poe's time at college, he returned home, but after a short stretch of working for and arguing with John Allan, he broke north for Boston, and soon after joined the army. In his two years toting a gun around, he was stationed at three different East Coast forts. At this point I'd only been to Fort Independence in Boston, where I had a somewhat disappointing experience, Poe-wise, at least. My time at Fort Monroe, his last of the three forts, was the opposite.

Fort Monroe is located in Hampton, Virginia, about eighty miles southeast of Richmond. The familiar pentagonal stone structure took fifteen years to build, from 1819 to 1834. It is the largest stone fort ever built in the United States.

Poe arrived at Fort Monroe in December of 1828 and was stationed there for only about four months. That short time period of his life was marked by two major occurrences. The first was the death of Frances Allan. The second was his successful attempt to leave the army three years before his term ended to get into West Point.

Fort Monroe is at the south end of the checkmark-shaped peninsula that is Old Point Comfort, right at the mouth of the Chesapeake Bay. As I neared its walls, looking for a parking lot, fort batteries slid by on the bay side of the road, black and decrepit like ghost ships in one of Poe's seafaring stories.

At one point I overshot the fort and found myself at the Old Point Comfort Light, the second-oldest lighthouse on the bay, and the oldest that's still working. It predates the fort, being built in 1802, so it's seen some stuff with its single bright eye. Strangely, the white lighthouse was short, maybe three or four stories high, and stuck close between two houses on a residential street like it was the abode of some eccentric architect. Apparently the house nearest it was the light keeper's home long ago.

Eventually, I realized I was supposed to actually drive right into the fort. That meant crossing a narrow bridge that stretched above a moat and passing through a single-lane hole in the fort wall. In place of the usual welcome sign,

*Entrance to Fort Monroe*

a sign warning what to do if I came across old munitions on the ground greeted me. "Grab it and jump up and down in excitement" was not the answer.

Inside, instead of the wide, green lawn I had seen at Fort Independence and at other old coastal forts in my life, there was . . . a town. An entire town. There were homes and street lights and roads and buildings and parks, all surrounded by the moat and fortress wall. It made me want to write a pitch for the next season of *The Walking Dead*.

Turns out, Fort Monroe had only recently been converted into a historic site, and had been an active fort until 2011. Today, people still live and work there. The brochure for the place calls it a "park in progress."

I was headed specifically for what was called the Casemate Museum. A casemate is a fortified structure from which guns can be fired, and which apparently can be turned into a museum.

As I drove around the inner circumference of the fort wall, I passed the parade ground that today is famous for being home to the Algernoune Oak, a five-hundred-year-old tree named after the original wooden fort that was built in 1609 on the site of the Jamestown colony.

I was there on Black Friday, the day after Thanksgiving, and the streets were empty. Eventually, I found a parking spot right by a historical sign that pointed out a particular house as the home of Robert E. Lee, who, at 24, was stationed to oversee the final construction of the fort in the early 1830s. His first child was born in that house.

Inside, the museum was a warren of brick rooms, connected by low archways that wended an impressive distance along the fort wall (although the enclosed space made it seem like I was under the fort) and told the history of the place in chronological order with artifacts and reconstructed rooms and mannequins in costume. I mentally rewrote the pitch for *The Walking Dead* season into a straight-to-Netflix horror movie. Working title: *Dark Fortress.* Maybe *Fort Darkness.*

The centerpiece of the museum is the prison cell of Jefferson Davis, the president of the Confederacy. He was held at Fort Monroe for two years after the war, both for his involvement in that and for suspicion of complicity in Abraham Lincoln's assassination. He spent his first four and a half months in that large cell in the casemate, which visitors can enter through iron-barred doors. The whitewashed room has wide, dark planks for a floor and a bed, desk, and chair roped off in the corner. Taking up one whole wall is a massive thirty-five-star American flag in a frame, the actual one that had been placed in Davis's cell to taunt him. A small exhibit case outside the cell shows off a couple of Davis's personal items, most notably a massive meerschaum pipe, yellow with age and carved into the shape of a vicious-looking eagle talon holding an egg-shaped bowl. He wasn't good at choosing a side, but, man, he sure had taste in pipes.

But what I was really at Fort Monroe to see predated the Civil War, and in fact was much closer to the beginning years of the fort.

Only a couple of rooms deep into the museum, in a corner by a window and roped off from the rest of the room, was a nondescript mannequin in a white shirt and dark lamb-chop sideburns. He was sitting at a writing desk, a soldier's coat thrown over the back of his chair and a shako on the sill of the window. On a white perch above him was a small, black raven. It was the only sign that this bare-lipped man was Edgar Allan Poe . . . just kidding. There was a placard the size of a window that bore the heading: EDGAR ALLAN POE: A SOLDIER OF CONFLICT.

I got closer to the desk and saw a picture of his birth mother and an inkwell. In his hand was a feather quill, and the papers on the desk included a duty roster under one hand and the beginning of a letter beneath the other.

*Poe exhibit, Casemate Museum, Fort Monroe*

The full text of that letter was printed on the placard. It was his plea to John Allan to help him get into West Point. In it, he mentions Fort Monroe and talks about how his army knowledge at West Point would be an "unprecedented case in the American army" and that getting his cadetship would be a mere formality. The letter ends with Poe's usual excuses, blame-casting, and begging for favors that mark the majority of his surviving correspondence with his foster father.

The placard also stated that Poe visited Fort Monroe later in life. A painting reproduced on it depicted Poe standing on an elegant patio with tall columns and moonlight reflecting off water behind him. Around him was seated a group of listeners, mostly women in white dresses, while above his head the ghostly images of angels and planets and bells and a raven wound upward. The caption read:

> **Poe returned to Fort Monroe as a civilian in 1849. In this watercolor drawing by Allan Jones (1954). Poe is performing for his friends on the veranda of the Hygeia Hotel. Two of the poems he recited that evening were "Ulalume" and the unpublished "Anabell Lee." [sic] Less than a month later he was dead.**

The Hygeia was demolished in 1862.

I've seen some amazing, sophisticated tributes to Poe on this journey, but something about this display charmed me. A mannequin, a placard, and some set dressing—that's all it takes to contribute to the physical legacy of Edgar Allan Poe . . . you don't even need a mustache.

The museum continued through the long length of the casemate. It covered everything from ironclad ships (the USS *Monitor* and CSS *Virginia* fought just off-shore here) to artifacts from every major war and civilian life in the fort. Honestly, it was much, much more than I expected from a free museum dedicated to a single pentagon of land.

Once I was through the Casemate Museum, I doubled back to the entrance, where I had spied a set of steps that led to the top of the fort's ten-foot-thick walls. From that vantage point, I could see Hampton across the moat.

But then I looked down and saw a flat stone the size of a book in the grass that topped the wall. Then another. And another. Each one bore names like Mitzy or Blacky or Tippy.

The top of Fort Monroe was a pet cemetery.

Running a good length of the wall was a single line of graves, each marker unique and continuing through the stone arcs of old gun mounts that intermittently lined the wall. The oldest grave I saw was from 1936, and there were dead animals representing just about every decade since then. Some were given relevant names, like Jefferson Davis Talbot, an unknown species who died in 1984. Or Sarge, who was "faithful for 15 years" before dying in 1969.

Looking into it later, I found that there were some four hundred remains of pets atop the walls of the fort. It stopped allowing animal interments in 1988, although some have snuck in animal carcasses since that time.

As I have been programmed to do since starting this project, I looked for Poe references on the small gravestones of the pets. Didn't find one. That's cool, though. The fort has a mannequin.

## *Oh, the Places You'll Poe*

After leaving for Boston and a short military career, Poe would return to Richmond here and there over the next eight years and eventually move back in the summer of 1835 at the age of 26, a year after the death of John Allan.

The Edgar Allan Poe who moved back to Richmond was a drastically different person from the youth who had left it. By this time, he had served in the army, attended West Point, published two more books of poetry, *Al Aaraaf, Tamerlane, and Minor Poems* and *Poems,* and had lived in Massachusetts, New York, Maryland, and South Carolina. Most recently, he had lived in Baltimore, where he had met the two women who were to play the largest roles in his life, Maria Clemm and her daughter/his future wife, Virginia. Poe had even gotten his first literary break by winning a short story contest in Baltimore for his "MS. Found in a Bottle."

But the reason for coming back to Richmond was to start his literary career in earnest at the *Southern Literary Messenger*.

I returned to Richmond for a much different reason: to meet a man named Holt Edmunds.

I found Edmunds at the office of the small real-estate business that he owns. He was tall, thin, and in his sixties, with a head of thick, white hair and an incongruous pink plastic digital watch on his wrist.

His office was located on West Main Street in the Fan district, in a row of colorfully painted residences and businesses. He told me in his strong Southern drawl, "My wife and I moved to the area in 1973. Back then it was pretty rough. We had to sleep with the mattress against the front door for security." Today, Richmond is in a pretty great spot, maintaining the uniqueness of a small town, but bustling with the economy of a larger city.

We got into his car to get some lunch. As we drove, he pointed out many Richmond sites, both Poe-related and not. The former site of Pratt's Castle, the eccentric medieval-looking home of William Pratt, who took Poe's last daguerreotypes. Belle Isle in the James River that was the home to a Civil War POW camp. A good place to get a steak.

At one point, he apologized and informed me that he had to stop and call his wife, whose name is Virginia. She was having a birthday lunch with some of her friends and was under the mistaken impression that he gave one of his employees too much work to attend. He just wanted to clear it up so that she wouldn't be cross with him.

When he got off the phone, I mentioned I'd heard that one of his forebears had attended the University of Virginia during Poe's time there.

"Yeah, his name was Sterling Edmunds. Horsewhipped another student after losing $240 to him at cards because he thought he cheated. He got suspended." He laughed. The incident is mentioned in the Arthur Hobson Quinn biography of Poe.

Eventually, we ended up at an Italian restaurant that had no name on the outside, and which I would never have entered were I not led in by a local. Once we were seated and had our order in, I asked him for his Poe story.

"As a teen I loved Poe, even wrote a book of short stories that were Poe-like. I printed it out on a mimeograph, passed it out to students." He then inadvertently traced Poe's route from Richmond to Boston when he went to college at

Boston University to study photojournalism. He explained his temporary departure from the South, "I was a child of the 60s—minus the drugs—and I'd grown
up in a boys-only school, so I wanted the big city . . . and girls."

After graduation, he got back into Poe on his return to Richmond, when he
threw a Poe-themed party complete with dramatic readings because, well, it was
Richmond and it seemed to fit. Mostly, though it was "an excuse to have a drunk."

Eventually, that sliver of Poe in his life grew until he found himself on the
board for the Richmond Poe Museum (we'll get there, I promise), where he's
been for about thirty years.

"When I joined, I was by far the youngest on the board, and I remember
joking at my first meeting, 'I'm happy to be here . . . because it looks like as long
as I stay on the board I'll live until I'm 80.' Didn't go over well."

He even served as president for a couple of those years, but found it not to fit
his inclinations. "I'm not president material. Not a scholar or administrator. I'm
a businessman. So when the Poe Museum needs business, I can be the hit man
for them. I'm okay with that." He then explained what he meant by "hit man." At
one point the museum was down to a mere $10,000 dollars in its bank account,
which wasn't enough for payroll, so he and a colleague went out and raised the
money it needed, basically saving the museum.

I then found out Edmunds was the man who salvaged the bricks from the pile
of rubble that New York University had turned the Greenwich Poe House into,
throwing some seven hundred into the bed of his truck. I told him I had seen a
few of those numbered bricks in my travels. "I have number one. Somebody gave
it to me. I didn't grab it for myself."

It became apparent pretty fast to me that Edmunds was into the Poe community just as much for the community as the Poe. Then he flat-out stated it. "My
big payoff with Poe is that I've met a lot of neat people." It just so happened that
his Richmond community included Poe, expanding his community beyond the
city. As an example, he told me that the next day he was traveling down for a Poe
conference. "Boring stuff with interesting people" is how he described it. "I'm
going for the free meals and to see good friends. I'm not a scholar, so the topics
look dull to me. Not enough of them are about Poe's dark side. Poe would've been
forgotten if it weren't for his dark side."

"Then what does it say about people like you and me, then?" I asked.

He laughed. "That we have a case of arrested development."

Once we'd finished our meal, he asked me if he could show me anything
Poe-related while I was in town. I told him I'd seen the major sites of Richmond,
had been to the Poe Museum, Shockoe Hill Cemetery, Eliza Poe's grave, as well
as some of the minor sites.

"Have you seen where the office of the *Southern Literary Messenger* was?"

"No."

"All right. Let's go."

The *Southern Literary Messenger* was a periodical originally owned by a man named Thomas Willis White that ran from 1834 to 1864. However, it's only really notable today for two of those years . . . the years that Poe was its editor. In 1835, Poe joined the young magazine, and quickly his voluminous contributions and publishing instincts earned him the editor role, one which White was somewhat loathe to part with.

But, first, Poe had to stumble out of the gate because, well, he was Poe. Apparently, he was fired within a month for his drinking habits and general moodiness. After Poe left, White called Poe a "victim of melancholy" and said that he wouldn't be surprised to discover that Poe had committed suicide.

Granted, it was a hard time in Poe's life. Even though he finally had a job that could put food on his table and respect in his soul, he was alone in a city full of bitter memories, working at a building that was next door to what had been the office of his foster father. Worse, he was far removed from the Clemms, who had been his family for the past four years. To top it all off, it looked as if Maria and Virginia were heading to the household of his not-broke lawyer cousin, Neilson Poe, who had offered to take them into his care.

Basically, Poe was a terrible bachelor.

But Poe took advantage of his unemployment and headed back to Baltimore to pick up Virginia and Maria and bring them back to Richmond to be his bride and mother-in-law, respectively. White gave the new family man another chance, and he went back to work at White's magazine with passion.

It was here, at the *Southern Literary Messenger*, that Poe honed his tomahawk as a literary critic, where he started to make connections in the literary world, and where he finally saw a future for himself. It was in the pages of the *Southern Literary Messenger* that many of his famous works first saw printer's ink. Like "Berenice," "Morella," "Loss of Breath," "The Unparalleled Adventure of One Hans Pfaall," the much-undervalued "King Pest," and the beginning sections of his only novel, *The Narrative of Arthur Gordon Pym*.

In one letter he sent much later in his life, Poe brags that under his editorship he increased the number of subscribers to the *Messenger* from 700 to 5,000 in his short time there. Knowing Poe and knowing people, that's certainly an exaggeration. But he did put the new magazine on the map. In fact, White was nervous with the reputation the mag was getting as a result of the highly critical Poe, as well as the fact that the reputation was overshadowing his own role in the magazine. In 1837, by mutual agreement between the two, Poe left the magazine, although he still contributed to it for the rest of his life and long after White himself had died.

*Site of the* Southern Literary Messenger *building*

Poe also left the state, taking his little family and heading to New York to see what opportunities a couple of years of publishing experience could get him and to start pursing this idea he was having for a new magazine. Not long after his stay in New York, they would move on to Philadelphia.

I didn't think the *Southern Literary Messenger* building was still standing. As we drove, I said as much. Edmunds only shrugged it off and asked me, "Do you drink?"

"Yeah."

"Good. I really hope this place is open."

We pulled up to an ugly, blocky white building with no windows on the first floor at 15th and Main Streets. The large building that housed the offices of the *Southern Literary Messenger* had indeed been torn down, as well as the building next to it, which housed the offices of Ellis and Allan. Both were demolished in 1916.

Old pictures show the *Southern Literary Messenger* building taking up the whole corner of 15th and Main. This building, whose parking lot we were pulling into, was farther down 15th Street by a few dozen feet, although a low shed-like annex elongated the building to the end of the corner. However, the footprint of this building and Poe's first real office job certainly seemed to overlap.

But it wasn't architectural plans I was thinking about as I suddenly realized where Edmunds was taking me. An almost embarrassed neon sign above the door, the feeble light of which worked valiantly against the afternoon sun, proclaimed LADIES AND GENTLEMAN'S CLUB. Beneath it, another sign named it CLUB ROUGE. Holt Edmunds, the man who, not two hours earlier, was mortified that his wife would be upset over a social mix-up around her birthday luncheon, was taking me to a strip club. As I write this, I can only think of driving around Baltimore with David Keltz, laughing at the story of Poe and a stripper named Lenore.

"Now," he said, as he led me confidently to the dark portal that was the open door of the club, "I don't usually drink this early in the day." Inside, my eyes took some time readjusting from the summer sun outside. I could just barely make out the sight of pale buttocks divided by dark thongs clustered around the bar. Edmunds walked in there like he was the landlord, found out the drink special, ordered us two beers, and asked for dancers. We were the only customers there.

As we settled down in front of the room-sized stage, Sparkle started doing her thing to the crunchy electronic strains of AWOLNATION's "Sail." "Good song," Edmunds whisper-yelled to me. Sparkle would tell us later she was attending Virginia State University near Petersburg, a predominately black college in a city where I would have a Poe appointment in a couple of hours, although I couldn't offer her a ride since it was the beginning of her shift.

*Talavera, site of Poe's last known reading of "The Raven"*

"You want to know something funny?" Edmunds asked. "My nephew owned this place two years ago."

"Not anymore?"

"No. Serving six years in Otisville. Tax evasion. He was the most infamous man in Richmond. Used to drive around town with a big sound machine and ads plastered all over his car offering girls money to dance. The place was called Velvet back then. He wanted to open a second strip club right across the street from the Children's Museum. What kind of man wants to do that? Even brought a gun to my father's ninety-fourth birthday party. My nephew."

We only stayed for a couple of dances. Edmunds had to get back to work, and I had to figure out if a stripper story would be jarring in the middle of my Virginia chapter. Once back in the judgmental light of day, I asked him, "So if I write in the book, 'Holt took me to a strip joint,' you're okay with that?"

"Of course. Why not? It's funny."

On our way back to his office, he took a slight detour to a yellow house at 2315 West Grace Street. Built in the 1830s, it was an old house called Talavera that had been the home of Susan Archer Talley, a friend and neighbor of Rosalie Poe. Back then, it was surrounded by farmland but had been moved to where it stood today . . . just another distinguished-looking house on a high-end city street. It was in that house that Edgar Allan Poe gave his last reading of "The Raven," just two weeks before his death . . . a fact which, without nude dancing, was a lot less interesting than it would have been two hours before.

## *Hey, Little Sister*

Poe's wife, Virginia, died a few chapters ago, but now it's time to marry her. According to some of the more extreme and Griswoldian interpretations of Edgar Allan Poe, that might have been the order he wanted anyway.

Fresh off his ill-fated matriculation at West Point, Poe moved in with relatives who were all already living in poverty in a crowded house in Baltimore.

It was there that he got to know his eight-year-old cousin, Virginia, and her mother, Maria Clemm. After four years living with them, he moved to Richmond and realized he didn't want to live with anybody else. When he found out that his cousin Neilson Poe had offered to become their caretaker, he panicked. There's just no other word for it. He needed both of those women in his life. He was twenty-seven years old and had already lost two of his families. But he wanted more than a cousin and an aunt. He rushed up to Baltimore to grab a bride and a mother-in-law to live with him in Richmond.

But nothing I write will illustrate his state of mind at that time better than a letter he wrote to his aunt that contained a secondary letter to his cousin. This was the correspondence, the original of which mesmerized me at the Enoch

VIRGINIA     297

Pratt Free Library in Baltimore. Just about every book about Poe prints it in full
because it's the most important surviving letter of his that we have. I mean, this
is Edgar Allan Poe:

> My dearest Aunty,
> I am blinded with tears while writing thi[s] letter—I have
> no wish to live another hour. Amid sorrow, and the deepest
> anxiety your letter reached—and you well know how little I
> am able to bear up under the pressure of grief. My bitterest
> enemy would pity me could he now read my heart. My last
> my last my only hold on life is cruelly torn away—I have no
> desire to live and *will not*. But let my duty be done. I love,
> *you know* I love Virginia passionately devotedly. I cannot
> express in words the fervent devotion I feel towards my
> dear little cousin—my own darling. But what can [I] say?
> Oh think for me for I am incapable of thinking. Al[l my]
> thoughts are occupied with the supposition that both you
> & she will prefer to go with N. Poe. I do sincerely believe
> that your *comforts* will for the present be secured—I
> cannot speak as regards your peace—your happiness. You
> have both tender hearts—and you will always have the
> reflection that my agony is more than I can bear—that
> you have driven me to the grave—for love like mine can
> never be gotten over. It is useless to disguise the truth that
> when Virginia goes with N. P. that I shall never behold her
> again—that is absolutely sure. Pity me, my dear Aunty, pity
> me. I have no one now to fly to. I am among strangers, and
> my wretchedness is more than I can bear. It is useless to
> expect advice from me—what can I say? Can I, in honour &
> in truth say—Virginia! do not go!—do not go where you can
> be comfortable & perhaps happy—and on the other hand
> can I calmly resign my—life itself. If she had truly loved me
> would she not have rejected the offer with scorn? Oh God
> have mercy on me! If she goes with N. P. what are you to do,
> my own Aunty?
>      I had procured a sweet little house in a retired situation
> on Church Hill—newly done up and with a large garden
> and [eve]ry convenience—at only $5 month. I have been
> dreaming every day & night since of the rapture I should
> feel in [havi]ng my only friends—all I love on Earth with

me there, [and] the pride I would take in making you both comfor[table] & in calling her my wife. But the dream is over[.] [Oh G]od have mercy on me. What have I *to live for?* Among strangers with *not one soul to love me.*

The situation has this morning been conferred upon another. Branch T. Sunders. but White has engaged to make my salary $60 a month, and we could live in comparative comfort & happiness—even the $4 a week I am now paying for board would support us all—but I shall have $15 a week & what need would we have of more? I had thought to send you on a little money every week until you could either hear from Hall or Wm. Poe, and then we could get a [little] furniture for a start for White will not be able [to a]dvance any. After that all would go well—or I would make a desperate exertion & try to borrow enough for that purpose. There is little danger of the house being taken immediately. I would send you on $5 now—for White paid me the $8 2 days since—but you appear not to have received my last letter and I am afraid to trust it to the mail, as the letters are continually robbed. I have it for you & will keep it until I hear from you when I will send it & more if I get an[y] in the meantime. I wrote you that Wm. Poe had written to me concerning you & has offered to assist you asking me questions concerning you which I answered. He will beyond doubt aid you shortly & with an effectual aid. Trust in God.

The tone of your letter wounds me to the soul—Oh Aunty, aunty you loved me once—how can you be so cruel now? You speak of Virginia acquiring accomplishments, and entering into society—you speak in so *worldly* a tone. Are you sure she would be more happy. Do you think any one could love her more dearly than I? She will have far—very far better opportunities of entering into society here than with N. P. Every one here receives me with open arms.

Adieu my dear aunty. I *cannot advise you.* Ask Virginia. Leave it to her. Let me have, under her own hand, a letter, bidding me *good bye* —forever—and I [m]ay die—my heart will break—but I will say no more.
EAP.

Kiss her for me—a million times[.]

For Virginia,

My love, my own sweetest Sissy, my darling little wifey, thi[nk w]ell before you break the heart of your Cousin, Eddy.

I open this letter to enclose the 5$—I have just received another letter from you announcing the rect. of mine. My heart bleeds for you. Dearest Aunty consider my happiness while you are thinking about your own. I am saving all I can. The only money I have yet spent is 50 cts for washing—I have 2.25 left. I will shortly send you more. Write immediately. I shall be all anxiety & dread until I hear from you. Try and convince my dear Virginia. how devotedly I love her. I wish you would get me th[e] Republican [which] noticed the Messenger & send it on immediately by mail. God bless & protect you both.

Poe's relationship with his wife, Virginia, is second only to Poe's death in its mystery. Besides the above sub-missive, the only surviving records of any written communication between the two are an 1846 poem she wrote for him on the occasion of what would end up being their last Valentine's Day together and a letter he wrote in June of that same year. The Valentine was another piece, the original manuscript of which I had seen at the Enoch Pratt Free Library. The Valentine:

Ever with thee I wish to roam—
Dearest my life is thine.
Give me a cottage for my home
And a rich old cypress vine,
Removed from the world with its sin and care
And the tattling of many tongues.
Love alone shall guide us when we are there—
Love shall heal my weakened lungs;
And Oh, the tranquil hours we'll spend,
Never wishing that others may see!
Perfect ease we'll enjoy, without thinking to lend
Ourselves to the world and its glee—
Ever peaceful and blissful we'll be.

The letter:

> **My Dear Heart, My dear Virginia! our Mother will explain
> to you why I stay away from you this night. I trust the
> interview I am promised, will result in some *substantial
> good* for me, for your dear sake, and hers—Keep up your
> heart in all hopefulness, and trust yet a little longer—In my
> last great disappointment, I should have lost my courage
> *but for you*—my little darling wife you are my greatest
> and *only* stimulus now, to battle with this uncongenial,
> unsatisfactory and ungrateful life—I shall be with you
> tomorrow P.M. and be assured until I see you, I will keep
> in *loving remembrance* your *last words* and your fervent
> prayer!
> Sleep well and may God grant you a peaceful summer,
> with your devoted
> Edgar**

But in all the mystery around his relationship, we do at least know one thing about Poe and Virginia: They honeymooned. And, today, you can visit their honeymoon suite.

Petersburg, Virginia, is located about twenty miles south of Richmond. It's a small city of about thirty thousand, and most of its stories are related to the Civil War. It's also one of the cities that Poe's parents toured as actors.

What I was looking for was on West Bank Street, and before I was too far away, I saw the sign. Hanging from the second story of a building was an image of Poe beside an image of Virginia, the latter being her death portrait. The pair bookended a small raven like the proud parents of a child. The only words on the sign were ALL THAT WE SEE OR SEEM IS BUT A DREAM WITH A DREAM in a tiny banner in the bird's beak. Below it all was the year 1836, the year the two honeymooned on the second floor of that building.

Back then, 12 West Bank Street had been the location of Hiram Haines Coffee House, although it had a different house number at the time. Hiram Haines was a poet, a newspaper editor, and a friend of Poe's. He married one of Poe's childhood friends, and both men pushed each other's publications in their own.

However, the only times Haines is really brought up as part of the Edgar Allan Poe story is when he let Poe use his place to honeymoon, and then later, when Poe was in Philadelphia, when Haines offered Virginia a fawn for a pet, which they turned down. That's pretty much all anyone ever cared about Hiram Haines.

Until a man named Jeffrey Abugel moved to Petersburg in 2005.

Today, instead of the Hiram Haines Coffee House, the name above the door is, well, Hiram Haines Coffee and Ale House. It's not that Haines's place had survived the past 180 years, but that it was reincarnated in 2010 (with ale . . . it had been good in its previous life), thanks to Abugel.

I walked in and found an extremely cozy literary establishment. Early Tom Waits was playing over the sound system. On the walls surrounding the tables were shelves full of books and antiques, pictures of authors such as Kerouac and Twain and Sartre and, of course, Poe. Library lamps lit the booths. A large black sign descended from the ceiling that proclaimed, HISTORIC SITE OF HIRAM HAINES' COFFEE HOUSE 1829–1836 on one side and HISTORIC SITE OF EDGAR ALLAN POE'S HONEYMOON, MAY 1836 on the other.

The place was, in a word, cool. The kind of place you want to hang out in and discuss literary points that otherwise would embarrass you if somebody overheard the conversation. I had timed my visit between the lunch and dinner, so the place was empty.

Abugel walked out from somewhere in the back and greeted me. He had a gray mustache and talked with a New York accent, only somewhat softened by his years in the South. He seemed a bit tired to me, although over the course of the afternoon, I would discover he was more world-weary.

I immediately complimented him on the ambiance of the place. "I grew up in Brooklyn and lived in Greenwich Village, where there were a lot of literary pubs . . . like the White Horse, where Dylan Thomas had his last drink and then died at St. Vincent's across the street. It's where I had my first drink. I wanted that same literary pub feel." Minus the comatose poet on his sidewalk, I assumed.

He had attended New York University, where he majored in journalism, and had written a few books on the topic of depersonalization, a cousin disorder to depression that is

*Hiram Haines Coffee and Ale House*

more specifically defined as a detachment from oneself where, I guess, all that you "see or seem is but a dream within a dream."

He introduced me to his wife, Beverly, who came in briefly through a doorway to the adjoining building, where she ran an antique shop and interior design business. That building had been Haines's actual home, where he lived with his wife and six children. The two buildings were Siamese back then, too.

I knew most of Abugel's Hiram Haines story from the short book he had just published called *Edgar Allan Poe's Petersburg*, which detailed him coming to this city and hearing from locals about the connection this building had to Edgar Allan Poe. The first chapter opens:

> **I confess. I was never Edgar Allan Poe's biggest fan. I respected his place among American poets but pretty much left what I'd read behind in high school. Too many Hammer films, too much Vincent Price had long dissociated me from the body of work that went so far beyond "[The] Cask of Amontillado" and "The Raven." Over time, the words of my favorite authors—Borges, Camus, Miller and Mishima—became sacrosanct. Poe, somehow, seemed more Halloween than hallowed.**

That changed in Petersburg, as he devoured everything Poe wrote, seeing echoes of his own studies on depersonalization, and then researched the building we were both standing in. Eventually, the research backed up the rumors and he bought it. Although by then he pulled a move I'd seen before with Poe guys. His loyalty changed.

"By the time I finished reading Hiram's letters, I really liked the guy and was sad that he was dead." Haines died in 1841 at age 39. "He seemed very modern, was crazy about his wife. And there was just a lot to learn about him. Nothing new came out to me regarding Poe. Everybody's kind of done him to death. But Hiram, he became my guy." In fact, the publicity he brought to Haines convinced nearby Blandford Cemetery, where Hiram and his wife are buried, to restore the husband's and wife's fallen, broken headstones.

As we talked, a couple of people walked in and sat at a table. While he served them, I wandered into the back room, which a sign above the entryway called the Rue Morgue. The room had originally been the back alley of the place before it was roofed over at some point in the past.

Small and narrow, the room had walls that were made up of what had one time been the exterior of buildings, and still looked that way, with rough bricks and windows. There were carpets on the cement floor, and the space was crammed with whisky barrels, a couch, an old piano, and a couple of larger tables. Above, a wooden plank had been lodged through the upper story windows and a ceiling fan was affixed to it. After the Civil War the place was a bakery, and the ovens were located in this section.

When he came back from his duties as server, he said, "This place isn't about French fries. You can get that type of stuff across the way at Longstreet's." Longstreet's was a casual restaurant without any known past literary legacy.

Turns out, Abugel wasn't looking for a permanent project with the coffee house. He just wanted to restore it and secure the history, really.

"Who wants to run a restaurant? It's fun sometimes, but it's a pain in the ass all the time." His father owned a restaurant when he was younger, and he worked there, afterward promising himself that he'd never own one. But, now, because of Edgar Allan Poe, he was doing just that. "My whole purpose was to bring back the history. That's what gets me excited."

Unfortunately, he soon discovered that Petersburg doesn't really have the demographics to support the type of place he wanted to establish, making him less world-weary, I guess, and more Petersburg-weary. Still, he was persevering with his coffee and ale house.

He took me to the second floor, which wasn't a part of the restaurant. Most of the two upper floors were original, with horsehair plaster and pine flooring. The evidence was in the decay. As we got to the top of the stairs, I found myself on a small landing. Plaster had fallen in chunks from its ceiling, and fissures spread along the walls. A door with glass painted green had the words CENTRAL CREDIT AGENCY painted on it, barely discernible through large cracks. Beside the door a sign read, E.O. WILKERSON, SURVEYOR.

On the other side of that door was the honeymoon suite of Poe and his child bride, where they stayed for anywhere from a few days to two weeks, depending on who's telling the story.

Inside, it was as decrepit as the landing, although brighter, thanks to the windows that faced West Bank Street. The only furnishings in the room were a mattress-less bed frame and a portrait of a woman above the fireplace. The paint on the walls, what hadn't peeled off at least, was pale green, and electricity had been installed on the outside of the walls through old conduits.

Outside the window I could see the sign with Edgar and Virginia Poe's portraits on it. Across the street was the incongruous Siege Museum. The white, colonnaded Greek Revival museum building had been built around 1839, a few years after the Poes had their honeymoon, and was originally intended to be a marketplace. It was dedicated to the Siege of Petersburg, when Ulysses S. Grant and the Union army took over the city after ten months of battle. During that long siege, exhausted and sick Confederate soldiers had rested and convalesced in the very room where I was standing. Abugel pointed out another building visible from the window. "That was the home of Elizabeth Keckley. She was the dress maker for Abraham Lincoln's wife at the White House."

Adjoining the bedroom was a large sitting room painted in the same pale green. A couch, a coffee table, and some chairs had been set up in front of the large fireplace, and a table against the wall held a couple of Poe's books. An adjoining dining room was open and empty.

"It's all original: the mantels, the molding, the paint. There's a claw-foot tub in the bathroom. He pointed at a long, narrow room off the dining room that was filled with building refuse almost to the point of hiding the tub. "I thought about outfitting these rooms so that people could actually stay in them, and maybe I will since I'm still here, but it'd be a pain to maintain the history and to deal with modern regulations for a living space."

*Bedroom of Edgar and Virginia's honeymoon suite*

He left me to wander the decrepit rooms like a lost soul while he went downstairs to take care of the restaurant. I snuck up to the third floor just briefly and found it in a similar condition of decay.

Returning to Poe's honeymoon suite, I had the time and the perfect place to really give some thought to Poe and his bride.

Biographers of Poe usually handle this aspect of Poe's life pretty well. And by aspect, I mean the fact that the twenty-seven-year-old Poe married his thirteen-year-old first cousin. I'm not sure how well I'll do. It's icky. At its worst, it's incestuous pedophilia. At its best, we have to say something vague about cultural norms in the nineteenth century and true love.

Poe married her in Richmond (although some say he had a civil ceremony in Baltimore first and then a more traditional ceremony once they moved south), and he lied about her age by a good eight years to do so. Most writers about Poe caveat this the same way. That it was certainly young for that time period, but only two to three years too young. That first cousins regularly married each other back then. Certainly, in most states today, marrying a first cousin is legal, as is an adult marrying someone as young as sixteen. But again, Virginia was thirteen, and he had lived with her since she was eight.

Some of the more imaginative rationalizations for this relationship are that Poe never consummated it, or didn't until she was older. That he wanted an ideal woman to adore or a sister (and the mother she came with) that would never leave him, not a partner or someone to share flesh with. Certainly, the two never bore children. And, certainly, he was known to call her "sis" and "sissy."

But to me, much like the usual rationalizations for his moments of drunkenness—that his natural constitution made him extremely susceptible to small quantities of alcohol—the explanation for marrying a girl thirteen years from the womb seems weak. I have to trust the experts that this was more-or-less okay back then, and certainly, from the historical record, Poe didn't get any public disapprobation for the situation, but a lot of bad things were okay back then.

Poe was, in many ways, a broken person. Maybe Maria and Virginia were too. And broken pieces often can form a whole. But good thing he was a great writer. And good thing it's two-hundred-year-old news. And good thing ickiness contributes to the Myth of Poe more than it takes away from it.

I guess that was why I wasn't too skeezed by standing in the room where the two might have taken it all to the next level . . . if it was really their honeymoon suite.

*Living room of the Poes' honeymoon suite*

At some point in my travels, somebody told me that this wasn't the original building where Hiram Haines had his coffee shop. That the original building had been torn down and replaced long ago with the one I now stood in.

Abugel dealt with that pretty convincingly in the book and seemed to have found plenty of evidence to the contrary. Certainly, these rooms felt extremely old. Even so, it didn't really matter to me. I mean, the grave of Poe's biological mom is a guess. His college dorm room has a fifty/fifty chance of being the wrong one. Today, they are more important as monuments to Poe than as historical traces of him. Made me wonder what would have happened if Boston had claimed the still-surviving house next door to the site of Poe's birth home as his, shoved it full of artifacts, and stuck a sign in the grass of the Common stating, POE'S BIRTH HOME, THIS WAY.

On my way out, I asked Abugel about his plan for the Hiram Haines Coffee and Ale House. He told me he wanted to sell it.

"What would you do then?"

"I'd travel, write. I'm always trying to finish my novel. It's set in Petersburg, but it's not about Hiram and Poe, although it does mention them. Once I got that done, then I could really move on."

Between the pleasant and bookish atmosphere of the coffee house and the legacy of the room upstairs, I don't think I'd ever want to move on from a place like that . . . although I would get tired of serving French fries.

## *Center of the Poe-verse*

The small, dark stone house on Main Street is the oldest surviving building in Richmond. Built sometime around 1737, it edges out the Craig House by close to fifty years. By itself, it has nothing directly to do with Edgar Allan Poe. The place was around during his time, obviously, and only blocks from where he lived, so he more than likely knew the house. Back then the Old Stone House was an unremarkable and slightly younger place. However, in modern times, it has become the gateway to a Poe experience unequalled anywhere.

You've already read my case for Poe's Baltimore grave being the number one Poe site on the planet, but that judgment, I must admit, must be taken into context with my macabre interests and home-field biases. Even if it's true, it doesn't change the fact that the center of the entire Poe-verse is the Edgar Allan Poe Museum of Richmond. It has more authentic Poe per square inch than Poe himself probably had.

The museum started as the Edgar Allan Poe Shrine back in 1922 and was made up of the Old Stone House and the garden behind it. Because it was in a place where Poe spent so many years, there were quite a few Poe artifacts for them to access from private collectors and other sources in the area. Still, it was

*Edgar Allan Poe Museum in Richmond*

less a museum at the time and more like Poe Park in the Bronx currently is, with a twist that we'll get to in a second.

I've visited the Richmond Poe Museum twice so far in my life. The first time, in 2012, was before the start of the book project, so my role was just to gawp. This time, less than a year later, my role was to gawp and take notes.

We opened the door of the Old Stone House and found ourselves in the gift shop—T-shirts, plush toys, key chains, glassware, tote bags, air fresheners, lunchboxes—anything you could fit Poe's face on was for sale. However, as much as I wanted to pull my car up to the door and take it all home, my wife and I were there for a personal tour from Chris Semtner, the manager and curator of the museum.

Since 2000, Semtner has had the task of taking care of the largest and most important public collection of Poe artifacts in the world. He's the only full-time employee of the museum, with the rest of the staff rounded out by a handful of part-timers who run admissions and do tours. As a result, most of the work falls on Semtner, whether it's organizing events or cataloguing artifacts or crunching the data from the hygrometers in the exhibit cases to ensure an ideal environment for the priceless artifacts.

He opened a door in the gift shop to show us the single exhibit space therein. It was mostly furniture. That's kind of how I remembered it from my first visit. There were a lot of pieces that had belonged to Rosalie Poe, including her piano, as well as some furniture from Poe's boyhood home.

However, what was different from my last visit is the centerpiece of the room, one of the centerpieces of the whole collection, in fact: Poe's boyhood bed. It had been displayed somewhere else in the museum on my previous visit. Certainly, the bed where Poe dreamed his earliest dreams within dreams was a great place to start a tour of the museum.

It was a simple, low wooden bed, with spheres on each post. We'd probably call it a cot these days, and then we'd choose to sleep on the floor instead of on such an uncomfortable-looking thing. A grungy, old, khaki-colored blanket patterned with faded red diamonds was placed neatly over it. The placard in front of it explained its whole chain of custody. From Poe, it went to the daughter of John Allan's business partner Charles Ellis, who then gave it to her own daughter when she grew up, who then gave it to her grand-nephew, who bequeathed it to the Raven Society at the University of Virginia, which, realizing a childhood bed didn't go in a college dorm room, I guess, gave it to the museum, where it's been since 1979.

On the wall of the room was a pair of original life portraits of John and Frances Allan. The museum is the only place in the world with original life portraits of Poe's guardians. There's a lot of stuff like that in the museum.

After that room, we exited behind the Old Stone House into a long courtyard. The first thing I noticed was, well, what I quite logically took to be mutant hornets the size of my thumb swarming us. Semtner smiled. "Oh these. They're nice. They're called cicada killers." And then he promptly stuck out his hand and let one of the white-and-black giants alight peacefully on his palm. We had timed our visit for the seventeen-year cicada resurrection.

*Poe's childhood bed, Edgar Allan Poe Museum*

To either side of us were buildings, and in the back of the courtyard, past a central fountain, was a brick shrine made up of a row of archways that formed a pergola. Inside was a white bust of Poe, a copy of the Edmund Quinn version at the Fordham Cottage. The copy actually replaced another copy donated by the Bronx Academy of Arts and Science that had originally been in the shrine. It was stolen in 1987, but then later turned up at a biker bar. According to a book Semtner wrote, called *Edgar Allan Poe's Richmond: The Raven in the River City,* an unknown man in a cowboy hat walked in with the missing eighty-pound-bust, heaved it onto the bar, and ordered it a drink before leaving it there.

The last time I had seen the courtyard, it was set up for a wedding, with rows of white chairs and the Poe bust presiding.

But the garden isn't merely dedicated to Poe; it's almost created out of him. The whole museum is a Frankenstein's monster of Poe's life in Richmond. The red brick of the pergola was from the original *Southern Literary Messenger* building. The ivy growing around us had been taken from Eliza Poe's grave. A live oak just off the garden was a reference to "The Gold-Bug," although I saw no skull nailed to any of its branches. Benches in the garden were from Mrs. Yarrington's boardinghouse, where Poe and his family lived while he worked at the *Southern Literary Messenger.* And somewhere, they have the load of seven hundred bricks that Holt Edmunds nabbed from Poe's Greenwich Village place, ready to incorporate into the museum at the first opportunity.

The whole thing is like the ingredients of some witch's potion meant to resurrect Poe. The guiding light of this landscape was Poe's poem "To One in Paradise," the first stanza of which goes:

> **Thou wast all that to me, love,**
> **For which my soul did pine-**
> **A green isle in the sea, love,**
> **A fountain and a shrine,**
> **All wreathed with fairy fruits and flowers,**
> **And all the flowers were mine.**

The buildings surrounding the courtyard were actually part of the museum complex. Today, the Poe Museum is far from just the small stone house and garden it was in the early 1920s. It's now made up of four different buildings. From the Old Stone House, we were to visit the buildings in a clockwise direction. Our next stop, the building on our left, was called the Model Building.

The small, almost-hallway of a room had quite a few amazing pieces. The fireplace mantel from Poe's boyhood bedroom. The only known manuscript in Poe's handwriting of his original "To Helen," which was penciled in an album, the words differing slightly from all published versions. There was a red leather trinket box and a wall mirror that belonged to Virginia. The letter from Poe to Hiram Haines declining the fawn. Poe's handwritten quotes from the works of Shakespeare and Milton.

This room is also where I saw his 1831 volume *Poems*, which he put together with funds from his fellow West Point cadets, and which the owner had written on its title page "This book is a damned cheat."

The room also featured a few relatively strange pieces. There was a sterling silver fingernail file that Poe had gifted to someone who helped him do some proofreading on the *Southern Literary Messenger* and a thick bun of white or pale blonde hair from the head of Eliza White, the daughter of Thomas White, who owned the *Southern Literary Messenger*. Rumor has it that Poe was interested in her, but if so, it was short-lived as he, of course, married Virginia soon after moving to Richmond.

However, the building gets its name from the massive artifact taking up most of the narrow room: a miniature model of Richmond as it would have appeared in Poe's day. Of course, miniature is relative, because the model is about eighteen feet long. It sits behind a sheet of glass, and relevant Poe sites are marked. It was great for getting a sense of Poe's Richmond, especially after touring the modern and much-altered version earlier that day.

It was also because of this model that Chris Semtner was the person leading us through the museum.

Semtner was born in the small town of Blackstone, Virginia, about fifty miles southwest of where we were standing. He went to art school at Virginia Commonwealth University, as well as at the Pennsylvania Academy of the Fine Arts. That's right. Semtner was genetically an artist, not an administrator.

He found himself at the Poe Museum to do restoration work. The model of Richmond had caught fire in 1999. Lead pipes had melted all over it, damping the flames but further damaging the piece. The museum wanted it repaired, so Semtner spent six months restoring one small section per day behind the glass wall. Basically, Semtner started as an exhibit and worked his way up to curator.

From this building we continued around the garden, past the Poe Shrine and into the building in the back corner. On our way in, we passed a horse-headed hitching post made of wrought iron, one of many that lined the streets of Richmond back in the day. There's a famous picture of Gertrude Stein posing beside one in 1935. A couple of pictures from that same visit show her at the Poe Shrine itself.

This two-story building was called the Exhibits Building. The main room on the first floor is a stage for temporary exhibitions. On my first visit, it had been

*Edgar Allan Poe Shrine, Edgar Allan Poe Museum*

filled with a life-sized diorama from "The Pit and the Pendulum," complete with a rat-covered mannequin victim. Very haunted house.

This time, it went more elegant with a *Poe in Paris* exhibition, showcasing artifacts that explored Poe's influence in France and beyond. There was original Poe-inspired artwork by Édouard Manet and Henri Matisse and Paul Gauguin. Rare French translations of Poe's work by Charles Baudelaire and Stéphane Mallarmé. Even a first edition of the novel *An Antarctic Mystery,* Jules Verne's sequel to Poe's *The Narrative of Arthur Gordon Pym of Nantucket*, and the most persuasive reminder yet that I needed to reread that book.

The top floor of the building featured an open space with a rotating selection of Poe portraits on the walls from a variety of years and artists. There was an 1884 frontispiece image by Elihu Vedder for "The Raven" that featured Poe's profile, a 1930 drawing of the poet by Disney illustrator Ferdinand Horvath, a 2007 sketch of him by Ville Valo, the lead singer of the Finnish rock band HIM, and a 1972 reverse silhouette by Bob Harper.

On our way out, Semtner opened what seemed like a random door on the first floor and out raced an honest-to-God black cat. He quickly grabbed it and held it up for us to pet. It had white spots on its stomach and neck. "This is Pluto. We expect the white spots to turn into a gallows at some point."

They had found the cat as a kitten out in the garden, along with two other littermates. The trio were all given proper Poe names, Catterina went home with a staff member, and Edgar and Pluto became permanent residents of the museum.

Finally, we went to the last building of the museum complex. Directly across the garden from the Model Building stands the Elizabeth Arnold Poe Memorial Building. Named after Poe's mother, the building was constructed in 1928 to mimic the look of the last home where Eliza Poe lived. Later, and after it was too late, the museum staff learned the building they used for a model had nothing to do with Eliza and wasn't even built until after her death.

Nevertheless, this building holds the mother lode of Edgar Allan Poe. Inside, multiple exhibits take up the first floor. I'd list the highlights, but literally everything in this room is a highlight. There is his walking stick that he accidentally left behind before heading north to his death in Baltimore. (The story goes that he grabbed the wrong walking stick at a friend's house on his way out.) His vest was there, as were his stock-

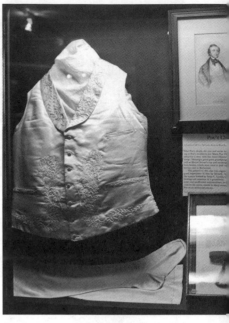

*Poe's vest, stockings, and boot hooks, Edgar Allan Poe Museum*

ings, boot hooks, a trunk, and a key that was found in his pocket after his death. A brass ladle from his Fordham home.

Let me take a breath.

The pair of candelabra under which he wrote "The Bells." His desk chair from the *Southern Literary Messenger,* its back sawn off to help him with his posture. The last known letter he ever wrote, on September 18, 1849, which was to the poet Marguerite St. Leon Loud, whom he was supposed to meet in Philadelphia to edit her manuscript. Even a small cutting of his hair, less like the full lock I'd seen in Baltimore and more like a highly attenuated smattering of filaments. It had been taken by Dr. Joseph Evans Snodgrass on Poe's deathbed.

On one wall is a magnificent marble monument called the "Actors' Memorial to Poe." It's ten feet tall and shaped like a heavily ornamented door. On the top half, stark against the white marble, is the face of Edgar Allan Poe in dark bronze. A marble wreath encircles it, and the full-sized marble statue of a woman leans against it. It looks like a woman visiting Poe's grave and is even reminiscent of Poe's grave marker.

It was sculpted by Richard Henry Park in 1884 and originally installed at the Metropolitan Museum of Art in New York before finding a new home Richmond. The inscription on its bottom half reads:

THIS MEMORIAL, EXPRESSING A DEEP AND PERSONAL
SYMPATHY BETWEEN THE STAGE AND THE LITERATURE OF
AMERICA, WAS PLACED HERE BY THE ACTORS OF NEW YORK
TO COMMEMORATE THE AMERICAN POET
EDGAR ALLAN POE,
WHOSE PARENTS—DAVID POE, JR., AND ELIZABETH
ARNOLD, HIS WIFE—WERE ACTORS, AND WHOSE RENOWN
SHOULD, THEREFORE, BE CHERISHED, WITH PECULIAR REVERENCE
AND PRIDE, BY THE DRAMATIC PROFESSION
OF HIS COUNTRY.
HE WAS BORN IN BOSTON, THE 19TH OF JANUARY, 1809;
HE DIED IN BALTIMORE, THE 7TH OF OCTOBER, 1849.

HE WAS GREAT IN HIS GENIUS; UNHAPPY IN HIS LIFE;
WRETCHED IN HIS DEATH. BUT IN HIS FAME HE IS IMMORTAL.

SAEPIUS VENTIS AGITATUR INGENS
PINUS, ET CELSAE GRAVIORE CASU
DECIDUNT TURRES, FERIUNTQUE SUMMOS
FULGURA MONTES.

The last few lines are from the *Odes* of Horace. In English, it reads, "'Tis oftener the tall pine that is shaken by the wind, 'tis the lofty towers that fall with the heavier crash, and 'tis the tops of the mountain that the lightning strikes."

Here also is the original bust that was recovered at the biker bar.

This is another one of those Poe sites that is extremely hard to exit, but fortunately, I was only going upstairs . . . up stairs, by the way, that had been pulled from Poe's boyhood home. The second floor isn't part of the exhibition, and is used instead as a back-office space. There was a conference table for meetings and a small reference library full of books that would have been extremely valuable to somebody writing a book about Poe had he not lived nine hours away.

Poe's Trunk
Poe left this trunk in Richmond on his last visit to the city. It contained most of his worldly possessions: some clothing, a mirror, and some manuscripts. The key to the trunk was found in Poe's pocket after his death two weeks after leaving Richmond.

Key to Poe's Trunk

*Poe's trunk and key, Edgar Allan Poe Museum*

Semtner showed me a few things they had sitting around, waiting to get cat-alogued or validated or incorporated into an exhibit. A piece of plaster from the Poe House in Baltimore, various Poe-inspired artworks, a painting rumored to have been owned by Poe at some point. He even showed me a severed hand in a box that was used as an invitation for a museum event.

But eventually, we sat down at the conference table for the "tell" part of our show-and-tell afternoon. I started with what has become my standard ice-breaker, even for strangers on the street. "Tell me your Poe story."

"I was introduced to him by a librarian in fifth grade. The stories weren't the usually ones kids first read when it comes to Poe. They were stories like, 'Never Bet the Devil Your Head' and 'Hop Frog,' also some of his humorous pieces."

"How difficult is it to be the only full-time employee of the Poe Museum?"

"It can be rough, but I do like working in a small museum. I can come up here and do research and then go down and talk to Poe fans, show them around. That's pretty great."

"Since you're an artist running a literary museum, have you become more of a lit guy?"

"Well, first let me say that reading is the one art form that's also a part of our daily life. You can survive without paintings or music. I had to, at least when it came to paintings, since I grew up in a small town with no museums. But you can't survive or get ahead in work or life without reading. You do it every day without even thinking of it as an art form because it's so integrated into your life through every e-mail, text, or advertisement.

"But, no, I'm still an art guy, although managing a museum dedicated to Poe helps me with that."

"Yeah?"

"I mean, we remember 'The Tell-Tale Heart' vividly. Why? There's a scene in which the victim is awakened in the middle of the night by a slight sound his murderer makes outside his bedroom door. Then the old man sits up in total darkness for the better part of an hour, terrified of the unseen, unknown danger he senses—but does not see—just outside his room. Poe takes an ordinary room, changes the whole atmosphere. That's what artists do. Like what Hitchcock did with showers or Van Gogh did with wheat fields. You can't look at those things the same anymore. It's about seeing the world in a new way.

"In Poe's best stories and poems, he's able to do that. Half of 'The Raven' takes place before the raven even enters the room. The narrator and the reader spend this time imagining, even fearing, what could be tapping on his chamber door. That great passage 'Deep into that darkness peering, long I stood there, wondering, fearing, doubting, dreaming dreams no mortal ever dared to dream before' is all about the narrator staring into the impenetrable darkness, terrified of what could be there. It's the details that Poe leaves out that really make his best work effective. They're like paintings in that way.

"Paintings don't have a beginning, middle, or end. Everything's there at the same time. But they can communicate what's about to happen or what is happening elsewhere. In my own work, I was doing staircases for a while because they imply somewhere else, something unseen, just outside our field of vision at the bottom or something at the top or on the other side of a closed door. Portraits, too. The human face has that same power of suggestion."

The last time I was at the museum, I'd actually seen some of Semtner's work on the second floor of the Exhibits Building. A portrait of Poe himself against a vivid red background was the one I remembered. I brought the painting up.

"Yeah, I also painted one of his sister, Rosalie. I painted her as an older woman because there was just something about her look. They really knew how to grow old in the nineteenth century.

"But the visual arts aren't just relevant to a place like this philosophically. My art education is a great fit here, practically. I want to do exhibits that are as visually appealing as they are intellectually stimulating. I don't get to do that much with the buildings that show the artifacts, but that's fine. Those buildings should show their age. They're trips back in time. But like the Exhibits Building, I get to do a lot with that."

"The last time I was here it had a man about to get sawn in half by a pendulum blade."

"When I first started here, the museum board didn't want to address the darker side of Poe. They didn't even want to have any events in October. Anything to do with what they called the occult was not allowed."

"That must've been hard. Even apart from his work, he died in October. That's automatically a Halloween party."

"Exactly. I mean, in their defense, only a tiny fraction of his stories are horror tales, but these are the tales he's known for, the ones that draw the popular audience to him. And, honestly, that's where he excelled as a writer.

"It's also universal. Poe has that famous quote 'Terror is not of Germany, but of the soul,' and then he went and elevated the genre. He understood the mechanics of fear and constructed his stories like mousetraps to spring in just the right way at just the right moment to elicit the desired emotional response. Unlike, say, Mary Shelley, who created a story based on a terrifying dream she had and, in putting it to paper turned it into a not-scary morality tale by diluting it with extraneous detail. The potential was there, though. Later, other storytellers got hold of her concept, and the horror of *Frankenstein* was finally teased out."

"So it seems the museum is struggling, or at least in the past it was, with the thing I love the most about Poe. That he's an icon, especially of horror."

"Well, my whole philosophy for how I kind of see the Poe Museum comes from the title of a Bigfoot book I had as a child." At this point the pen I was taking notes with scribbled off the page like an errant record needle. "It was called something like, *Bigfoot: Man, Myth, or Monster?*

"Here, the 'man' part of Poe is the historical personage, the 'myth' is the legend of the tormented artist that is the public image Poe, and the 'monster' is the caricature of Poe that is a creation of our popular culture, the purely fictional character who appears in comics like *Batman: Nevermore* or on television shows like *South Park*. Poe is all three, but none of these alone tells the whole story. The mission statement of the museum is about interpreting Poe's life and influence, but in the past the museum was almost totally biographical, so it was missing the influence. The Exhibits Building is all about that, as you saw with 'Poe in Paris.'

"But we're still kind of figuring out how to deal with how often Poe pops up in popular culture. Do we support it? Correct it? Like the John Cusack movie." He was referring to *The Raven,* a major studio picture that came out in 2012 and depicted an extremely pop culture version of Poe trying to solve murders based on his stories. "Are we happy for the publicity? Yes. Should we become more involved in any conversations around it or let them be, or pick and choose? I don't know. I mean, in the end, it didn't have much of an impact, so who cares? Or take *The Following.*" This was a prime-time network show starring Kevin Bacon that I alluded to in the introduction. "That one's easier because Poe isn't in it. It's just Poe-inspired."

"So how much of Poe do you, personally, take home? I know you've done portraits of him, but how much of your life is Poe-inspired?"

"I try to find a balance. At home I don't think about him. I'll do paintings, sure, but I'll also go out of my way to paint anything else or avoid the topic completely. Sometimes I tell people I sell insurance to get around the inevitable questions about my favorite Poe story."

"Your fault for having a cool job. So what's the best thing about being the official caretaker for just about all things Poe?"

"The kids. We work a lot with school groups, and we try hard to catch their imaginations and inspire them. Obviously, the fact that we're a Poe museum helps a lot. I had one teacher tell me, 'He's creepy enough to be cool for the kids.' They tell me it's like pulling teeth to get them to read until they get to Poe." It took large amounts of will power not to interrupt with a "Berenice" joke. "Poe feels dangerous to these kids. He had problems with his parents, career uncertainties, wrote about being alone. Of course adolescents identify with that."

What he said reminded me of the famous T. S. Eliot quote about Poe: "That Poe had a powerful intellect is undeniable: but it seems to me the intellect of a highly gifted person before puberty." As much as I love Poe, that insight always kind of exposed him a bit for me.

Semtner continued, "Kevin Williamson is a good example of that. He visited the Poe Museum when he was young and living in North Carolina. Then he goes on to write the *Scream* movies, and now he has *The Following*, which he said was inspired by that early visit to the Poe Museum.

"That's why we have a Young Writer's Conference every year. It's that legacy of inspiration. Poe didn't just write literature, he crafted philosophies about art and literature and innovated new genres. He wanted others to follow him by making their own contributions to the development of art and literature."

"So let's say it's my first time here at the museum. I come in, I take pictures of the bed, try to find his house in the model, see his stockings and then I leave. What would make that a successful visit from the perspective of the museum?"

"Well, Poe was obsessed with effect, with having an emotional impact on his readers. Not just in his fiction, but everywhere else. He wrote about furniture and decor, about punctuation and landscaping. He thought that a sustained, unbroken effect was all-important. And I guess we want guests to have some kind of memorable emotional experience, as well, not necessarily a feeling of terror or melancholy but one of inspiration. We want people to leave inspired to read a good book or to write the next great poem or story."

It was a good talk, and I'm not at all, or only partially, biased by the fact that it was ten feet above Poe's hair and walking stick. As we exited the front door of the Old Stone House, I spied a chipped, plain block of granite bearing Poe's name and birth and death years. It was just sitting in the weeds beside the house, like it was somehow being thrown out and preserved simultaneously.

Later, I'd learn that the block was discovered in 1973, with the general theory of its origin being that it was intended as a pedestal for the Poe statue in Capitol Square and just didn't work out.

And, yet, the museum holds on to it. Like Poe's honeymoon suite, like his college dorm, like his military assignment at a fort, like the final resting places of those who were close to him, like the overwhelming number of artifacts on display and in the vaults of the Poe Museum . . . it just had to be held onto. Because it's connected to Poe.

And Virginia is for Poe lovers.

*Poe's Tavern fireplace*

# CHAPTER 8

# South Carolina

*From Grief and Groan to a Golden Throne*

IT DIDN'T AT FIRST FEEL LIKE one of my Poe trips. I was outside of Charleston, South Carolina, driving the Mark Clarke Expressway to Sullivan's Island. It was the middle of February, but the temperature was in the fifties. Palm trees lined the road, and as I neared my destination I started passing through wetlands. Then, right before the bridge to the barrier island, I saw a small white sign on the side of the road accented by two deflated balloons. It said GOLD BUG ISLAND. This was definitely a Poe trip.

It wasn't until I explored Sullivan's Island a bit more that I realized why it hadn't felt that way. This place was pleasant.

No other location I'd visited on this journey could I describe as "pleasant." Sure, the colleges I'd seen—the University of Virginia, West Point, Columbia University—were all stately, beautiful institutions, but I'm too old to find any college campus pleasant. "Alien" is a better term.

But Poe-Land is mostly an urban place. Sure, its cityscape is varied, and it's impossible to confuse the streets of Richmond with the streets of Baltimore or Philadelphia, or Providence or Boston with the Bronx or Manhattan, but all are dominated by the usual hallmarks of the city: advanced decay and progress, the far ends of poverty and riches, the practical too often winning out over the beautiful. And, its biggest identifier, the exploded anthill of people that cover every square concrete and metal inch.

In the past, I've shunned the tropical climes. Partly, it's because I dig seasons, but mostly it can be blamed on my college years, which were spent in Florida. Along with my degree, I came out of that state with an intense distaste for palm trees (which too often look like ratty dusters to me), sweating for no good reason, and unsightly beaches paved in semi-nude people.

These days, I've softened more to it and see much of its appeal. And, anyway, I was visiting this beach community in the winter, which is a different world than a beach community in the summer. I was also coming from eighteen inches of snow back at my house in New England.

Sullivan's Island caught me in a good mood. But it also kept me there.

There are two reasons why Poe-Land extends as far south as South Carolina: Poe's time here and Poe's tale here.

Edgar Allan Poe spent thirteen months on Sullivan's Island, from November of 1827 to December of 1828, just shy of two Christmases. It was the farthest south he would ever go. He was stationed at Fort Moultrie. It was his middle assignment between Fort Independence in Massachusetts and Fort Monroe in Virginia and formed the largest chunk of his military career.

But if the story of Poe's time in South Carolina were only a military one, it would be a boring one, especially since we know so little of it. Fortunately, there's more to the story . . . or more of a story . . . or, well, a story.

Poe mentioned this area of South Carolina in three of his tales. In "The Balloon-Hoax," a faux-journalistic piece on what is purported to be the first trans-Atlantic flight by balloon, Poe has the adventurers finish their journey from England on Sullivan's Island and at Fort Moultrie specifically. In "The Oblong Box," the ship on which the story takes place departs from Charleston, and it is there that the narrator first sees the mysterious titular container. Neither is a South Carolina story, though, as in both cases the locale is merely used as an end and start point, respectively.

But then there's "The Gold-Bug." Not only is this one of Poe's major stories, but it also takes place completely on Sullivan's Island and, even better, is intrinsically a South Carolina tale, taking advantage of the locale in many ways, from its pirate lore to its native flora. Here's Poe's description of the island from the story:

> This island is a very singular one. It consists of little
> else than the sea sand, and is about three miles long.
> Its breadth at no point exceeds a quarter of a mile. It is
> separated from the main land by a scarcely perceptible
> creek, oozing its way through a wilderness of reeds and
> slime, a favorite resort of the marsh-hen. The vegetation,
> as might be supposed, is scant, or at least dwarfish. No
> trees of any magnitude are to be seen. Near the western
> extremity, where Fort Moultrie stands, and where are some
> miserable frame buildings, tenanted, during summer, by
> the fugitives from Charleston dust and fever, may be found,
> indeed, the bristly palmetto; but the whole island, with the
> exception of this western point, and a line of hard, white
> beach on the seacoast, is covered with a dense undergrowth
> of the sweet myrtle, so much prized by the horticulturists of
> England. The shrub here often attains the height of fifteen
> or twenty feet, and forms an almost impenetrable coppice,
> burthening the air with its fragrance.

But let's start where Poe himself did, building bombs on the beach.

## Fortified in South Carolina

On my treks to Fort Independence and Fort Monroe, I discovered that the two forts couldn't be any more different from each other, sharing only the commonalities of really thick walls and a powder-burnt poet. As I pulled into the parking lot of the Fort Moultrie Visitor Center, I was about to find myself in a fort as different from the other two as they were from each other.

The story of Poe's time in South Carolina is a blank spot in his history. Most biographers expend no more than a few lines on his time here, wanting to get from the interesting reasons he joined the Army in Massachusetts to the interesting reasons he left it in Virginia. Or, of course, they just take advantage of the opportunity to talk about "The Gold-Bug."

More than likely, little happened in those thirteen months at the fort other than the usual daily army activities. Like the rest of Poe's time in the military, it was peace time, so the life of a soldier was merely one of vigilance. That meant a lot of routine, but also a lot of not fearing for one's life. We know Poe was good enough at his job to get promoted while at Fort Moultrie to sergeant major and that he was entrusted with both clerk duties and artificer duties, which had him writing reports, as well as assembling and inspecting the shells for the big guns.

He may have still been holding onto certain romanticized ideals that

*Fort Moultrie*

entranced him as a youth, the same inclinations that had him joining the Rich-mond Junior Volunteers when he was a teenager. The same inclinations that inspired him to write one of his first poems about the conqueror Tamerlane. The same inclinations that made him proud of the military heritage bequeathed him by his grandfather David Poe, who was the Baltimore quartermaster in the army and friend of Lafayette.

On the other hand, we also know that it was here that produced the first evi-dence of his burgeoning dissatisfaction with a soldier's life. One letter he wrote from Fort Moultrie survives, and it was written to John Allan at the end of his assignment there, just days before embarking for Fort Monroe. It's a long one, some three pages, so I won't pad the book's length with the whole thing, but it's the usual Poe-Allan affair. Here is a relevant enough selection of it:

> **I have been in the American army as long as suits my ends or my inclination, and it is now time that I should leave it—To this effect I made known my circumstances to Lieut Howard who promised me my discharge solely upon a re-conciliation with yourself— . . .**
>
> **The period of an Enlistment is five years—the prime of my life would be wasted—I shall be driven to more decided measures if you refuse to assist me.**

You need not fear for my future prosperity—I am
altered from what you knew me, & am no longer a boy
tossing about on the world without aim or consistency—I
feel that within me which will make me fulfil your highest
wishes & only beg you to suspend your judgement until you
hear of me again.

You will perceive that I speak confidently—but when
did ever Ambition exist or Talent prosper without prior
conviction of success? I have thrown myself on the world,
like the Norman conqueror on the shores of Britain &, by
my avowed assurance of victory, have destroyed the fleet
which could alone cover my retreat—I must either conquer
or die—succeed or be disgraced.

Being past the prime of my own life, I didn't mind
spending some of what I had left at the fort, especially since
what I found there was absolutely idyllic.

Fort Moultrie is located at the western end of the island and has guarded the
Charleston Harbor since before this country was a country. The fort that stands
today, and which is the one Poe would have known, was built in his birth year of
1809. Two other forts at the site predated it, including an original wooden fort
that saw action during the Revolutionary War. It was during one of the battles
of that war that the current fort and its predecessors got their name, after Colonel William Moultrie. He led the forces that protected Charleston during a 1776
battle with nine British warships that came to be called the Battle of Sullivan's
Island. It was also how South Carolina got its state flag, with its crescent moon
and palmetto tree. Moultrie chose the blue color and crescent moon for the war
effort, and then the state added the palmetto about a hundred years later to symbolize his victory.

Fort Moultrie played a part in the battle that started the Civil War, the Battle
of Fort Sumter, which was named after another fort in the middle of the harbor.
Fort Moultrie remained a fort through both world wars, before finally easing into
civilian life in 1947.

The visitor center is across the street from the fort. Upon entering I found a
room full of exhibits that covered the broad history of the fort and island, from
the three wars it took part in to the slave trade in which it was so prominent
(almost half of all African slaves brought to North America came through this
island). But no Poe. I didn't even see anything related to him in the gift shop.

I talked to the attendant at the desk and mentioned that my interest was
Edgar Allan Poe. I asked her if there were any plaques or commemorations or

Fort Monroe-like mannequins dedicated to him that I should look out for. She said no, vaguely mentioned a "Gold-Bug tree" somewhere on the island, and then went and got one of the rangers to try to help me out. He came back with an identical "no," although he did mention a couple of sites already on my itinerary. He told me there's not much on the island, other than a single street of restaurants. "It's mostly residential," he explained. "Expensive houses that are in high demand . . . except during hurricane season."

They did hand me an official Fort Moultrie brochure dedicated to Poe, although even that doubled-sided page had to be filled out with information from his non-South Carolina life.

Undeterred, I crossed the street for the sally port, the main entrance of the red-brick fort. In doing so, I passed the grave of Osceola, the Seminole leader who died while imprisoned at the fort, and the Patapsco monument, a short obelisk inscribed with the sixty-two names of the men who died aboard the U.S.S. *Patapsco,* an ironclad monitor ship that hit a Confederate mine in the harbor toward the end of the Civil War. Five of the men are buried there.

Inside, I followed the signs through the white tunnels that wended and deadended in empty, claustrophobic powder magazines. I would later be told that in past years, an arts society would turn the fort into a Poe-themed haunted house/ performance art piece of sorts called *Edgar Allan Poe: Back from the Grave.* For the event, the fort was set up with lighting and sound effects. Actors performed his works at stations throughout. The subterranean vaults were particularly useful for such stories as the "The Premature Burial," while the view of the harbor from the ramparts made for a compelling backdrop for a rendition of "Annabel Lee."

Eventually, the tunnels let me outside, into the center of the fort. Instead of having a green expanse of blank ground like at Fort Independence or being an entire town like Fort Monroe, it was a compact, hilly area, with each hill hiding an underground chamber. The brick structures above ground were painted a welcoming shade of yellow that contrasted with the big, black death machines on the walls. Only a few other visitors were walking the fort, all of them retired military men with their wives, their branch of service emblazoned on caps on their heads.

The most prominent part of the fort was the World War II—era Harbor Entrance Command Post, which rose far above the fortress walls like the bridge of a battleship. A set of stairs descended deep inside that tower. There, behind a big metal door, was a long, yellow hallway filled with glassed-off rooms. There were war bond posters and pictures of Eisenhower on the walls, helmets and uniform jackets on hooks, and old-fashioned telephones and clipboards. Big Band music played on the loudspeakers. It felt like going back in time.

When I surfaced, I went back further in time to some of the remaining inte-

*Foundation of the barracks from Poe's time at the fort*

rior structures from Poe's day. In the northwest corner of the fort was a small yellow-painted powder magazine building, its entrance guarded from detonation by a matching and thick freestanding wall of stone called a traverse. In front of it, a yellow cement rectangle filled with grass outlined the footprint of what had once been the enlisted barracks, where Poe would have lived. Cannons from his era sat on the wall just above.

At some point the path through the fort deposited me outside the walls, where I followed it to the beach and then to the original site of the wooden fort and then finally to an exterior battery. From the shore I could see Charleston across the harbor, as well as Fort Sumter.

The walk ended at a massive black battery, one of many dotting this area of the island, some abandoned, others turned into town landmarks. A historic sign informed me that nearby, in 1864, during the Civil War, the *H.L. Hunley* became the first submarine ever to sink an enemy in combat.

The Confederate submersible sank during the attack, killing its entire eight-man crew, who sank in their cast-iron tomb to the bottom of the harbor, where the submersible was lost for 130 years. In 1995, the location of the historic submarine was confirmed and it was then raised in 2000. The *Hunley* is now on display in a tank at a defunct naval base in North Charleston, the men inside interred with previous crewmen (the *Hunley* killed two of its previous crews, as well) in Charleston's wonderfully atmospheric Magnolia Cemetery.

From there, I went back to the visitor center, where I climbed the stairs to its rooftop observation deck to take in the whole of the compact fort and the harbor beyond. The fort seemed almost quaint, with its bright yellow interior structures and the beach beyond. My first stop on Sullivan Island, the one with the only definite historic connection to Poe, was disappointingly Poe-less. What made not finding any real references to Poe at the fort strange, though, was that I found them everywhere else on the small island.

## Hunting for Poet Treasure

All right. Let's talk pirates. When it comes to classic tales of Jolly Roger'd ships, we immediately think of Robert Louis Stevenson. With his first book, *Treasure Island,* Stevenson gave us Long John Silver and fifteen men on a dead men's chest and black spots and marooned pirates and everything we needed to make pirate stories exactly the same from that point on.

For that, we can partially credit Edgar Allan Poe . . . or at least Stevenson did. In an essay he penned about writing the book, Stevenson directly mentions Poe's influence:

> On a chill September morning, by the cheek of a brisk fire, and the rain drumming on the window, I began THE SEA COOK, for that was the original title. I have begun (and finished) a number of other books, but I cannot remember to have sat down to one of them with more complacency. It is not to be wondered at, for stolen waters are proverbially sweet. I am now upon a painful chapter. No doubt the parrot once belonged to Robinson Crusoe. No doubt the skeleton is conveyed from Poe.

Later in the chapter, he would say of that same skeleton, "I had called an islet 'Skeleton Island,' not knowing what I meant, seeking only for the immediate picturesque, and it was to justify this name that I broke into the gallery of Mr. Poe and stole Flint's pointer."

"Flint's pointer" in Stevenson's tale was the skeleton of Allardyce, one of the pirate crewman killed after burying treasure and whose body (and eventually bones) is arranged as a compass to literally point the way to it.

In all this, Stevenson isn't referencing Poe's penchant for the macabre. He's directly citing Poe's story, "The Gold-Bug," which is unique in Poe's body of work for being, well, a fun tale of pirate adventure. Sort of.

"The Gold-Bug" was published in 1843 in the *Philadelphia Dollar Newspaper.* He had submitted the story to the periodical as part of a contest, which he won, the prize being both publication and $100.

It became his most popular story while he was alive and was even turned into a stage performance in Philadelphia not long after it was published. In fact, its popularity was only rivaled by "The Raven," which came out a year and a half later. In a letter dated May 1845, Poe wrote, "The bird beat the bug . . . all hollow."

"The Gold-Bug" is about a man named William Legrand. Some say this Legrand was based on a naturalist named Edmund Ravenel, who at that time would stay the summers on Sullivan's Island and collect specimens, although zero documentation of a meeting between Ravenel and Poe exists. Others take the first few lines about Legrand, who was in a fallen state socially and financially and was basically living in hiding on the island, and use them to interpret Legrand as a stand-in for Poe himself.

Anyway, Legrand catches gold fever of a sort after finding a new species of scarab and an old encrypted map in the marshes around his house. The map, he believes, points to the buried treasure of Captain Kidd. A bushwhack, a skull nailed to a tree, and two men on a dead man's chest later, he finds exactly what he's looking for.

It's a strange one for a Poe story. Nobody dies. The appearance of madness is actually cleverness. And everybody gets rich and lives happily ever after. The only real Poesque trait to the story is the deciphering of the map, which plays into Poe's love of cryptograms, and which is similar to his stories of ratiocination.

Poe wrote a few seafaring tales—"MS. Found in a Bottle," "The Descent into the Maelstrom," *Arthur Gordon Pym,* and (technically) "The Oblong Box"—with none of them being pirate tales. And the one he does compose, "The Gold-Bug," is completely landlocked . . . and on Sullivan's Island, no less.

Which is another strange aspect of this tale. Most of Poe's works, when a location is even given, could have been lifted and placed anywhere else with just a scratch-out of a pen without harming the story. However, in "The Gold-Bug," the setting is crucial to the story, especially since it was born out of pirate legends from the 1700s. As such, it is very much a story that could have only been set near the southeast coast of the United States, and especially in the Charleston area.

Sullivan's Island is where the Gentleman Pirate Stede Bonnet was caught. He and his men were hung across the harbor at White Point Garden in Charleston. Anne Bonney started her life of nautical crime there in Charleston. Edward Teach, bad old Blackbeard himself, held the city siege by blockading the mouth of the harbor with his fleet of ships (his ransom demand was medicine). He would later get beheaded about three hundred miles up the coast, off Ocracoke Island in North Carolina.

That makes Sullivan's Island, which during Poe's time was a no man's land, a perfect place to hide a treasure, and a perfect place to go bucking off into the brush to find one.

I had a few things to find myself on the island, now that I was done with Fort Moultrie. It was going to be pretty easy. The entire island is only about two-and-a-half square miles, with much of that being wetland. My first stop was the library, not to brush up on "The Gold-Bug," as would have made sense, but because it was named "Edgar Allan Poe Library."

It's a tiny community library for a tiny community, and half of it is a children's room. But, man, it's a unique place. The whole thing is built inside an old fort battery. That means outside it's pretty ugly, looking to all the world like anything but a library. Parking signs on the gun emplacements. Abandoned batteries adjacent to it. Massive metal doors painted black flanking the entrance. Inside, the ceilings are claustrophobically low, the doorways arched, and the block walls all painted in what I was coming to think of as "Gold-Bug yellow" after my time at the fort.

Inside, there were touches of Poe everywhere. Stencils of ravens and his face and name in the windows, a niche with a small bust of Pallas topped by a cheap Halloween-decoration raven. Behind the check-out desk on the wall were pictures of Poe, his wife Virginia, and his mother Eliza, as well as illustrations from a couple of his works.

It took about twelve seconds to see the whole place, but it was a good refresher for me. It might seem odd, but in my treks, it was easy to forget I was chasing down the physical traces of a literary figure. Of all the Poe memorials, naming a library after him makes the most sense.

*Edgar Allan Poe Library*

*Poe Avenue*

From there I was off to Gold Bug Island. I hadn't known about the place prior to my visit. The small, white sign I saw on the road earlier had been a surprise to me. I followed the black arrow beneath the name to a turn off . . . but there wasn't much to see. I drove through the open metal gate, where a blue-and-yellow sign proclaimed the island HOME OF EAST COOPER OUTBOARD MOTOR CLUB. Elsewhere I saw its symbol, a yellow and black bug with large pincers. I drove down to a parking lot, next to which was a clubhouse and a pavilion, but couldn't go much farther, as MEMBER ACCESS ONLY signs prohibited any trespassing by people without yellow insects tattooed on their forearms. Also because there was nowhere else to go on the small island. Later, I would find out it's basically a private boat launch and event rental site, primed, I guess for Edgar Allan Poe–themed oyster roasts.

I crossed the bridge back onto Sullivan's Island and made my way to the neighborhoods. The streets of Sullivan's Island form a narrow grid slightly off-kilter in spots. Its north-south streets are all named after stations (Station 29 Street, Station 30 Street, etc.), and it's divided by Middle Street, which is more or less held down by Fort Moultrie at one end and the bridge to the Isle of Palms on the other. The streets are marked with white stone posts of varying heights staked into the ground, the names written vertically down the shafts.

I was looking for three streets in particular: Poe Avenue, Raven Avenue, and

*Goldbug Avenue*                    *Raven Avenue*

Goldbug Avenue. Apparently Balloon-Hoax Avenue and Oblong Box Avenue were just too weird. Obviously it took seconds to find with a GPS. Poe Avenue starts at Fort Moultrie and merges with Middle Street. Raven and Goldbug Avenues are completely residential and full of the large hurricane-victim houses mentioned by the park ranger to me at Fort Moultrie. They also parallel each other, with the shorter Raven Avenue being the farthest north of all the island's east-west streets. Beyond it is marsh, waterways, and then the mainland.

But I wasn't just looking for signposts in the vicinity. The "Gold-Bug tree" that I was told about at the fort had struck a muted chord in my head, like I had heard that story before. A little bit of smartphone searching later, and I had the address.

It can be found at the intersection of Goldbug Avenue and Station Street 27, which is near the east end of Goldbug. It had been described to me as a beautiful live oak, and it was exactly that, as live oaks so often are.

It took up the entire front lawn, and was as wide as it was long, with its thick, serpentine branches dipping down to brush the grass and then continuing on. It almost looked more animal than plant, more octopus than oak. This ancient tree for sure had been around during Poe's time here.

But it wasn't the tree from the story, not the one that Jupiter climbs to drop the gold-bug through the eye socket of the skull nailed to the branch. (If you haven't read the story, hopefully that one sentence compels you to.) That one, Poe describes as:

> an enormously tall tulip-tree, which stood, with some eight
> or ten oaks, upon the level, and far surpassed them all, and
> all other trees which I had then ever seen, in the beauty of
> its foliage and form, in the wide spread of its branches, and
> in the general majesty of its appearance.

The description was only one word away from a pretty accurate description of that tree: that word being "tulip." Another strike against the tree is that it looked extremely easy to climb, while scaling the tree in the book took some effort. Of course, I never believed it could be the one from the story, but I at least was hoping it was a reasonable facsimile. Still, should whomever owns that tree want to nail a skull in a branch or hang a bug from its bough, or just throw up a plaque, I'd be way okay with it. I was starting to feel like the entire "Gold-Bug" story should be mapped out on the island, with people from the visitor center, when asked about Poe, handing out encrypted maps with goats on them that visitors can follow.

And right in the center of that map, marked with an X, would be Poe's Tavern.

## Poe Burgers with a Poe Scholar

I admit, what I'd seen thus far of Poe's South Carolina wasn't worth going out of the way for unless you have a special shade of obsession with Poe. But the one

*Gold-Bug Tree*

thing on the island that every Poe fan should swing by if they get the chance is Poe's Tavern.

It's on Middle Street, a mile away from the fort, in a small cluster of restaurants and stores that forms the entire center of commerce for the island. From the outside, it looks like your typical beach joint, with palm trees wrapped in string lights, outdoor seating surrounded by a white picket fence, and a tiny gravel parking lot.

It's the sign, though, that gives it away as something different. It bears a pair of eyes and a mustache connecting a hint of a nose with a hint of lips. His hair was a black bird. It was unmistakably Edgar Allan Poe.

In front of the restaurant, cut into the concrete walk, was the shape of what would have been anywhere else on the planet an anonymous-looking insect. The steps it pointed to led to a porch, where more tables were set up. Since this was technically winter, the porch was covered with plastic sheeting held in place by metal snaps.

Above the door to the porch was the first half a Samuel Johnson quote that was completed above the inner door to the restaurant: THERE IS NOTHING WHICH HAS YET BEEN CONTRIVED BY MAN, BY WHICH SO MUCH HAPPINESS IS PRODUCED AS BY A GOOD TAVERN.

Inside, the place was packed, even though it was a Friday afternoon in the middle of February on a tiny island community in the winter offseason.

But despite the loud throngs of patrons, the place seemed extremely comfortable. It had two main spaces: the front half was a large bar, and the back half was restaurant seating.

And the whole place was just covered in Edgar Allan Poe.

If it had his face or name on it and could be framed, it was on the walls. Whether that was a facsimile of "Annabel Lee" in his handwriting, a print of Joe Coleman's painting *A Descent into the Maelstrom of Edgar Allan Poe* or an old advertisement for Bell's whiskey that featured the poet and played off his poem of the same name. There were posters from movies based on his work. First-day covers of his stamps. Under glass on a stand in the corner was a fist-sized rock painted with his face. Above the bar was a mask of Poe that had been used as part of the PR campaign of the television series *The Following.*

There was so much Poe that it didn't seem like just a random marketing angle to give the place some local flavor and the opportunity to sell T-shirts (which they did). It almost seemed curated.

The signature image of the restaurant, though, the one that always pops up when you Google the eatery, is the fireplace. It's in the bar area and surrounded by a couch and chairs. On the red brick, above the hearth, as if it had been burnt there naturally by the hot soot, was a large image of his face. No matter what I scrutinized in the place, my eyes kept returning to that fireplace image.

But on first entering, I wasn't doing much scrutinizing. My purpose for visiting Poe's Tavern was two-fold . . . well, three-fold, counting the fact that I was hungry. I wanted to see the place as a stop on my Poe tour of Sullivan's island, but I was also there to meet a Poe scholar. And I was pretty excited to meet the guy.

When I first started this book project, one of the potential titles for it was *The Afterlife of Edgar Allan Poe.* A quick online search, however, turned up that it had already been taken in 2004 by a man named Scott Peeples . . . Scott Peeples, PhD, to be precise.

Peeples was a professor and the chair of the English Department at the College of Charleston, not ten miles away from Poe's Tavern, and it was this man I was there to meet. Partly because I needed a local expert, but mostly because his Poe interests probably intersected with my book project more than anybody I'd yet met.

We happened to walk in at about the same time and grabbed a table in the back, right by a large sheet of frosted glass bearing the tavern's Poe logo on it. My first impression of Peeples was that he didn't come off too professorial, honestly. He was laid back, casually dressed, and I probably would have guessed a range of professions before I landed on professor.

Menus were placed in front of us, and he joked, "You might want to steal that." The thin, laminated, single-folded sheet bore the logo of Poe's Tavern on the outside. Inside, everything on the menu was named after the poet, from Edgar's Nachos to the Annabel Lee, a Charleston-style crab cake sandwich topped with remoulade.

I didn't know whether to choose my order based on what I was craving or my favorite story. I ended up with a Gold Bug Burger. He ordered the black bean burger, but didn't call it by its full name: Poe's Black Bean Burger.

I explained the project to him and how I had found him. "So I was looking for somebody knowledgeable about Poe in South Carolina and it seems to be your domain."

"It's not much of a domain."

I started in. "Tell me your Poe story."

"Well," he began, his tone measured

*Poe's Tavern sidewalk*

but not infused with any southern drawl that I could detect, "I always liked Poe, but my academic interest really started in grad school." Peeples had done his graduate work at William and Mary in Virginia and his undergraduate work at Georgetown University in D.C. He picked up his PhD at Louisiana State University. "I was taking a class on the modern short story, and I became interested in how the short story developed in magazines in the early to mid-nineteenth century, and that was just kind of a new thing for me. I guess it seems fairly obvious now, but the rise of the modern magazine sort of created the short story genre. And Poe is a central figure in that, so I got into him in a very geeky academic way." He was beginning to seem professorial to me.

"It was a big realization for me, that you could look at Poe as a person in history who did what he did because he was in a certain place and time where there was a demand for it, as opposed to thinking about Poe as detached from everything and writing about the 'terror of the soul' and being the stereotypical tragic/romantic artist. His stories had to be written where and when they were written."

"That's the disconnect between the popular Poe and the academic or historical Poe, right?"

"Yeah, and at some point, I kind of swung back to the creation of this popular Poe as one of my interests in him."

This was the reason I was excited to talk to Peeples. Throughout the course of this book, I'd purposefully talked to only two scholars. The first was Dr. Paul Lewis, back in Boston. Peeples was my second. Both had shifted somewhat from a completely academic view of Poe to something else. Lewis embraced advocacy that incarnated itself in the campaign for the Boston Poe statue. With Peeples, his focus had broadened beyond academia to Poe as a modern phenomenon.

"Did your interest in the popular Poe come about as a result of *The Afterlife of Edgar Allan Poe?*" I still wanted that title, at least as a subtitle.

"The publisher was looking for a book that covered the literary criticism of Poe since his death, and that's what I wrote, but I wanted to do at least a chapter on Poe in pop culture and snuck that into the end."

The whole book is actually one of the more accessible scholarly works that I've come across, but certainly what elevates it for a layman like myself is the last chapter. If you ever borrow my copy, you'll see about ten dog-eared pages in that part of the book.

"Of course," he continued, "ever since it came out, I spent the last ten years thinking how I could have done a better job at that chapter and all the things I left out. It seems clear now that it could have been the basis of a whole book. And from then on I was more interested in Vincent Price movies and the history of commemorations in other cities. I even got to talk to younger school audiences about Poe, because of the book.

"Do they ask you to tone down Poe or play it up for them?"

"Mostly they just want you to entertain the kids for an hour. So I brought props. It's like Lisa says in that *Simpsons* Halloween episode where they do 'The Raven': 'Don't worry, Bart, you won't learn anything.'

"In some ways you could do a pop culture project like that with any famous author, but there's something strange and unique about the popular perception of Poe and the way he's marketed. Maybe Mark Twain comes close. Maybe Hemingway, just in terms of how there's this branding that's associated with the writer, but there's still something far more unexplainable around Poe's appeal."

Peeples had other academic interests, of course, including crime novels of the nineteenth century . . . like George Lippard's *The Monks of Monk Hall*. However, he always ends up coming back to Poe. "In my experience, it's easier for me to publish things with Poe's name on them than any of my other interests." And all this despite the fact, he told me, that few people in academia these days want to be pigeonholed to one author.

"But I thought literary academia was like science. You know, a guy spends his entire career analyzing newt skin."

"To some degree that's true, but coming out of grad school with a focus on a single famous author is just not good for marketing yourself academically."

"Nice phrase."

"It's really the way it is."

At some point in the conversation, we made the inevitable shift to the various people I'd talked to for the book. This happened generally with every conversation I had for this project, but in this case, since Peeples was close to the last person I talked to for the book, the list was long at this point. Most of them had met each other, or at least heard of each other, and it didn't take me long after starting this project to realize I was an outsider in a cult of Poe . . . it just took me this long into the book to admit it.

"It's interesting," Peeples continued. "You've got sort of two overlapping Poe communities. I don't think there's a firm line between them, but you've got academic Poe scholars, and you've got people who sort of work in what you could call the Poe industry—if you can call a labor of love an industry, since that's what it is for most people—museum curators, collectors, people who aren't academically trained, but who share an interest with academics. I came up through the academic side, but especially in recent years, I've been spending as much time with people on the other side. I think it's kind of cool how those two realms have become less segregated over the years. You can stay at a certain level with Poe or go deeper, but there are a lot of ways to go deeper."

"As a college English professor, you probably get to explore that a lot with students, right?"

"It depends on the course and how much time we have. I do teach Poe pretty regularly in different contexts. Often, it' just a superficial survey, so we just hit a major work or two, but when I have more time, I usually go into the college archive, where we have an original copy of *Burton's Gentleman's Magazine*, in which Poe was published. It's a well-preserved copy, so I can pass it around to illustrate what I was saying before about the context in which Poe wrote his stories.

"I also did a course called Poe, Place, and History, where we talked a lot about how significant place is to studying him, particularly given his reputation for not being concerned with locale or history."

"What did you discuss in that class?"

"We tackled questions like, 'Where is the house of Usher?' or 'What difference does it make that "The Assignation" takes place in Venice?' Why does he set a story in a place that he's never been? What is Venice supposed to signify to his readers in 1834? Same with Paris in the Dupin stories. He wrote these classic stories set in places he never visited. In addition to that, you have the significance of the different cities he lived in during his life and career."

Peeples pointed around, where Poe glowered at us in a wide array of artistic styles from every flat surface. "The last day of class we all came here, actually."

"This place is amazing. How often do you get down here?"

"A few times a year," he replied.

Without looking, I pointed in a random direction secure in the knowledge that I was pointing at something Poe-related. "It seems to me to illustrate a whole other point regarding the pop culture Poe. He's marketable. The owners wouldn't do this if they didn't think it would bring in customers. Boggles my mind. Like the Baltimore Ravens: 'A Poe connection will make us money.'"

"I'm actually working on a paper right now for a comparative literature conference about Poe as commodity. Especially since the notion of his marketability often depends largely on him being neglected or underestimated in his lifetime. He was the perennial underdog and that turns out to be a paradox. A place like Poe's Tavern will make a lot of money trading on the fact that Poe is this tragic figure."

"And Poe gets no licensing fees."

"Right. Obviously, this place has done extremely well. Been here for around ten years, so it predates the Poe Bicentennial, when he got really popular. They've even opened another one in Florida." That's right. The owners had recently franchised Poe in 2011 . . . in Atlantic Beach, Florida, which has zero connection to Poe. That's how much they thought that the image of a gloomy writer of spooky stories and poetry could be a money-maker for a maker of hamburgers.

"Yeah," Peeples continued, "and this is an area, even though it's touristy or maybe because of it, where businesses used to not last very long. In fact, I know that this building housed a number of restaurants that failed prior to Poe's Tavern. It's just been hugely successful. This isn't unusual for a lunch crowd." It was such a huge crowd that toward the end of our meeting, we had to move outside by the concrete gold bug because the din was just too loud.

"Tell me about Poe in South Carolina. Obviously, that's why I'm here."

"It brings up an interesting question: What happens when you've got almost no documentary evidence of Poe's time in a place? We know that Poe was stationed at Fort Moultrie for a year, but that's it. Most of our knowledge of his time in the area is culled from the traces that show up in his few stories that mention the area. I'm actually working on an article around that as well. What is Poe's afterlife in Charleston?" Now he was just rubbing the title in my face.

"I've been to Charleston before, but I'm really just visiting Sullivan's Island on this trip. How much legitimate Poe stuff is there in Charleston?"

"Not a thing. People like to think he spent time in Charleston wooing southern belles, that he was active in the social scene because he was Poe, but he was nineteen. He wasn't that Edgar Allan Poe yet."

"Are you from the area?"

"Yes, I grew up in Charleston. It's strange that I ended up finding a job at a college in the place where I grew up. It rarely works out that way."

"So you grew up hearing some of the rumors of Poe in Charleston? About a year ago, I visited the Unitarian Church Cemetery, just because I like cemeteries, but that place is often mentioned as having an 'Annabel Lee' connection."

"I went to that church for a while, and heard the docents expressing their frustrations a few times that visitors are coming thinking they're going to find Annabel Lee's grave."

The story went that Poe was interested in a girl in Charleston. Her father didn't approve, so they met in secret at the cemetery of the Unitarian Church on Archdale Street. Interestingly enough, some of the versions of the tale give the girl the name "Annabel Ravenel," as in daughter of the naturalist . . . or because it's cool for Poe to date a girl with "Raven" in her name. Eventually, Poe was transferred and years later the girl died of fever. Poe returned to visit her grave, but the father, in a fit of inexplicable pettiness, either dug up the entire family plot and moved it to an unmarked part of the cemetery or arranged the family plot so that it was impossible to tell which grave was Annabel's. Distraught at not being able to find his lost love's grave, Poe penned his poem "Annabel Lee." Meanwhile, her ghost obviously haunts the cemetery.

If Annabel Lee did have a grave, I imagine it would be in a place like the cemetery at the Unitarian Church. It's a revelation of a cemetery. The large, Gold-Bug-yellow Gothic church was built at the beginning of the Revolutionary War by a religious group called the Society of Dissenters. Today it's Unitarian Universalist and not at all an abandoned property. They just happen to dig a shaggy cemetery.

A few thin pathways allow visitors to navigate this thicket of palm trees, magnolias, Spanish moss, and all kinds of other plants and trees thriving on a soil rich with death. The tiny cemetery seems both abandoned and exquisitely caretaken at the same time. I visited it in November a year or so earlier, but I've heard it's even more striking in the spring, when all the wildflowers are blooming. The place has a secret garden feel. It's hemmed in on all sides by buildings, except for where it connects to the adjacent St. John's Lutheran Church cemetery, yet four steps into it I felt as if I were making an archaeological discovery on some distant jungle continent.

And it's in great contrast to the rest of historic Charleston, where every historic home shows off ridiculously manicured gardens in what I assume is some never-ending competition for the covers of local guidebooks.

Peeples continued, "My mom used to point at Breach Inlet, where the bridge

*Unitarian Church cemetery*

is from Sullivan's Island to the Isle of Palms, and warn me, 'Don't ever swim there. That's where Annabel Lee drowned.'"

"That's awesome. 'Annabel Lee' as a cautionary tale. So Sullivan's Island is a legitimate Poe site, and they seem to have grabbed Poe's physical legacy in a unique way."

"It has, but with mostly faux-Poe sites. Like this restaurant or the street names. I mean, it's not the only place to do that, but it's interesting because they're paying tribute only because they're near something related to Poe in some degree.

"But one of the cool things about Sullivan's Island as a Poe site is that you can take a walk on the beach, and if you don't look in the wrong direction—you know, toward modern-day Charleston—you can say, 'Poe took a walk on this beach in 1828, and it probably looked just like this.' You can't really do that in any of the cities that he lived in or near.

"I guess my take on Poe in Charleston and Sullivan's Island is that there's nothing to really go on, so we make it up. And it's been a pretty successful attempt at mythologizing. Maybe I should follow Boston's example and start a campaign to get a monument to Poe on Sullivan's Island."

We eventually parted ways, me and Peeples, with me wondering yet again if this was somebody who should have been doing this book instead of me. But I wasn't yet done with Poe's Tavern.

My hotel was about twenty minutes away, in North Charleston, but I wanted to hang out some more on the island, tie up a few loose ends, pretend to be Poe on the beach, like Peeples had suggested. So Poe's Tavern became my basecamp for the day. I would return to sit on the couch in front of the Poe fireplace and watch the server in his Poe Tavern T-shirt struggle with building the fire while I downed gin and tonics, scribbled notes, and answered e-mails on my phone. Every once in a while, I would yank myself out of that cozy nook to take pictures and examine more closely the Poe decor while trying not to be too much of an ass for the patrons and staff.

And then, fortunately, I had to use the restroom.

The facilities at Poe's Tavern are marked with a raven for guys and a black cat for gals. Inside the men's restroom, it was cramped . . . there was barely room for two people. But the walls were papered in pages from Poe books in a glorious collage of words and pictures. Then, as my ears adjusted from the din of the crowd outside, I realized that I was listening to the voice of Vincent Price reading the text of the "The Gold-Bug." I have never washed my hands so thoroughly.

My overall impression of Poe's treatment on Sullivan's Island is that the town had primed itself with a single coat of Poe, and that at some point in the future maybe it would be ready for a second coat. It already seemed to me that the small sign I'd seen for Gold Bug Island should have been a reference to Sullivan's Island as a whole. That the palm tree on the WELCOME TO SULLIVAN'S ISLAND sign that is used on just above every locale in the Southeast United States should be replaced by a burnished bug for a more unique community identity . . . and maybe to help get that bug a rematch with the bird.

Even more than providing the community a unique identity, it could be an opportunity for a more unique Poe identity. Everybody thinks of ravens and black cats when it comes to Poe. But just as integral to his works are the gold-bug and the orangutan and the mummy and a bunch of other icons that haven't yet been rendered a Poe cliché.

Sullivan's Island could get a leg up on that, and that second coat of Poe could be to give a reality to the fictional world of "The Gold-Bug" or to erect a monument of Poe at the fort or maybe even, after enough franchising, to paint the phrase HOME OF THE ORIGINAL POE'S TAVERN on its welcome sign.

Sullivan's Island was my last major trek for this book you hold in your hands.

Crossing the bridge back to the mainland was extremely bittersweet for me. But in many ways, the island was a fitting end for this book.

After all, we're setting him down safe and sound on Sullivan's Island, just like the crew in his "The Balloon-Hoax."

In the introduction to this book, I mentioned that the downside to telling Poe's story geographically is how confusing that makes his timeline. Well, there's another downside . . . that it ends in anticlimax, under the shady palm trees and Spanish moss on a balmy island in South Carolina.

Then again, by arranging the book this way, we give Poe the happy ending he never got in life, and which he probably deserved, just by dint of what he's given to culture as a whole, and what he's personally given to those of us who proudly call ourselves Poe fans.

And this is where we should leave him, just like his characters in "The Gold-Bug," who have to go through macabre pointers like human skeletons and mistaken insanity to achieve a happy ending. We wouldn't have found Poe as intriguing if this were his real end, but, hey, screw us.

STEFANIE ROCKNAK

*Life-sized clay sculpture of the Boston Poe statue*

# Epilogue

*My Days Have Been a Dream*

YOU'RE GOING TO HAVE TO finish this book for me.

From the first word I typed in this story, I was hoping to time my year-long trek in Poe-Land to end at the unveiling of the Boston Poe sculpture. I imagined a large, black sheet, maybe like the one at the H. P. Lovecraft bust unveiling, hiding the full-sized human form in the middle of Edgar Allan Poe Square. I imagined myself milling through the crowds around it, reuniting with many of the people in this book . . . certainly everybody from the Boston chapter: Norman George and Paul Lewis and Rob Velella and Brad Parker and Robert Davis. Maybe Ed Pettit would come up from Philadelphia or Scott Peeples from South Carolina. Jeff Jerome and Kristen Harbeson and David Keltz from Baltimore. Holt Edmunds and Chris Semtner from Virginia. Perhaps Peter Fawn from across the ocean. Or some of my more Lovecraft-obsessed friends I met in Providence.

But, no. As I write this, Bad-Ass Poe has yet to be anchored into the bricks of his birth city. I went back to the square one last time to at least close the loop on this book. It was late February 2014, and the city was between snowstorms. That meant piles of dirty snow flecked with asphalt ate through the streets and sidewalks like alien blobs, and cars driving by were rimed with ghostly veneers of salt. The Central Burying Ground was doubly buried, with just the crowns of the gravestones visible above the snow. The branches of the Callery pear trees above me were bare. Honestly, I'm not even sure what kind of trees they are.

The electric box was still painted Poe, and he still had the graffiti bullet hole in his head, although the patch of flaked paint had grown to behead the raven atop the bust of Pallas. Norman George's Poe plaque, the foundation stone for the rest of Poe in Boston, seemed to be shining more brightly than I remembered. I don't know if that was psychological on my part or if someone had burnished it as a result of my many queries into its existence.

But Edgar Allan Poe is definitely coming to Boston. Come October, probably by the time you're splitting the pages of this book, he'll be strutting across Edgar Allan Poe Square, looking for all the world like a man ready to reinvent literature again.

He had already grown from the 19-inch wooden maquette I had seen at the 204th Poe birthday event at the Boston Public Library to a full-sized clay sculpture. The maquette had traveled to Texas, where it was digitally enlarged and incarnated into full-sized urethane foam pieces. These were shipped back to Massachusetts and assembled around a custom-made armature and base. That work was performed by none other than Robert Shure of Skylight Studios, who twenty five years earlier was involved in the 1989 Poe plaque.

Stefanie Rocknak, the sculptor who had hard-won the opportunity to bring Poe back to Boston, took that foam and metal skeleton and used it as the core for a beautiful clay sculpture that, at the exact moment I stood on the icy brick and bemoaned it not yet being at its permanent home, was being hacked into forty or fifty pieces on the floor of a foundry in Chelsea, Massachusetts, about five miles away from the square.

Like Edgar Allan Poe himself had, the statue was going through a lot.

I knew all these particulars from talking to Rocknak. Since I couldn't see the sculpture, I could at least talk to the sculptor. So I gave her a call.

Honestly, it was a long time coming. Even though I didn't get to talk to Rocknak until the end of this project, I had felt somewhat of a kinship with her throughout it. After all, we'd both been working on Poe for the past year or so.

Rocknak was from Maine, had earned her PhD from Boston University, and was currently a professor of philosophy at Hartwick College in Oneonta, New York. She had become a finalist for the Boston Poe project on her portfolio alone, and then once she'd achieved that, had created the winning design, one which I learned was formally called "Poe Returning to Boston" and not, as I had gotten into the habit of calling it, "Bad-Ass Poe."

"How do you divide your brain between teaching philosophy and sculpting?"

"I've always been interested in art, always been active with it, and that naturally translates into big questions like 'Why do we make art?' or 'Why does art have such an effect on us?' That's how I became interested in philosophy."

"Do you have an interest in Poe at all, or were you just eager to jump at the chance to do a major public sculpture, regardless of the subject matter?"

"My undergraduate degrees are actually in American studies, art history, and studio art. I only turned to philosophy at the PhD level. As an undergraduate, I spent a lot of time on Poe—I've always loved his work. So it was kind of the perfect project for me."

"Are you freaked out by how prominent this statue is going to be? I mean, it's right on Boston Common."

"Yes, but I try not to think about that as I sculpt. I just want to make it the best I can regardless of where it's going. That said, it is the most conspicuous piece I've ever worked on and the first time I've sculpted a historic figure, so I am a little nervous. I was very anxious about just exposing the pictures of the statue that I took in my studio to the entire world."

"How did you come up with such an intrepid design?"

"Well, most of my work is very motion-oriented, so that's how I approached it, but the constraints I was given by the Poe Foundation of Boston also directed it. They told me the story behind Poe in Boston and said that they didn't want another sculpture of a guy on a horse. They've enough of those in the city. So I gave them . . ."

"Bad-Ass Poe, right."

Of course, he wasn't looking too bad-ass at the moment. He'd been divvied up into small parts as part of the lost-wax casting process that would transform the design into the durable, bronze creation that future generations of Poe fans and Bostonians would walk past, making the strutting Poe look even more a part of the downtown scene.

I don't know if she realized it, but Rocknak was joining a hefty legacy of sculptors who turned their formidable talents to Poe's visage, many of whose work I'd seen over the past year: George Julian Zolnay, Moses Jacob Ezekiel, Rudulph Evans, Edmund T. Quinn, Richard Henry Park, Charles Rudy, Daniel Chester French. Whoever does the grand tour of Poe-Land next gets to add Stefanie Rocknak to that list.

But I'm not too down about not being able to include the finished Boston Poe statue in this book. I mean, I will see it. But it's a great reminder that Poe-Land is vast and impossible to fully explore in one book over one year. Heck, the minute I sat down to write this epilogue, I got a message from Bryan Moore, the sculptor of the H. P. Lovecraft bust at the Providence Athenaeum, and in-general cool guy. He wanted to tell me that his next project was to sculpt a bust of Edgar Allan Poe for the Boston Public Library. It's to be installed in late October of 2014, just a couple of weeks after Rocknak's statue, only two miles away. The physical legacy of Edgar Allan Poe just keeps growing.

But just because I need you to finish this book for me doesn't mean this book doesn't get an ending. For, quite to my surprise, I was awarded an audience with the queen herself.

## Queen of Poe-Land

The name "Susan Jaffe Tane," with its eerily identical meter to "Edgar Allan Poe," haunted my entire journey through Poe-Land. In Boston, it popped up during the 204th Poe birthday celebration because she'd just donated a sizeable chunk of money to the Boston Poe statue. In Rhode Island, the Providence Athenaeum staff was meeting with her the week after I talked to them. In fact, Tane was the intended recipient of the Poe-ka dot pocketbook I was shown. In New

York, a third of the artifacts in the Morgan Library and Museum exhibition bore her name. I also saw her being interviewed in the video on the second floor of the Fordham Cottage. In Virginia, Holt Edmunds was taking her to a Poe conference the day after I met him. In England, Peter Fawn brought her up multiple times as context for his own collection. And just about everybody in this book asked me, after I explained my project to them, if I had talked to her.

You see, Susan Jaffe Tane is the preeminent collector of Poe artifacts on the planet. She has the most valuable private collection of Poe-phernalia, one that at least rivals and probably beats all institutional collections, as well.

Now, obviously, you don't just call up a woman like that and ask entrance into her sanctum to see her and some of American literature's most prized possessions. It took a good word from Peter Fawn for me to get an e-mail from her that said, "Why don't you come meet me at my Manhattan apartment? That's where I keep all my Poe treasures."

So, for the seventh time in this journey, I found myself driving into the state of Poe's final residence. It was my last Poe trip for the book, squeezed in a week before my deadline.

Tane actually lives in Connecticut, but keeps a place (and her Poe collection) on the Upper East Side of Manhattan. I entered her building, was checked in by the doorman, who sent me to the elevator man, who took me to her floor, where I was directed down a long hall lined with framed prints of Gustave Doré illustrations of "The Raven."

Pressing the doorbell elicited a buzz and a bark. The latter belonged to a small, black, curly-haired dog named Misha that was a Russian variety of poodle. Tane was holding it in her arms, calming it down, when she opened the door.

She offered me tea from a polished, wooden Fortnum & Mason box in a black mug decorated with Edgar Allan Poe's signature and apologized for not having any cookies on hand. She was just back from a vacation on the opposite end of the world, to Australia and New Zealand, and hadn't yet reacclimated to normal life. As we sat at the counter in her kitchen, I explained my project to her and then learned about her background.

She grew up on Long Island and went to Boston University in the 1960s, where she got an education degree. "I was a school teacher. That's what I was allowed to be back then." After teaching school for a short time, she took a break to raise a family, and then worked as the vice president of marketing for a company that manufactured tanks and other containers. Later, she married Irwin R. Tane, who died in 2001. These days, she has Edgar Allan Poe . . . and all that comes with that.

I quickly learned why Tane was such a part of the contemporary world of Poe, as opposed to some wealthy collector walled in from the masses by display cases. "Why has everyone I've talked to about Poe wanted to know if I talked to you?"

"Well, my name is most associated with Poe because of my collection, but my role in the Poe community is much broader than that. I support the museums, the societies, the scholars. I'm not a scholar myself, but through the Poe Studies Association, I offer scholarships for people all over the world to attend Poe conferences to deliver papers and meet each other and exchange ideas. I'm on the board of trustees for the Richmond Poe Museum, and they count on me. Poe Park in the Bronx counts on me. I'm sure I'm leaving things out. But the point is, I want to keep the Poe community vibrant and alive."

And, of course, she exhibits her artifacts for the public. Hers isn't a collection that collects dust. It does stuff. Goes places. Had I visited her just a week or two earlier, well, she would have been away on vacation. But I would also have missed out on about twenty percent of her collection.

After we finished our tea, she led me into the dining room. I've used the metaphor of feasting on Poe artifacts a couple of times in this book, but here were some of the greatest treasures of Poe-dom covering every square inch of a long dining-room table, most of the artifacts and manuscripts still cocooned in bubble wrap. They had been shipped from the Morgan Library and Museum, where they had formed what was arguably the core of the now-shuttered *Terror of the Soul* exhibition. I just needed a fork and knife and a random manuscript to tuck into my shirt as a bib. Maybe something ripped out of *Arthur Gordon Pym*.

We walked around the table, unwrapping this piece or that. Most of what I called out from my visit to the Morgan exhibit in the New York chapter of this book was Tane's. And the only real defect of the exhibition—that each amazing piece was the forever-distant width of a glass case away from me—was now remedied. Here I was holding and scrutinizing up close such pieces as Poe's coffin fragment, the issue of the *Evening Mirror* that is generally considered the first time "The Raven" saw print, and Poe's personal copies of *Eureka* and *The Conchologist's First Book*, both of which bore his notes, edits, and corrections throughout the pages. Poe didn't believe in the notion of a final version, even after publication.

I picked up a framed manuscript portion of "The Rationale of Verse" and said the only thick-tongued thing I've been able to muster those few awe-struck times I've gotten the experience of holding such things over the course of the book: "I can't get over how neat his penmanship is."

"Yeah, and it keeps on changing," she observed, as only someone who owned many samples of his handwriting from across his life could.

One of those samples was Poe's letter to Washington Irving, written on October 12, 1839—one horror story writer to another, two weeks shy of Halloween. "This is one of my favorite letters. Basically, he asks Irving to make him famous," she said, as we picked out this passage from his inhumanly exact handwriting:

> Now, if, to the very high encomiums which have been
> lavished upon some of my tales by these & others, I could
> be permitted to add *even a word or two* from yourself,
> in relation to the tale of "William Wilson" (which I
> consider my best effort) *my fortune would be made* . . . I
> am deliberately convinced that your good opinion, thus
> permitted to be expressed, would ensure me that public
> attention which would carry me on to fortune thereafter,
> by ensuring me fame at once . . . what will be an act of
> little moment in respect to yourself—will be life itself
> to me.

Another letter we looked at was to an aspiring poet named Abijah Metcalf Ide, Jr., of South Attleboro, Massachusetts. The young man, who was a farmer, wrote to Poe in October 1843, a year before the publication of "The Raven," to become friends and seek advice from the poet, which Poe was happy to give:

> I would say to you, without hesitation, aspire. A literary
> reputation, it is true, is seldom worth much when
> attained—for by this time the appetite for applause is
> sated—but in the struggle for its attainment is the true
> recompense. You are young, enthusiastic, and possess high
> talents. You will not fail of success. Be bold—reach much—
> write much—publish little—keep aloof from the little wits,
> and fear nothing.

Tane then showed me an actual daguerreotype of Poe in a thin, hinged, decorative case. I've used the term daguerreotype in multiple places throughout the book, but, honestly, I had no idea what it was. The images I'd seen of them online and in books and in photographs taken from the "dags" look like static photographs, and I didn't remember looking too closely at it at the Morgan. However, the small artifact she handed me suddenly illuminated the concept for me. So I can call it a dag now, I guess.

The image of Poe looked like it had been lightly burned onto a mirror, and you could make out Poe only by looking square at the image. When you did that, it looked like a photograph, and this was how I saw every photograph of them. When I turned it a few degrees, the image became a photo negative until the extreme angle made it disappear completely, leaving only the tilted, silver mirror. It was like a hologram.

The particular one Tane showed me is known as the Players Club dag. It was created five years after Poe's death from the Thompson dag, which was taken of Poe by William Pratt three weeks before Poe died, in Richmond. It was then donated to New York's Players Club, where it was kept at the organization's Hampden-Booth Theatre Library. At some point, probably in the 1980s, it disappeared, and then showed up in 2004 on the PBS show *Antiques Roadshow*. It was brought on by a woman named Sally Guest, who had picked it up at an antiques shop in Walnut, Iowa, for $96. The show gave it a conservative estimate between $30,000 and $50,000.

Of course, the national exposure caught the attention of both the Poe community and the FBI, who retrieved the stolen dag and returned it to the Players Club. The organization leveraged the publicity to put it up for auction. "I didn't realize it at the time," said Tane, "but I was bidding against the National Portrait Gallery. Had I known, I would've walked away . . . I think."

Then she showed me her copy of *Tamerlane and Other Poems,* the rarest book in American literature. Hers is one of only two copies in private hands; the other was the one that went for $660,000. "It wasn't as nice as mine," she told me proudly. Tane had picked hers up in 1991 for less than $150,000. Her copy is the one purchased for $15 in a junk shop in Hampton, New Hampshire, less than an hour from my home, where I'm writing this epilogue. I've told that story dozens of times in my life, so I was excited to have such a close-up experience with its subject.

Tane's copy is unmistakable, as it bears a large, circular discoloration right in the center of the front cover. Basically, some guy used it as a drink coaster. As a joke, a friend of the previous owner of the book made up a set of actual drink coasters featuring the front cover of the *Tamerlane,* which were than given to Tane. She let me have one as a token of my visit.

"Do you ever panic? You're responsible for a big chunk of Poe's original legacy. What if something happens to it on your watch?"

"Oh, it's already happened. There've been fires. I've loaned things out that got lost. You protect it as best you can, but stuff happens; what can you do?"

"So what's the motivation to put these invaluable pieces on display? I mean, if I had these items, I would build an exhibit room in my house and then wander among the cases by myself with a glass of port and a smug look on my face. I'd hoard it, I guess, like a dragon on a pile of gold. Why keep sharing it? Especially since it's a risk every time you let part of it out into the world?"

"I feel like I'm lucky to own it, so I feel this responsibility to share. And not just so that people can see the artifacts themselves, but as a way to push Poe's legacy overall and to bring the Poe community together.

"A lot of collectors don't share what they have, and that just doesn't seem fair, because pieces like these belong really to the culture and can be used to do good. Every time I exhibit them, it benefits a cultural institution—a museum, a library—what with the publicity and the visitors and the admission."

"But do you still come home one day and are like, 'I'd really like to see *Tamerlane.*' And then you have to go, 'Damn it, that's in Richmond for the next six months. Oh, well.'"

"Oh, I've had empty walls here for months thanks to the Morgan exhibition." She was talking particularly about her massive *Spirits of the Dead* movie poster, which took up one whole wall in her foyer. On my visit, it was already hung back up, where it matched a similarly sized poster of Roger Corman's *The Raven* on another wall in her apartment. I think that was the last Vincent Price reference in this book. Sad.

In my naiveté, I then asked her if she gets a cut of the admissions or any type of rental fees from offering her collection to outside parties to exhibit. Part of me thought there must be an ulterior motive for putting the collection out there besides mere pride of ownership.

"I've never made a penny on the exhibitions. Even if I publish a catalog, I'll give it to the museum to sell." Turns out, not only does she not make money, she actually loses money every time one of those pieces leaves her apartment, since she covers insurance and transportation. Apparently, you can't just toss a piece of Poe's coffin in a manila envelope and shove it in a mailbox. And the financial considerations pale next to the fact that she's risking an irreplaceable artifact that's precious both to history and her.

Even so, Tane says she rarely says no to legitimate requests for her pieces. During the 2009 Poe Bicentennial, so many items in her collection were crisscrossing the country at a high rate that she had to keep a spreadsheet to know where it all was and where it all was going next. Sometimes she'll deliver them herself or bring some with her to one of the talks she gives on collecting, in which case she hand-carries the artifacts on the plane or the train or in the car.

"Are you worried about people stealing it off you when you're travelling?"

"Not a chance. Most don't know what it's worth. They would step on it to steal my iPhone."

"So where do these all go when you're done unwrapping them?"

"My library. I'll show you. It's a bit of a mess since the pieces here on the table are missing from it."

As we walked across the apartment, we passed a drink service, on the counter of which was a simple decanter and brandy glass set. She told me it had belonged to Poe's foster father, John Allan. Just sitting there with the rest of the glassware. If she had told me to make myself a drink, I would probably have grabbed one of the glasses.

Her library was both open and cozy, with plenty of warm wood, comfortable chairs, and a couch on which was a pillow with Poe's face in a repeated pattern all over it. It was obviously a place exquisitely maintained, but it wasn't so distant that you would think twice before pulling a book on the shelf and plunking down to read it.

Framed on the wall, above the couches, were the three large pages from the *Baltimore Saturday Visiter* that featured Poe's first paying writing gig, "MS. in a Bottle." At each end of the fireplace mantle were Poe-shaped Edgar Awards from the Mystery Writers of America, one from 1946 and the other from 1952, like I had seen at Peter Fawn's house. Above them was a framed letter from Baudelaire, in which he tells his publisher that he is about to send in his translation of Poe's "The Man of the Crowd." Busts of Poe were here and there, including the more-than-a-century-old Rudulph Evans bust I had seen at the Morgan. A couple of blank spots on the wall revealed other items that had been on display at the Morgan and were now on her dining room table. I guess that's what she was referring to as a "mess."

But the thing that first arrested my eyes upon entering was the nineteen-inch wooden maquette of the Boston Poe statue sitting on the desk. It was the sculpture I had seen at the Boston Public Library in January 2013. Stefanie Rocknak had visited Tane just a day or two before to give it to her. I had wondered where it was going to end up. It was this item that had temporarily displaced John Allan's brandy set.

"So what do you want to see first?"

"Lady's choice."

Interestingly, the first thing she pointed out in the room, before any priceless artifact, was a framed picture on the wall of Poe in a casket. She was seated in the background with other mourners, slightly blurry and dressed in black funeral-wear. She had attended Jerome's and Redfield's Poe funeral in Baltimore. Had even framed her ticket right there beside the photo.

Also on that same wall was another of those bricks from the Greenwich Village Poe house, this one mounted on a wooden plaque with a brass plate that had Tane's name on it.

She showed me a check for $30, endorsed by Poe, and then an L-shaped piece of wood from Elmira Royster Shelton's house that had been saved from the trash during a renovation. It was a gift to her from Harry Lee Poe, also known as Hal Poe. Hal Poe is big in the Poe community. He's a descendent of one of Poe's cousins, and a real Poe proselyte. He's a collector, an author, an academic, and a minister. Honestly, he should have been in this book, but he lives in Tennessee. "He's a real southern gentleman, that Hal, and it makes me laugh to think of him upside down in a dumpster rooting around for pieces of Elmira's house."

We then went through a whirlwind of original Poe manuscripts and books. A handwritten copy of his poem "Spirits of the Dead" from 1828, making it one of the earliest Poe manuscripts we have. Or she has. Another of "Epimanes," from 1833. She showed me "The Conqueror Worm" manuscript . . . the same one I brought up in the introduction to this book, which went for $300,000. I had no idea when I included it that I would be face-to-parchment with it a year later.

At one point she said to me, "You're a writer. Where are your original manuscripts?"

I've never really thought of my books in those terms. The closest I came was "latest file." "Well, they're on my hard drive, which is backed up to the cloud. So I guess they're at my house and in a datacenter in Oklahoma."

"Right. You don't have a handwritten manuscript. And I bet all your correspondence for the book was completely through e-mail." I nodded. "One day soon, there won't be any such thing as a literary artifact, so these items aren't just important because of who they're connected to, but because of the way of life they represent."

Tane also had original editions of all Poe's books, including the 1829 *Al Aaraaf, Tamerlane, and Minor Poems* and the 1845 *The Raven and Other Poems,* as well as entire runs of every magazine he wrote for, including the *Southern Literary Messenger* and *Burton's Gentleman's Magazine.* These were kept in glass-fronted, temperature-controlled shelves low to the floor. To access them, she sat on an extremely low stool that couldn't have been more than a couple inches tall to pull the books out. I tried to crouch beside her, but couldn't hold out as long as she could and kept having to stand up to make sure I still had knees.

Then Tane pulled out a mysterious little upholstered box made up of small compartments. It turned out to be somewhat of an Ark of the Covenant of Poe. In one compartment, was a silver spoon monogrammed HEH on the handle that had belonged to Henry Herring, Poe's uncle, who was awarded it for a prize pig at a county fair. It also had an actual lock of Poe's hair, much like the tress in the Enoch Pratt Free Library collection. That would have been the most interesting artifact had it been my first glimpse of Poe's DNA. But it was topped in this case (and, in this case) by a delicate gold circlet inscribed on the interior with Poe's first name. It was the ring he gave to Elmira Shelton near the end of his life and is further evidence that the two intended to marry. Tane's current catalog entry for the piece refers to it as Poe's engagement ring. Poe's friendship ring doesn't have the same ring.

The next item blew me away in a totally different way. It was a large, thin, sleeve-like case. After the two of us wrestled with it for a while, we were able to slide out an original version of *Le Corbeau (The Raven)*, translated by Stéphane Mallarmé, and illustrated by Édouard Manet. Of course, I'd seen scans of the illustrations before, but never was I so intimate with the original. It was massive for a book, about the size of a small poster. Flipping through the large pages created slight breezes, and the book was autographed by both men. Actually, *book* doesn't describe it. It was a work of art.

My list of favorite Poe things was growing so long as a result of this visit that *favorite* was starting to lose all meaning. Fortunately, we shifted to other nineteenth-century authors. One whole niche of the library was taken up by Mark Twain items. "So you collect other authors, as well?"

"Yes, I do collect some nineteenth-century authors. I have a good collection of Twain. He's easier to collect than Poe. He lived almost twice as long as Poe and is a more recent author, so there's a lot more Twain out there. I also collect Melville."

"So are you *the* Melville collector like you're *the* Poe collector?"

"I have a very fine collection of Melville," she answered vaguely. "But I don't get as involved with those authors as I do Poe. Just don't feel them as much."

I wondered to myself what the difference was. Certainly, it could have merely been a case of plain favoritism. But I also wondered if it went back to Poe's draw and status as an icon of culture. I mean, she could grab anybody off the street outside her building, march them up to this room, and say, "Look, Poe's hair, Poe's handwriting," and they'd be amazed. I'm not sure she could do that with Melville or even Twain, who's still well known in popular culture, and receive the same reaction.

At one point, she pulled open a drawer and I saw peeking out some original comic book art. I'd also noticed here and there, in the otherwise elegant study, a Poe action figure or a Poe doll sitting on a ledge.

"So how often do you collect modern Poe items?"

"Well, I don't usually, but the comic book art is because I'm prepping for a Grolier Club Poe exhibition. I'm going to call it *Poe to Pop*. I want it to be different from the Morgan exhibition, so it'll be more about Poe's continuing influence on modern culture.

"These other things are usually gifts. I get Poe gifts all the time, even from people I don't know." While we had been in the kitchen, she had picked up a package that turned out to be a PR packet for the FOX series *The Following*, complete with a rubber Poe mask with realistic hair. She wasn't sure yet who sent that to her.

"So you've got this beautifully appointed library, adorned with invaluable pieces of literary history, and then somebody sends you an action figure or a Halloween mask. What do you do with that?"

"I think it's cool, a riot. I love it. Here, look." And she led me into one of the bedrooms, where a tall, elegant glass case was filled with Poe-themed tchotchkes . . . more action figures, bobble-heads, earrings, small pillows. "A riot."

And with that, it was time for us to eat. We hit up an Italian placed called Tony's, a few blocks away.

"Tell me your Poe story."

"I discovered him when I was young, in school. We had to memorize a long poem, and most of us picked 'The Raven' because the meter and rhyme made it easy to remember. And it just stuck with me, and I always loved it, even though I didn't become a real Poe fan until after I started collecting."

"How did that start?"

"With just one book. In 1987, I was browsing through the New York Antiques Show at the Seventh Regiment Armory on Fifth Avenue. I loved going to antique shows. I never bought anything, I just loved walking the aisles. But then I saw this beautiful, original copy of *The Raven and Other Poems.* And I kept going back to it. They probably thought I was casing the joint. I was afraid to ask to see it. I mean, I didn't know an individual could own something like that. I thought only museums and libraries could. But I had to have it. I don't really know why. It just spoke to me. Like I said, I wasn't what you could call a Poe fan at the time. I just loved the look and idea of this book and I had this relationship to the subject matter that went back to my childhood. So I bought it."

"Was that the one you showed me at your library?"

"No. I sold that one because I recently was able to obtain one in better condition. I don't usually keep multiple copies of a book."

"So then you had one book on your shelf, you're not yet a collector . . . how did you cross over?"

"I became friends with Stephan Loewentheil. He owned the Nineteenth Century Shop, which had the booth where I bought *The Raven.* He had a Poe collection, too, and had some pieces he wanted to divest himself of. At the time I was still figuring out whether I wanted to start a collection and what it would cover. I mean, that book could have launched me into a more general nineteenth-century collection, but then I decided to really focus on Poe. It was a great decision in hindsight, and it's the first thing I tell collectors who are just starting out . . . it's more important to focus on one thing than to have some of this and some of that, because then you're a library."

Of course, with her purchase of Tamerlane in 1991, she was officially "all in" when it came to Poe collecting.

"How has collecting changed since you started with that one book?"

"Well, a lot. I've been collecting now for about twenty-five years. It's become more global. Poe's appeal is international, of course, but other countries have started taking an interest in collecting Americana in general, and it's a lot easier to be aware of and involved in auctions and sales anywhere in the world thanks to the technology.

"I think the biggest thing is that you can't really build these collections anymore. Pieces just aren't available because you don't know who has it or who the collector is or what they have. And that's on top of the fact that it's always been the type of environment where major pieces often only hit the market once in a lifetime, like when a collector dies or needs money."

"Do you ever get tired of your role as, I don't know, duly recognized representative of all things Poe?"

"Oh, no. It's actually turned into an important role in my life. I mean, who would have thought? Twenty-five years ago, I bought a Poe book. Today, I'm defined as a collector. I never started out as a Poe fan. Never started out as a collector. I was at an antiques show."

"It sounds like you got pulled into all this."

"I did. I really did. All of a sudden, I was a Poe collector. It's amazing how your life changes . . . teacher, marketing, now this, owner of the Susan Jaffe Tane collection."

"Does that make you uncomfortable at all?"

"I am okay with it, but only because I've gone with it. I've found my niche."

"So what happens now? Do you just go from one exhibit to the next? Keep adding to it? Start a different collection?" I always want to know about the depressing part of collecting.

"I'm almost at the end of my collecting career . . . well, you're never at the end of it. Every collector says that. I don't know why I just said it, so just scratch that.

"But what happens to my collection now has been a question on my mind for the past ten years . . . and I still don't have an answer. My kids don't really want it. They're happy to be part of what I do, but it's not their thing. Nor do I want to saddle them with the responsibility and headache of these extremely valuable objects. I could give it away in my lifetime to make sure it goes to the right place or give some other collectors the opportunity to own it, but . . ."

"I assume that goes against your every instinct. You'd have to go from being a collector, how you define yourself right now, and what's been an important part of your life for a quarter century, to suddenly getting rid of everything and not being a collector. Sounds genetically impossible."

"Yes, there's a lot of emotion to this. You're giving away pieces of yourself, basically, in that case. But there are practical problems, too. I mean, most institutions and private collectors simply can't afford this collection, especially the way the market is today. I don't think I could afford it today. And I don't want some institution to stuff it all in a box in a vault and bring out only some of it every once in a while. I mean, seriously, what would you do? Well, you wouldn't even want to show it to anybody in the first place, so . . ."

"Right, buried in my coffin with me or maybe under a big tomb like a pharaoh."

"Well, that's another option," she said. "It all goes back into culture that way, too. Every museum has an Egyptian wing."

"On the other hand," I said, "it's kind of a good dilemma. It means you've invested yourself in something that you cared about immensely. The fact that it's a tough decision sort of validates the whole thing, to me anyway."

I had been tweaking Tane about how much better it would be for her to keep her collection to herself just for fun, but in some ways collecting is extremely private. The act of collecting is basically the act of externalizing parts of yourself. Not to quote the band Yes, but you kind of surround yourself with yourself. Of course, in other ways, collecting is extremely public because we always want to show people this new thing we got and connect with them. And, to me, that's humanity in a nutshell. We all have these private inside lives that we'd love to open up to the right person or persons. We want people to get us, the real us. A collection is one of the bridges we build to make that connection.

But, like Tane said, it's also a responsibility. Her role as a collector is to show people reality. We can read in Kenneth Silverman's biography of Poe that Poe published *Tamerlane and other Poems* in Boston in 1827 at the age of seventeen or eighteen, and it's a fact that you absorb or you don't. But Tane can walk you over to the actual book and say, "Look, this really happened. Here's the evidence, right off Calvin F. S. Thomas's press. That book exists, which means Poe existed. Need more proof? Here is his hair. He loved; here is his engagement ring. He died; here is a fragment of his coffin. When we say he wrote 'The Conqueror Worm,' we mean that literally with a pen on a piece of paper. Here is that manuscript." Without these pieces, it's all just a story. And Tane is making Poe and literature and history real for the rest of us.

Poe-Land is a real place.

Today, we live in a society of collectors, although most of those collectors seek out demographic-targeted, off-the-shelf, mass-marketed baubles and trifles solely created to be collected. But to collect actual, irreplaceable pieces of history and human culture is a unique calling, one that Susan Jaffe Tane does with a unique passion.

Poe could have used somebody like her in his actual life.

In the last chapter of this book, we left Poe relaxing in the shade of a palm tree, idly batting at a bug on the end of a string. It was a good place to leave him. But thanks to the collectors and institutions that preserve pieces of him and his work, his stuff keeps pretty busy.

## Why Is Poe So Cool?

You're going to have to finish this book for me.

Sure, I need you to visit things like Boston's Bad-Ass Poe and Moore's Poe bust at the Boston Public Library and Tane's Grolier Club exhibition in New York and whatever Poe exhibitions and shows follow every autumn after that, but I need you to finish this book in another way . . . by answering its central question. Honestly, it took the duration of the project for me to really even form the question the way I wanted to ask it, much less get it answered. In the end, I just wanted to know the answer to this: "Why is Poe so cool?"

I realize that there is never only one reason for anything, and certainly not for something as far-reaching as Poe's influence, but I still want, however foolishly, a unified theory of Poe. Still, over the course of this book, I did find many explanations that throw their simple dim rays of light through the crevices of their lanterns to at least partially illuminate the answer.

Like local pride. Every town has a statue of somebody whom only diehard locals know. For whatever reason, we like people who come from our own town or city or state or country. With Poe, he lived in so many states (and England) that he inadvertently hedged his bets in this regard. Had he lived in just one city for his whole life, Poe-Land would be a much less impressive place.

Related to that reason, when Edgar Allan Poe is part of your local community, that means you share an interest in common with a much large community of Poe aficionados across the country and world. One of the discoveries that surprised me over the course of the book is that everybody I talked to knew everybody else that I was talking to. Geographically, the physical legacy of Poe might be a predominately East Coast phenomenon, but Poe himself is an international one, and he transcends interests and age and personality. That kid with the *Texas Chain Saw Massacre* T-shirt and that ancient academic with a copy of *Sappho* in the original Greek tucked under his arm can sit down on a bench together and talk about Edgar Allan Poe.

I didn't talk to too many Poe artists or writers over the course of this book, but I think I learned that, strangely enough, Edgar Allan Poe also offers hope. What he wrote while alive wasn't fully appreciated in his time, and basically not appreciated at all compared to how it's appreciated now. That's a precedent and a touchstone. You can die alone far from your friends in an unmarked grave and still have people love you or your work 150 years later. At least you can hope. Make sure you live in more than one state, just in case.

One of the more important answers to this question of "Why is Poe so cool?" is that his life validates his work or, at least, as it was put to me earlier in the book, intersects it. Poe doesn't disappoint us when we look behind the silken, sad, uncertain rustling of his purple curtains. We've all had that experience where we love a piece of work, be it a song or a story or a painting, but then in learning more about the artist suddenly find the work tainted or inauthentic in some way and are disappointed. Which is strange, since we also simultaneously value the creative and imaginative faculties of the mind.

Still, we'd rather our artists match their work . . . or, more accurately, our impressions of their work. And Poe was a writer of tragedies while living them. A man who penned mysteries while spawning them in life and death. A man who wrote of struggles while struggling. Even if those tragedies and mysteries and struggles have become mythic past the bounds of accuracy, there is still enough tragedy and mystery and truth behind them to validate his work in a way that we are never disappointed by him.

And speaking of validation, he validated an entire genre. The horror story, which often even today is a disparaged one, in large part owes the legitimacy it has to Edgar Allan Poe. He proved that enlightenment sometimes works best in the gloom of a spooky room, that awe has much of terror in it, that the dark side of life is still a side of life, that the morbid can be magnificent. And the horror genre is one of intense dedication from fans who don't forget their icons.

Which brings up Halloween . . . and this is going to seem silly, but bear with me. Every year his relevancy in culture gets renewed through a holiday already steeped in black cats and madmen and tombs. Once you find yourself part of a holiday, part of a tradition, you're close to immortal. And Halloween has gotten big, second only to Christmas, in this country. Every year come October, you can find Poe on the stage and on television screens and in supermarket aisles and all over the Internet. The fact that he died in October only helps.

Being the grandfather of so many genres of literature doesn't hurt him, either. The most reliable way to achieve immortality is by having as many descendants as possible, and his are so numerous that he'll never be forgotten. Every detective and spacefarer and psycho killer and explorer in our fiction lays wreaths at his tomb annually.

And, of course, the themes he focused on are still the themes most relevant and most intriguing today: death and the mind.

Anybody who struggles with the idea of death, whether it's their own or that of one of their loved ones, and looks to literature and poetry to help with that struggle must, at some point, run the gauntlet of Poe's work. His mastery over death was only on the page, of course, but that might be as close to mastery over death as we can ever get.

As to the mind, from modern psychology to artificial intelligence, the blob of pink tofu in our heads is one of our central mysteries. As Poe showed us many times, the same brain that can fall prey to a sheer hoax can also masterfully concoct one. The same brain that can perceive and connect and deduce and produce with such genius can also misperceive and break and destroy with insanity. I'm not saying that the narrator of "The Tell-Tale Heart" could've been C. Auguste Dupin, but how many brain cells away were the two? Also, the narrator of "The Tell-Tale Heart" could've been C. Auguste Dupin.

There is also the ineffable quality of Poe. So many times over the course of this book I heard in reference to his work, "It was so different than anything I'd experienced." This difference is not quantifiable. Sure, he was a master of his craft, and that reason for his current place in our culture would deserve its own paragraph if it weren't too obvious to elaborate on here. But in this case, I don't think they meant "Nobody has ever written like him" or "Nobody writes about what he writes about." Especially today in a world of art and literature completely influenced by him. As scholars and historians have showed us, he was writing on topics that were popular in his day. And today those topics are even more popular. Those who talk about how different he seems mean . . . I don't know. The only way to get insight into this aspect is to read Poe.

Finally, it's the enigma of Poe. We still don't understand him, even as we tout his work as genius and his life as strange. We just don't get him. And as long as he's this unsolved cipher, we will continually take him down from the shelf and attempt to solve it every now and then. Of course, if we ever did solve him, it would be the very next day that we forgot about him.

While working on this book, I finally got around to rereading *The Narrative of Arthur Gordon Pym of Nantucket,* the closest thing Poe wrote to a novel. In my introduction I said I didn't think I could ever read it again because my first experience with it years ago was so bad. Poe himself called it a "very silly book." Over the course of this other very silly book you hold in your hands, *Pym* came up enough times and in enough interesting contexts that I did reread it. In doing so, I found many of my original impressions remain unchanged—namely, that too much of it is bland filler and its ending is still something that I cannot forgive (although it certainly has stuck with me all these years).

But throughout the book were scenes of such exquisite gruesomeness and vividness and even comedy (the fake ghost scene still makes me laugh), that I do have to revise my opinion. More importantly, in reading it during a year that I was at my most intimate with its author, I fancied I saw a peculiar similarity between the two. Like Poe's life and work, *Pym* is a journey of wild unevenness.

It has moments of brilliance bracketed by moments of absurdity and inanity, all of it climaxing in a mysterious ending that scholars are still debating today. That's Poe.

I didn't fully answer my own question of "Why is Poe so cool?," one which had me traveling far from my home, meeting and talking to dozens of people outside of my comfort zone, and reading and researching and writing within every square inch of clock face I had available to me. However, I feel like I found Eldorado 20 times over. My days over the past year have truly been a dream.

Never RIP, Edgar Allan Poe.

# Acknowledgments

I'D LIKE TO THANK EVERY PERSON whose name is mentioned in this book. Each one took time out of their lives for my project, whether that was hauling out artifacts from archives or touring me around sites or just chatting with me for an hour or two. A few even invited me into their homes. Many of them kept in touch with me throughout the course of the project, lending me help when I needed more information. I'm happy to say I've made a few new friends thanks to this book.

I'd also like to acknowledge a few people specifically who either didn't appear in the book, or whose debt goes beyond what is mentioned within its pages.

Like David Goudsward, whom I contacted years ago for my first book project when trying to find the Vermont grave of the man who wrote the script for the 1922 film *Nosferatu,* and whom I finally met in person for the first time at NecronomiCon Providence. He put aside his own esoteric book projects to review a few pages of mine. Maybe one day we'll find that grave, Dave.

All the people at Countryman Press for helping me do something a little different and a little riskier than what I usually do for them, despite the fact that their salespeople don't know what to do with it at all: Kermit Hummel, who gave me the go-ahead and sagely knocked down some of my original titles for the book until we arrived at the perfect one we have now; Lisa Sacks, who managed the project; and Dan Eisner, who had to deal with my many quirks of composition.

Brian Weaver, who accomplished the impossible task of portraying Edgar Allan Poe in a fresh way with yet another amazing cover for one of my books that makes me more excited than the story it represents.

Everyone who follows me on my OTIS website (oddthingsiveseen.com) and the related socials. My books so far have all been an outgrowth of OTIS, which wouldn't have worked without a readership. I want to specifically thank those of you who sent me words of encouragement and excitement about the project, even while putting up with the lack of new content on OTIS during the final months of deadline push for the book.

My parents, Edward and Nancy, whose house in Maryland became my headquarters and jumping-off point for the southern half of this book, and who helped me out in many other ways, not the least of which was inadvertently giving me the book that introduced me to Poe.

Rob Velella, whom we all met in the Boston chapter. He took an interest in the project beyond his part in the book and ended up being one of only two people to read a full, early draft of the manuscript. I am considerably grateful for his expertise and insight. I've never met anybody more dedicated to and knowledgeable of nineteenth-century American literature than Rob. If you ever get the chance to see him as Edgar Allan Poe, do so.

That other person who read the manuscript is, of course, my wife, Lindsey, who deserves special recognition. Anytime there is an undefined "we" in this book, it's probably her, as she accompanied me on many of these treks. When she couldn't, she held down the house while I took off on trips that are hard to justify in any rational way. And she did all this while baking a baby, our second daughter, Hazel Lenore, to whom this book is dedicated.

And my first daughter, Esme, who hit four years old during the writing of this book. She was also sometimes part of that undefined "we." She now says, "Poe," every time she sees a picture of a man with a mustache.

*Fortunato, the author, and Montresor—Westminster Hall, Baltimore, Maryland*

# Selected Bibliography

**I**HAD ONE YEAR TO WRITE THIS BOOK. More precisely, I had one year to travel to seven states, D.C., and a country across the ocean. I had one year to visit somewhere around ninety sites, to interview two dozen people, to research a well-known and much-distorted topic thoroughly enough to not look like too much of an ass at the completion of the project. And, of course, I had one year to write this book. Meanwhile, all of this Poe-foolery was happening while trying not to get fired from my day job, keeping my family from hating me, and not getting too far behind on any of my television programs. Many things suffered over the course of this project, not least of which is this bibliography.

But that might have been true had I a decade of leisure to put together this book. There are libraries full of works based on Poe out there (which I fully realize I am adding a straw to), and I'm the slowest reader to ever claim an English degree. But I think I read enough that I can suggest a core curriculum for anybody who wants to up their Poe game a level or two. The below list does not include the bevy of great standalone essays and online materials that I read (with one important exception), nor the few wrong turns I took reading works about Poe that proved of little value to this particular project itself or were redundant with other works, nor does it include the few local-interest books that were helpful in tracking down some of the more obscure bits of Poeana (those works are mentioned in the relevant parts of this book).

Bittner, William. *Poe: A Biography* (Boston: Little, Brown and Company, 1962). I pulled a beat-up and stained copy of this book off the shelf of my local library when I first started preparing for *Poe-Land*. It was the only Poe biography the library had, but it provided me a satisfying-sounding starting gun for my project and was a good way to later triangulate Poe with the other two biographies.

Brower, Brock. *The Late Great Creature: A Novel* (New York: Athenaeum, 1972). This is the closest I came to reading any Poe fiction. It's not Poe fiction. It's technically the story of a low-budget horror movie inspired by Poe's "The Raven," but it's really about truth and horror (as opposed to truth and beauty). I'm indebted to Norman George from the Boston chapter of this book for suggesting it to me.

It's now one of my favorite books, period, for reasons not related to Poe, whose literary and physical legacy is just a single theme running through this dark wonder of a book.

Hoffman, Daniel. *Poe Poe Poe Poe Poe Poe Poe* (Baton Rouge: Louisiana State University Press, 1998). One of my regrets with *Poe-Land* was that I didn't get to play inside Poe's stories and poems really at all in these pages. The upside to that is I had no chance of doing it better than Hoffman did with his analysis of Poe's work in *Poe Poe Poe Poe Poe Poe Poe.* Unfortunately, Hoffman passed away early in 2013, right at this start of this book project. Had I gotten the chance to meet him after *Poe-Land,* I would have told him how much more of an appreciation for the title of his book I have. The *P, O,* and *E* keys on my keyboard are almost completely worn blank.

Ostrom, John W., Burton R. Pollin, and Jeffrey A. Savoye, eds. *The Collected Letters of Edgar Allan Poe in 2 Volumes,* 3rd ed. (New York: The Gordian Press, 2008). Probably the most helpful books in this whole freaking project, and not just because of the huge amount of labor the editors took to organize all of Poe's surviving private correspondences, but also because of all the invaluable supplementary material—the commentary after each letter, the short biographies of his correspondents, the chronology of Poe's life. If I had been forced to write this book with only one resource, these would be a solid second. First place would go to the website at the end of this selected bibliography.

Peeples, Scott. *The Afterlife of Edgar Allan Poe* (Rochester: Camden House, 2004). I effused over this one already, in the South Carolina section of this book, but it really is a great way to acclimate yourself to the lay of the land in Poe criticism and culture, even for a layman.

Poe, Edgar Allan. His Collected Works. I don't have a preference for any particular collection of Poe's work, and I read and referenced multiple versions throughout the course of this trek. Every time one of those public domain collections is printed with a new cover, I end up buying it somehow. It was the largest share of my reading and included all of his fiction, poetry, and available essays. The only thing I cheated on was *Eureka.* That got skimmed. Not enough time in the universe, unfortunately.

Quinn, Arthur Hobson. *Edgar Allan Poe: A Critical Biography* (Baltimore: Johns Hopkins University Press, 1941). Of the metric tons of Poe biographies out there, this volume was the one most recommended to me. After reading it and a few others, it's impossible for me to even kind of disagree. It's balanced, restrained, and researched with astounding thoroughness. Quinn somehow presents Poe's story both objectively and without masking his underlying ardor for Poe.

Silverman, Kenneth. *Edgar A. Poe: Mournful and Never-ending Remembrance* (New York: Harper Perennial, 1991). This biography is the most accessible and recent of the in-depth biographies. Gets weird in a few places around how he draws some of his insights into Poe, but it's undeniably a work in complete service to Poe's legacy.

Thomas, Dwight and David K. Jackson. *The Poe Log: A Documentary Life of Edgar Allan Poe, 1809–1849* (Boston: G. K. Hall & Company, 1987). Part of the *American Authors Log Series*, this valuable book tells Poe's story using a comprehensive and curated selection of original documents, such as personal letters, newspaper accounts, and legal documents, to tell Poe's story. Basically, it's a paper trail of Poe.

www.eapoe.org: Don't let the front page and format fool you. This site is the [#]1 resource for all things Poe. You just gotta dig a little. It's got everything, even digitized versions of some of the books in this bibliography. Officially run by the Edgar Allan Poe Society of Baltimore, it's really the passion project of Jeffrey A. Savoye, the independent Poe scholar whom I saw at The Cask of Amontillado Wine Tasting Among the Bones. He's also, as you no doubt noticed, the common denominator between this resource and *The Collected Letters of Edgar Allan Poe in 2 Volumes.* If this book was more about Poe's life and/or literary legacy and less about Poe's physical legacy, he'd have been the first person I interviewed. As it stands, I probably should have interviewed him anyway . . . but, man, am I scared of his Poe knowledge.

*Annabel Lee Tavern side door*

# Poe-Land

## *The Abridged Version*

## MASSACHUSETTS

*Former Site of Edgar Allan Poe House*: 62 S. Charles St., Boston

Edgar Allan Poe Square, Plaque, and Statue: Boylston St. and Charles St., Boston

*Edgar Allan Poe Condominiums/Grolier Club Medallion*: 15 Fayette St., Boston

*Former Site of Calvin F. S. Thomas's Print Shop*: 1 State St., Boston (where Tamerlane and Other Poems was printed)

*Frog Pond Poe* (referenced to disparage Boston as Frogpondium): Boston Common, Boston (now a playground and wading pool/ice rink with cartoony bronze frogs)

Former *site of Federal Street Theatre/Odeon Theatre*: 1 Federal St., Boston (where Poe's mother performed while pregnant with Poe and where decades later Poe lectured)

*Fort Independence*: Castle Island, South Boston (plaque with Poe's face etched on it is at the adjacent playground)

*Former Site of Washington House and Tavern*: Church St. and Central St., Lowell (marked with engraved stone column)

*Wentworth Building*: Shattuck St. and Merrimack St., Lowell (Poe lecture site)

*Annie Richmond Grave:* Lowell Cemetery, 77 Knapp Avenue, Lowell (located on Verbena Path)

*Boston Public Library, Central Library*: 700 Boylston St., Copley Square, Boston (Poe's name is engraved on the side facing Boylston St. and is the soon-to-be home of Bryan Moore's Poe bust.)

*Westford Poe Marker*: 11 Graniteville Rd., Westford

## RHODE ISLAND

*Sarah Helen Whitman House*: 88 Benefit St., Providence

*Cathedral of St. John Cemetery*: Church is on 275 N. Main St., Providence, but cemetery is accessible via path behind it, at 66 Benefit St. (site visited by Poe and Whitman during their romance)

*Providence Athenaeum*: 251 Benefit St., Providence

*Sarah Helen Whitman Grave*: North Burial Ground, 5 Branch Ave., Providence
(Coming from cemetery entrance, you'll see it on the left side of Dahlia
Path, adjacent to an identical small block of stone marking her sister Susan
Anna Power, which is in turn adjacent to a table monument.)

## H. P. Lovecraft Sites

*Lovecraft Bust*: Providence Athenaeum, 251 Benefit St., Providence

*Fleur-de-Lys Studios*: 7 Thomas St. (used as address of Henry Anthony Wilcox in
"The Call of Cthulhu")

*First Baptist Church of America*: 75 N. Main St., Providence (where Lovecraft
attempted to play "Yes, We Have No Bananas" on the organ)

*Site of Lovecraft's Funeral*: 187 Benefit St., Providence (was Knowles Funeral
Home back then)

*Shunned House:* 135 Benefit St., Providence (used as the titular haunted house
in "The Shunned House")

*Cathedral of St. John Cemetery*: Church is on 275 N. Main St., Providence, but
cemetery is accessible via path behind it, at 66 Benefit St. (site visited by
Lovecraft because it was a site visited by Poe)

*Halsey House*: 140 Prospect St., Providence (used by Lovecraft as the home of
the titular character in his novella *The Case of Charles Dexter Ward*)

*Little White Farmhouse*: 133 Prospect St., Providence (house briefly mentioned
in *The Case of Charles Dexter Ward*)

*Lovecraft House*: 10 Barnes St., Providence (where Lovecraft wrote "The Call of
Cthulhu")

*Brown University Ladd Observatory*: 210 Doyle Ave., Providence (Lovecraft was
given regular access to the observatory by a family friend, and it is perhaps
here that he gained his awe and terror of the cosmos.)

*Prospect Terrace Park*: 60 Congdon St., Providence (frequently visited by
Lovecraft; home to statue and remains of Providence founder Roger
Williams)

*Lovecraft's Last Home*: 65 Prospect St., Providence (also used as the house in
"The Haunter of the Dark")

*H. P. Lovecraft Memorial Square*: Prospect St. and Angell St., Providence

*Hamilton House*: 276 Angell St., Providence ("sumptuous but hideous French-
roofed mansion" referenced in "The Shunned House")

Former Site of Lovecraft's Birthplace: 454 Angell St., Providence

*Lovecraft House*: 598 Angell St., Providence

*Butler Hospital*: 345 Blackstone Blvd., Providence (hospital where both his parents died insane, 23 years apart)

*Brown University John Hay Library*: 20 Prospect St., Providence (site visited by Lovecraft, and which holds his papers and artifacts)

*Lovecraft Plaque*: 20 Prospect St., Providence (on a stone in front of the John Hay Library)

*Brown University Van Wickle Gates*: College St. and Prospect St., Providence (site of picture of Lovecraft, sitting at the gates)

*Lovecraft Grave*: Swan Point Cemetery, 585 Blackstone Blvd., Providence (at intersection of Pond Avenue and Avenue B)

## New York

*Poe Arch/Laura Gardin Fraser History Panels*: Bartlett Hall, United States Military Academy, Thayer Rd., West Point

*Edgar Allan Poe St.*: W. 84th St. between W. End Ave. and Broadway, New York (Manhattan)

*Shakespeare Society Raven Plaque*: 255 W. 84th St., New York (Manhattan)

*Eagle Court Raven Plaque*: 215 W. 84th St., New York (Manhattan)

*Edgar's Cafe*: 650 Amsterdam Ave., New York (Manhattan)

*Poe Mantel/Butler Library Façade*: Butler Library, Columbia University, 116th St. and Broadway, New York (mantel is in the Rare Book and Manuscript Library; Poe's name is carved on the left of the building façade; Manhattan)

*Greenwich Village Poe House Memorial*: W. Third St. between Sullivan St. and Thompson St., New York (entrance is on Sullivan St.; Room 112 is inside; Manhattan)

*Original Site of Poe Greenwich House*: 85 W. Third St., New York (Manhattan)

*Poe Park/Poe Cottage*: Grand Concourse between E. 192 St. and E. K St., New York (Bronx)

Original Site of Poe Cottage: Poe Pl., New York (Bronx)

*High Bridge*: 40.842346, -73.930487, over the Harlem River (Bridge across which Poe used to walk; Bronx/Manhattan)

*University Church/Edgar Allan Poe Way/Original Old Edgar*: Rose Hill Campus, 441 East Fordham Rd., New York (church is site of two plaques naming its bell "Old Edgar"; Edgar Allan Poe Way is site of main building dating to Poe's time; original bell is in the Department of Archives and Special Collections in the Walsh Library; Bronx)

*Hall of Fame for Great Americans*: Gould Memorial Library, Bronx Community College, 2155 University Ave., New York (Bronx)

## pennsylvania
*Former Site of Moyamensing Prison*: E. Passyunk Ave. and S. 10th St., Philadelphia
(historic sign)
*Moyamensing Wall Remnant*: Reed St. and S. 11th St., Philadelphia (behind
grocery store)
*Free Library of Philadelphia*: 1333 Wagner Ave., Philadelphia (home of Grip the
Raven and the rest of the Richard A. Gimbel Poe Collection)
*George Lippard Grave*: Lawnview Cemetery, 500 Huntingdon Pike, Rockledge
(near the south corner)
*Poe Mural*: Green St. and N. 7th St., Philadelphia
*Edgar Allan Poe National Historic Site:* 532 N. 7th St., Philadelphia

## maryland
*M&T Bank Stadium*: 1101 Russell St., Baltimore (home of the Edgar Allan Poe
Ravens)
*Westminster Hall/Poe Proscenium/Catacombs/Poe Grave Sites:* 519 W Fayette St.,
Baltimore (Poe Proscenium is in the hallway adjacent to the auditorium; the
catacombs are below; Poe's original gravesite is behind the building, and
his current grave that he shares with his wife and mother-in-law is at the
front corner of the cemetery, where Fayette St. and Greene St. intersect.)
*Edgar Allan Poe House and Museum*: 203 Amity St., Baltimore
*Enoch Pratt Free Library Central Library*: 400 Cathedral St., Baltimore (home of
locks of hair from both Poe and his wife, a piece of Poe's coffin, various
important letters, a George Julian Zolnay bust, and the Poe Room)
*Poe Statue*: Maryland Ave. and W. Mt. Royal Ave., Baltimore
*Former Site of Odd Fellows Hall*: 30 N. Gay St., Baltimore (where Poe once
lectured)
*Latrobe House*: 11 E. Mulberry St., Baltimore (site where *Baltimore Saturday
Visiter* contest was decided, in which Poe won for best short story with "MS.
Found in a Bottle" and the editor of the paper himself won the prize for best
poem; currently marked by plaque)
*Former Site of Baltimore Saturday Visiter Building*: Baltimore St. and Gay St.,
Baltimore (where Poe had an altercation with the editor for awarding
himself the first prize for poetry)
*Annabel Lee Tavern*: 601 South Clinton St., Baltimore
*Site Where Poe Was Found in "Great Distress"*: Somewhere around 900–904 East
Lombard St., Baltimore (The old address of what was Gunnar's Hall was
844 Lombard St.)
*Poe Death Site*: 100 N. Broadway, Baltimore (historic sign marks the building
wherein Poe perished)

# GREAT BRITAIN

*Flowerbank Guest House*: Millcroft Rd., Minnigaff Newton Stewart, Wigtownshire, Scotland (site of supposed Poe visit)

*David Poe and Ann Allan Tombstone*: North Ayrshire Heritage Centre, Manse St., Saltcoats, Ayrshire, Scotland

*New Laigh Kirk*: John Dickie St., Kilmarnock, East Ayrshire, Scotland (churchyard where Poe supposedly copied epitaphs)

*Poe Plaque*: Kilmarnock, East Ayrshire, Scotland

*Former Site of Misses Dubourg's Boarding School*: 146 Sloane St., Chelsea, London, England

*Former Sites of Allan Homes*: 39 and 47 Southampton Row, Camden, London, England

*Tower of London*: Tower Hill, London, England

*Stoke Newington Library Poe Plaque*: Stoke Newington Church St., London, England

*Poe Bust/Former Site of Manor House School/The Fox Reformed Restaurant*: 176 Stoke Newington Church St., London, England

*St. Mary's Old Church*: Stoke Newington Church St., London, England

# VIRGINIA

*Eliza Poe Grave*: St. John's Churchyard, 2401 E. Broad St., Richmond (against wall that borders N. 25th St.)

*Shockoe Hill Cemetery*: 2nd and Hospital Streets (graves of John and Frances Allan, Jane Stith Craig Stanard, and Sarah Elmira Royster Shelton)

*Sarah Elmira Royster Shelton House*: 2407 E. Grace St., Richmond

*Jane Stith Craig Stanard House*: E. Grace St. and N. 19th St., Richmond

*Former Site of Moldavia, John Allan's Home*: 5th St. and Main St., Richmond (site of Poe plaque)

*Poe's Pub*: 2706 E. Main St., Richmond

*Monumental Church*: 1224 E. Broad St., Richmond

*Richmond Randolph No. 19 Masonic Lodge*: 1805 E. Franklin St., Richmond (site where Eliza Poe performed and Edgar Allan Poe performed guard duty for Lafayette)

*Poe Statue*: 9th St. and Franklin St., Richmond

*Poe Dorm Room*: 13 West Range, University of Virginia, Charlottesville (Historic sign is just across the lawn on McCormick Rd.)

*Jefferson Society Meeting Room*: Jefferson Hall, University of Virginia, Charlottesville

*George Julian Zolnay Bust of Poe*: Alderman Library, 160 McCormick Rd., University of Virginia, Charlottesville

*Albert and Shirley Small Special Collections Library*: University of Virginia, Charlottesville (site of Poe signature from the Jefferson Society meeting minutes and a pane of glass from his dorm room etched with a poem rumored to have been his handiwork)

*Fort Monroe/Casemate Museum*: Hampton

*Hiram Haines Coffee and Ale House*: 12 W. Bank St., Petersburg (site of Edgar and Virginia Poe's honeymoon suite)

*Hiram Haines' Grave*: Blandford Cemetery, 319 S. Crater Rd., Petersburg

*Former Site of* Southern Literary Messenger *Building*: E. Main St and N. 15th St., Richmond

*Talavera:* 2315 W. Grace St., Richmond (site of Poe's last public reading of "The Raven")

*Edgar Allan Poe Museum*: 1914 E. Main St., Richmond

## washington, d.c.

*Rosalie Mackenzie Poe Grave*: Rock Creek Cemetery, 201 Allison St NW, Washington (Section D, approximately the middle, in a row of small plaque-like stones flush with the ground)

## south carolina

*Fort Moultrie*: 1214 Middle St., Sullivan's Island

*Edgar Allan Poe Library*: 1921 I'on Ave., Sullivan's Island

*Gold Bug Island*: 1560 Ben Sawyer Blvd., Mt. Pleasant

*Poe Streets*: Poe Ave., Raven Dr., and Goldbug Ave., Sullivan's Island

*Gold Bug Tree*: Goldbug Ave. and Station 27 St., Sullivan's Island

*Poe's Tavern*: 2210 Middle St., Sullivan's Island

*Unitarian Church Cemetery*: 4 Archdale St., Charleston

# Index